HISTORY AND . . .

HISTORIES WITHIN THE

HUMAN SCIENCES

HISTORY AND...
HISTORIES WITHIN THE
HUMAN SCIENCES

━━►⊷◉⊶◄━━

Edited by

RALPH COHEN AND
MICHAEL S. ROTH

UNIVERSITY PRESS OF VIRGINIA

Charlottesville and London

ACKNOWLEDGMENTS   The essays by Carolyn Porter, Rena Fraden, Rosalind E. Krauss, Leo Treitler, Clifford Geertz, Renato Rosaldo, Ian Hacking, David A. Hollinger, Lillian S. Robinson, Robert Dawidoff, and Carl E. Schorske were originally published in *New Literary History* 21 (1990). Michael S. Roth's Introduction is a revised version of the original in that issue. The essay by John Brenkman was previously published in *New Literary History* 23 (1992). Carolyn J. Dean's essay is reprinted with the permission of Wesleyan University Press from *History and Theory* 33, no. 2 (1994). The other essays all appear here for the first time. The editors wish to thank Charlotte Bowen for her help in assembling the essays and reading proofs, and Gerald Trett for his thoughtful and meticulous editing of this volume.

THE UNIVERSITY PRESS OF VIRGINIA

First published 1995

Library of Congress Cataloging-in-Publishing Data

History and— : histories within the human sciences / edited by Ralph Cohen
and Michael S. Roth.
        p.   cm.
    ISBN 0-8139-1498-1 (cloth). — ISBN 0-8139-1499-x (paper).
  1. History—Philosophy.   2. Historiography.   I. Cohen, Ralph, 1917–   .
            II. Roth, Michael S., 1957–
                D16.8.H62418   1995
            901—dc20   94-38653
                    CIP

Printed in the United States of America

CONTENTS

HISTORY AND...
HISTORIES WITHIN THE
HUMAN SCIENCES

INTRODUCTION

Michael S. Roth

SEVERAL OF THE essays in this collection were originally presented at
a conference sponsored by the Scripps College Humanities Institute. In
organizing that meeting and in helping to prepare this volume, I hoped to
create a forum in which some of the important uses and abuses of history
in the human sciences would be discussed. All of the essays which follow
contribute to this discussion, although they do so in very different ways.
The status of historical knowing is directly addressed in regard to some of
the disciplines, while the disciplinary or theoretical context of contemporary discussions of history is stressed in other of the essays. The result is
an eclectic collection tied together by common themes and issues. In this
Introduction I shall try to underline some of those themes to say something about what is at stake in the controversies about these issues. First,
however, I must say something more about a history common to several
of these papers, thereby creating a context for the discussions contained
therein.

All of the contributors received a similarly structured invitation, the
first page of which stated the general goals of the conference and volume.
Each author's invitation continued with some specific questions, depending upon the relevant discipline and the author's previous work. Since
some of the authors refer to this letter, I cite the first, common page, here:

> I am writing to invite you to participate in a conference . . . on the
> place of history and historical thinking in the human sciences today. "His-
> tory and . . ." will examine the various ways in which history informs
> some of the crucial aspects of contemporary culture and our attempts to
> understand it. Panels such as "History and Literature" and "History and

Philosophy" will focus on how comprehension of the past informs our ways of knowing and acting. . . .

"History and . . ." takes place at a time of critical importance for our understanding of how consciousness of and rhetoric about the past contributes to our ability to make sense of our cultures. Whereas a historical appreciation of the sciences and humanities was once seen as a necessary component of a liberal education, in the wake of structuralism's and functionalism's celebration of the synchronic, the significance of historical knowing is far from clear. More recently still, poststructuralism's playfulness sees no virtue in making meaning from memory, and it is doubtful that deconstruction will clarify the importance of a sense of the past for our ability to come to terms with the present.

"History and . . ." will address the status of historical knowing in the humanities today. We trust that by bringing together some of its most thoughtful scholars to concentrate on this theme we will all better understand not only how our disciplines are connected to professional historiography but how our attempts to understand cultures are connected to our pasts.

Thus, the agenda for the conference, and hence for this volume, was not confined simply to an examination of the status of historical knowing but included as its presupposition a certain historical matrix for the examination. History has been displaced by contemporary developments in the human sciences, and yet these developments do not adequately address the importance of what I called "a sense of the past." We are, I claimed, at a critical moment in our efforts to understand the importance of history. Thus, a history is told here to legitimate and lend importance to an inquiry into the status of historical knowing in the human sciences.

As we shall see, for some of our contributors this use of history was abusive. Nonetheless, almost all of the papers in this volume make this same move more or less explicitly. That is, they all set up the present as a historical moment so as to consider the status of the historical. Of course, there are differences among the contributors about where we are now when we speak about "history and . . . ," as there are differences about who "we" are. The tension between "history of" and "history and" is very fruitful, for a discussion of the status of the historical which did not reduce that status to nothing is more persuasive when it enacts a use of history as it considers the value of historical knowing.

Of course, the discussion of the value of historical knowing has its own history. In the United States from the 1940s through the 1960s, discussions by philosophers of the value of history were discussions about the quality of historical knowledge as a science. As the star of pragmatism waned, the dominant model for testing the scientificity of a discipline was taken from logical positivism. Historical writing, Carl Hempel had argued in an article that set a paradigm which lasted twenty years, must yield general laws if history was a science.[1] Indeed, as Louis Mink remarked, "it could be said without exaggeration that until about 1965 the critical philosophy of history *was* the controversy over the covering-law model."[2] In the late 1960s, however, there developed more interest in understanding what historians did when they wrote about the past and less effort to tell them what they must do to behave like scientists. Philosophers began to look again at the "autonomy of historical understanding" and thus at the forms in which that understanding was expressed. Rather than concentrating on history as a form of knowledge, there was a shift to a focus on history as a kind of writing. Even analytic philosophy of history can be said to have taken a "linguistic turn."[3]

A parallel series of changes can be seen in France during roughly the same period. In the 1940s Hegelian Marxism had a crucial effect on thinking about the connections between history and knowing. For the Hegelians, history was the reservoir of all truths and values; as dramatic pragmatists, they saw in History the court of world judgment. By the end of the decade, Hegelian historicizing declined with the loss of faith in the meaningfulness of history. Contemporary events made a mockery of the idea of history as a reservoir of significance and direction, and the development of sophisticated methodologies of the synchronic in linguistics, anthropology, and cybernetics legitimated a retreat from the historical.[4]

Perhaps the most famous attack on historicizing came with Levi-Strauss's critique of Sartre in *The Savage Mind*. For the structural anthropologist, as for the logical positivist, historical narratives might not do any harm, but they seemed to have little to commend them as forms of knowledge. However, as structuralism's scientific pretensions were themselves made objects of criticism by thinkers we have come to call post-structuralists, history could be and was recuperated: not as a form of knowledge, but as a text, a kind of writing.

Although these are histories painted with a spray can, I trust they are familiar enough to help orient the reader for some of the discussions to follow. Of course, the French and American stories are not unrelated. For example, a writer on history whose work responds both to the French and American contexts just described is Hayden White. White's rhetoric of history aims to show how historical writing achieves what Barthes called the "reality effect." By bracketing the question of correspondence and by examining the rhetoric of the great historians and philosophers of history, White showed that the criteria for distinguishing among texts (or actions) could not be found in an appeal to history. A great "undoer" in the sense that Ian Hacking uses the term in his essay in this volume, White demolished the notion that history can be a neutral testing ground for judgment by showing that historical writings create criteria of realism that themselves cannot be judged *according to history.*[5] Major developments in the critical philosophy of history and in poststructuralist literary theory seemed to agree in the undoing of history as a kind of knowledge to be set off against texts, or writing or discourse.[6] No longer were we to ask about the sense of a history, but to puzzle out how it was put together, how it worked. In an intellectual world cheerfully removing privileged places as quickly as it shook up foundations, historical understanding has been seen not as a neutral or necessary context but as a trope to be used, a literary device to be employed for proper (or subversive) effect. Even the New Historicism's effort to return to history (or to histories) presupposes the linguistic turn just described. That is, it presupposes a necessary if not arbitrary connectedness that allows the historical to be read in much the same way as literary texts.

The linguistic turn, or functionalism, in regard to the historical has given us a much richer understanding of the ways in which the discourse of history performs; how the "history-machine" runs. Questions remain, however, about why one turns to history in the first place. What do we want from the past, and what shall we do with our history once we understand that it cannot function as a neutral court of appeal? All of the papers in this volume are self-consciously written after the linguistic turn of the historical; in other words, the contributors all use and comment upon historical discourse knowing that *H*istory has been undone. The histories they tell in relation to their subjects (and sometimes *of* their subjects) should help us to better understand how history can be coupled to the human sciences other than as background or as natural context. They should also help us see how this coupling responds to specific questions in particular areas of the humanities today, and how it satisfies, avoids, and represses those desires to make meaning and direction out of the past.[7]

The study of literature has been one of the areas in which the use of history has been (and remains) a source of great controversy. Formalism has many guises, Carolyn Porter's essay reminds us, and the retreat from the historical that was legitimated by the methods of close reading identified with the New Criticism has its own history. Porter's essay is a sharp criticism of formalism and aestheticism as techniques to escape the subversive power of literature. The contemporary effort to return to history via the marginal and the esoteric that is characteristic of the new historicism is seen as yet another displacement of literature's many-voiced potential for opposition and resistance.

Porter sets up her paper and her critique of new historicism with a historicization of the contemporary juncture in theory and criticism. That is, in looking at history *and* literature, she offers a history *of* the recent study of literature. "We have reached a moment" and "we have no choice about where we are"—these are telling expressions of her own use of a history to legitimate her criticism of those who deny or neglect the power of the past.

Porter does not, however, want to offer a history that would be beholden to a teleological end or a universal. Apparently convinced by the criticisms mounted against such monologic or essentialist abuses of the past, she tries to find a format for conserving the potential for subversion and resistance that would not depend on them. A historical story should be a contestatory tale. The model of the "flat discursive field" introduced at the end of her essay is an attempt to find a way of talking about marginality, otherness, history and literature without creating a privileged place for some of the components of the discussion. In her response to Porter, Rena Fraden questions whether "flatness" allows one to determine which oppositional practices were worth encouraging or condemning. Fraden asks whether it is inevitable that the embrace of historical multiplicity means conceding hierarchy to the traditional humanists. The paradoxical status of authenticity in both new historicism and in Porter's critique of it continues to cast a shadow over all claims on the past.

The limits between literature and history are at the center of Robert Alter's essay, "Imagining History in the Bible." Alter's title indicates that he accepts no neat distinction between fictional and historical texts; history is *imagined* in the Bible, and Alter is interested in how that imagining both grows out of and remains faithful to a connection with known empirical realities. The difficulty with this enterprise is that we can very rarely (if at all) know when a fidelity to the real has been maintained. The chain of inference from evidence to interpretation that a writer such as Thucydides seems to provide access to has no direct counterpart in the Hebrew Bible. Instead, we have a seamless garment of interpretation into which are woven many-colored strands of what may be historical facts. Alter asks us to consider the ancient Hebrew narratives as an alternative strategy of representing historical experience in a persuasive form.

This approach to the historicity of biblical texts is a sharp departure from the dominant strains of historical criticism of the Bible. Since the eighteenth century, biblical criticism has consistently sought to separate the "true" and "real" elements of these ancient texts from those that fabricated (fabulated?). Sometimes the "true" and always the "real" elements of the texts were indentified with (or as) their historical components. Rather than aiming at a distillation of the historical, Alter shows us how biblical criticism integrated historicity into its moral, psychological and political (and, perhaps we can add, aesthetic) concerns. His chief example is the David story, in which the imaginative elaboration is put in the service of a "historical search" in order to reveal the meanings of events and experience.

Alter's approach depends on the shifts in the status of historical understanding discussed above. Historical criticism was put in the service of modern secularism throughout the nineteenth century—historical research could expose the human invention and revision to undermine claims of revelation. But when historicism itself became the object of criticism, when the failed scientific pretensions of historical writing were made apparent, the question of the historicality of biblical narrative seemed decidedly beside the point. Alter returns to the question of history and the Bible not in order to divide texts between the fictional and the real but to understand how these ancient narratives confront the "moral dilemmas of living in history". For Alter, the writers' invention in the Bible "springs from certain historical seeds," thus using history to imagine a meaningful way of responding to these dilemmas.

Rosalind Krauss's paper offers sharp criticism of contemporary efforts to "return" to the historical via the anecdotal, and—in good deconstructive fashion—she weaves her discussion of "history and art history" into a more general challenge to some of the presuppositions of this volume as a whole. Krauss's "Story of the Eye" is a story of how art history and modernism both grew out of assumptions about the optical and its independence from the body and from desire. For modernism this led to a privileging of reflexivity, and for the discipline of art history this led to an isolation of art from nonart. In Krauss's view Duchamp is a crucial figure because he cannot be accounted for through the "founding optic" of modernism and art history without missing the power of his work. Nor, she emphasizes, can we begin to understand him through appeals to the difference between diachronic and synchronic understanding.

Deconstruction is important in this regard because it undermines the kinds of distinctions crucial for modernism and traditional historical understanding. As Krauss's essay reminds us, Derrida's critique of Husserl, like Duchamp's critical place in modern art, shows how the instantaneous is an illusion bound up with the idea of being-fully-present. There is never a "now" without some form of retention and protention; never a "neat little distinction" between the synchronic and the diachronic. Krauss joins in Duchamp's critique of modernism's "fetishized autonomous realm of the visual" and emphasizes the artist's exploration of not just the retina but the body "in all its thickness and temporality."

Krauss's paper not only criticizes some of the terms in which we consider the historical, it offers a history of its own. Modernism and the discipline of art history are tied together—prisoners of their optical histories. They continue to act out the stories of their pasts, blind to their own ways of seeing, their own eyes. The alternative to this history of imprisoning opticality is found in the postmoderns Duchamp and Derrida. Deconstruction powerfully shows that there is always-already a trace, "a not-now infecting the now," in Krauss's phrase. But is a trace a history? It is clear from her essay how deconstruction can be wed to a postmodernism that always keeps open the possibility of the historical. How deconstruction can be useful in the construction of a history (which would include consideration of how it was useful in the construction of the history that forms part of the "Story of the Eye") continues to be a subject of intensive reflection for those unwilling to isolate or ignore the contributions of what we call "theory" to the humanities. After we say that the "not-now" is there (the "not-now" also can be thought of as Duchamp's idea of "grey matter" or as the unconscious, or desire), how does deconstruction help us to say anything more about the body or about history "in all its thickness and temporality?"

In "History and Images in Medicine," Sander Gilman examines the status of visual representations in the construction of medicine's history. The use of "illustrations" in writing the history of medicine has been ubiquitous, but their function in the creation of a usable past for modern medical science has been given little attention. Gilman provides a taxonomy of the uses of these images and an analysis of the various kinds of work they do in modern efforts to legitimate medical practice by constructing its history as a story of progress.

Images have been important in histories of medicine because they allow the past to be presented as a collection of curiosities. The strangeness of past medical practices is bound together with the strangeness of disease itself. Both are contained in visual representations that can function as "windows on the world" of the past that give readers a sense of immediacy and distance. The immediacy stems from the image's (especially the photograph's) implicit claim to present the world "as it really was"; the distance stems from the *normal* (i.e., objective, detached) perspective from which the image is seen (by the photographer and by the reader of the history). The exotic is brought near by the image, but there is no threat of contamination.

The decisive phase for the history of medicine was the end of the nineteenth century, when Charcot tied his own clinical work to the construction of a history out of which it was said to emerge. Both his clinical practice and his historical construction relied heavily on visual presentations because they shared the epistemological conviction that seeing something made it real. History was made to show the superiority of contemporary French medical science, a science which had finally been able to see things clearly. Images could punctuate the path from obscurity to clarity.

Gilman shows how German historical models departed from Charcot's heavy reliance on visualization. A reliance on pictures might be appropriate for unscientific anthropology, but history was rigorously about documents. When Meyer-Steineg and Sudhoff write illustrated histories of medicine the images were there to point to the evident superiority of German science. But German science itself had no need of images, or of visualization, for its own powerful practices. The historian pictures it from outside the boundaries of the science he or she describes.

Gilman's essay shows how images are contained by the histories which use them. In the history of medicine, images are the field on which debates about scientific status and national identity and prestige are played out. Multiple meanings can be reduced by simple photographic illustration, as multivalence is filtered into a single narrative line. As Gilman notes, narrative history, often with a self-congratulatory, progressive dimension, is used to control the ambiguity of the image itself.

John Brenkman's essay on psychoanalysis and history reexamines the strategies that Freud used to control ambiguity by reinscribing history's political and social crises into the dynamics of the middle-class family. Brenkman rehistoricizes psychoanalysis by showing how Freud reduced the "tangle of cultural identities and social relationships" in fin-de-siècle Vienna to an Oedipal "I-mother-father" reference point against which he read all conflicts on the individual and social levels. For Brenkman, "Exemplary forms of personal suffering . . . [are] ciphers of the social relationships in which we wittingly and unwittingly participate." His essay attempts to show that the psychoanalytic effort to explain social relationships through an analysis of personal suffering was in fact an effort to avoid political crises.

Brenkman uses a variety of historical recontextualizations to make his theoretical point about psychoanalysis: Freud's experience of the crisis of liberalism in the late nineteenth century (as described by Carl Schorske), his participation in the discourse of contract theory in political theory (as described by Carole Pateman), his place in the changing conflict of patriarchy (as described by Franz Kafka). The theoretical point is that psychoanalysis, like many forms of discourse within an individualist frame, deflects the narrative of community into the narrative of family. The narrative of family is structured by compulsory heterosexuality and male dominance, and these structures are not seen by Freud as products of history but as necessary ingredients of the normal psychological development of humans. The investment in the family narrative neglects community as it avoids the political.

Thus, Brenkman's ambitious account of the "Freudian structure of feeling" moves among various historical levels: from Vienna to the history of patriarchy, to Freud's biography, to the intellectual controversies surrounding crucial psychoanalytic texts. All of these levels bring us back to what he calls "social relationships" and to politics. But it is important for Brenkman that these dimensions of history are not reducible to one another: there is no ur-history (such as Freud thought he had found in the Oedipus Complex) that explains all the others. Brenkman enacts and would have us pursue multidimensional historical investigations to uncover the "norms and pathologies that typically occur in the making of the socialized individual." The current crises of the socialized individual and the increasingly evident multidimensional construction of identity make this pursuit seem particularly compelling.

One of the most fertile areas for historical scholarship in recent years has been the history of sexuality. Thinking history and sexuality together has been an important avenue for denaturalizing a broad range of human activities but also for reimagining the human itself. Carolyn Dean's essay, "The Productive Hypothesis: Foucault, Gender and the History of Sexuality," examines how a dominant paradigm for thinking about the history of sexuality is both constrained and stimulated by the work of Michel Foucault. Dean discusses how historians and theorists of sexuality are divided about the very nature of the object they study. Is there something called sexuality that is given different forms in different cultures over time, or is sexuality itself produced by forces as the sign of power relations within a culture as it develops? Those scholars who work within the former model tend to show how the sexual self was forced to fit into the emerging forms of modern life, thereby constraining desires and limiting the body. Those scholars working within the latter model tend to show how the sexual self (and the idea of the repression of sexuality) is itself a creation that serves modern hierarchies of power.

Dean situates both of these models in relation to the work of Michel Foucault. Foucault's critical work in the history of sexuality challenged basic notions like repression and freedom, calling into question historicist faith in the possibility of liberating sex from cultural constraints. Dean in turn historicizes Foucault, showing how his approach to the past emerges out of and against particular early twentieth-century ideas about the construction and dissolution of the desiring male self. She thus "links Foucault specifically to a historical context in order to explore his limitations," especially in regard to understanding the history of women's sexuality.

Dean's essay thus reconfigures crucial contemporary debates in the history of sexuality in relation to Foucault and then reinscribes Foucault's own work in the history of those who wanted to reimagine the *male* subject for specific political purposes. The subtle strategies or games of resistance and pleasure that Foucault locates as possibilities even within dominant cultural forms assimilate women's desire to the male subject, if their desire has any place at all. By locating Foucault's work in the history of the creation of a male subject, Dean hopes to clear a space for imagining how the shapes of sexuality are gendered and how they might be created or expressed in new cultural practices.

Like the history of sexuality, film studies have been driven by theoretical concerns over the last few decades, especially in regard to the formation of the subject. These concerns, whether in regard to the cinematic apparatus or in regard to psychoanalytic issues of identification (or both) have often tended toward ahistorical, formalist analysis. E. Ann Kaplan makes use of these theoretical developments to connect film and history in new ways, especially in regard to questions of race, transference, and identification in American cinema. Kaplan is interested in the intersections among cinema, imperialism, and psychoanalysis. She draws on recent writing about postcolonialism and race to question notions of spectatorship that grew out of a structuralist application of psychoanalysis to the mechanisms of cinema. Kaplan is interested in models that situate the spectator historically (which she seems to think is akin to delineating the spectator's "positionality") so as to uncover the agency with which one makes sense of movies.

Kaplan underlines the importance of historically situating the reading of films, and not only their production, and she locates her own readings in a particular present. Thus, the turn to history must be self-conscious, reflexive. From our densely layered present, are we capable of understanding the positions of the past, or are some of them lost to us? Kaplan does not pursue this question but instead focuses on the possibilities for nontraditional modes of spectatorship which take into account the complexities of identity. If multiple spectator-positions are available to us in watching a film, then there are possibilities of diverse forms of identification. Kaplan wants to take race into account in understanding these identifications, but she does not want to constrain them with racialist assumptions. Race becomes part of the transference between viewer and movie, and the transference is always located in complex historical situations.

The history embedded in Kaplan's essay is one of the deepening awareness of the importance that race plays in (differently) determining our lives, and of the possibilities of not being determined in culturally stereotypical ways. The dilemma here is that history should reveal the depths of racism and the persistence of race as a cultural filter of consciousness. But history should also reveal how we might create "models for exploring and negotiating ethnic conflict." In other words, Kaplan connects history and film by showing how a historical position shapes who we are and what we can say, but also that a historical position allows for potentially powerful agency. We can make our history, even if it is not just as we please.

As Leo Trietler notes, musicology has until recently been left untouched by many of the theoretical controversies that have enlivened and sometimes plagued the rest of the human sciences. However, his paper on history and music has connections with others in this volume in that it aims to overcome the distinction between the diachronic and the synchronic as separate modes of understanding. The synchronic or structural account of music provides an account of that against which the expressive qualities of music work, but it cannot provide an adequate description of that which draws us and ties us to music in the first place: "its beauty, its expressiveness, its power to move people." On the other hand, a naive diachronic approach to music may lock us into a romantic attitude to performance and the authenticity of a "work" which blocks our sensitivity to its power in the here and now.

Treitler addresses questions concerning how notions of authenticity and originality affect the status of the musical work. In speaking to this general topic, he also wrestles with how performance (and the history of performance) is considered by the musicologist as part of what a "piece" of music is. How else to consider certain kinds of music—such as medieval—which had no other original form *but* performance? However, Treitler discusses the dangers of a fetishized approach to early music; an approach that would not realize that we can only approach the work through the concepts of our present. The contribution of early music studies "cleansed" of authenticity is that they would teach us to use the present to reach not only the "original" music but our own relation to it, our own historicity.

Treitler is thus an advocate of a hermeneutic approach to music and to history in thinking about the conjunction of the two. This approach gives up the search for certainty and origins, and it is free from the drive for progress that was so crucial for modernism. Instead, the past becomes neither an object for study nor a commodity to be used but a reservoir of sounds and structures to be appropriated. In articulating this approach to music and history, Treitler sketches very briefly a history of his own. This history is rather whigish: younger musicologists are breaking away from the fetters of their disciplinary pasts: principally, analytic formalism on the one hand, and the romantic search/need for originality on the other. The hermeneutic approach to music emerges *from* the history of musicology to offer a conceptualization *of* the history of musicology to legitimate its present concerns and styles.

W. D. King extends some of Treitler's concerns about performance and history in his discussion of history and theater. What is the *object* of theater history? *Which* performance is *the* performance, and which context is relevant to the understanding of a play? How is the written play relevant to this history? These are some of the theoretical and practical questions that arise in trying to understand the curtain line—"telling production from reception, the past from the present, the manifest from the latent"—on which traditional theater history tries to stand. How does theater history bring the curtain down on a play in order to allow us to see what has gone on behind it?

These are theoretical questions, or at least questions that can be pursued in regard to the very possibility of a critical retrospective understanding of theatrical performance. King pursues three conceptual models for theater history in relation to the curtain: theater history translates performance and is continuous with it; theater history necessarily misreads performance and is discontinuous with it; theater history can incarnate performance, becoming its sign. The first two models are familiar in the philosophy of history. The first is a confident historicism, connecting past and present through cannons of criticism that allow for the use of evidence to legitimate understanding. The second is a confident skepticism, exposing the wishful thinking behind any attempt to use history to understand or explain any occurrence in the past. We are not, according to this skeptical position, able to cross the curtain of time through our methodologies, no matter how sophisticated. The third model owes much to mystical traditions that allow us to recognize how an attempt to understand performance, and perhaps any action, is in defiance of time. This last model does not reject the possibilities of understanding because of this defiance, as does skepticism. Nor does it shrink from the outrageousness of this defiance, as does historicism.

It is important to note that King does not organize these three models historically. There is no diachronic progression from one to another. On the contrary, the third approach to the past can arise at any time—and has. King quotes Walter Benjamin: "The past can be seized only as an image which flashes up at the instant when it can be recognized and is never seen again." [8] The apprehension of the past on this side of the curtain is an act of creation and recovery, a hermeneutic performance in the present that might allow us, belatedly, to grasp a drama of the past.

Perhaps more than anyone else, Clifford Geertz has been effective in bringing the styles and power of hermeneutics to bear on the methods and subjects of social science. His work has had an enormous impact on historians, and his paper here is concerned with the confrontation of historical and anthropological ways of knowing. Like Treitler and King, Geertz has investigated how the shifting status of the knowing subjects and objects of knowledge affect interpretation. Geertz's essay in this volume underlines the fact that when historians and anthropologists try to comprehend the "the Other," not only do they differ in how they constitute the object of study, but their self-constructions are not at all the same. "To the historical imagination," he writes, " 'we' is a juncture in a cultural genealogy, and 'here' is heritage. To the anthropological imagination, 'we' is an entry in a cultural gazetteer, and 'here' is home." Geertz's essay explores a body of work that combines both modes of comprehension; work which in order to understand specific problems (the disequalibration of ways of being in the world; the connection of symbolic practice and institutional power) redefines anthropology and history in relation to one another. The emphasis here is not on a theoretical reappraisal of the possibilities or autonomy of ethnographic and historical understanding but on the "textual tactics" used to illuminate particular issues.

Geertz, too, has a history to recount in his essay, although it might be seen more in terms of legacy than in terms of genealogy. We have moved from a world in which anthropologists were thought to have "space" and historians, "time," to one in which we must find a place for the particular modes of construction of space and time, continuity and change, meaning and action typical of each discipline. The differences between the "backward glance" and the "sideways glance" remain; what is new and promising and anxiety-producing is that in the service of particular ends we might use both in trying to (re)focus our vision. Renato Rosaldo's response to Geertz emphasizes how the differences between the anthropological and the historical "glances" have become increasingly blurred so that it is no longer clear how the two fields can retain their respective identities as they work in combination with one another. Those who work on the borderlands—methodological, but also national, ethnic and political—are less interested in a happy marriage between disciplines than they are in challenging patterns of identification with various dimensions of the status quo.

Roger Abrahams's essay, "History and Folklore," examines the borderlands where politics and play, power and freedom, authenticity and imitation overlap to form dense patterns of cultural cross-fertilization. Of course, such cross-fertilization can be productive for some groups and extremely dangerous for others. He concentrates on the wild costuming and carousing that erupted in culturally controlled situations in colonial America. For the social historians working on premodern popular culture, these carnivalesque revels provided insight into the "ways particular peoples acted under specifiable political, economic, or social conditions." In other words, historians used these extraordinary moments as revelations of the normal rhythms of life in a specific time and place. Folklorists, on the other, had until recently assimilated these anomalous events with one another, tending to emphasize not historical specificity but connections over long stretches of time and space. Critical cultural studies—what Abrahams calls "the cultural critique"—have in recent years underlined how cultural difference has been articulated in the historical past. The diverse expressions of dominant power and resistance to it condition this articulation of difference.

Abrahams would like to encourage and tries himself to practice a form of inquiry that would combine folklore, social history, and the cultural critique. We start with some signifying practice in the past—"playing Indian" is the example in Abraham's essay—and begin to see how it serves a variety of cultural functions in different contexts. The ubiquitous symbol certainly does not make for univocal meaning. Regional, economic, and gender difference all figure in the ways in which meaning is constructed in a context of contested power relations. The multifocused research that Abrahams sees as the salutary outcome of combining cultural criticism with history and folklore would pay attention to the ways traditions of imitation and revelry as protest are passed down over time, as it would show how these traditions are constructed and reconstructed at specific moments and places for particular goals. A fertile combination of these modes of inquiry would attempt to understand these traditions as serving ideological as well as broadly cultural goals, and it would insist that one be cognizant of how one's own work is conditioned by and perhaps participates in the history one is constructing.

As Geertz's and Abraham's essays show how some of the best recent work in history, folklore, and anthropology provisionally redefines the disciplines, Ian Hacking's article shows that a historicist nominalism can help in the construction of an arch that historians and philosophers might pass through together. Hacking presents the case not for a global historicism and philosophy as conversation à la Richard Rorty but for "taking a look," investigating how ideas have been constructed in culture and society. How, I had asked Hacking in my invitation to the conference, are forms of historicism in contemporary philosophy related to the philosophical task of problem solving? As Hacking explains in his essay, "taking a look" helps one to understand how problems got to be considered as such, perhaps abandoning the idea of problem solving as little more than a ripple in the sea of the history of philosophy. David Hollinger, in his response to Hacking, suggests that a historical appreciation of the construction of philosophic problems is not a substitute for the effort—perhaps always provisional—at problem solving. In his brief look at the history of philosophy, he suggests that this effort may not be as ephemeral as Hacking at one point suggests. It is interesting to note how much weight both Hacking and Hollinger are willing to attach to the historical endurance of a facet of philosophy.

As Hacking's paper calls for an approach to philosophic questions that would detail their genesis and acceptance as problems, it also situates this approach in the history of philosophy. Hacking would link the Lockeian imperative to understand a concept or knowledge by its origins with the Kantian tradition, understood as critical of philosophy as such. A key term in this regard is *undoing,* showing that a doctrine or dogma is neither true nor false. By linking undoing and historicism together without the idea of progress, Hacking, like Foucault, wants us to understand not whether a doctrine is true but how concepts gain currency and power. The schematic history recounted in his paper is not aimed at legitimating his view as being the latest embodiment of history as progress but only at giving a more than local account of how his own concepts of historicist nominalism and undoing are linked with the traditions of philosophy. When we see ourselves in the tradition of the undoers of philosophy, we can "take a look" at the cultural construction of various kinds of concepts as philosophically minded historians or historically minded philosophers. Indeed, we would want to take a look at what difference this distinction was meant to establish.

But here it is appropriate to raise what has become, at least since the

1970s the question common to most meetings in the humanities: *who is this "we"?* Just as one(?) must be wary of thinking about *History* as an object already-made awaiting our discovery of parts of it, one must be suspicious about a universalized knowing subject. In other words, in thinking about an appeal to history, I want to know who is doing the appealing and for what ends. A concern with this question is certainly part of what animates the papers of Lillian Robinson and Robert Dawidoff.

Women's studies have certainly had a crucial impact on expanding our understanding of what counts as historical. Lillian Robinson's paper presupposes this contribution and goes on to consider how the appeal to history (and history's appeal) is today affecting women studies as a field of inquiry and feminism as a political movement. Robinson is also concerned with distinguishing between inquiry/knowing and politics; that is, in distinguishing, as she says, between understanding and liberation. Historical comprehension, we are reminded, is not enough.

But Robinson also wants to consider the politics of separating understanding and action. This is where the history of women's studies becomes relevant to the connections between history and women's studies. Robinson describes how the contributions of feminist historians have now created evidence and narratives about the history of women that can be appropriated for a variety of ends. The history of women's studies can be told as a success story: so much has been uncovered about the history of women in a short period of time. But scholarly success has come to have ambiguous political significance. How to consider the use of women's history to support a politics that appears to be antifeminist? If we can analytically separate historical understanding and political action, we must also push historical inquiry toward a reflexivity that allows us to consider the politics of "objective" historical understanding. Reflexive historical understanding, Robinson emphasizes, is still not a substitute for liberation, but it does help to preserve critical vigilance. Although this position raises more questions than it answers, it is probably appropriate for a politics of inquiry that refuses to substitute inquiry or even understanding for politics.

In "History and Cultural Studies" Elazar Barkan traces the development of a new counterdisciplinary mode of inquiry in the academy. Barkan is particularly concerned with the fate of a successful counterdiscipline: namely, to be successful is to be made a discipline. So cultural studies, which cut its teeth on the battle of marginality versus a hegemonic center finds itself at the center of the action. And, for the most part, the new centers of academic action are the same as the old ones, although the people in those prestigious institutions look different (and may even sound different). Barkan focuses on Edward Said's extremely successful challenge to the Eurocentric approach to culture and society, and he is interested in how the critic can maintain his voice as a radical outsider when his work has so deeply conditioned our contemporary approach to the West and its others.

Barkan shows how historical understanding has been important for identity studies as they have developed into cultural studies. History was a mode of empowerment, revealing the brutal facts of political, sexual, and social oppression and the resistance of those who were to write themselves into the narratives that describe who we are and how we might change. History could be used to show the fissures in the edifice of Western white power, to destabilize it. It could also be used to show the resilience, even the nobility, of those who suffered from that power. But as the historical narratives were rewritten (again), new approaches to recounting the past and its complex relations to the present became increasingly important. Cultural studies concentrate less on establishing an empowered subject than on revealing the historical construction of a heterogeneous and relatively unstable identity. The historical discipline has been picked over by those in search of a usable (or discardable) past. But, as Barkan shows, it has also been reseeded by the new methodologies and diverse political concerns of those who have returned to history. The eclectic "new cultural history" results from this cross-fertilization.

Barkan's history of cultural studies goes from the margins to the center, from the radical to the establishment. There is co-optation here and a moderation of political demands. There is also a reinvigoration of scholarship and a shuffling of methodological, political and aesthetic allegiances. Cultural studies have been a potent challenge to the ways we were used to talking about our past, and they have joined with a theoretical critique of narrative understanding to undermine our conventional modes of representing history. But cultural studies depend on some form of historical consciousness to validate their own critical-political enterprise, and so they will have to legitimate new modes of recounting the past. The future of cultural studies may thus lie in the connections they can forge to the past.

Robert Dawidoff's essay picks up on some of the themes important to Robinson's and Barkan's contributions. If the latter explored the diverse and overtly political uses of understanding the past, the former is concerned with the costs of any historical knowing. Dawidoff writes as a historian about the discipline's necessarily destructive effects. Whereas most of this volume's discussions concern the elements which history brings to other disciplines in the humanities, hence the leitmotif of coupling which runs throughout, Dawidoff reminds us of the loss that always is part of the effort to make present in intelligible form some aspect of the past. As he says, we may want a happy inventory of "history and . . . ," but we ought to recall our experience of "history . . . but."

Every act of historical imagination makes connections, even if it is aimed at criticism. Connections are made *at least* temporally: it matters that some thing happened after something else. Whether one thinks the historian discovers these connections or constructs them, Dawidoff wants us to recognize that the result always includes some effacement of the original components. One might say that Dawidoff raises the idea of a historical unconscious. That is, he raises the idea that the past remains inaccessible to us despite the quality of our politics, our methodologies, or our self-consciousness. He is not making a theoretical point here about the ontology of the past. Rather, he wants to call our attention to an anxiety that may go along with historical comprehension; an anxiety for both the historian as the person representing the past, and (if we identify with the object of the inquiry, as citizen, as woman, as black, as Jew) for that about which the history is told. Dawidoff wants us to attend to this anxiety because he thinks that working through it may enrich our stories and our lives.

Carl Schorske's essay may be read as a response to, even a defense against, the anxiety Dawidoff discusses.[9] In responding to an invitation to discuss history and the study of culture, Schorske provides a history of history using Herodotus as the point of departure and return. He emphasizes the necessarily collaborative dimension of the historian's enterprise: the historian's need for materials provided from other sources. This collaborative dimension is at once Clio's great strength and the source of her vulnerability. She has legitimate access to all facets of human experience once they are distanced by being considered as past. However, she is limited to and by the past as such as the only properly historical subject; and the past as such is empty. No concepts or experience are inherently historical, they become historical only when they are woven into continuity and change. The historian, Schorske emphasizes, "reconstitutes the past by relativizing the particulars to the concepts and the concepts to the particulars, doing full justice to neither."

Here is one of the chief sources of the anxiety Dawidoff discusses. A condition of historical reconstruction is an injustice to particulars and to concepts. If one is writing a history of a group with which one identifies or about which one cares deeply, consciousness of this injustice produces pain, or perhaps resentment toward the historian doing the "relativizing." We are all aware that in telling the history of the United States, for example, historians have until recently paid scant attention to the past experience of women and minority groups. The history of these groups was "relativized" in regard to the story of the nation as a whole. Over the past twenty years the trend has been in the opposite direction: reconstructing the histories of these groups and refusing the perhaps illegitimate demands of a more totalizing History. If Dawidoff and Schorske are right, however, history *necessarily* relativizes particulars. In other words, the stories that historians tell of past experience will always be stories in which the object of the narratives (or their descendants or comrades) sometimes fail to find themselves (or those they identify with).

Schorske not only discusses the necessary components of history, like the other contributors to this volume he tells us a history. In other words, he makes connections between "history and the study of culture" by weaving together a brief account of the history of history. This account emphasizes the links between the status of historical knowing and the idea of progress. With the decline of the idea of progress and concomitant rise of modernism's emphasis on the autonomy of particular practices, faith in a general account of the meaning and direction of change over time all but disappeared. The notion that understanding was achieved through an account of how things were and how they changed became illegitimate in a culture that no longer assumed that changes were moving in the same direction. This is the story of the decline of a global historicism; the replacement of history as the queen of the human sciences. However, in recent years various dimensions of using history to illuminate specific problems and possibilities have emerged in a striking way. The present collection is evidence of an interest in histories which is tied neither to the idea of progress nor to a totalizing History. Schorske concludes that "history is . . . proliferating a variety of subcultures at the expense of its synoptic function." Clio's loom is tested, but strengthened, by the experience of fragmentation in contemporary culture.

Indeed, the loom is strengthened, if one takes Schorske's essay seriously. After all, despite his cheerful appreciation of particularities, fragmentation, and what he calls the *glasnost* of contemporary interdisciplinary work by historians, his own paper here is a striking example of history's synoptic function. Even if the profession and the academy have moved to accept the proliferation of diverse discourses and practices, the form of Schorske's essay still testifies to the belief that history is "the ground on which the problems of [our] destiny must be debated." In other words, even in a playfully fragmented, or woefully mutilated culture, Clio makes connections. The decline of the idea of progress does not necessarily entail the decline of history (even of History). To be sure, without the pattern of progress the historian's weaving must become yet more versatile. However, this makes Dawidoff's question loom even larger: where is my (or our) thread?

From a Schorskeian perspective, history can be made into the field on which we find ways to talk and listen to one another. The historian's response to the anxiety produced by the historical unconscious is to keep talking and listening; trying to bring into the historical conversation those who hitherto have not found themselves in the products of historians. No longer tied to the narrative of progress or to any other *particular* narrative, history can be seen as the quintessential talking cure. This cure does not efface the past as unconscious; it can only confront the anxiety of never really connecting with that which is no more by acknowledging the distance (and conflict) between our representations and our desires and memories.

If Clio has no real data or concepts of her own, not even a genre, nothing can be excluded in principle from a historian's embrace. This raises fears of annexation, or of being forced into a story that is not one's own. These fears are real and important: "taking a look" at history teaches us not only about the politics of what is left out but also about the prices paid for being included in a narrative of the past. This dizzying historical reflexivity is the condition of historical conversation today. But the potential inclusiveness of history (as a political, moral, and aesthetic aspiration) is part of its great claim on us; part of its legitimate power. In other words, to answer a question posed at the beginning of this Introduction, the aspiration to connected inclusiveness is one of the elements that bring us to history in the first place. Connected inclusiveness (as a practice, a construction, not as a given) can be used for critique as well as for legitimation. The desire to make and test connections and the actions that may spring from this desire are risky; we can make mistakes as well as connections. But the will to make the links that form the basis for debating our destiny may be the core of history's cultural contribution: the content of the conjunction between history and the human sciences.

NOTES

1. Carl G. Hempel, "The Function of General Laws in History," *Journal of Philosophy* 39 (1942): 35–48.

2. Mink, "The Divergence of History and Sociology in the Recent Philosophy of History," in *Historical Understanding,* ed. Brian Fay, Eugene O. Golob, and Richard T. Vann (Ithaca, 1987), 169.

3. In this regard, see F. R. Ankersmit, "The Dilemma of Contemporary Anglo-Saxon Philosophy of History," *History and Theory* 25, no. 4 (1986): 1–27.

4. See Michael S. Roth, *Knowing and History: Appropriations of Hegel in Twentieth Century France* (Ithaca, 1988).

5. See ibid., "Cultural Criticism and Political Theory: Hayden White's Rhetorics of History," *Political Theory* 16 (1988): 636–46.

6. On changes within the American historical profession that are connected to these developments, see Peter Novick, *That Noble Dream: The "Objectivity Question" and the American Historical Profession* (New York, 1988), and my review essay, "Unsettling the Past: Objectivity, Irony and History," in *Annals of Scholarship,* 9, no. 1/2 (1992): 171–81.

7. This volume does not take up in any detail the extraordinary exfoliation of histories to legitimate ethnic and national identities or to empower what has come to be called "identity politics." I hope to address some of the issues raised by these developments in forthcoming collections on nationalism and post-colonialism.

8. Walter Benjamin, "Theses on the Philosophy of History," in *Illuminations,* ed. Hannah Arendt (New York, 1968), 255.

9. An earlier version of Dawidoff's essay was the response to Schorske's paper at the History and . . . conference.

HISTORY AND LITERATURE: "AFTER THE NEW HISTORICISM"

=➤-◉-◄=

Carolyn Porter

IN A PAPER I delivered well over a year ago at the University of California, Irvine, I addressed some of the problems I saw with new historicism under the title "Are We Being Historical Yet?" The answer was a provisional no.[1] In calling my remarks here "After the New Historicism," I may seem unduly optimistic, or pessimistic, as if in the brief interval of a year or so, new historicism had become "history." Clearly this is not the case. So let me gloss my title for a moment.

In alluding to Frank Lentricchia's *After the New Criticism,* I have in mind in particular the point Lentricchia made in his preface when he noted that even though New Criticism as a movement was officially "dead," its formalist legacy remained virulent in contemporary theory. Finding the "traces" and "scars" of New Criticism in the "evasive antihistorical maneuver[s]" by which various literary theorists accomplished an "often extremely subtle denial of history," Lentricchia made clear the marked extent to which a state of affairs "after the New Criticism" had still to be reached. Indeed, his book was itself offered as a mode of transportation to get us under way, at least, toward that promised land. Coming as I do from what a visitor to Berkeley once called "the land of the new historicism," I can report that it is not that promised land. Lentricchia predicted that the fate of that "heavily contested and abused term," *history,* might well "determine the direction of critical theory in the years just ahead," a prophecy whose partial fulfillment has taken an ironic turn with new historicism.[2] For if some of us have found it necessary to "go after" the new historicism, it is partly because this movement has generated forms of critical practice that continue to exhibit the force of a formalist legacy whose subtle denials of history—as the scene of heterogeneity, difference, contradiction, at least—persist.

23

My title, then, like Lentricchia's expresses a wish, and indeed the same wish, for a genuinely historicized critical practice. In addition to its temporal meaning ("subsequent to in time or order") and its aggressive meaning ("to go after x"), however, "after" can also be used to state resemblance, as in "after the manner of, or in accordance with x." My title is intended to carry this third meaning as well, since new historicism has forced me to reformulate questions in accordance with the terms it has used and the models it has deployed.

Let me begin by briefly elaborating on the point I have already mentioned about the persistence of formalism. Needless to say, any model of literary studies carries with it a set of political implications, and New Criticism was no exception. In particular, as an academically institutionalized critical practice, New Criticism generated politically resonant contradictions that are still with us. For example, in its capacity to provide a pedagogically functional solution to the problems posed by the numbers and kinds of new college students poured into the American academy by the G.I. Bill after World War II, the New Criticism legitimized—and was in part legitimized by—its power to focus exclusively on the literary text, to detach it from the literary history that had traditionally formed the disciplinary field of philological studies. If New Criticism's isolation of the text from its context enabled the techniques of close reading to be taught—if not to "the masses" then at least to increasing numbers of them—it also installed an ahistorical ideology of the autonomous text at the center of literary studies in the United States. This ideology clearly, if indirectly, served the interests of a nation now well positioned to reaffirm—after 1945, in a newly ironic sense—its long-held belief that America's mission was to bring an end to history. For Americans approaching what Daniel Bell called the end of ideology, history became, in Toynbee's words, something unpleasant that happened to other people. Literature, meanwhile, was something pleasant that could happen to us, if we accepted the formalist proscriptions of various "fallacies" that served to sever text from context, sanctioning a view of the poem as verbal icon infused with tension and ambiguity, the canonical author as unknowable genius, and the reader as passive and awestruck worshipper of literature. Whether conceived as Joyce's escape from the nightmare of history or as Stevens's supreme fiction, literature served as the repository of the transcendent, among whose functions was to silence or to marginalize any political imagination inclined to roam beyond the liberal consensus.

This contradiction—inscribed in a critical model that facilitates mass education and at the same time fosters a dehistoricized and apolitical vision of literature—remains sedimented in our critical practice and teaching today. For more than two decades now, the formalist isolation of the text on which New Criticism based its critical practice has been relentlessly attacked and discredited. Yet close reading remains the central skill taught in most undergraduate literature classes. More directly pertinent to my concerns here is the degree to which graduate programs in literature by and large continue to be structured by demands that derive from a formalist model awkwardly grafted onto a residue of old-fashioned literary history. Such programs compel students to read a large body of canonical literature, to read the major "readings" in the critical canon, and to suppose for themselves a literary history linking it all up. Somewhere along the way, on the momentous occasion of specialization, they are to grasp the chain of this literary history firmly at two proximate and prespecified points bounding a historical field, and hang on for dear—that is, professional—life.

Two points are worth making about this disciplinary structure. First, the "mastery" of the canon of English and American literature from Beowulf to Faulkner is sustainable, even as the illusion it is, only because what "mastery" actually means is a trained and sophisticated reading ability. (The specific version of the good scholar—who may not know the answer, but knows how to find it—which graduate programs in English are designed to produce is someone who may not have read some specific text, but is trained well enough to know *how* to read it on demand.) In short, reading has remained the heart of the critical enterprise.

Secondly, as far as the curriculum was concerned, once formalism became dominant, literary history soon became functionally little more than a practical means of dividing literary studies into manageable segments. The literary academy has until very recently relied on T. S. Eliot's "Tradition and the Individual Talent" as an adequate sanction for studying the talents and letting the tradition fend for itself, opting for what the late Henry Nash Smith used to call the well-placed oriental carpet approach over the wall-to-wall carpet school of curriculum revision. As for nonliterary history, until recently, and except in marginalized fields like American Studies, it has played a role in literary studies only as a backdrop—a series of "worldviews" magisterially unfolding from the fourteenth to the twentieth century, a base you could pretend to touch whenever you realized you were stealing them all, but of no direct consequence to the main enterprise of reading the text.

In short, formalism has remained institutionally inscribed, despite the fact that we ritualistically denounce it at every opportunity. In view of the serial ordeal that literary studies have experienced as a result of all the "new-isms" and "post-isms"—as Derrida recently called them—it is rather disheartening to note that the formalist agenda, as well as the politics of containment it represents, has remained hegemonic at least as an institutional framework for graduate training in literature.

No doubt one reason for this is that proposed by Frank Lentricchia: the American brand of "deconstruction" centered at Yale defanged the monster of Derridean theory, anesthetizing its political threat and appropriating its fertile analytic power for a reproduction of the formalist program. But this story, which has itself gained virtually canonical status in recent years, needs to be amplified and revised in the light of another. For if formalism has been able to absorb and appropriate certain kinds of poststructuralist theory, it has also had to marginalize other forms of critical practice, notably those oppositional, alternative, and sometimes strongly antagonistic forms that have emerged since the 1960s, first from Marxist, then from Afro-Americanist and feminist, and finally from Third World Studies. This story has yet to be told, and I will not try to tell it here. But I think that once it is told, it will reveal how the growth of these oppositional and antagonistic practices, both within and without departments of literature, has exercised a mounting pressure on the formalist framework of literary studies. Once told, this story may help to account for the present scene, in which such oppositional critical practices have now repositioned themselves so as to undermine the boundaries beyond which they have been marginalized.

In short, it seems to me we have reached a moment at which the antiformalist projects emerging from within the dominant quarters of literary studies (new historicism, cultural criticism, and so on), and the oppositional critical practices marginalized by formalism (Marxist, feminist, Afro-Americanist, and Third World Studies) have found themselves occupying a common ground, a ground we have come to call "discourse" or "the social text." In calling this a "common ground," I am of course ignoring the fact that it is also currently a battleground. Among both feminist and Afro-Americanist critics, for example, there are major debates going on right now about whether they want to share this ground at all. Many do not, since they regard it as the property of a colonizer called "Theory" which they have good reason to suspect as a tyrant and usurper. Meanwhile in its most general and diffuse sense, the new historicism is regarded by many as affording us at last the weaponry to clear the field of deconstructionists, and Derrida himself has, in response to certain insidious forms of attack on his political credentials, found it necessary to remind us of the political stakes implicit in his approach to language.[3] The battlefield is large and it is not a pretty sight. If it sometimes displays what Barbara Christian has called a "race for theory" among the previously marginalized, it also reveals scenes of colonization in progress.[4] For example, having finally compelled the attention of dominant groups of literary critics, feminist criticism becomes part of gender studies, where it can readily sanction the remarginalization of women. As Afro-American, ethnic, and Third World Studies present new applicants for the status of subjects, they are collectively reified as the "other," licensing what Houston Baker has called the study of the "dynamics of 'othering' engaged in by a self-indulgent Western soul."[5]

Nevertheless, it seems to me that we have no choice about where we are, unless we want to retreat to the traditionalist encampments that still dot the landscape. We confront what Raymond Williams has called "language in history, that full field."[6] The question before us is not whether to explore this field but rather how it should be constituted and framed for analysis. If from the standpoint of oppositional critics there is risk, there is also enormous promise in this moment. We confront a virtually horizonless discursive field in which, among others, the traditional boundaries between the literary and the extraliterary have faded, so that those trained to "read" a text need no longer be constrained by the canon. The "document" and the "archive" are open wide to them, not as the repository of background materials, but as texts in their own right. Herein, I think, lies the danger of a short circuit, in the shape of a license that authorizes literary critics to explore this discursive field by announcing, "Worry no more about how the text is related to reality. Reality *is* a text and you may read it at will." As I shall try to illustrate in a moment, in the practice of some kinds of new historicism, this can mean that the social text turns out to be read as we have been trained to read a literary text, that is, in traditional formalist terms.

I want, then, first to address new historicism, or at least a certain widely recognized tendency in this movement, in order to focus more specifically on how the discursive field can be framed so as to produce a "historicized" critical practice that serves finally to resecure a formalist agenda and the politics of containment it serves. My aim is to clarify the grounds as well as the need for an alternative model, one that would take seriously those multiple and heterogeneous "others" that oppositional forms of scholarship and critical practice have made visible.

One way of approaching the new historicism is to understand it as emerging from the contradiction it purports to overcome—that between a formalist agenda and an "old historicist" framework. Louis Montrose, for example, opposes his own work as a new historicist to that of a formalist view of literature as "an autonomous aesthetic order that transcends the shifting pressure and particularity of material needs and interests," and Stephen Greenblatt describes the old historicism he rejects as "monological" in that it posits an "internally coherent and consistent" "vision" which then "can serve as a stable point of reference, beyond contingency, to which literary interpretation can securely refer."[7] Rejecting both of these approaches, new historicism instead wishes to explore, in Greenblatt's phrase, "both the social presence to the world of the literary text and the social presence of the world in the literary text."[8] In the process, however, new historicism has brought upon itself the opprobrious charge of being Marxist. This is not surprising, since Marxist criticism has for many years flown a flag saying "Only Historicize." But whatever form this historicizing procedure has assumed in the work of Marxist critics, its leftist political orientation has remained clear. The same cannot be said for the new historicism. That is, although there may be for Marxist critics a political necessity to historicize, in and of itself to historicize literary studies is not necessarily to foster or support either a Marxist or a more generally leftist politics. Both Montrose and Greenblatt have insisted that their kind of new historicism, at least, is also opposed to Marxist criticism. The point here is that although new historicism may well foster what Edward Pechter calls a "new politicization" of literary studies, it is by no means a given that its alliances will lie on the left.[9]

If new historicism, then, at least in the hands of some of its practitioners, is opposed to Marxism, to formalism, to old historicism, what makes its project distinctive, and distinctively historicizing? What most clearly legitimizes its claim to being a literary historicism is that it addresses nonliterary, marginal, and often quite esoteric documents as well as canonical

texts. But what new historicists then do with such documents can sometimes be disquieting.

For example, in "Invisible Bullets," Stephen Greenblatt delivers a compelling analysis of Elizabethan culture by deploying Foucault's model of
power to argue that power produces the very subversion it contains. The
essay's title comes from Thomas Harriot's *A Brief and True Report of the new
Found Land of Virginia* (1588), which Greenblatt describes as a "tract for
potential investors in a colonial scheme."[10] In making his pitch, Harriot
records the "alien voices" and "interpretations" of the Algonkian Indians,
among which is the report's most riveting revelation, the natives' belief
that the massive deaths that follow in the Europeans' wake are caused by
"invisible bullets" floating in the air. Greenblatt suggests that "the recording of alien voices, their preservation in Harriot's text, is part of the process whereby Indian culture is constituted as a culture and thus brought
into the light for study, discipline, correction, transformation" and concludes that this "momentary sense of instability or plenitude—the existence of other voices—is produced by the power that ultimately denies
the possibility of plenitude" (51).

Now clearly enough, the Europeans did not "constitute" the Algonkian
culture "as a culture," nor—just as clearly—does Greenblatt mean to deny
that the Algonkians existed as a culture before the arrival of the English.
He makes a point of the fact that he is only addressing "events as reported
by Harriot" (47). But although such a disclaimer helps to account for the
textualization of "the existence of other voices" as identical to a "momentary sense of instability or plenitude" (or ambiguity and tension?) *in* a text,
it also excludes the very discursive space of "English Algonkian relations"
that has served to accord the analysis its claim to being historicist (51).

In effect, what happens here is that the cultural domain of "English
Algonkian relations" is rhetorically invoked only to be itself marginalized.
Foregrounded by the colonial encounter between Harriot and the Algonkians, the paradox of power is not treated as an expression of colonial
power. Rather, the drive to focus on a set of texts in which subversive elements are both produced and contained effectively marginalizes the very
site of the essay's most vividly "historicizing" discourse.

A more extreme version of this problem may be found in Steven Mullaney's essay "Strange Things, Gross Terms, Curious Customs: The Rehearsal of Cultures in the Late Renaissance." Mullaney's procedures sug-

gest that if the colonized other is not at least recognized as having a separate existence, as in Greenblatt's essay, then it is all too easy for the analysis to reenact the discursive practice of effacement and appropriation it is ostensibly disclosing. For Mullaney, the alien, the marginal, the other, is an already constituted category of analysis, and a remarkably commodious one at that. The "strange things" of his title refer not only to the "curiosities gathered from around the world" that are collected and exhibited in Walter Cope's "wonder-cabinet" but finally to everything and everyone "perceived as alien, anomalous, dissimilar, barbarous, gross, or rude" at the time.[11] The marginal is, in short, always already a cultural product of a dominant discourse: "What the period could not contain within the traditional order of things, it licensed to remain on the margins of culture" (44), where it was "maintained and produced, as something Other" (43).

The crux of Mullaney's argument concerns the means by which this production and maintenance of the other is effected, namely, through a "process of cultural production synonymous with cultural performance" (43), which he designates as a "rehearsal of cultures" (48), whose purpose is accomplished when the "distinction between the alien and its representation . . . virtually cease[s] to exist" (45). An extended anecdote serves to describe what is meant by "rehearsal." At Rouen in 1550, a highly elaborate and detailed reproduction of Brazil was erected but then destroyed during the dramatized enactment of tribal battles performed for Henry II and Catherine as they entered the city. Thus Rouen tells the same story as the wonder-cabinet: "The New World is both recreated in the suburbs of the Old and made over into an alternate version of itself, strange but capable of imagination" (46). Further, it adds a dramatic new element to the picture of the "rehearsal of cultures," for the "consumption of Brazil," as Mullaney calls it, demonstrates not only the re-presentation of an "alien culture," but its "erasure" as well (48).

Just as Greenblatt moves from Harriot's *Report* back to Elizabethan England and Shakespeare's stage, Mullaney promptly notes that Rouen's treatment of Brazil "was by no means reserved for New World cultures" (49) and shifts the scene to England, where the "genealogy" of the "rehearsal of cultures" is traced to "the reign of Edward I, whose colonization of Wales in the thirteenth century" is described as a rehearsal of the "subcultural excursions of sixteenth-century England" (49). Despite the rather breathtaking leap back in time, this transition felicitously accomplishes at once two strategic imperatives: it shifts the focus from the "merely colonial" to English domestic culture, and it regrounds the analysis in "the larger dramaturgy of power" (49) which we will eventually learn is "being performed, as it were, by history itself" (61).

The strategic function in the essay of those "strange things" brought home from abroad thus becomes clear. That is, the use made here of the colonial as a resource for telling anecdotes reveals that such choices serve to constitute the "marginal" as always already subordinated, dominated, othered. It matters not in the slightest whether the "alien culture" being "represented" and "effaced" (48) at Rouen occupies some discursive space of its own or has resisted the European's domination, since what is true of the Europeans being analyzed is also true of Mullaney's analysis—for both, that is, the "distinction between the alien and its representation" has "ceased to exist" (45). The Europeans' "rehearsal of cultures," after all, amounts finally to a discursive practice of appropriation and effacement aimed at the "erasure or negation" of the alien cultures they were trying to subordinate (48). Properly speaking, it is part of what will produce and sustain a colonialist ideology. But in Mullaney's essay, a similar discursive "erasure or negation" of the heterogeneous cultural spaces in which those being subordinated may also have been engaged in their own discursive practices (both resistant and collaborative, no doubt) is not only presupposed, as a historical inevitability, but also reenacted, at least in the sense that the entire discursive space of the colonial is raided for cultural examples and then marginalized as "merely colonial" (49). This anecdotal procedure, then, enables him at once to exclude from his frame and to appropriate as exemplary of the "historical" the already muted other.

The tendency of some new historicists to deploy riveting anecdotes has been widely noticed. By no means all such anecdotes are drawn from colonialist discourse, but when they are, the results tell us something about both the methodological limits and the political import of new historicist practices. Here, for example, colonialist discourse provides anecdotes that serve as a "marginal" upon which literary analysis itself operates in very much the same way that Mullaney's argument operates on the events at Rouen—to appropriate the "strange things" to be found outside the "literary," while effacing the social and historical realm that produced them, at once plundering and erasing the discursive spaces to which the argument appeals for its historicist status. But since this operation effectively retextualizes the extraliterary as literary, its results seem to me more properly designated as Colonialist Formalism than as new historicism.

I am suggesting, then, that insofar as new historicist work relies upon the anecdotalization of the discursive field now opened for interpretation, it can only expand the range of the very formalism it so manifestly wants to challenge. According to Walter Cohen, this anecdotal technique reflects a principle of "arbitrary connectedness" at work in new historicist criticism in which "the strategy is governed methodologically by the assumption that any one aspect of a society is related to any other." [12] If such a principle serves to legitimate a suspect functionalism in the social sciences, in literary studies it serves to legitimate an equally suspect formalism that can treat the social text in much the same way it has been accustomed to treating the literary one, that is, as the scene of tension, paradox, and ambiguity. Further, it is not only marginal groups and subordinated cultures that can be occulted, whether by exclusion or incorporation, by effacement or appropriation, but the "social" itself as well. Insofar as this happens, the "social text" remains a text in the formalist sense, rather than the literary being historicized as itself a form of social discourse.

In some cases, however, it is clear that what informs these procedures is less a general principle of "arbitrary connectedness" than a specific model of power derived from Foucault. In "Invisible Bullets," Greenblatt obviously constructs his analysis on the basis of certain of Foucault's discussions of power. For example, when Greenblatt says that "theatricality . . . is not set over against power but is one of power's essential modes" (56), he echoes the Foucault who says that power is not simply "a law which says no" but rather something that "traverses and produces things," something that "induces pleasure, forms knowledge, produces discourse." [13] In *The History of Sexuality*,[14] Foucault undertakes to transpose sexuality from something against which power works, as a negative, proscriptive, censoring force, to something which he describes in "Truth and Power" as "a positive product of power" (120). Greenblatt invokes the same logic of inversion from negative to positive when he transposes "theatricality" from the site of opposition to "power" to the site of "one of power's essential modes" in the process of rejecting formalism's belief in the "self-referentiality of literature" (56). But if theatricality, literature, or art in general is understood as *either* "set over against power" *or* "one of power's essential modes," and if, as here, this "either/or" allies the first choice with a formalist belief in literature's autonomy, then only formalists can believe that literature might harbor any socially resistant or oppositional force. Meanwhile, to believe that literature might have social or political weight as a form of cultural agency entails also believing that such agency as it has is by definition already co-opted by "power." What is thus excluded is the possibility that literature might well—at least occasionally—occupy an oppositional cultural site at specific historical moments. It is this possibility that has been foreclosed by the reading of Foucault at work here, a reading in which power is absolutized as a transhistorical force that relentlessly produces and recontains subversion so that any resistance or opposition to such power always presents itself as already contained and thus neutralized.

This reading of Foucault is credible, though not inevitable. Foucault's work can certainly authorize this essentialized model of power, one that serves not to historicize the object of analysis but rather to dehistoricize it as one mode in which power is manifested. But Foucault can also be read quite differently, especially if we attend to the political conditions in and against which his project took shape. I am not prepared to offer such an alternative reading of Foucault here, but I do want to address more fully the debilitating choice offered us by Greenblatt's "either/or" as a means both of evoking this alternative Foucault and of moving us forward to the question of how we might begin to formulate an alternative approach to the discursive field.

The choice between a formalist view of the literary as "set over against power" versus a putatively historicist view of the literary as "one of power's essential modes" readily invokes the ideologically charged constellation of values clustered around the formalist construction of the literary as transcendent, that is, as a medium in which the creative imagination of a supposed author operates to emancipate us from the constraints of social reality and thereby to secure and legitimate a realm of aesthetic pleasure outside history, impervious to power, and untouched by the material conditions of production, consumption, and exchange. But this somewhat caricatured view of the literary and the aesthetic more generally has a history, and a fairly well documented one. According to Raymond Williams, for example, among the manifold ways in which the dominant culture of nineteenth-century Britain established and maintained hegemony was to "specialize as aesthetic" those "visibly alternative and oppositional" elements it could not readily incorporate within "the ruling definition of the social."[15] Foucault alludes to a similar process when he refers to "all those experiences which have been rejected by our civilization or which it accepts only within literature."[16]

In short, if the values of transcendence relegitimated by formalist ideology themselves emerge from a historically specifiable set of developments
in a hegemonic process, then the need of a dominant culture to displace
the literary from the "social," to locate it in a marginalized space of the
aesthetic, could not have arisen in the first place had literature posed no
threats to that culture. "Transcendence," in other words, is not equivalent
to, but in fact—historically speaking—is an ideological defense against,
literature's potential as a discursive site of subversion, resistance, or antagonism. We cannot, therefore, ally the belief in a transcendent realm
of a literature "set over against power," in autonomous isolation from
history, with a belief that literature harbors culturally resistant or oppositional forces. Of course, this is not to say that literature cannot also serve
to support and legitimate the dominant culture's power. It is only to insist
that once stripped of its ideological function as transcendent, it is by no
means, in principle, stripped of its active force within the discursive field.

The confusion of transcendence with opposition might be explained
in the light of post-1960s critical discourse, in which the vocabulary of
transcendence seems to have been cross-fertilized with that of liberation.
That is, once the politics of liberation proved inadequate, and particularly
in reference to the French case of May 1968, a whole body of political and
cultural theory was thrown into doubt—not merely that which supported
a liberal humanist ideology, but also that which offered a Marxist or
broadly leftist critique of bourgeois liberalism and state power. Certainly
among the most radical participants in the rethinking of politics and critical theory to emerge from these events was Foucault, whose project was
centrally concerned with finding a means to work our way out of a thoroughly discredited politics of liberation—a politics, to designate rather
than to define it fully, which promised to liberate the repressed humanity
of the individual from the bourgeois state and family. Closing all the escape hatches offered by the theoretical framework supporting such a politics, Foucault charted the new territory of the discursive by means of a
"genealogy" he once described as a form of "tactics" designed "to emancipate" "subjugated knowledges," to "render them, that is, capable of
opposition and of struggle against the coercion of a theoretical, unitary,
formal and scientific discourse."[17] Characteristically, Foucault here translates emancipation into the radically different register of "opposition" and
"struggle," activities taking place within a discursive field from which
there is no escape. Foucault's work is rich with the vocabulary of war

and politics—insurrection, resistance, domination, opposition, struggle, tactics—a vocabulary itself deployed in a concerted attack on the discourse of liberation politics, with its vocabulary of repression, subjects, truth, humanism, and freedom. Thus for Foucault, at least, the possibilities for resistance, opposition, subversion must lie in a different register than that which liberation politics occupied. Whether such possibilities in fact emerge in the course of Foucault's work, the point to be underscored here is that he pursued these possibilities without benefit of liberation as a value or as a viable political program.

I am suggesting, in other words, that to cancel out transcendence or liberation is by no means to eliminate the potential for subversion and resistance in the discursive field. Foucault mapped this field as a circulatory system of power relations that can be tracked across the boundaries imposed by the discursive regimes he identified in order to discredit. The "insurrection of subjugated knowledges" he fostered exposed the "memory of hostile encounters" he found still "confined to the margins of knowledge" (81, 83). What makes his work indispensable to us in literary studies is that it undermines the boundaries dividing the literary from the extraliterary, the canonical from the popular, the dominant from the marginal and subjugated. His account of power as omnipresent and immanent throughout the discursive field can, as we have seen, open the "trap" he recognized when he remarked on the "danger of ourselves constructing" a "unitary" discourse capable of annexing the marginalized and subjugated knowledges whose history of struggle it has revealed (86). But if Foucault's work can be used to limit the very possibilities it makes visible, it also sanctions the effort to find new ways of keeping those possibilities in sight.

How, then, could we construct the discursive field so as to avoid a relapse into formalism, which remarginalizes both the social and the "others" whose voices it should make audible? I want merely to offer some suggestions that might prove helpful in such a project, whose accomplishment would obviously entail a collective effort.

Cultural and political analysis has in recent years provided us with a variety of theoretical means for constructing an alternative model of the discursive field. In addition to the work of Foucault and Raymond Williams, we might look to that of Michel de Certeau, to the critique of everyday life associated with the work of Henri Lefebvre, to feminist film theory, and to LaClau and Mouffe's post-Marxist interpretation of hegemony.[18] Drawing on some of these sources, I want here very briefly to hypothesize a continuous but continuously heterogeneous discursive field in which dominant and subjugated voices occupy the same plane, as it were. Indeed, the first point to be made about this construction of discursive space is that it can be most immediately figured, if only for heuristic purposes, as flat.

Fredric Jameson's discussion of the postmodern may be useful here. Jameson argues that the entire range of conceptual models dependent on depth (for example, essence/appearance, latent/manifest, authenticity/ inauthenticity, signifier/signified) has given way to a "new kind of flatness or depthlessness" that he finds characteristic not only of postmodernist art but of contemporary theory as well.[19] In constructing the discursive field as flat, we could usefully imagine ourselves reenacting the process of looking at a cubist painting, as John Berger has described it. That is, according to Berger, we recognize a spatial relation on the surface that sends the eye into the depths of the painting, only to be returned again to the surface, where we deposit the knowledge gained from our passage.[20] Whatever the value of this description in regard to cubism, it can figure for us a crucial feature of our situation as readers of the social text. The process by which we look into the depths, as it were, only to be returned to the surface where, as it turns out, we always were, teaches us to rescore depth as surface. We learn, that is, that what seems to lie in the "depths" must be restored to the surface, deposited there as new knowledge — a maneuver very much like that "genealogy" that Foucault describes as a tactic for restoring subjugated knowledges to the visible space of discourse. To envisage this space as effectively depthless is a means at least of defending against a set of problems arising from the residual belief in transcendence, liberation, and so on. We thereby might guard against the tendency that Tony Bennett identifies in certain strains of deconstruction and that we have found in certain strains of new historicism — the tendency to "keep alive the demand for transcendence simply by neverendingly denying its possibility — a criticism of essentialism which can rapidly become a lament for its loss, a consolation for the limitations of the human condition which is simultaneously a recipe for political quietism."[21]

To make this point in a different register, we could turn to Lukács's analysis of Kant's thing-in-itself as a formalized barrier of rationalist thought that serves to place off limits the irrational realm previously recognized as, or propitiated through, magic, ritual, or religion (as in "Fortune is a woman"). According to Lukács, Kant's thing-in-itself ren-

ders this realm unknowable, by definition, to the rational subject of modern science. The binary "phenomenal/noumenal" henceforth functions
to repress as unknowable all that cannot be comprehended within Kant's
rational system.[22] Functioning as an epistemological proscription, the
thing-in-itself legitimates by exclusion the unitary discourse of science,
rather like the "repressive hypothesis" Foucault attacked. Other binary
oppositions, such as, langue/parole, form/content, operate in similar
ways: that is, they serve to repress and occult the area designated by the
second term as unknowable in itself. If this repression is a precondition
for the coherence and luminosity of the first term, then seeing them both
on the same plane would enable us to bring again into view the "memory
of hostile encounters" such binaries serve to deny, to erase from memory. (Derrida's transposition of signifier/signified to the single plane of
the text effects a similar shift; that is, to say that there is nothing outside
the text because there is no transcendental signified is precisely to cancel depth in order to foreground a signifying process that operates in and
constitutes a horizonless plane.)

Figuring the discursive field as a plane, however, is at best a crude ap-
proximation of the theoretical operation conducted by LaClau and Mouffe
in their radical reconceptualization of hegemony as a "field of articulatory practices." In *Hegemony and Socialist Strategy* their aim is "to dissolve"
all forms of a "differentiation of planes" which sanction that "topography of the social" presupposed not only by classical Marxist theories of
base/superstructure but by the "fundamentalism of [all] the emancipatory projects of modernity."[23] It would require another essay to address
adequately the promise of, and the problems with, LaClau and Mouffe's
poststructuralist revision of Gramscian theory, but I would suggest that,
among its several theoretical advances, their project offers us some terms
for working out rigorously the implications of Foucault's effort to shift
from the register of repression and emancipation to that of opposition
and localized struggle. In their analysis, a host of dualisms grounded in
the essentialist logic of modernity's emancipatory projects are not merely
erased or deconstructed but redeployed as features of a "general field of
discursivity." Rather than occupying "two different ontological levels," for
example, "hegemonic and hegemonized forces" are understood to "constitute themselves on the same plane," a discursive field whose characteristics demand a vocabulary of unstable "frontiers" and "antagonistic forces"
rather than one based on ideology and superstructure.[24] These discred-

ited concepts, according to LaClau, are "essentially topographical." That is, they assume a "a space within which the distinction between regions and levels take place" which "implies . . . a closure of the social whole" enabling "it to be grasped as an intelligible structure" with "precise identities" assigned to "its regions and levels." By contrast, the discursive field as it is construed by LaClau and Mouffe presents "practical-discursive structures" that "do not conceal any deeper objectivity that transcends them, and, at the same time, explains them," but rather "forms *without mystery,* pragmatic attempts to subsume the 'real' into the frame of a symbolic objectivity that will always be overflown in the end."[25]

What is at stake here is the possibility of "contingency" in the field of articulatory practices, a contingency that follows from the related claims that "power is never *foundational*" and that "no discursive formation is a sutured totality."[26] The tactical force of *suture,* it seems to me, is particularly notable, here as in the work of feminist film theorists. Not only, as it is deployed in film theory, does *suture* afford us a way to restore a recognition of what has been occluded from our view by the cinematic apparatus, but further, given its root meaning, *suture* enables us to view the social text as inscribed by wounds, by signs of those "hostile encounters" that Foucault describes as the "ruptural effects of conflict and struggle" that "functionalist and systematizing thought is designed to mask."[27]

Finally, this approach to the discursive field might enable us to reexamine both those voices engaged in "othering" and the voices of those "othered" in the process. This move might profitably begin with Bakhtin. If there is, at any historical moment, a heterogeneous array of discourses, it is also the case that the voices made audible by those discourses are themselves heterogeneous, "double-voiced" in Bakhtin's sense.[28] That is, since social discourses compose a heteroglossia, any discursive subject must revoice the multiple and contradictory discourses to which s/he has been subjected, and indeed by which s/he has been constituted as a subject.[29]

Now if both "othered" discourses and "othering" ones exhibit what Bakhtin called double-voicedness, and both occupy the same heterogeneous discursive space at any given moment, two consequences follow. First, the voices of those "othered" by the dominant discourse acquire a new authority, no matter how marginalized or effaced they may have been. Further, because they are double-voiced, they may be understood not as always already neutralized by the ideologies they must speak through in order to be heard but rather as inflecting, distorting, even appropriating such ideologies, genres, values so as to alter their configuration. Secondly, since the dominant voices engaged in "othering" are also double-voiced, heterogeneous voices in struggle with each other become audible even in the texts of canonical authors, texts that can therefore come unsutured, revealing the wounds left from the hostile encounters which "othering" requires.

If Lacanian theory posits the "other of discourse," this approach suggests the possibility of an other *in* discourse, one that can erupt from the sutured fabric of the dominant culture's discourses. As I hope to demonstrate in another place, Mark Twain's *Pudd'nhead Wilson* can be read as the scene of such an eruption, specifically one that occurs on the site of the central black female character, Roxana. Similar analyses could be made, I believe, of Melville's *Pierre* and Faulkner's *Absalom, Absalom!,* where Isabel and Rosa Coldfield, respectively, function less as characters than as sites of disruption, where the wounds inflicted and sutured over by a white patriarchy come unsutured. If such analyses prove viable, they might, incidentally, provide a way of addressing formalism itself as a kind of critical suture, for the texts such an approach would probably valorize are either those, like *Pierre* and *Pudd'nhead Wilson,* which have never made it to canonical status because of their failure to achieve organic form, or those, like chapter 5 of *Absalom, Absalom!,* which have until quite recently been marginalized as incomprehensible.[30]

As for those "othered," the American slave's narrative is widely seen as rehearsing the dominant white culture's ideologies, such as the self-made man's rise to fame and fortune. But this does not necessarily mean that the subversive agency of such voices is contained by the ideologies they deploy. *The Narrative of Lunsford Lane* (1842), for example, is not unique in sounding Franklinesque in its record of how self-discipline and an enterprising inventiveness can foster the accumulation of money and independence, although it is a more detailed account than most.[31] Lane reports that he acquired the $1000.00 necessary to buy himself out of bondage by selling peaches at $.30 a basket to begin with, and then escalating his commercial enterprise by selling pipes of his own design and tobacco mixed to his own special formula, both at prices that undercut his competitors. But the central fact of Lane's entrepreneurial career is that it is motivated by the desire not to *make* but to *buy* himself. In the voice of the ex-slave narrator, the harsh facts of a commodified society are blurted out. Lane's narrative internalizes the authority of his white audience by speaking within the terms of its ideology; at the same time, it refracts that ideology through a language peculiar to a man who has been a slave—a language in which both manhood and freedom have a precisely stated price.

The point is that there is a difference made when the voice rehearsing the dominant culture's ideology is that of an ex-slave. I don't mean to suggest that these oppositional discourses are pure expressions of resistance; they are, rather, multivoiced discourses in which both dominant and oppositional ideological strains are at work. By no means are they invulnerable to the neutralizing forces of incorporation and recontainment. But once they are seen as belonging to the same heterogeneous discursive field as their dominant opponents, while they may finally be contained, they cannot be denied agency.

I am keenly aware that I have provided little more than some notes toward an alternative model. I am even more keenly, and painfully, aware that the necessarily collective task of addressing Williams's "full field" of "language in history" within the current framework of literary studies, not to mention the current political context of the academy itself, poses formidable problems. On the one hand, it seems melodramatic to take ourselves and our tasks so seriously as to believe that it matters that much how we approach them. On the other hand, to use the readily available tools that modernism has granted the intellectual for ironic self-effacement in order to refuse a responsibility whose measure we cannot take with any certainty poses other kinds of risks. The dilemma was posed by Henry Adams when he remarked, "A parent gives life, but as parent, gives no more. A murderer takes life, but his deed stops there. A teacher affects eternity; he can never tell where his influence stops."[32] Adams himself resolved the problem by using self-effacement as a mask for a hubris he could neither tolerate nor escape. In his recent testimony regarding "Paul de Man's War," Jacques Derrida addresses, and reveals, the costs and the implications of the same dilemma.[33] It is very easy to regard Derrida's treatment of "responsibility" as a display of astonishing hubris; the opening pages of the article elevate the "war" over de Man's early journalism to the rather improbable level of a world-historical event. But it is less easy, and more important, to recognize that such a dismissal of Derrida's response can serve to relieve us of the kind of responsibility he is urging us to confront, the kind of responsibility Paul de Man evaded. We may not experience ourselves as agents, but as Derrida puts it, we may still "have to answer [*repondre*] for what is happening to us" (594).

NOTES

1. This paper reprises and tries to move beyond the argument conducted in "Are We Being Historical Yet?" *South Atlantic Quarterly* 87 (1988): 743–86.

2. Frank Lentricchia, *After the New Historicism* (Chicago, 1980), xiii.

3. See Jacques Derrida, "Racism's Last Word," *Critical Inquiry* 12 (1985): 290–99; and "But Beyond . . . (Open Letter to Anne McClintock and Rob Nixon)," *Critical Inquiry* 13 (1986): 155–70.

4. See Barbara Christian, "The Race for Theory," *Cultural Critique* 6 (1987): 51–64.

5. Houston Baker, "Caliban's Triple Play," *Critical Inquiry* 13 (1986): 183.

6. Raymond Williams, *Writing and Society* (London, 1984), 189.

7. Louis Montrose, "Renaissance Literary Studies and the Subject of History," *English Literary Renaissance* 16 (1986): 8: Stephen Greenblatt, Introduction, *The Forms of Power and the Power of Forms in the Renaissance* (Norman, Okla., 1982), 5.

8. Stephen Greenblatt, *Renaissance Self-Fashioning: From More to Shakespeare* (Chicago, 1980), 6.

9. Edward Pechter, "The New Historicism and Its Discontents: Politicizing Renaissance Drama," *PMLA* 102 (1987): 292.

10. Stephen Greenblatt, "Invisible Bullets: Renaissance Authority and Its Subversion," *Glyph* 8 (1981): 49; hereafter cited in text.

11. Steven Mullaney, "Strange Things, Gross Terms, Curious Customs: The Rehearsal of Cultures in the Late Renaissance," *Representations* 3 (1983): 43; hereafter cited in text.

12. Walter Cohen, "Political Criticism of Shakespeare," in *Shakespeare Reproduced: The Text in History and Ideology,* ed. Jean E. Howard and Marion F. O'Connor (New York, 1987), 34.

13. Michel Foucault, "Truth and Power," in *Power/Knowledge: Selected Interviews and Other Writings, 1972–1977,* ed. and tr. Colin Gordon (New York, 1980), 119; hereafter cited in text.

14. See Michel Foucault, *The History of Sexuality,* tr. Robert Hurley (New York, 1978).

15. Raymond Williams, *Marxism and Literature* (Oxford, 1977), 125.

16. Michel Foucault, "Revolutionary Action: 'Until Now,'" in *Language, Counter-Memory, Practice,* ed. Donald F. Bouchard, tr. Donald F. Bouchard and Sherry Simon (Ithaca, 1977), 222.

17. Michel Foucault, "Two Lectures," in *Power/Knowledge,* 81, 85; hereafter cited in text.

18. See Michel de Certeau, *The Practice of Everyday Life,* tr. Steven F. Rendall (Berkeley, 1984); and *Heterologies: Discourse on the Other,* tr. Brian Massumi (Minneapolis, 1986). On the critique of everyday life, see the excellent collection edited by Alice Kaplan and Kristin Ross for *Yale French Studies* 73 (1987). The recent work in feminist film theory is especially rich, too much so to do justice to it here, but among the many excellent sources are Teresa de Lauretis, *Technologies of Gender* (Bloomington, 1987), Kaja Silverman, *The Acoustic Mirror* (Bloomington, 1988), and Mary Ann Doane, *The Desire to Desire* (Bloomington, 1987). Good collections are *Studies in Entertainment,* ed. Tania Modleski (Bloomington, 1986) and *Feminism and Film Theory,* ed. Constance Penley (New York, 1988). The central text by Ernesto LaClau and Chantal Mouffe is *Hegemony and Socialist Strategy: Towards a Radical Democratic Politics,* tr. Winston Moore and Paul Cammack (London, 1985). See also "Building a New Left: An Interview with Ernesto LaClau," *Strategies* 1 (1988): 10–28. Paul Smith's *Discerning the Subject* (Minneapolis, 1988) provides a useful argument and overview in relation to the issue of the discursive subject.

19. Fredric Jameson, "Postmodernism, or the Cultural Logic of Late Capitalism," *New Left Review* 146 (1984): 60.

20. John Berger, "The Moment of Cubism," in *The Look of Things,* ed. Nikos Stangos (New York, 1971), 150–59.

21. Tony Bennett, "Texts in History: The Determination of Readings and Their Texts," in *Post-Structuralism and the Question of History,* ed. Derek Attridge, Geoff Bennington, and Robert Young (Cambridge, 1987), 66. Such a lament, for example, emerges in Greenblatt's rephrasing of Kafka: "There is subversion, no end of subversion, but not for us" ("Invisible Bullets," 53).

22. See Georg Lukács, *History and Class Consciousness,* tr. Rodney Livingstone (Cambridge, 1971), 111 ff.

23. LaClau and Mouffe, *Hegemony and Socialist Strategy,* 134, 139; "Building a New Left: An Interview with Ernesto LaClau," 20.

24. LaClau and Mouffe, 134–35, 136.

25. "Building a New Left: An Interview with Ernesto LaClau," 17–18.

26. LaClau and Mouffe, 142, 106.

27. Foucault, "Two Lectures," 82.

28. See Mikhail Bakhtin, *The Dialogic Imagination,* ed. Michael Holquist, tr. Caryl Emerson and Michael Holquist (Austin, 1981).

29. In *Discerning the Subject,* Paul Smith has refocused the vexed issue of the subject from a related vantage point, arguing that "ideological interpellations may *fail* to produce 'a subject' or even a firm subject position. Rather, what is produced by ideological interpellation is contradiction, and through a recognition of the contradictory and dialectical elements of subjectivity it may be possible to think a concept of the agent" (37). See also Teresa de Lauretis's description of a "heterogeneous and heteronomous" "identity" that might be usable as a "strategy" for a feminist criti-

cal practice, in *Feminist Studies, Critical Studies,* ed. Teresa de Lauretis (Bloomington, 1986), 9. But see also Kaja Silverman's questioning of these pluralist models in *The Acoustic Mirror.*

30. For a provocative treatment of Rosa Coldfield's chapter in *Absalom, Absalom!,* see Linda S. Kauffman, *Discourses of Desire* (Ithaca, 1986), 241–78.

31. See Lunsford Lane, *The Narrative of Lunsford Lane* (Boston, 1842).

32. Henry Adams, *The Education of Henry Adams,* ed. Ernest Samuels (Boston, 1974), 300.

33. Jacques Derrida, "Like the Sound of the Sea Deep within a Shell: Paul de Man's War," tr. Peggy Kamuf, *Critical Inquiry* 14 (1988): 590–652.

RESPONSE TO CAROLYN PORTER

Rena Fraden

HISTORY AND LITERATURE have made the headlines recently. The middle-brow press—*Newsweek,* the *Nation,* and the *New Republic*—have all printed articles concerning the de Man affair, scandal, or crisis, depending on your point of view.[1] In the face of revelations about de Man's historical past—he seems to have written about 100 articles and book reviews for Nazi collaborationist journals in 1940 and 1941, a small number of which were explicitly anti-Semitic—the reconstruction of the meaning of deconstruction is underway. Friends of de Man and enemies of deconstruction are hotly debating what connections there are, if any, between de Man's history, his politics, and his theory.

Geoffrey Hartman in the *New Republic* defends deconstruction from the charges of historical amorality at least in the realm of theory. Hartman also offers a reading of de Man's later, theoretical writings that is rhetorically remarkable for its generosity toward his ex-colleague, its sympathy with de Man's particular historical burden. Hartman is careful not to assert but only to suggest that it "may yet turn out that in the later (de Man) essays we glimpse the fragments of a great confession" (30). What emerges is a new reading of de Man, the allegories turned into the confessions. Hartman sees now in his work something that was not there before because he now knows something about de Man's history. Another voice, an oppositional voice comes into the record.

David Lehman in *Newsweek* skewers de Man and deconstruction and trumpets de Man's theories as nothing but a highfalutin' cover-up of historical immorality. With deconstruction defeated, what will be attacked next? Lehman writes:

> Opponents of deconstruction think the movement is finished. As one Ivy League professor gleefully exclaims, "deconstruction turned out to be the thousand-year Reich that lasted 12 years." What's next? Berkeley professor Frederick Crews sees the rise of "the new militant cultural materialism of the left." That school prescribes the study of books not because of their moral or esthetic value but because they permit the professor to advance a political, often Marxist agenda. Crews contends that there's more than a trace of deconstruction in "the new historicism"—which is the one reason traditional humanists hope that it, too, will self-deconstruct in the wake of the de Man disgrace. (65)

Well, this might strike some of you as beneath contempt, too stupid to address, but I wonder how this point of view will figure in the histories of deconstructive criticism that will be written ten, twenty, thirty years from now. Lehman's suggestion that Marxists have a political agenda, but not a moral and aesthetic one, is absurd. Marxist aestheticism has always been accused of too strict a reading of the relationship between politics and aesthetics. But revisionary or post-Marxists like Raymond Williams and Stuart Hall have developed a theory that gives much more autonomy to art or culture and that makes the base/superstructure model more circulatory than it once was. Surely morals and aesthetic values are enmeshed in political considerations. The dismay over politics entering the "free zone" of literature is palpably expressed in this article. And though I do not share this particular dismay, and even embrace the intertwining of moral and aesthetic with an overt declaration of political values, I feel I must, at some point, speak to this anxiety: that those of us outside the realm of traditional humanism have *abdicated* a moral position.

As simplistic and paranoid as *Newsweek*'s report is, it addresses something else I find troubling: the way that our own histories become obsolete so quickly, so useless, dismissed, laughed at, scorned. When certain words become suspect, guilty by association, contaminated by contact, and tainted by unhappy history, they are quickly and absolutely abandoned. Deconstruction may be one of these words, formalism seems to be another. Is it possible though to salvage what is useful and retain what is right from what has been hastily discarded as politically or morally diseased, naive, stupid, or dangerous?

Here, I turn to Professor Porter's paper. Specifically, is there not something worth saving in, say, the practice of close reading? Isn't close reading at the nucleus of even our advanced, historically informed literary pedagogy? If there is everything for those of us in literature to learn from these discussions of history—that language is always already embedded in culture or history or politics—surely the one thing that the study of literature can return to the world is a sensitivity to the mechanics of language and rhetoric, the tropes and trips of speech. Professor Porter's "close reading" (am I right to use the term?) of the texts of the new historicists, the political implications and contradictions in their work, is incisive, a devastating analysis. We see how new historicists have used a certain reading of Foucauldian power as a way to assert yet once more a monolithic worldview, one that once again denies agency to "others." Against a kind of history that privileges a single narrative strand, she urges us to move away from the theater of power to focus instead on the site of struggle between subjects or narratives. And then begins to describe what this "alternative field" of discursive sites would look like.

I have enormous sympathy for this alternative field—it is one I explore in my own work—but I'd like to sketch briefly some of the problems I have found, some of the contradictions, the theoretical shortcomings of the notion of the alternative or oppositional model. Every movement, after all, comes with its own set of contradictions, no matter how politically correct we attempt to be. Faced with the complexity of the particular—historical specificity—the moral force of opposition Carolyn Porter implicitly invokes may not be the sure guide we hope for.

Raymond Williams owned up to some of these problems in his theoretical book *Marxism and Literature.*[2] Williams acknowledged that although it is necessary to theorize about the alternatives to culture, it is not always easy to recognize the real thing. "It is exceptionally difficult to distinguish between those which are really elements of some new phase of the dominant culture . . . and those which are substantially alternative or oppositional to it: emergent in the strict sense, rather than merely novel" (123). This is not to say that he denies that alternatives exist, only that one can be easily fooled. The pivotal question, of course, is how can we judge what is truly oppositional?

I'd like to take a minute to develop one historically specific event that might show how difficult some of these judgment calls are to make. In the same *Newsweek* issue with the piece on de Man was a review of Spike Lee's new film *School Daze.* Spike Lee is a young black filmmaker; *School*

Daze is his second picture; the first was *She's Gotta Have It. School Daze* is set in a black college and the plot revolves around the confrontations between different coalitions of students—wannabees (wannabee white) and jigaboos (dark and proud)—and between those who mean to get their education and others who are willing to be kicked out in order to protest the school's investments in South Africa. The film has received a lot of reviews, mostly good ones by white critics, but much opposition from some portions of the black community. Some believe that Spike Lee was just plain wrong about the black colleges; he spent too much time on fraternity and sorority life, causing the film to degenerate into an *Animal House*. Others believed that in airing the conflicts about color prejudice among blacks, Spike Lee was painting an "unflattering" portrait, politically damaging to blacks. I was just in a seminar where one woman said that if there were ten movies out about black kids in college then she wouldn't mind this portrayal, but since this is the *only* one around she's suspicious about its probable effects. It may feed the prejudices of the white majority (who, by the way, aren't going to see it anyway). Spike Lee has argued that that sort of "negativism"—that you could only portray a people in a "positive" light (that is, a white light?)—was a trap he wasn't going to fall into.

The last line of the film is a Brechtian moment, as the actors turn to face the audience and shout at us, "Wake Up!" Who does the film mean to wake up—black, white? Are we waking up to different situations and to different answers? Do you judge this film on its aesthetic merits (whether it conforms to or breaks the mold of the *Animal House* genre, for instance) or on its politics? And can we agree on what its politics are? Who determines the criteria for judgment? Spike Lee has made certain voices audible, voices that had been internally suppressed as a political strategy. What are the costs of maintaining that repression, and what are the costs of bringing it to the public's attention?

The other problem that causes me a good deal of anguish is the suspicion that no matter how politically correct I try to be—how many voices I am able to bring to the surface which weren't "there" before because they had been thought to be unimportant or had been actively suppressed—that I am by virtue of my critical power to choose (and limited by my historical blindness) still practicing some version of colonization. I agree that our alternative critical role must be to "make audible" those other voices, but is it possible to listen to that "other" without somehow recontaining it in our discourse, academic or otherwise? I just don't see how we get

around the semantic implications of the power play implicit in the phrase
and activity of "making audible."

Once I have situated myself as a critic of a discursive field, a field of
contending forces and voices and histories, and have mapped out some of
the contentions, I still find myself mapping some sort of narrative. If we
are willing to entertain the notion that something like subjects still exist
for us to describe, I think we also find ourselves making judgments upon
them. Flat as the landscape may be, we still privilege, by giving more
space or more moral support to one voice than another. Surely, the act
of dredging up from the depths those previously inaudible voices is one
not innocent of power—the power of analysis, of choice, and therefore
of politics and morality. I can see the merit of the flat metaphor, although
it has rather depressing connotations. I agree that what is important is
giving agency to those who have been ignored or have been actively denied it. The pressure from ethnic and women's studies to bust up the
traditional disciplines and their canons has been salutary. And the alternative canons these studies and movements have inspired have had practical
repercussions I applaud. They have given us new voices, new questions,
new classes, and new requirements.

Even as I welcome the analysis of other voices and of the heteroglossia in all voices, I wonder whether it is inevitable that the embrace of
multiplicity means that I must concede hierarchy or metaphors of depth
to the traditional humanists. Depth may not be something I am willing
to give up altogether—at least with respect to morality and politics, if not
aestheticism. Are we saying that giving agency to those who have been
denied it is the extent of our intellectual morality? Are exclusion and inclusion the sole grounds on which we base morality, aesthetics, politics?
Sometimes I think that what is being articulated in the vision of multiplicity is utopian democracy. Frank Lentricchia and Dominick LaCapra
join Carolyn Porter in promising us that if we free ourselves from a static
world view, we will be able to participate in a cultural conversation, a dialogue, one that changes when new people walk into the room. In the wake
of de Man I sometimes think that conversation or even revision doesn't
satisfy. Jean Howard has argued that the practice of history is more active
and urgent than the word *conversation* implies. She insists that any move
into history is an intervention.[3] In the fallout of the de Man affair, it seems
to me the question must always, if not always already, be turned around:
How are we as critics implicated in our own social texts? My final offering

on the subject of history and literature is a word that has a deeply troubling history: the word *discrimination*. It is a word that cuts both ways, but forces us to consider the consequences of the acts of interpretation.

NOTES

1. David Lehman, "Deconstructing de Man's Life: An Academic Idol Falls into Disgrace," *Newsweek,* 15 Feb. 1988, 63–65; Jon Wiener, "Deconstructing de Man," *Nation,* 9 Jan. 1988, 22–24; Geoffrey Hartman, "Blindness and Insight: Paul de Man, Fascism, and Deconstruction," *New Republic,* 7 Mar. 1988, 26–31; hereafter cited in text. Since writing this response in late February of 1988, the headlines have moved a notch upwards into the highbrow press, most notably Jacques Derrida's essay "Like the Sound of the Sea Deep within a Shell: Paul de Man's War," *Critical Inquiry* 14 (1988): 590–652. This is not the occasion, tempting as it may be, to respond to Derrida along with Professor Porter. I only began this specific occasion alluding to the Paul de Man affair because it seemed to me to bring up the importance of responsibility. It is gratifying to see that Derrida's essay in defense of his friend and colleague also turns on this word.

2. Raymond Williams, *Marxism and Literature* (Oxford, 1977).

3. See Frank Lentricchia, *Criticism and Social Change* (Chicago, 1983), 113–63; Dominick LaCapra, *History and Criticism* (Ithaca, 1985); and Jean Howard, "The New Historicism in Renaissance Studies," *English Literary Renaissance* 16 (1986): 13–43.

RESPONSE TO RENA FRADEN

———◆◦◆———

Carolyn Porter

THE FINAL PARAGRAPH of my paper was written largely in response to Professor Rena Fraden's incisive commentary at the conference. The questions she poses are all salient and difficult, but the most pressing, for me at any rate, is her final one, "How are we as critics implicated in our own social texts?" This question seems to me to articulate the commentary's most fundamental and pervasive concern—with the issues of values and judgments we have to confront and the ethical anxieties that must attend them. The most salutary aspect, perhaps the only salutary aspect, of the revelations about, and the debates over, Paul de Man is that they compel us to confront this question of complicity and responsibility, as Derrida has recognized with more force and cogency than anyone else, in my view.

Beyond invoking Derrida's published response, I would add here only a few more remarks, which can neither do justice to the gravity of Professor Fraden's commentary nor deal adequately with her specific criticisms. To begin with, there is no question about the fact that we are "implicated in our own social text," since we participate in creating and sustaining it. This view, of course, presupposes some version of a belief in agency, a term whose displacement of "freedom" in our discussion of these matters signals how keenly aware we have become of the limits on our powers as subjects. It is a sense of those limits that Professor Fraden's response makes me realize that I failed to stress sufficiently in my paper.

Among the curious ironies of our critical debates these days is the extent to which the left, with its long and tortured record of deterministic theories, has developed a stake in defending agency rather than determinism. Although I think there are now strong cases being made for agency, of which LaClau and Mouffe's is a good example, it's also worth turning the question around, as Professor Fraden suggests. That is, in arguing for some kind of agency, we may be merely defending against our sense of complicity in a world we lack the power to change. Yet the alternative defense is to evade responsibility for the choices we do make by insisting that they are always already constructed. Between these two defenses, there is—for me at least—a clear ethical choice.

Second, in the more concrete domain of literary studies, where Professor Fraden locates her questions about what it means to "make audible" the voices of the marginalized and silenced, it seems to me that our power is severely limited. Whether we invoke the old model of the culture industry, or newer ones such as Baudrillard's simulacra, we have ample grounds for demonstrating that our power to "make audible" anyone's voice is at best slight, at worst delusory. Our "critical power to choose," when developing a syllabus for example, is itself circumscribed in a variety of ways, from the level of prescribed curricular structures all the way to that of publishers and their marketing programs. Further, there is no question that adding the works of Afro-American women writers, say, to a syllabus for an American literature course offered in an English department works to recontain their oppositional force. I would agree, in other words, that we are "practicing some version of colonization," but add that this is a condition less of our power than of our relative lack of it; such colonization is built into the educational system we serve, one with apparently infinite resources for deflecting oppositional voices.

Our choices are almost entirely local ones. There is a choice, for example, between including Petry's *The Street,* Nella Larson's *Quicksand,* and Zora Neale Hurston's *Their Eyes Were Watching God* in an American fiction course, or not doing so. The choice here is not whether to "make" such voices "audible"; they have been made audible by others, largely by Afro-Americanist scholars (and sometimes by editors such as Toni Morrison when she worked at Random House). Rather, the choice is whether to recognize them—to attend, to pay attention. No doubt, in teaching such texts we foster their incorporation and recontainment, but what do we do by not teaching them? I can beg the question still further by noting that such choices, though heavily controlled, can also have consequences, if only by making slight differences in the structure of choices available to students. If the shape and content of that structure were wholly irrelevant, why would William Bennett have been out and about his obsessive business?

Third, as scholars, critics, teachers, or as subjects of any description one chooses, we cannot be understood as "giving agency." Again, the issue is recognition, not endowment; only God can (allegedly) endow human beings with agency. This is clearly enough not Professor Fraden's point in using such a phrase. I call attention to it here in order to correct any impression my paper may have left that I would argue for so much power. (Arguing for agency is difficult enough; arguing for its reproduction or transmission would be impossible.) *Her* point is the far more difficult one about judgments and discriminations that are neither "innocent" nor certain (for example, "How can we judge what is truly oppositional?").

As I have already indicated, we are surely not innocent, though we *are* responsible—which is one dilemma. Another is that there is no "sure guide" by which to judge not only what is oppositional but also what our moral judgment of any oppositional discourse should be. In this context, it is worth reiterating a point I made at the conference about the ethically undefined status of the term *oppositional* as I, at least, understand it. To put it rapidly, fascism was an oppositional cultural formation, and probably "emergent in the strict sense" as well, not to mention subversive of a certain form of state power. There is nothing intrinsically positive, on an ethical register, about any of these terms.

As to the grounds for the judgments we *do* make, I can only respond— lamely enough—that I cannot answer the question, but then—in defense of my lameness—I think it is unanswerable. I do agree with Professor Fraden that we perforce make such judgments with "historical blindness," not to mention a host of other blindnesses. Among these sometimes, I would add, is a desire to be "politically correct." Living as we do in contradiction, such an ideal is utopian. As a criterion for judgment, whether ethical, aesthetic, or even political, it is seriously flawed—as Professor Fraden has persuasively demonstrated, and nowhere more forcefully than in her discussion of Spike Lee's film, toward which there is clearly no finally "politically correct" response.

Finally, I completely accept the charge of being a "close reader," and am very grateful to Professor Fraden for being such a good one.

IMAGINING HISTORY
IN THE BIBLE

———⟫‣•◦‣⟪———

Robert Alter

DO THE PURPORTEDLY historical narratives of the Hebrew Bible have anything to do with history, or are they rather chiefly the product of ideological fabrication, dubious oral traditions, collective fantasy, and the tangled
threads of ancient Near Eastern folklore? With only a few notable exceptions, academic investigation of the Bible over the past two centuries has
placed the weight of emphasis on the second, more skeptical, of thse two
alternatives. The origins of Western historiography are typically traced
back to Herodotus and Thucydides rather than to the Bible because, as
Bruce Mazlish argues, plausibly enough, it is the Greek writers who devised an investigative method that "allow[ed] the reader to share both
the evidence and the inferences, the facts and the speculations that lead
to [their] conclusions."[1] Such empirical tentativeness is obviously alien to
the procedures of the biblical writers. Nevertheless, at a moment when
theoretical reflection on the writing of history has raised questions about
the drastic selectivity and bias and the incipient fictionality of every act of
identifying, sequencing, and interpreting historical data, it may be time to
reconsider whether the ancient Hebrew narratives might offer a comple-
mentary strategy to that of the Greeks for the persuasive representation
of historical experience.

A great deal of intellectual energy has been misdirected through a
dozen generations of biblical scholarship to determining the historicity
of the biblical texts, which in practice usually turns out to mean exposing their lack of historicity. The root of this misdirection was incisively
defined two decades ago by Hans Frei in his somewhat forbidding but
essential study of modern intellectual history, *The Eclipse of Biblical Narrative*. Until the eighteenth century, Frei argues, the historical, moral, and

symbolic "levels" of the biblical text were generally conceived to exist together in a single divinely warranted concordance, and the historical accuracy of Scripture thus posed no intellectual problems. During the eighteenth century, a cluster of developments in European thought — Frei singles out deism, empiricism, and skepticism — challenged the traditional assumptions about the multilayered matrix of truth of the biblical texts:

> In effect, the realistic or history-like quality of biblical narratives, ac-knowledged by all, instead of being examined for the bearing it had in its own right on meaning and interpretation was immediately transposed into the quite different issue of whether or not the realistic narrative was historical.
>
> This simple transposition and logical confusion between two cate-gories or contexts of meaning and interpretation constitute a story that has remained unresolved in the history of biblical interpretation ever since.[2]

One should note that Frei proposes as equivalents "realistic" and "history-like," two terms that are central to the argument of his whole book. Elsewhere, he offers a thumbnail definition of the concept under-lying the terms: "Realistic narrative is that kind of narrative in which subject and social setting belong together, and characters and external circumstances fitly render each other. Neither character nor circumstance separately, nor yet their interaction, is a shadow of something else more real or more significant."[3] Frei's definition of "history-like," or realistic narrative unfortunately works as well for *The House of Mirth* or for *The Golden Bowl* as for the Joseph story, and so in itself the concept will not help us decide whether there is anything in the Bible that might qualify as history writing. Frei is, however, quite acute in observing a "transposition and logical confusion between two categories or contexts of meaning" that has bedeviled biblical studies for two centuries. Let me hasten to add that the question of what may have actually happened in history (to the degree that such happenings are at all accessible to us) is obviously of great intrinsic interest, and I am by no means dismissing the prodigious efforts of modern historians of ancient Israel. But Frei's contention is that the focus on the issue of historicity has encouraged habits of misreading or underreading the biblical text, or rather reading through it, against the grain of its own semantic intentions, to conjectured things that might lie behind it.

Vivid confirmation that this confusion of categories is still very much with us is provided by Robin Lane Fox's *The Unauthorized Version,* a critique of the historicity of the narratives of both Testaments published as recently as 1991. Lane Fox, an eminent historian of Late Antiquity, is not a biblical scholar by profession, but he has done his homework with admirable thoroughness. He has a nice sense of how to weigh historical evidence, and some of his arguments against the historical character of the biblical stories are shrewdly conducted. The main problem is that this book, which is subtitled "Truth and Fiction in the Bible," has a woefully inadequate notion of both those key terms. He draws a confident equation between truth and history (an equation between truth and the history-like would have been more defensible), and he possesses two perfectly simple criteria for measuring the truth of all ancient narratives—whether they are internally consistent and whether they answer to the facts. These are precisely the assumptions of modern biblical scholarship rooted in a nineteenth-century positivist mindset that is very little inclined to interrogate its own presuppositions. The idea of "the facts" is left as unexamined as that of truth and fiction. The limitation of the notion is something to which I will address myself momentarily. Suffice it to note that Lane Fox, wielding the two-edged sword of his truth-criteria, is able to state flatly that "as they stand, the stories of the Creation and the Nativity are untrue: they do not correspond to the facts or cohere between themselves."[4] Perhaps *The Unauthorized Version* may seem something of a special case—the work of a keen intellect energized by the terribly simplifying impulse to play the village atheist. From another point of view, however, the book is a grand recapitulation of attitudes that have dominated biblical criticism since the nineteenth century, extruded here in the unnuanced vocabulary that enthusiastically speaks of the "falsehood" of Scripture, describes the late-biblical practice of pseudopigraphy as "a forger's paradise," and again and again proclaims that "all of this was untrue."

One must concede that history has something to do with facts and that any narrative that is blatantly, willfully counterfactual cannot be historical. (Thus Jonah and the frame story of Job are clearly not historical narratives, and the Book of Genesis probably has no more than a few historical kernels, however much the ancient audience may have accepted it as an authoritative account of the origins of the human race and of the people of Israel.) But history is a great deal more than the record of facts, and it is precisely for this reason that some of the major biblical narratives may qualify as serious history writing. The "facts," that is, in principle are verifiable or falsifiable details of action, chronology, biography, topography, geography, social institution, and the like, the neatest of them actually quantitative data, which are embedded in historical narratives. It is a fact that people in the Patriarchal Age rode donkeys and not horses because the Hittites had not yet introduced the domestication of the horse to the region. The consistent use for transportation of donkeys in the Patriarchal tales might give them an air of authenticity (were it not for the anachronistic camels seven centuries before their actual domestication) but does not automatically make them historical. Conversely it is in all likelihood a considerable exaggeration that 600,000 Israelites were involved in the exodus, but that unfactual statistical detail does not automatically mean that the account of national origins in the liberation from Egypt of a mass of Hebrew slaves is totally unhistorical.

Now, the historical narratives of the Bible fairly bristle with "facts," and, given the lack of corroborating or disconfirming evidence, there is no way of knowing whether most of them are concoctions, approximations, or accurate reports. We are told of the Judean king Azariah (2 Kings 15) that he assumed the throne at the age of sixteen, that he reigned for fifty-two years, that his mother's name was Jecoliah, and that he was quarantined with leprosy to his dying day while the prince-regent Jotham ruled in his stead. Beyond these ostensibly factual matters, we are given only the Deuteronomist's evaluation that Azariah did what was right in the Lord's sight, though the cult in the proscribed "high places" continued during his reign. This particular king, then, is really the subject of an annalistic notation rather than of history writing proper, and the factual details scarcely affect this status. The true historian, ancient or modern, is concerned in varying degrees with facts but is driven by the desire to make sense of them. He is concerned, in other words, with the causes of the events with which he deals, with the ways in which they may manifest lawlike properties or patterns of recurrence, and with their meanings. It is obviously meaning that is the special concern of the Hebrew historians. As Yosef Hayim Yerushalmi has put it with aphoristic concision, "If Herodotus was the father of history, the fathers of meaning in history were the Jews."[5]

Yerushalmi qualifies this remark in a note by explaining that what he is referring to is transcendent meaning. Everything in the Bible is, I suppose, at least ultimately or implicitly transcendent, but I will argue that this unmoving horizon of the divine in biblical literature in no way diminishes its urgent concerns with aspects of human experience that are political, social, moral, psychological, and as such profoundly pragmatic and this-worldly. The abiding biblical interest in these spheres draws the biblical historians rather closer to their Greek counterparts. Yerushalmi's sharp antithesis might be usefully balanced with this counterstatement by Amos Funkenstein, who also argues more broadly that Yerushalmi's suggestive book overdraws the contrast between history writing and collective memory: "A new type of historical images emerged, in antiquity, out of collective memories: it consisted not only in a reminder of the past in order to forge a collective identity and to maintain it, but in the attempt to understand the past, to question its meaning. That historical consciousness in this precise sense developed first and primarily in ancient Israel and in Greece."[6] The understanding of biblical history that I will try to develop here definitely leans toward Funkenstein's view, but to be fair to Yerushalmi, it should be observed that he evinces a fine appreciation for what he calls the "concreteness" of biblical historiography and for the prominence it gives to the scene of human action. Nevertheless, I think he places excessive emphasis on cult and collectivity—an emphasis that leads to assertions such as this: "The biblical appeal to remember has . . . little to do with curiosity about the past. Israel is told only that it must be a kingdom of priests and a holy people; nowhere is it suggested that it become a nation of historians."[7] In context, this claim is perfectly justified because Yerushalmi has just rehearsed a catalogue of biblical injunctions to remember and of rites or liturgies of remembrance. But if remembering as a covenantal obligation is a matter not of intellectual inquiry but of reaffirming God's election of Israel and Israel's historical destiny, there is abundant evidence in the actual historical narratives of a desire to know what went on in history, what impelled its principal actors, and what multiple and perhaps contradictory lessons might be learned from the historical record. Israel is of course not enjoined to become a people of historians, but it is also nowhere enjoined to become a people of poets and master storytellers, though the literature it produced reflects a powerful vocation for both those literary activities.

It may be our own tacit prejudice, referring to a model of knowledge borrowed from the natural sciences, to imagine that history writing proper should deal with causes rather than with meanings, but in fact the two are not separable in the historical realm, and no historian can entirely exclude considerations of meaning. I am of course not suggesting that history writing is intrinsically didactic, but it rarely escapes being thematically structured. How much writing, for example, on the mass murder of European Jewry by the German state can avoid pondering the nature of totalitarianism, the human capacity for evil ("banal" or otherwise), the character of racial hatred, the moral ambiguities of submissive victimhood or attempted resistance? These are all to some degree questions that address causes of the phenomenon, but they also speak powerfully to the condition of those of us who come after the events, deeply implicated as we are in the processes of history, and thus are considerations of meaning as well as causation. The indeterminate, and also overdetermined, multifaceted, elusive realm of causes and meanings is preeminently the arena of the biblical historians. Their narratives, precisely because they are devised for the purposes of historical understanding, are ones in which, as Frei says, "subject and social circumstance belong together, and characters and external circumstances fitly render each other."

There are, as I intimated at the outset, many biblical narratives that fulfill these conditions of the historylike but that, at least from our modern retrospective viewpoint, are fictional invention. Since among my own putative past sins I have been upbraided for attaching the term *fiction* to biblical narrative, let me observe here that a distinction needs to be drawn between the conscious intention of the writer and the actual relation to history of the story he produces. I have no idea what a Hebrew writer in Jerusalem court circles during the ninth or tenth centuries B.C.E. might have thought about the categories of history and fictional invention. Perhaps, in reworking literary or oral traditions to produce his own version of the Joseph story—let us say, that of the hypothetical J figure—he was convinced that he was merely crystallizing an authoritative account of what had actually transpired in the fourth generation of the nation's forebears, when the people of Israel was still no more than a clan. But to lend credence to the historical character of his story, one would have to assume, against what is known about ancient traditions everywhere, that the folktales, oral sagas, literary fragments, or whatever else the writer had at his disposal, really conveyed to him an accurate detailed account of events that occurred in the household of Jacob some seven centuries earlier. One may enthusiastically agree with Tolstoy and all those who have described this story as one of the greatest in the whole Western tradition and yet remain quite skeptical about its status as history.

Where, then, does real history writing begin in the Bible? There must surely be what I have called kernels of historical memory, small or large, and unevenly distributed, in Genesis, Exodus, Numbers, Joshua, and Judges, but the bulk of these narratives is more plausibly attributed to the complex elaboration performed by national traditions and individual literary imaginations. In all that follows, I shall concur with the conclusion of Gerhard von Rad, in an important article published, astonishingly, in Germany in 1944, that history writing proper, both in the Bible and in the Western tradition, begins with the David story.[8] (Since I remain stubbornly skeptical about the existence of an independent Succession Narrative, an axiom of German analytic scholarship since the 1920s, I include as an inseparable first phase of the history of David the stories of Samuel and Saul.) Von Rad instructively contrasts the purportedly historical narratives in Judges with the kind of story we encounter when we get to David. In Judges, the stories, which he calls "hero-sagas," though they may embed certain historical details, begin to look, under the light of form-critical analysis, like a redacted, retrospective conglomeration of earlier tales that were not originally related to the lives of their supposed historical protagonists. (Thus the Gideon cycle appears to string together a series of cultic etiological tales.) When we reach the Succession Narrative—and somewhat earlier, in my contention—the narrative is no longer an assemblage of discrete stories loosely or ingeniously attached to the central figure. Instead, all the details fit together in one large multifaceted thematic unity (von Rad expresses keen enthusiasm for the complex artistry of the narrative), and everything is subtly informed by a double system of causation: events are determined by human motives and actions, without miraculous intervention as in Judges, yet through these all-too-human instruments God's larger purpose is inexorably carried out. History writing, von Rad assumes, requires the context of politics, both as the subject of its narrative and as the setting of its authors. He frames this observation in Hegelian terms: "Only a state, which itself makes history, can write history."[9] Von Rad does not directly address the question of the historical accuracy of the David narrative but he seems to assume it.

His sketchy reconstruction of the historian remains, after half a century, the consensus view, though there are some vigorous dissenters: the writer is conceived to have flourished in the ambience of the Davidide court, in a hypothesized Solomonic Enlightenment, perhaps no more than two or three generations after the events he reports. Let me suggest that he would then have had access to abundant accounts of the events, some even going back through a relatively short train of transmission to actual witnesses. It also seems reasonable to assume that at a distance of perhaps only a few decades from the events, their broad public outline would have been common knowledge—the civil war between the House of Saul and David, the creation of a small Davidic empire through the action of expeditionary forces, Absalom's rebellion, and so forth. A general adherence of this sort to historical actualities of course does not preclude the introduction of episodes that may have a questionable relation to history, but I will not be concerned here with the attempt to make such discriminations. What seems to me more relevant to the task of locating the origins of history writing in ancient Israel is to see how the writers, in the artful articulation of materials that may have been by and large historical, created complex means for *imagining* history—which is to say, integrating a report of historical "facts" with an effort to understand their elusive causes and multiple meanings. In 1 and 2 Samuel and on into Kings, the historylike, elsewhere an attribute of narratives that have a rather tenuous anchorage in actual historical events, is associated with at least some significant degree of historicity. When the biblical writer, perhaps in collaboration with antecedent tradition, invents the chief narrative events whole-cloth, we have what Herbert Schneidau has called "historicized fiction"[10]—a story that has the uneven feel of historical experience, that conveys something of what it is like to live in history (Frei's "realism"), even though most of what is narrated may never have happened. But even when the narrative is founded in historical events, it needs historylikeness, or realism, in order to transcend the limits of a schematic chronicle of happenings and to become historiography—which involves making connections, discriminating patterns, addressing causes and meanings. The writer of historicized fiction, or any kind of fiction, has access to the realm of motive and psychology, to the inwardness and intimate transactions of his characters, and to the ambiguities of determination or overdetermination of events, because he has invented them. The biblical historian creates for himself this access to historical personages and events in his compelling effort to understand them. Thus, the historical narratives and the historicized fictions of the Bible deploy the same techniques of narrative artistry, and with very similar intentions, though the former is by and large founded in historical actualities while the latter works with many materials that may have been only imagined to be historical.

The defining principle I would like to propose for the history of Saul and David is this: the story is demonstrably an interweave of historical fact and invention, but the transition between the two is seamless because factual details like invented ones are never inertly reported but rather imaginatively elaborated in order to get at their meanings, while invention itself is for the most part discreetly managed not to violate the historical search but, on the contrary, to provide insight into it.

Let us briefly consider a few actual or purported "facts" in 1 and 2 Samuel. If scholarly consensus is correct in its assumption that the historian responsible for the narrative lived as close as two or three generations to the actual events, then there would obviously have been some body of general knowledge about the events familiar to his audience which he was not authorized to transgress. To cite a broad-gauge instance, the historian could not have been free after reporting Absalom's coup d'état to send David and his loyalists down to Philistine territory along the Mediterranean because it would have been common knowledge that the flight from Jerusalem, together with the ensuing battle against Absalom, was to the east, into trans-Jordan. What the writer does do is to thematize brilliantly the spatial deployment of the story that is one of his historical givens. In a grand panorama, rather unusual in biblical narrative, we are made to see the sad procession of David and his men, advancing on foot, down across the Kidron Brook up the Mount of Olives and then onward to the Jordan. Along the way, David has dramatic encounters with figures who are variously devoted to him or despise him, and the panoramic space through which he flees comes to be an image of his drastic loss of power, David ironically retracing in ignominious defeat the route over which he once sent expeditionary forces in pursuit of conquest.

It is of course no more than a plausible inference that the flight to trans-Jordan is a historical fact. Many of the details of the story remain undecidable in this regard because, for all the zeal of the scholarly detectives of historicity, the evidence outside the biblical text is very scanty. Let me cite a couple of instances of more minute narrative data. Was King Saul really "head and shoulders taller than all the people"? There seems to me a reasonable likelihood that he was, for if this narrative was originally framed just several decades after the events, it is the sort of notable detail that might have been retained in collective memory, and the writer would not have had an easy time giving artificial elevation to a monarch, say, who people remembered standing under five feet. But even if my surmise is right, what is important about Saul's tallness is hardly its sheer factuality but its figuring as a nexus of signification. Saul's physical stature is repeatedly used as an emblem for his ostensible fitness and actual unfitness for the throne.[12] This thematic point is made theologically explicit in 1 Samuel 16 when Samuel is sent by God to Bethlehem to anoint one of Jesse's sons in place of Saul. Just as the prophet is tempted to choose the hulking first-born, God (who actually does almost no intervening of this sort elsewhere in these stories) warns him not to make the same mistake he made with Saul: "Look not to his appearance and to his lofty stature, for it is not what man sees — man sees with the eyes and the Lord sees with [or, to] the heart." (1 Samuel 16:7). Coming from God, this is a lofty enough state-ment of the opposition between outward and inward, physical strength and spiritual worth. But, especially if one keeps in mind von Rad's notion of a double system of causation, human and divine, informing this history, bigness as a misleading sign of fitness for leadership also has more frankly pragmatic implications as a focus for the interpretation of political his-tory. Physical force may prove far less useful for the exertion of political power than adroitness, resourcefulness (think of David with his slingshot, having declined to don Saul's bulking armor when it was offered), perhaps a certain degree of ruthlessness and disquieting flexibility about principle and appearance (for example, David taking refuge among the Philistines, and playing the drooling madman when his life is at stake). Thus Saul's bigness is associated with his rigidity, his inability to seize circumstances or adapt to them, with a kind of tragic bumbling quality, while the less physically looming (though handsome) David proves to be the first full-scale portrait in Western literature of a Machievellian prince.

Since we have followed Samuel on his clandestine mission of king-selection to the household of Jesse, what are we to make of the report that David is the youngest of eight sons? Is this a historical fact? Until some lucky archaeologist unearths the Bethlehem town registry from the middle decades of the eleventh centure B.C.E., there is obviously no way of knowing for sure, but this detail of the story looks suspiciously formulaic. The first three of Jesse's sons are named — interestingly, the first two have names that include the component *'av*, "father" — and then a total of seven are mentioned, each to be rejected in turn, until the youngest is called in from the flock and is anointed. Instructively, the second, much less styl-ized account of David's debut in the next chapter, though it also mentions eight brothers and reports the same names for the first three, invokes no procession of one to seven, leaving David, the youngest, at home with an anonymous group of four siblings while the three oldest are serving in

Saul's army. (The anonymous four seem so irrelevant to the second story that I am almost tempted to succumb to an impulse of redaction-criticism and wonder whether an editor may have introduced the reference to them merely in order to harmonize the second story with the first.) My own hesitant inference is that the historical David probably was not a firstborn, though how many brothers he really had is anybody's guess. What the historian has obviously done is to assimilate whatever he may minimally have known about the facts of David's birth with a familiar archetype in the literature of ancient Israel repeatedly inscribed in Genesis: the deflection of primogeniture. The more common setting for that deflection is a head-on conflict between two brothers. In this instance, the reversal of primogeniture is heightened by the association with the formulaic number seven (just as the type scene of the betrothal by a well in a foreign land is heightened in the case of Moses in Midian when not one maiden but seven sisters come to the well). Would the historical authority of the story be undermined if we could somehow demonstrate that David actually had just three brothers, or five, or nine? Certainly not from the biblical standpoint, which in any case is strongly inclined to use numbers not as mathematically precise markers but as conventional approximations: seven is an integrated few, ten a minimal communal unit, forty a round good many, seventy (as the product of seven times ten) an imposing group, and so forth. David's seven older brothers, then, are a means of highlighting his belatedness, which mirrors Israel's historical role as a latecomer among the peoples of the Fertile Crescent, and of underscoring his surprising spring from youthfulness and obscurity to power, his enactment of that repeated destiny in which the last becomes first. I don't think the historian would have thought he was merely inventing, or distorting, the historical record: the seven siblings help explain the meaning of David's career, how it fits into a recurrent pattern that is a kind of law of Israelite history.

Beyond the relatively mechanical phenomenon of the elaboration and shaping of details to make sense of the historical record, a pervasive and more complex feature of biblical history is that the way the story is told — its formal narratological contours — exerts constant subtle pressure on the historical data, leads us back and forth restlessly through the labyrinth of motives and causes and the intersections of character and circumstance in order to illuminate the bewildering meanings of historical experience, making us contemplate the moral dilemmas of living in history.

Although biblical narrative is by Greco-Roman and later Western standards extraordinarily laconic, the Hebrew narrator when he chooses can provide perfectly lucid access to the inner experience of the historical personages, either reporting their feelings and motives or offering little bits of interior monologue. If we ask ourselves the crude question, how did the historian know what Saul or David said to himself, the simple answer is that he knew because he invented it. The notion of invention, however, requires conceptual complication: although the narratological function of interior monologue in these stories may be virtually the same as in entirely fictional narratives, the writer gives us the unvoiced speech of his protagonists not as free-standing fabrication but as a means of artfully focusing his insight into their nature as historical figures. The writer exercises, in other words, a certain freedom of stylization that is loosely analogous to the liberties Thucydides takes in contriving speeches for some of the leading figures of his history. The difference is that Thucydides is chiefly concerned in the oratory he devises with political principles and questions of policy, whereas the biblical historian is also urgently interested in individual psychology and moral character and how they play out in the historical arena.

A textbook illustration of the deployment of shifting narrative perspectives, inward and outward, to shape the meanings of the historical account, is the story in 1 Samuel 18 of Saul's bungling effort to get David out of the way by sending him off on the supposedly suicidal task of getting a bride-price of a hundred Philistine foreskins so that he can marry the king's daughter.[13] Throughout the episode, Saul's feelings and intentions are made perfectly transparent. We are told explicitly that he is afraid of the spectacularly successful David. When he devises his plan to have David killed in battle (a stratagem that will return to haunt David later when he hits on a roughly similar scheme to get rid of Uriah), his calculation is exposed to the harsh light of direct quotation in interior monologue: "For Saul thought, 'Let not my hand be against him, let the hand of the Philistines be against him.'" Meanwhile, David's motives and intentions remain steadily opaque. We get no report of his feelings, no interior monologue, but only, as throughout the first half of his story, public speech (here, his protestation of unworthiness to marry into the royal family) that lends itself to multiple and conflicting interpretations. What emerges from this narratological difference in the presentation of Saul and David is a sharply contrastive perception of how the two figures move through the political arena. The young David is a supremely political, and politic, man: all we really know of him is the speech he frames for the public realm, which may have its private motives but always serves his political ends. As for Saul, it may be that in the history's theological system of causation he will lose the throne because God has "diselected" him through Samuel the prophet, but in the pragmatic system of causation he seems altogether too transparent, too heavy-handed in his devisings and his revealed intentions, to hang on to power.

Dialogue, one of the chief modalities of all biblical narrative, is the most pervasive technical means through which the writer adumbrates the multiple and often murky human implications of the historical record. Let us consider one characteristic instance. In their flight from Absalom, David's forces set up headquarters east of the Jordan in the walled town of Mahanaim. At the insistence of the troops, David remains in Mahanaim while they go out to face Absalom's pursuing army. The king gives explicit instructions to Joab, his commander, and to Joab's brother Abishai, to do no harm "to the lad Absalom." Joab, of course, who remains ruthlessly Machievellian while the aging monarch is softened by paternal compunction, is not going to leave so dangerous an adversary around and will kill Absalom, delivering the first blow with his own hands after the rout of the rebel forces. An eager young man, Ahimaaz the son of Zadok, insists on running off to bring the news of the victory to David, though Joab tries to dissuade him. Joab himself sends off a certain Cushite with the report. (It should be noted that the foreign messenger at moments of disaster is a recurring motif in these stories.) There follows a spectacular visual set piece, in which David sits between the inner and outer gates of the city while a lookout posted on the wall above the outer gate espies first one figure and then a second running toward them. (Did it really happen that way? Perhaps. In any case, the scene serves as a brilliant representation of David's desperate grasping for knowledge through the instrument of others.) Here are the concluding lines of the scene (2 Samuel 18: 27–32):

> The lookout said, "I see the first one running like Ahimaaz the son of Zadok." And the king said, "He is a good man, and he comes with good tidings." And Ahimaaz called out and said to the king, "All is well," and he bowed low with his face to the ground before the king and said, "Blessed be the Lord your God who has delivered over the men who raised their hand against my lord the king." And the king said, "Is all well with the lad Absalom?" And Ahimaaz said, "I saw a great tumult sending the king's

servant Joab and your servant and I know not what." And the king said, "Turn aside and stand here." And he turned aside and took up his stance. And now the Cushite arrived, and the Cushite said, "Let my lord the king receive the tidings that the Lord has vindicated you this day against all who rose against you." And the king said to the Cushite, "Is all well with the lad Absalom?" And the Cushite said, "Like that lad may be the enemies of my lord the king and all who rose wickedly against you."

As with most of the dialogue in the David history, it would be extremely far-fetched to imagine that anyone present could have heard these words and transcribed them for the subsequent use of the historian. Rather, the historian has invented the dialogue, just as elsewhere he has invented interior monologue, to represent the clash of motives and David's emotional anguish in the resolution of Absalom's rebellion. The old king clings talismanically to the illusion of hope while we, the audience, know there is no hope: Ahimaaz is a good man, he will bring good tidings. Immediately, in a little narrative ellipsis, the good man appears within the gate with his tidings, the first word he utters being *shalom,* "All is well." Prostrating himself, his language a model of deferential address to the king, he then reports the victory in the most general terms. David immediately addresses his darkest fear: "Is all well [*shalom*] with the lad Absalom?" That question works as a painful formal refrain through the whole scene, while the repeated designation of the decidedly adult Absalom—both a fratricide and a usurper—as "lad," *na'ar,* not only focuses David's feelings of paternal tenderness but also picks up a literary echo, the words of the angel to Abraham as he is about to slaughter his own son, "Do not reach out your hand against the lad, nor do anything to him" (Gen. 21:12). Ahimaaz chooses to evade David's terrible question about his son. The syntax of the Hebrew at this point is incoherent, and I would conclude that this is not a problem of faulty textual transmission but a mimesis of Ahimaaz's stammer of confusion: great tumult—to send the king's servant—your servant—I don't know what. David realizes he will get nothing more out of him and so orders him to stand aside. The Cushite messenger exhibits little of Ahimaaz's extreme deference before royalty. He does not prostrate himself; he moves quickly in both his speeches from the deferential third person to second-person address;[14] and he does not begin his report with *shalom,* "All is well." (Through all this, the Hebrew reader can scarcely forget that *shalom* forms the last two syllables of Absalom's name, *Avshalom*.) When David puts to him the crucial anxious question about the fate of the lad Absalom, the Cushite, perhaps because he is a foreigner, does not seem aware of the abyss he is uncovering; and though he, too, does not directly state that Absalom is dead, he conveys the information confidently in a triumphal formula that follows the general biblical pattern, thus may perish all your enemies. As witnesses of this awful revelation, we, the audience, are no doubt invited to recall the moment when the Amalekite messenger thought he would gladden David's heart by reporting Saul's death, claiming, to boot, that he himself had finished off the king. Those ill tidings resulted in David's peremptory order to kill the messenger. Here, at a much later juncture in David's long struggle in the deadly coil of politics and family, he instead breaks down, now climbing to that outpost over the gate, repeating his single stutter of grief: Absalom, Absalom, my son, my son.

If one concedes that the biblical historian's drive to understand the political, moral, and psychological predicaments of the historical personages leads him to shape the events, amplifying what is known through shrewd literary elaboration, there remain bothersome instances of invention plain and simple. There are, in other words, at least a few episodes reported in the history of Saul and David that almost certainly never happened. The easiest way to dispose of these would be to say that the Israelite literary imagination, only imperfectly engaged in the recording of history, failed to distinguish between the historic and the fabulous or folkloric and so made a promiscuous mélange of all three. There is probably some truth in that characterization, but the notion of a haphazard commingling of materials does not allow for the firm continuity of interpretive purpose, manifested in literary shaping, between the probably historical episodes and the occasional episodes that are probably invented.

A case in point is the story of the witch of Endor (1 Samuel 28), the only ghost story in the whole Hebrew Bible. We, of course, know that the episode could not be historical because we—or at least, most of us—no longer believe in ghosts. For most of us, then, the story has the same fictional status as Macbeth's encounter with the three witches—and, in fact, as we shall see, its narrative function is somewhat akin to that of the scene in *Macbeth*. In terms of biblical notions of reality, it is not at all clear that the summoning up of a departed spirit would have been thought of as a supernatural event, and so the unhistorical character of the episode would not have been so evident to the ancient audience as it is to us. In the somewhat fluctuating biblical conception, the dead either sank into extinction in the Pit, Sheol, or lingered there as insubstantial spirits that might perhaps be addressed by necromancy. The *yid'onim,* or necromancers, were banned not because they were dealing in wholly empty superstition but because they were exercising a technology of the spirit realm independent of God's imperatives. He was "the God of spirits for all flesh" whereas they presumed to operate on spirits beyond the pale, without divine authorization. Thus, the introduction to the Endor episode provides us two crucial pieces of information for what follows: the death of Samuel, Saul's one-time anointer and implacable foe, which is bracketed with Saul's rooting out (reported in a pluperfect) of necromancers in the land.

Now, a key theme of the whole Saul history, including its most naturalistic episodes, is the king's constant reaching for withheld knowledge in a futile attempt to control the uncertain and perhaps ominous future. Saul calls on oracles and omens and prophets, pronounces rash vows, all in vain. (The first time we encounter him in the story, he is looking for a seer to help him find his lost asses. This will be his last success in a quest for knowledge.) In the parallel narrative track, the fugitive David travels equipped with an *ephod* (a divining instrument) and a priest to consult it in proper form, and he is able to get the requisite yes-or-no indication from above whenever he stands at a crossroads of decision. The story of the necromancer of Endor culminates this representation of Saul hopelessly seeking knowledge. He has rooted out the necromancers—one of the two Hebrew terms for the profession is derived from the root *yad'a,* to know, which figures importantly here and elsewhere in the history of Saul. Now, he tries all means of predictive knowledge and gets no results: "And Saul inquired of the oracle, and the Lord did not answer him, and also in dreams, and also through the *'urim,* and also through prophets" (28:6). This leaves him one avenue, which he himself had proscribed. He bids his men to seek out a necromancer in the vicinity—his forces are encamped on Mount Gilboa, the night before the last battle with the Philistines—who presumably has gone underground and escaped the vigilance of the royal ban. This explains why he, the issuer of the ban, appears at Endor dressed as a commoner.

The woman needs to be urged to perform because she fears for her life. It is noteworthy that only she can see the figure she calls up from the dead, whom she is thus obliged to describe to Saul: even now, the knowledge he seeks is held at arm's length. When she tells him it is an old man "wrapped in a cloak [*me'il*]," Saul at once knows (*yad'a*) that it must be Samuel. The prophet is just as implacable as when he was alive. He begins by castigating Saul for disturbing his rest in the underworld, and when the king tells him he desperately needs to know what he should do in the imminent battle against the Philistines, Samuel responds with a verbatim reprise of the fierce speech in which, at the end of the Amalek episode, he told Saul that the Lord was irreversibly revoking his kingship. As to the knowledge of the impending future that Saul had sought, Saul responds with the grim finality of these words: "Tomorrow you and your sons are with me" (28:19).

The whole episode is beautifully fashioned, but the fashioning strikes one, at least in the first instance, as far more literary than historiographical. The use of the necromancer is in fact quite similar in function to the scene of the witches in Macbeth that it may well have inspired. Here, too, the man who would be king is caught in the inexorable trap of his own tragic destiny: seeking counsel or foreknowledge that will enable him to cope with the threatening morrow, he hears in the dead prophet's voice only his own imminent death sentence and that of his sons. An equally literary aspect of the story is its climactic use of a recurring motif. Garments and the divestment of garments play a crucial role in the story of Samuel and Saul almost from the beginning. When the woman of Endor describes the spirit as an old man wrapped in a cloak (*me'il*), Saul at once knows it must be Samuel because he is wearing his usual prophet's garb. But many decades earlier in narrated time, when Samuel's mother Hannah dedicated the child after weaning to serve in the sanctuary at Shiloh, we are given no direct report of her maternal feelings—instead, much more poignantly, we are told, "a little cloak (*me'il*) his mother would make him and she would bring it up to him each year when she came with her husband to offer the festival offering" (1 Samuel 2:19). The child Samuel is already enveloped in his future vocation. He will wear the little *me'il* as the token of his mother's love over the cultic *ephod* he girds round him as a priest's acolyte. As an old and wrathful leader, embittered by the imposition of the monarchy, he will be recognized by his prophetic *me'il* and, as we see here, he even bears it with him beyond the grave.

Saul, by contrast, is a man who cannot hang on to the garb of vocation. In the Amalek incident, he clings imploringly to the skirt of Samuel's robe (again *me'il* is the term used), and when it tears, Samuel immediately converts it into the symbol of kingship: "The Lord has torn from you this day the kingship over Israel and given it to someone better than you" (1

Samuel 15:28). (Samuel will echo most of these words when he speaks as
a ghost.) This bit of impromptu symbolic interpretation then serves as a
guide for a series of divestments in the Saul story. In the Goliath episode,
Saul offers his own armor to David. In the second of the two stories of
Saul among the prophets, the one that marks his devastating rejection by
Samuel, he is violently seized by "the spirit of God," and in an ecstatic
fit, strips off his clothes and rolls naked on the ground all that day and
night—the king shorn of his regalia, reduced to a bare forked thing in
this most ambiguous experience of "prophesying." And so when he appears before the woman of Endor dressed as a commoner, the disguise
may be dictated by practical considerations, but its resonant meaning is
one last self-divestment of the forms of kingship, before Saul's final and
fatal battle. And in the battlefield itself, after the defeat of the Israelites,
when Philistine soldiers find the slain king, what they do, plausibly but
also symbolically, is to strip him of his armor.

This intricate development of symbolic motif, culminating in a tale of
necromancy that could scarcely be founded in fact, would seem to take
our narrative a long way from the writing of history to the creation of literature. But what we need to remind ourselves, as several contemporary
theorists of historiography have proposed, is that those two categories
are not mutually exclusive oppositions. The story of the witch of Endor
seems to me in this regard a deeply instructive limit-case. It couldn't really
have happened, though it is at least conceivable that the writer's invention
sprang from certain historical seeds: perhaps what was transmitted about
the historical Saul included reports of an anxious and frustrated quest for
knowledge concerning his future through the available cultic and occult
means, and surely Samuel's grim adversial stance toward Saul, which as
prophet he would have manifested through imprecation and dire predic-
tion, might have been general knowledge. The scene of the prophet's
spirit summoned from the underworld to issue one final pronouncement
of doom might have been, from the viewpoint of the Hebrew historian,
not fanciful freewheeling invention but a kind of imaginative extrapola-
tion from what was historically known, endowing what was known with
a climactic focus.

All these events, let us remember, are deeply implicated in a web of
evolving political circumstances, as von Rad claims all true history writing must be. Samuel is not just a figure of folklore or a fictional idea but

the last, most powerful representative of the old political order of ad hoc charismatic leadership. He feels personally rejected, and is at first bitterly opposed, when the people demands a king. The tension and the eventual enmity between him and the man he initially selects as king are not just a matter of personal chemistry but reflect a historical clash between two different conceptions of the Israelite polity. The evolving play between the prophet's cloak and the king's changing or stripped clothing provides a technical means for focusing this clash of different political eras. And in the historian's extraordinarily subtle, dialectical understanding of politics, the historical necessity of monarchy is accepted but its grave moral dangers and abuses are searchingly examined—first in the sad fate of Saul, the man who tries desperately but is never adequate to the terrible challenges of kingship; and then in the complex career of David, whose resourcefulness fits him for the throne but who is also subverted by the very power he has succeeded in consolidating as he moves from battlefield hero to indolent monarch, casual adulterer, murderer, and impotent old man at the mercy of his sons, his wives, and his henchmen. In all this, as the historian moves back and forth from what may well have been factual materials to elaborations of detail and scene that exhibit intricate formal symmetries and developments, what he constantly attempts to do is not to report history—he is no annalist—but to imagine it. History in this body of narrative is represented in its concrete, often dramatic manifestations, in all the busy and bewildering transactions between personal destinies and public circumstances, between individual motives and psychology and collective ideologies. The goal is an account of what happened in history fused with the poignancy and the imponderability of being immersed with imperfect human resources in the powerful current of historical experience. To achieve this end, the writer worked with a hybrid form that was both imaginative literature and historiography. But as we come to understand certain lines of convergence between the two, we may be able to see more clearly that these superbly artful narratives are also a major point of departure for the writing of history in the Western tradition. To the extent that one can claim a continuous tradition of history writing in the West, its decisive origins are among the Greeks, not the Hebrews; and later readers approached the Bible in too strictly theological terms, as a unique and unprecedented text, to use it as a model for historiography. Nevertheless, these early Hebrew narratives, several centuries before Herodotus, were persuasively engaged in the writing of history, and as our own notions of historiography become more complicated, we are in a better position to appreciate their continuing relevance.

NOTES

1. Bruce Mazlish, "The Question of *The Question of Hu*," *History and Theory* 31 (1992): 151.

2. Hans Frei, The eclipse of Biblical Narrative (New Haven, 1974), 16.

3. Ibid., 13–14.

4. Robin Lane Fox, *The Unauthorized Version* (London, 1991), 36.

5. Yosef Hayim Yerushalmi, *Zakhor: Jewish History and Jewish Memory* (Seattle, 1982), 8.

6. Amos Funkenstein, *Perceptions of Jewish History* (Berkeley, 1993), 11.

7. *Zakhor*, 10.

8. Gerhard von Rad, "Der Anfang der Geschichtsschreibung in Alten Israel," *Archiv für Kulturgeschichte, XXXII:* 1–3, 1–42. I am grateful to my friend and colleague Amos Funkenstein for alerting me to this article and making the text available to me.

9. Von Rad, 29–30. My friend and colleague Michael André Bernstein has persuaded me of the Hegelian assumption behind this observation, against my initial impulse to link it with Nazi statist triumphalism.

10. Herbert Schneidau, *Sacred Discontent* (Baton Rouge, 1977).

11. For the importance of thematized space as an attribute of literary narrative, see T. G. Rosenmeyer "History or Poetry: The Example of Herodotus," *Clio* 2 (1982): 239–59.

12. I discuss the thematic use of Saul's bigness in greater detail in *The World of Biblical Literature* (New York, 1992), 99–101.

13. I devote closer attention to this episode in *The Art of Biblical Narrative* (New York, 1981), 115–20.

14. Biblical dialogue does allow for the shift from third person to second person. There is also one such shift in Ahimaaz's speech, when he mentions "the Lord your God," but for this particular locution it would be impossible in biblical usage to say "the Lord his God" in direct address. The Cushite is less deferential in simply naming the Lord, YHWH, and not attaching the deity to the king through a possessive.

THE STORY OF THE EYE

Rosalind E. Krauss

THE LETTER INVITING me to participate in this conference was very clear about its objectives. " 'History and . . .' takes place," it announced, "at a time of critical importance for our understanding of how consciousness of and rhetoric about the past contributes to our ability to make sense of our cultures. Whereas a historical appreciation of the sciences and humanities was once seen as a necessary component of a liberal education, in the wake of structuralism's and functionalism's celebration of the synchronic, the significance of historical knowing is far from clear. More recently still, poststructuralism's playfulness sees no virtue in making meaning from memory, and it is doubtful that deconstruction will clarify the importance of a sense of the past for our ability to come to terms with the present."

From those sentences, with their pessimism about the ability of the synchronic sciences to take culture seriously, with their certainty that poststructuralism is the opponent of both meaning and memory, the enemy of virtue in the name of playfulness, from those sentences I understood that I was being invited to a convocation of what has come to be called the new historicism. And thus I realized that whatever else I might say, I had better begin with an anecdote.

My anecdote, then, is drawn from the annals of the early sixties art world, a world just before it was about to be swept up into the hyperspace of minimalism and pop art. It is a story that was told to me by a critic—Michael Fried—about an artist—Frank Stella. It starts with a question.

"Do you know who Frank thinks is the greatest living American?" Michael asked me one day. And then, grinning with pride at the sheer brilliance of the answer, he said it was Ted Williams, the amazing hitter for the Red Sox. "He sees faster than any living human," Michael said. "His vision is so fast that he can see the stitching on the baseball as it comes over the plate. Ninety miles an hour, but he sees the stitches. So he hits the ball right out of the park. That's why Frank thinks he's a genius."

I remember the urgency in Michael's voice as his tone was divided by total hilarity at the image and utter seriousness about its import. But it was the early 1960s and I was in the grip of a certain view of modernism and so its import did not escape me either. I too found it a completely brilliant, wholly perfect idea: Ted Williams, the spectacular homerun hitter, the perfect metaphor for visual modernism.

There are some of you perhaps who do not find that image as completely intuitive as I did then—a failure that would not be surprising since the grip that modernism has on our intuitions has begun for some time now to slacken. But for me—then—the image performed the condition of an abstracted and heightened visuality, one in which the eye and its object made contact with such amazing rapidity that neither one seemed any longer to be attached to its merely carnal support—neither to the body of the hitter, nor to the spherical substrate of the ball. Vision had, as it were, been pared away into a dazzle of pure instantaneity, into an abstract condition with no before and no after. Yet in that very motionless explosion of pure presentness was contained as well vision's connection to its objects, also represented here in its abstract form—as a moment of pure release, of pure transparency, of pure self-knowledge.

Thus in the early sixties, the image of Williams's heightened vision conjured those very aspirations toward what Clement Greenberg had, at just about that time, outlined as modernist painting's self-critical dimension: its participation in a modernist culture's ambition that each of its disciplines be rationalized by being grounded in its unique and separate domain of experience, this to be achieved by using the characteristic methods of that discipline both to narrow and "to entrench it more firmly in its area of competence." For painting this meant uncovering and displaying the conditions of vision itself, as these were understood, abstractly. "The heightened sensitivity of the picture plane may no longer permit sculptural illusion, or trompe-l'oeil [Greenberg wrote], but it does and must permit optical illusion. The first mark made on a surface destroys its virtual flatness, and the configurations of a Mondrian still suggest a kind of illusion of a kind of third dimension. Only now it is a strictly pictorial, strictly optical third dimension. Where the Old Masters created an illusion of space into which one could imagine oneself walking, the illusion created by a Modernist is one into which one can look, can travel through, only with the eye."[1]

Lukács, deploring this technologizing of the body, this need to abstract and reify each of the senses in a submission of human subjectivity to the rigidifying model of a positivist science, Lukács would have found nothing to argue with in Greenberg's analysis. He would only have objected to its tone, to its position, which Greenberg shared with Adorno, that in this withdrawal of each discipline into that sphere of sensory experience unique to it, there was something positive, something utopian. For this utopianist modernism was insisting that the sensory stratum newly created as discrete, as self-sufficient, as autonomous, this very stratification permitted an experience of rescue and retreat, a high ground uncontaminated by the instrumentalism of the world of labor and of science, a preserve of play, and thus a model of freedom. And perhaps the pleasure for us at that moment in the sixties in the idea of a high-cultural ambition being allegorized through a baseball player was just this insistence on the seriousness of this very sense of play.

One thing was also unquestioned by us—and this, whatever their other differences, was also a shared assumption of Lukács, Adorno, and Greenberg—and that was that the modernist specialization and abstraction of the senses performed a radical break with an earlier phase of aesthetic experience, so that while nineteenth-century realist art could still be seen as continuous with a traditional artistic past, impressionism, for example, could not. And it was this discontinuity between what we could think of as art-historical art and what we would call modernist painting that formed an important part of the very definition we had of the becoming autonomous of art.

Now if the idea of a discontinuity between modernism and art history was important to both these enterprises—to the practice and criticism of contemporary art on the one hand, and to the historicist mission of art history on the other—it is the belief in that discontinuity that has begun to erode during the last two decades, under the analysis launched by poststructuralism on the one hand and through the critique mounted by certain postmodernist artistic practice on the other. For what has become increasingly clear is that modernism as a practice and art history as a discipline were born at the same time and developed out of certain assumptions that paralleled one another over the last hundred years. And one of these parallels is precisely the foundationalist assumption that it is in the nature of vision itself that any art practice (historical or modern) will be grounded.

What has become obvious, for example, is that between Greenberg's explicit characterization of modernism's self-critical stance as "Kantian" and art history's establishing of itself as a neo-Kantian project through which the visual arts are grounded categorically in the dimension of space and of vision's access to it, that between these two enterprises there are profound connections. Stephen Melville has described that moment in the early history of art history when a Hegelian model for the account of art's condition *as history* is exchanged for a Kantian model of the conditions of possibility for the permanently renewable experience of art through the modality of the visible. It is a moment of divide at which the work of Erwin Panofsky resets the agenda for the discipline. "Whereas in Wolf-flin," Melville writes,

> key terms ("thing in itself," "thing as it appears") can, from paragraph to paragraph and often undecidably, be given variously Kantian or Hegelian inflections, in Panofsky Kant unequivocally presides, and the explicit problematic of historicality recedes. The "Kant" in question here is also quite particular: given the state of Kant's German inheritance in the early part of this century, Panofsky could, in effect, have moved either toward the neo-Kantian tendencies that culminate in the work of Ernst Cassirer or toward the more radical revision of Kant set in motion by Heidegger. And Panofsky's choice was, clearly, for Cassirer. . . . This choice is clearly reflected in Panofsky's effort to read the necessarily hermeneutical activity of art history as a constrained passage from the "natural" to the "essential." In his essay "Perspective as Symbolic Form," with its explicit dependence on Cassirer . . . [Panofsky] finds in the Renaissance a period that delivers us from what might seem the debilitating fact of periodicity, or finds in it an optic that delivers us from our situations. History lies before us much as we might imagine nature to, available to our view. . . . This valorization of perspective opens the way to a new understanding of the objectivity of art history, one in which the becoming historical of art need no longer be an issue since we have now gained an apparently nonproblematic access to the rationalized space of the past. We can, that is, imagine ourselves henceforth as scientists of a certain kind, and it is within this imagination that Gombrich's work moves and gains its power. The grounds of privilege here become invisible and profoundly naturalized. The shift away from Hegel and toward the assumptions and interests of Anglo-American philosophy is an essential part of this reimagining

of art history, as in the psychologization of such key inherited terms as "schema."[2]

It is, then, this double grounding of both modernism and art history in the conditions of opticality—in conditions which for art history are invisible because they are "profoundly naturalized" and which for modernism have been made visible as the proud condition of reflexivity as a kind of natural legitimation—it is this grounding that forms the background to the case I want to present today.

Drawn from what we could refer to as the antioptical or antivisual option that existed within the artistic avant-garde in the first half of the twentieth century, this case is an example of a resistance to the visual that was performed in explicit critique of modernism's own privileging of opticality as the only way to ground or legitimate aesthetic practice. This resistance was never a movement. It was, rather, something like an underground studded with names like Max Ernst, Salvador Dali, Jean Dubuffet, Alberto Giacometti, and finding support in the theoretical work of others like Georges Bataille, Jacques Lacan, and Roger Caillois. It has been, however, an underground that has gone completely uncharted—not because these figures are unknown to us, but because the very idea of a resistance to the optical has for us—in the grip of art history's founding optic—been invisible.[3]

The case I am going to examine involves Marcel Duchamp, perhaps the earliest member of this underground, but a figure whose resistance to the visual—or what he called the retinal—has either been persistently overlooked or consistently misunderstood. Duchamp was outspoken about his impatience with what he termed "retinal art," and the following remark is typical of what he said again and again on this subject:

> I believe there is a difference [Duchamp told an interviewer] between a kind of painting that primarily addresses itself only to the retina, to the retinal impression, and a painting that goes beyond the retina and uses the tube of paint as a springboard to something further. This is the case of religious artists of the Renaissance. The tube of paint didn't interest them. What interested them was to express their idea of the divinity, under one form or other. Thus, without doing the same thing, there is this idea of mine, in any case, that pure painting is not interesting in itself as an end. For me the goal is something else, it is a combination, or at least an expression that only the grey matter can succeed in rendering.[4]

Now, this mention of the gray matter, ballasted as it is by the allusion to the Renaissance, has produced in certain Duchamp apologists the idea of Duchamp as an antimodernist who worked in support of an art of classical perspective, an artist who joined with Leonardo in locating painting's ambition in the production of a *cosa mentale*—the kind of diagrammatic mastery of reality made possible by the geometricization of space and light that Alberti had called the "legitimate construction." And indeed, this picture of Duchamp embracing perspective in a specifically antimodernist return to a historical style is buttressed by other passages in Duchamp's antiretinalist litany.

> Since the advent of Impressionism [he said in yet another interview], visual productions stop at the retina. Impressionism, fauvism, cubism, abstraction, it's always a matter of retinal painting. Their physical preoccupations: the reactions of colors, etc., put the reactions of the gray matter in the background. This doesn't apply to all the protagonists of these movements. Certain of them have passed beyond the retina. The great merit of surrealism is to have tried to rid itself of retinal satisfaction, of the "arrest at the retina." I don't want to imply that it is necessary to reintroduce anecdote into painting. Some men like Seurat or like Mondrian were not retinalists, even in wholly seeming to be so. (110)

But if Duchamp was cautious here that his strictures against retinal art did not imply a wholesale attack on the avant-garde and a merely reactionary return to historical art, certain of his interpreters have been less circumspect; and their reading, which reduplicates modernism's own vision of the profound rift between its synchronic regime and history's diachronous one, this reading, in positioning Duchamp *against* modernist art, locates him as being *for* the perspectivism of historical painting. That their reading also reduplicates the problematic set up by the letter describing this conference and its own opposition between synchrony and diachrony goes, I hope, without saying. And thus, even though here I am showing my cards in advance, what I hope to achieve by demonstrating the vulgarity—and in my view the falseness—of the perspectivist reading of Duchamp, is to raise doubts about the legitimacy of the very enterprise of this conference with its new historicist certainties about history's access to both "meaning and memory."

Duchamp's masterpiece is generally referred to as the *Large Glass*, although its official and much longer title is *The Bride Stripped Bare by Her*

Bachelors, Even. The dates given to the work are 1915, when the glass plates on which the work was executed were set up in Duchamp's New York studio, and 1923, when Duchamp (now returned to Paris) abandoned the project as officially "unfinished." But these dates are deceptive, since certain of the notes and sketches for *The Bride Stripped Bare* date from as early as 1912, and the last campaign on the *Glass* took place in 1920, shortly after which Duchamp left New York for Paris not to return until 1926.

That last campaign was probably the most laborious of all the various strategies of execution that Duchamp dreamed up for the application of matter to the surface of this work. For while other parts involved the careful laying down of lead sheet and metal wire—as in the element called the Chocolate Grinder—or the fixing of deposits of dust—as in the multiple appearance of what Duchamp called the Sieves—his last application produced the composite figure he called the Oculist Witnesses, and was made from the silvering of that part of the glass to render it a mirror surface, followed by the meticulous removal of all but the finest lines of silvering to create the three optical discs the *Glass* now bears. That these discs are in a rather dramatic perspective renders them homogeneous with the perspectival system that seems to reign in the lower half of the *Large Glass*. And it is the very assertiveness of this use of perspective that has always encouraged the revisionist, antimodernist reading of Duchamp.

But, far from being continuous with the rest of the field of the lower half of the *Glass,* the Oculist Witnesses represent a rather important rupture. In contradistinction to the apparatus occupying most of the surface, an apparatus through which Duchamp considered the mechanics of perpetual motion in what he termed the Bachelor Machine, the Oculist Witnesses are conceived within the domain of optics. And indeed this shift from mechanics to optics was accompanied in the late teens by a sequence of other works devoted similarly to issues of sight specifically set apart from motion: *To Be Looked at Close to, from the Other Side of the Glass, for Nearly an Hour* (1919), the *Handmade Stereopticon Slide* (1919), and the *Rotary Glass Plates* (1920). Thus it can be argued that if Duchamp left the *Large Glass* permanently unfinished, this was a result of his having set out in a direction somewhat at variance with the problematics of the machine. Optics had now become his "profession"—as was borne out by the business card he began to use throughout the twenties and thirties, giving his occupation as "spécialiste en oculisme de précision"—as it also became the medium of his opposition to painting. Thus, for example, in 1925 he wrote to the collector Jacques Doucet, for whom he had made the *Rotary*

Demisphere—a spiral-etched half-globe, which when set into motion created a pulsating optical illusion—regarding a request that the object be
exhibited: "To tell you the truth," he said, "I'd rather not. And I'll only
do it if you insist. All exhibitions of painting or sculpture make me sick.
And I would also regret it if anyone saw in this globe anything other than
'optics.'"[5]

It is of course the nature of this opposition, which seems like no
opposition at all, between retinalism and optics that creates at the heart
of Duchamp's enterprise a kind of interpretive paradox. For the retinalism that Duchamp rejected looks, at first glance, inseparable from the
very optics he embraced as its antidote. The retinalism Duchamp de-
tested was—as he stated above—the kind initiated by impressionism and
carried into the twentieth century by efforts to build abstract art on the
principles of just those color relations investigated by impressionism,
color relations that in turn depended on the discoveries of physiological optics, discoveries formulated in terms of "simultaneous contrast" by
figures such as Helmholtz or Chevreul. Yet—and here is where the confusion arises—physiological optics is exactly what one encounters in the
long series of works that permanently separated Duchamp from pursuing
the mechanics of his *Glass*. The whole enterprise of examining revolving
discs in order to measure the eye's physiological reaction to color, and the
equipment for mounting those discs in order to allow them to spin—this
belongs equally to the laboratories of nineteenth-century psychophysiological research and to Duchamp's *Rotary Demisphere* or his *Discs Bearing
Spirals* which were set into motion in either a filmic form—as in *Anemic
Cinema*—or in the guise of those curious optical phonograph records he
made and marketed in 1935 and called *Rotoreliefs*. Duchamp himself spoke
of this relation when he said the illusion of three-dimensionality unleashed
by the rotation of his discs was something achieved, "not with a complicated machine and a complex technology, but in the eyes of the spectator,
by a psychophysiological process."[6]

But if both Duchamp and impressionism exploited the data of physiological optics, their attitudes toward it were not the same. And it is here
that we begin to understand Duchamp's position as an antiretinalist.
Simultaneous contrast, which describes the interaction of the cones at
the surface of the retina and the way the color field is produced by their
mutual stimulation and innervation, is a phenomenon of sensory impact
at the level of the eye. It is not part of the different order of the encod-
ing and decoding of color experience that occurs at the level of cortical

synthesis. It is thus possible to envisage it as part of a model that separates eye from brain, as from other parts of the seer's body. It is oblivious,
for instance, to the fact that experiences of color can be produced from
within the body's own fabric, through the stimulations of other organs,
or mechanically by the electrical excitation of the optic nerve.

The principles of simultaneous contrast were first employed by impressionism. But as we know, by the beginning of the twentieth century, they
were taken as laws regulating a field of interactions—a surface of sensations which, on the one hand, could be described scientifically (that is,
mathematically), and on the other, could be analogized to the flat surface of the picture plane. It was thus that the becoming autonomous of
sight could be thought simultaneously in the field of positivist science
and in the domain of aesthetic culture. Armed, for example, with the laws
of retinal color interaction as formulated by Young and Helmholtz, one
could imagine that one now possessed the algorithm of vision, and that
this algorithm, this mathematical expression of relations, could serve as
an abstract generator for another field—that of the canvas—underwriting
and rationalizing the relations occurring on the plane of painting.

Two surfaces, the retinal and the pictorial, would then share a single
set of laws and both, in participating in the abstract language of positive science, would become independent, axiomatic, autonomous. Robert
Delaunay exemplifies this early twentieth-century expectation with his repeated declarations that the laws of simultaneous contrast and the laws
of painting are one and the same. "Color," he frequently wrote, "colors
with their laws, their contrasts, their slow vibrations in relation to the
fast or extra-fast colors, their interval. All these relations form the foundation of a painting that is no longer imitative, but creative through the
technique itself." What makes this possible, he would reiterate, is a scientifically wrought understanding of "simultaneous contrast." "To create,"
he insists, "is to produce new unities with the help of new laws." [7]

Delaunay's statement can stand for a whole conception of painting—
that of what we could call the reification of the retinal surface under the
logic of modernism. For this mapping of the retinal field onto the modernist pictorial plane with the positivist expectation that the laws of the
one would legislate and underwrite the autonomy of the operations of the
other, this is typical of the form in which high modernism established and
then fetishized an autonomous realm of the visual.

It was the idea of the self-sufficiency and the closed logic of this newly
conceived retino-pictorial surface that gave a program to early abstract

painting such as Delaunay's and a coherence to much of modernist theory. It is this logic that refuses to "go beyond" the retina to the gray matter, and it is to this refusal that Duchamp objects. But Duchamp's gray matter, though it undoubtedly refers to the cerebral cortex, does not thereby invoke a disembodied faculty of cognition or reflection, does not propose the transcendental ego's relation to its sensory field. The cerebral cortex is not above the body in an ideal or ideated remove; it is, instead, *of* the body, such that the reflex arc of which it is part connects it to a whole field of stimuli between which it cannot distinguish. These stimuli may come from outside the body, as in the case of normal perception, but they may also erupt internally, giving rise, for example, to what Goethe celebrated as "physiological color," or those sensations of vision that are generated entirely by the body of the viewer. The production of sensory stimulation from within the body's own field, the optical system's porousness to the operations of its internal organs, this fact forever undermines the idea of vision's transparency to itself, substituting for that transparency a density and opacity of the viewing subject as the very precondition of his access to sight. It is this density that physiological optics mainly explored, taking as its field the body in all its thickness and temporality, although as we have seen it is this aspect of physiological optics that modernist painting set aside.

The evidence that Duchamp thought about vision as arising from these multiple sources—that is, from both perceptual stimuli external to the body and from excitations deep within it—can be found everywhere in his work. But one statement about this comes from the notes to the *Large Glass*. There Duchamp describes the visual activity of the Bride's blossoming—that is, the orgasmic event toward which the whole mechanism of the *Glass* is laboring—in terms of a kind of circuitry through which the Bachelor Machine connects up to the system of the Bride. This circuitry is projected in the notes as an ellipse with two foci. The first of the foci, which Duchamp designates as the stripping by the Bachelors, seems to relate to the perceptual part of the arc he is mapping: the Bachelors are looking at the Bride. But the second focus, the Bride's "voluntarily imagined blossoming," connects the reflex arc of this ellipse to an organically conditioned source of the drive, an organ which Duchamp says "is activated by the love gasoline, a secretion of the bride's sexual glands and by the electric sparks of the stripping."[8]

Duchamp's view of the gray matter—that part that exists beyond the retina—thus cannot be separated from other kinds of organic activity within the corporeal continuum. And from this it follows that if the mechanism of the *Large Glass* obeys Duchamp's dictum of "going beyond" the retina, it does so not to achieve the condition of vision's transparency to itself—which is suggested by the model of classical perspective when applied to the *Glass*—but rather, quite obviously, to arrive at the threshold of desire-in-vision, which is to say to construct vision itself within the opacity of the organs and the invisibility of the unconscious.

By the time Duchamp became a full-fledged Precision Oculist—to use his term—this issue of mapping the visual arc's connections to its own conditions of desire had been rendered extremely pure. And in this fifteen-year-long exploration, the resources of physiological optics now became married to the theoretical domain of psychoanalysis and its own explanations of vision. For it is in that languidly unreeling pulsation, that hypnotically erotic visual throb of Duchamp's Precision Optics, that one encounters both the *body* of physiological optics' seeing fully enmeshed in the temporal dimension of nervous life, and something I would want to call an "optical unconscious." For it is here, as well, that one is made to connect to this body as the site of libidinal pressure on the visual organ, such that the pulse of desire is simultaneously felt as the beat of repression.

The rhythm of the turning discs in *Anemic Cinema* or the *Rotoreliefs* is the rhythm of substitution as, at an iconic level, various organs replace one another in an utterly circular associative chain. First there is the disc as eye, staring and insistent, which is then transformed into the erotic shimmer of trembling breast, itself giving way to the fictive presence of a uterine cavity and the implication of sexual penetration: "copulatory movements," one Duchamp scholar has euphemized it, "an in-and-out motion . . . in a literal allusion to the sexual act," says another.[9] And within this pulse, as it carries one from part-object to part-object, advancing and receding through the illusion of this three-dimensional space, there is also a hint of the persecutory threat that the object poses for the viewer, a threat carried by the very metamorphic rhythm itself, as its constant thrusting of the form into a state of dissolve brings on the experience of formlessness, seeming to overwhelm the once-bounded object with the condition of the nonformed.

Writing about "psychogenic visual disturbance" in 1910, Freud speaks of the various bodily organs' accessibility to both the sexual and the ego instincts: "Sexual pleasure is not connected only with the function of the genitals; the mouth serves for kissing as well as for eating and speaking, the eyes perceive not only those modifications in the external world which are of import for the preservation of life, but also the attributes of objects by means of which these may be exalted as objects of erotic selection." The problem for the organ can arise when there is a struggle between these two instincts and "a repression is set up on the part of the ego against the sexual component-instinct in question." Applying this to the eye and the faculty of vision, Freud continues, "If the sexual component-instinct which makes use of sight—the sexual 'lust of the eye'—has drawn down upon itself, through its exorbitant demands, some retaliatory measure from the side of the ego-instincts, so that the ideas which represent the content of its strivings are subject to repression and withheld from consciousness, the general relation of the eye and the faculty of vision to the ego and to consciousness is radically disturbed."[10] The result of repression is then, on the one hand, the creation of substitute-formations at the level of the libido, and, on the other, the onset of reaction-formation within the operations of the ego.

The sequence of substitutions within Precision Optics and the sense of perceptual undecidability projected through the object's condition as a state of perceptual disappearance, all this rehearses the Freudian scenario of the unavailability of what is repressed and the structural insatiability of desire. For desire-in-vision is formed not through the unified moment of visual simultaneity of the optical mastery of perspective but through the temporal arc of the body's fibers. It is an effect of the two-step through which the object is eroticized. Freud's theory of eroticization (or anaclisis), as set forth by Jean Laplanche, accounts among other things for the scopophilic impulse.[11] It is a theory of the two-step. According to the anaclitic model, all sexual instincts lean on the self-preservative or ego instincts, but they only come to do so at a second moment, always a beat after the self-preservative impulse. Thus the baby sucks out of a need for sustenance, and in the course of gratifying that need receives pleasure as well. And desire occurs at this second moment, as the longing to repeat the first moment, understood not as milk but as pleasure—understood, that is, *as* the satisfaction of desire. Thus it searches for an object of original satisfaction where there is none. There is only milk, which can satisfy the need, but cannot satisfy the desire, since it has become something that the little hiccup of substitution will always produce as insufficient. What this model clarifies is the way the need can be satisfied, while the desire cannot.

In relating this psychoanalytic model of desire's longing for a lost origin and a structurally irretrievable object to the experience of Precision Optics, I am attempting to capture the effect of this projection of desire into the field of vision. And I am trying to hold onto that field as something that is both carnally constituted and, through the activity of the unconscious, the permanent domain of a kind of opacity, or of a visibility invisible to itself. For the illusion of three-dimensionality that Duchamp's Precision Optics creates does not present a "legitimate construction" — a field set apart from the seer's body and mastered by his independent viewpoint. If Duchamp's illusion tunnels into depth, that depth is associated with the viewer's own body, with an exploration of its carnal core, and the tunneling implies an infinite regress, a constantly renewed act of disappearance, the operations set in motion by an insatiable chain of desire.

Thus, to those Duchamp scholars who want to connect his work to art history and to traditional perspective,[12] one would have to reply that Precision Optics is not only an attack on modernism's reified and fetishized "autonomous" vision but also a deconstruction of perspective's assumptions about the detachment and objectivity of "the viewer" it posits. And it is here that this Duchamp example needs more explicitly to be put into juxtaposition with the problematic of this conference.

I have said that Duchamp's deconstruction of modernism's conception of the visual field constituted a more general attack on what we could call the *politique of the visual*. It is thus not a regression backward into history — via traditional perspective — but a critique of modernism's own hidden congruity with the terms of history, that is to say, with the continuing model of vision that grounds and underwrites both kinds of art. And I now want to connect this with two more claims. They are interrelated. The first is that historicism — new and old — has consistently mistaken the nature of this critique, setting up not only the regressive reading of Duchamp, but far more generally elaborating historical narratives that, in their own dependency on the foundationalist visual model, fail, precisely, to historicize the visual. This indeed was the import of the passage by Stephen Melville that I read at the outset, in which we see the psychologizing and essentializing effects of the neo-Kantian basis of the discipline

of art history. The second is that if *history* has been guilty of this occulta-
tion of "meaning and memory," poststructuralism—and particularly deconstruction—has not. So that, at least for the extremely interesting and
complex history of the visual arts, the neat little distinction between the
synchronic and the diachronic within the human sciences seems to me to
be misguided.

Indeed, it is to deconstruction that we can turn for a critique of vision
that is extremely close to the one I have been sketching as Duchamp's.
The eye that stares, forever fixated, into the visual pyramid of the legitimate construction, the eye from which the perspective symmetrically un-
folds and to which it just as symmetrically returns, that eye as we know is
the logical guarantor that the plane of the projection—the painting—will
be the mimetically truthful double of any transverse plane in the original
field of vision. But that eye's logic guarantees more than the way that representation can always be folded back on itself in a miming that renders
itself transparent to the original experience, transforming re-presentation
into a calling up of the original, in a continually renewed presentation of
it, producing thereby a forever renewable present. That eye's logic speci-
fies that present as itself contracted to a point—occupying the geometry
of the limit, understood as the infinitely small or brief or contracted. The
vanishing point's infinity is mirrored in that of the viewing point, a concentration at *this* end into the infinitely short duration of the "now," a
present that is—as it achieves this limit—indivisibly brief and thus irre-
ducibly unassimilable to time. The rapidity of this point, this blink-of-
vision thus annihilates, structurally and logically, all possibility within it
of past and future. The eye of the legitimate construction regards its prospect from the vantage of a perpetual now.

We are, of course, familiar with Derrida's analysis of this "now" and the
role it plays in Husserl's phenomenology—an analysis that challenges this
"now" by calling it myth, spatial or mechanical metaphor, and inherited
metaphysical concept. Derrida's *Speech and Phenomena* acknowledges the
importance to Husserl's project of preserving the instant as a point, so
that the identity of experience will be seen to be instantaneously present to
itself.[13] Indeed, if self-presence must be produced in the undivided unity
of a temporal present, this is because it must have nothing to reveal to
itself by the agency of signs. As Husserl writes in *Ideen,* "Between perception on the one hand and the symbolic representation by means of images

or signs on the other, there exists an insurmountable eidetic difference."[14]

But this is an eidetic difference that is eroded by Husserl's own description of the experience of this "now" in its inextricable continuousness with a past prolonged into the present in the form of retentions and protentions, or memory and expectation. Husserl as he describes this gives it a surprisingly carnal form as he explains that "the now-apprehension is, as it were, the nucleus of a comet's tail of retentions," adding that "a punctual phase is actually present as now at any given moment, while the others are connected as a retentional train" (62). The fact of retention— as nonpresent carried into the present, as not-now infecting the now— suggests a temporality which, however, phenomenology cannot acknowledge. "As soon as we admit this continuity of the now and the not-now, perception and nonperception," Derrida writes, "in the zone of primordiality common to primordial impression and primordial retention, we admit the other into the self-identity of the Augenblick; nonpresence and nonevidence are admitted into the blink of the instant. There is a duration to the blink, and it closes the eye" (65).

And onto the screen of this closed eye is projected—against Husserl's will—the scene of writing and the structure of signs. Retention—which Husserl calls primordial memory in order to try to separate it from the re-presentation of secondary memory—retention, Derrida argues, has the same form of nonpresence that memory has, and thus shares with re-presentation a common root. This root—"the possibility of re-petition in its most general form, that is, the constitution of a trace in the most universal sense—is a possibility," Derrida argues, "which not only must inhabit the pure actuality of the now but must constitute it through the very movement of difference it introduces. Such a trace . . . is more 'primordial' than what is phenomenologically primordial. For the ideality of the form of presence itself implies that it be infinitely re-peatable, that its re-turn, as a return of the same, is necessary ad infinitum and is inscribed in presence itself" (67).

Derrida will thus not allow Husserl to detach the "now" of vision from the comet's tail of retention and protention—of expectation and memory—and ultimately, of course, from the issue of the unconscious. And it is vision's relation to this same comet's tail that is, of course, the story of Duchamp's optical unconscious as it is of the other members of the group I alluded to—the group of antivisualists within the avant-garde of the first half of this century. That their activity should have been unavailable up to now to historical analysis and that it has only become approachable through the kind of critical, deconstructionist operations launched, precisely, by poststructuralism, is the counterexample I wish to place on the table of this conference. For from my own experience as a historian of early modernism, I am more sure that poststructuralism, with the many strategies it has developed to outwit the innocent optic of "history," will be of far greater use in unpacking both meaning and memory than any historicism, old or new.

NOTES

1. Clement Greenberg, "Modernist Painting," in *The New Art,* ed. Gregory Battcock (New York, 1966), 107.

2. Stephen Melville, "Deconstruction and the Thought of New Perspectives," delivered at the meetings of the College Association, Houston, 14 Feb. 1988.

3. My own previous attempts to chart this territory have resulted in "Anti-Vision," *October* 36 (1986): 147–54, "Corpus Delicti," *October* 33 (1985): 31–72, and "No More Play," in my *The Originality of the Avant-Garde and Other Modernist Myths* (Cambridge, Mass., 1985). Ongoing work has appeared in "The Impulse to See," in *Vision and Visuality,* ed. Hal Foster (Seattle, 1988), 51–75, where the anecdote on pp. 283–85 above was published; and "The Blink of an Eye," a much expanded version of the Duchamp case discussed below (in *States of Theory,* ed. David Carroll [New York, 1989]).

4. Alain Jouffroy, *Une révolution du regard* (Paris, 1964), 115, my translation; hereafter cited in text.

5. Marcel Duchamp, *Salt Seller* (New York, 1973), 185.

6. Hans Richter, *Dada: Art and Anti-Art* (London, 1965), 99.

7. Robert Delaunay, *The New Art of Color,* ed. Arthur Cohen (New York, 1978), 35, 41, 63.

8. Duchamp, *Salt Seller,* 42–43.

9. Lawrence Steefel, "The Position of *La Mariée Mise à Nu par Ses Célibataires, Même,*" Diss., Princeton University 1960, 56; and Toby Mussman, "Anémic Cinéma," *Art and Artists* 1 (1966): 51.

10. Sigmund Freud, "Psychogenic Visual Disturbance According to Psychoanalytical Conceptions" (1910), in *Character and Culture,* vol. 19 of *The Collected Papers of Sigmund Freud,* ed. Philip Rieff (New York, 1963), 55.

11. Jean Laplanche, *Life and Death in Psychoanalysis,* tr. Jeffrey Mehlman (Baltimore, 1976), chs. 1 and 5.

12. See esp., Jean Clair, "Marcel Duchamp et la tradition des perspecteurs," in *Marcel Duchamp: Abécédaire,* ed. Jean Clair (Paris, 1977), 124–59.

13. Jacques Derrida, *Speech and Phenomena,* tr. David B. Allison (Evanston, 1973), 61; hereafter cited in text.

14. Edmund Husserl, *Ideen zu einer reinen Phänomenologie und phänomenologischen Philosophie* (Halle, 1913), 62.

HISTORY AND IMAGES
IN MEDICINE

⋙►·◦·◄⋘

Sander L. Gilman

THE QUESTION I want to address is why images—visual representations of all kinds—have remained a stepchild in the writing of the history of medicine. Certainly there seem to be enough illustrated histories of medicine to acknowledge the importance of the image in the writing of that history. And yet their function as part of the materials of medical history has always been peripheral at best. Recently, the Oxford art historian Francis Haskell, following the lead of cultural and art historians as diverse as Michael Baxandall, Irving Lavin, Peter Paret, Theodore K. Rabb, and Simon Schama, has again asked the important question of how and why cultural historians use visual images (Haskell, 1993; Baxandall, 1985; Lavin, 1993; Paret, 1988; Schama, 1987; Rabb 1975). Chroniclers of cultural and social change have used images as a source of material since the Renaissance. Drawing on the work of Arnaldo Momigliano, Haskell divides such writers into "historians," whose work consisted and consists of spinning narratives, and "antiquarians," whose work consisted of collecting and cataloguing objects from the past, many of which consisted of images in one form or another (Momigliano, 1950). In tracing the powerful need to reread these images from the standpoint of the narratives that are then spun about them, Haskell points out the danger of a misuse or suppression of images that would work against their correct meaning.

Deep in Haskell's sense of history, of his own project as an historian, therefore, is embedded the notion of the image as a fact that has a true as opposed to a false reading. (On this question see the papers collected in Rotberg and Rabb, 1988.) And that assumption becomes part of his analysis of the ways historians have used the visual. In seeing each reading of an image as one of a chain of readings, each of which has impact on

90

and alters all subsequent readings, Haskell presents the complex relationship between a sense of contemporary historical meaning projected into
the past and the extant meanings attributed to visual representation in the
past. This problem of the truth factor of visual sources haunts their use.
If read "correctly," do they provide a window into the past? Or are they
only the historian's projection of the visual culture of his own age into the
reconstructed past?

For the cultural historian writing after Johann Huizinga, who closes
Haskell's study, using, not using, or using visual sources incorrectly remains a contentious undertaking. But this is to no little degree the result of a tautology of which Haskell is quite aware, for the visual arts in
one form or another are part of the "stuff" of cultural history. To ignore
them or to "misuse" them means to violate the presuppositions of writing
"cultural history" as a history of culture in the public sphere. This undertaking means that the visual is intrinsic to the definition of culture (either
in its narrowest ["high art"] or in its broadest ["human production"] defi-
nitions). This tautology has not generally been a stricture on the writing
of the history of medicine. For the visual culture of medicine is not intrinsic to its "stuff" (either in its narrowest ["art/artist and medicine"] or
its broadest ["the visual culture of medicine"] sense). The visual arts have
only an ancillary relationship to the traditional definition of medical history as it evolved at the turn of the century. Haskell himself ironically
recapitulates this marginality in his introduction when he comments on
the central problem of his book, his critique of "some great historians for
not having paid enough attention to the arts and . . . explicitly criticizing others for having done so in an unconvincing manner." He observes:
"The historian of medicine is not expected to be able to cure a stomach
ache: should the historian of a particular historical method be required to
solve the problems raised by its use? . . . The aim of the chapters that follow is to explore how, when and why historians have tried to recapture
the past, or at least a sense of the past, by adopting the infinitely seductive
course of looking at the image the past has left of itself" (9). Historians of
medicine, according to Haskell's logic, are not physicians, but, according
to his logic, they are also not cultural historians. It is precisely that historians of medicine *are* cultural historians and that the culture of medicine is
as heavily involved with visual culture as any other aspect of modern cultural history that makes the anxiety about the use of the visual image in
the history of medicine a meaningful problem. Haskell's problem (if not

his absolute reading) is the use and abuse of the visual image, and it is a problem for the medical historian.

Haskell's own study does not overtly make reference to the visual culture of medicine. Yet he is concerned with the development of the relationship between appearance and character from the physiognomist Giovan Vincenzo Della Porta in the Renaissance through Johann Caspar Lavater in the eighteenth century to the historian Jacob Burkhardt in the nineteenth century. The fact that Della Porta and Lavater rooted their theories in "medical" models—models that defined somatic and psychological (or at least characterological) pathologies that had their antecedents as far back as the semiotics of Hippocrates—is not evident in reading Haskell's discussion. The visual cultural of medicine has been obscured by the very writing of medical history. And that because of aspects of its own history that are explicable and demonstrable. When we turn to the history of medicine for our models of the use of visual materials, four overlapping typologies for images can be found, typologies that bridge the gap between Momigliano's "historians" and "antiquarians."

In reviewing the illustrated histories of medicine or those histories of medicine that use visual images, the four major roles of visual images seem to divide nicely between the "antiquarian" and the "historical." The "antiquarians" use them (1) as illustrations, (2) as representations of facts about the real world, while the "historians" use them (3) as documents to show a self-contained visual language or iconography concerning health and illness present in specific traditions of visual representation, and (4) as objects to access cultural fantasies about health, disease, and the body. All of these roles overlap in one way or another in their presuppositions. This typology in the writing of the history of medicine is one that is not unique to the use of images in the writing of general history. But, following Haskell's argument, it is important to note that, for most historians of medicine through the close of the twentieth century, visual images are an untouched source material. Unlike Haskell's cultural historians, who know that this resource is potentially present and choose not to employ it, medical historians tend to avoid visual sources even where they would play an evident and simple role in supporting their arguments. The typology of the use of the images, therefore, reflects the limitations rather than the breadth of the medical historians' use of visual sources.

"Mere illustration" is the most common use of images in writing the history of medicine. Who has not enjoyed opening up such "coffee table" books? Such books, from the widely read illustrated medical history of Felix Marti-Ibañez, which first appeared as a series in *MD* magazine addressed to physicians, to the most recently packaged illustrated story of modern medicine, seem to use images as pictorial fillers (Marti-Ibañez, 1962; Carmichael and Ratzan, 1991; Smolan, 1992). No analysis of the images is given in the text; the images stand on the page as visual evocations of a mood or context. They represent an unmediated window into the world of medicine that seems to enable the mass reading market to observe the physician at work across the centuries. A large number of such titles exist, and they are clearly aimed at a mass reading (or, perhaps, better, viewing) market (see, for example, Bender, 1961; Lyons, 1978). In the history of psychiatry and psychology, the primary English-language illustrated history is that written by A. A. Roback and Thomas Kiernan (1969). All of these studies "find" images and scatter them through their histories like antiquarians discovering the remnants of the past.

Such antiquarian use of images as windows into the world of medicine harks back to Victorian popular illustrated books on the freakish aspects of the world of illness that in turn continued the early modern broadside traditions showing medical anomalies such as joined twins or unusual tumors. Like them, the frame for each image, the caption, or the text commenting on the image seems only to replicate in words the content of the image itself. The illusion is of an unbroken gaze into the past. But it remains the unusual and the different that are still captured in these illustrated histories and their images.

The twentieth-century use of this illustrative tradition has a clear ideological basis. By presenting an "unmediated" (that is, uninterpreted) representation of health and illness, the quaint practices of the past are "seen" by the reader cheek and jowl with portraits of the "Great Men," the medical innovators of the past. Thus in all of these heroic histories, a sense of the progress of medicine can be had by looking at the pictures. We, the lay viewer, can understand how far we have come by our own observation of these illustrations. In the case of views of contemporary medicine, such as the thematic picture story by Smolan that surveys the state of contemporary medical practice, the underlying assumption is a high level of contemporary medical competency as opposed to the unviewed but clearly less than adequate practices of a fantasy yesterday. Illustrations without overt analysis have the intrinsic ability to let viewers measure the realities of medical change for themselves, or so it seems. The use of images of health and illness is tied to an ever-improving reality of medical care of the patient in this model.

Such a naive use of illustrations is highly manipulated. The selection or editing of the material to tell a story means that the frame is a Procrustean bed. What is often unstated is the overt closure implicit in the use of such images. Such picture histories, however, employ an epistemology that assumes a relationship between the image and some reality external to the historian and the reader.

Such an uncommented window into the past is linked closely to the epistemological basis for the second use of images in writing the history of medicine. In this view the image functions as representations of facts about the real world, as in the work of Fox and Lawrence (1988) on British and American medical photographs. Mechanical reproduction is vital here. This use has no compunction in using any type of image, from the votive figures of Greek temples to the drawings of Andy Warhol, to illustrate the progress of medicine. Here, however, even the use of older forms of mechanical reproduction, such as the engraving or the lithograph with its evident aestheticization for the late twentieth-century observer, must give way to the photograph, a "real" window into the realities of the past. Once a naive, mid-nineteenth-century positivistic genre expectation of the photograph as a mimetic reproduction of reality is introduced, there is a heightened sense that such images have a true "proof" value, that is, they show you the way things really were. Here, it is not that the image is an index to a reality but rather that it permits the reader-viewer to open a window onto a past reality.

As in the illustrated history, the image and the reality are one. But unlike the illustrated history, where the illustration echoes the argument of the text, here the image is used as an overt part of the proof of the historian's argument. In such images, the historian says to the reader-viewer, you can see the truth of my statement for yourself, as you too have access to this objective window into history as it really was. Let us, however, the historian continues, be aware that these are images and that they also have a history. Such views of the medical image enter into the very use of images in medical textbooks, especially those in psychiatry that have a strong historical component. There the images claim to be a window on reality even when they attempt to represent internal psychic states such as depression (Kaplan and Sadock, 1989). The captions to these photographs all serve as frames to draw the reader's attention to the meaning of the photograph, a meaning that may not be apparent on first viewing. These images are now not "merely" illustrations of a lost world but part of the overt truth claim for the historian's ability to reconstruct the world as it really was. This medical antiquarianism echoes the antiquarian's claim for the overall validity of the visual object as a fragment of the reality of the past.

The "historians" of medicine use images in a more self-referential manner. The third model stresses the artistic medium itself and the internal iconographic tradition of the work of art. It is not the external world of medical practice and social reality that is evoked in the truth claims of this use but rather the internal rules of artistic representation. Here the reality that is conjured is that internal to the history of art. Such studies are often not clearly labeled as a history of representations and indeed seem to evoke a history of medical practice. Yet when they are examined they tend to be internal histories of medical representations. How well or poorly such images reveal the actual practices or beliefs of medicine is not central to these studies. Rather, it is the means by which the image is constructed, its internal vocabulary, that is central. This, as in the work of Robert Herrlinger on the history of medical illustration, emphasized the autonomous artistic vocabulary of the image (Herrlinger, 1967–72). Medical iconography was seen as separate from yet related to the general iconography of Western representational art following the guidelines laid down in the mid-nineteenth century in Ludwig Choulant's history of anatomical illustration and its relationship to high art (Choulant, 1852). The problem arises when the contemporary medical historian wishes to turn to contemporary, nonrepresentational art for images of internal, subjective states of feeling. Francis Haskell shows how even semirepresentational art can be and has been used as a source for cultural historians. But such a reliance on representational art (i.e., art that provides a recognizable visual analogy to visual experiences in the world) in medical history makes such a movement difficult.

The study of the representation of medical subjects, among them psychiatric ones, in high art is closely related to this approach to the iconography of medicine. Most often such studies examine themes in high art of medical significance as a means of examining the specific iconography that defines or is defined by that topic. Rarely is there any concern about whether what is being presented is "progressive" medicine or even "real" medical practice, though this is often assumed. What is important is the language of the image. Here the reality is that of the artistic tradition of representation. The captions often are used to point at specific references or to provide links among images (Zigrosser, 1959; MacKinney, 1965; Berger, 1970; Bauer, 1973; Seidenbusch, 1975; Grape-Albers, 1977; Schmidt-Voigt, 1980; Gerdts, 1981; Theopold, 1981; Jones, 1984; Jurina, 1985; Karp, 1985). Less frequently, the claims for a limited tradition of an autonomous medical iconography are examined as separate from the greater art historical one (Zglinicki, 1982). Specific studies of the relationship of given artists to specific themes in medicine also stress the iconographic tradition (Murken, 1979; Boeckl, 1984).

Related to such historical studies from the world of high art are the histories of popular medical caricature (Holländer, 1905, 1921a; Helfand, 1978, 1991). Here it is the analogy to medicine and its representation in other contexts, such as politics, that is of interest. No claims are made about the truthfulness of the image as a window into the world of medicine. What is stressed is the use of medical imagery as the internal vocabulary of the images. The genre expectation of the work of art (for example, the link between caricature and visual irony) and the specific visual devices (such as exaggeration) that are its means of expression are central to such studies.

The fourth means of employing visual materials is to make the image itself the means to allow the analysis of cultural fantasies of health, disease, and the body. Here the image serves as a mirror representing the self as formed by the fantasies of any given culture about illness and health. In my own studies of the visual representation of both the mentally and somatically ill, I stressed the close relationship between representations of illness and the cultural fantasies about illness (Gilman, 1976, 1982, 1986). This in no way undermined the question of the reality of illness, including mental illness, but rather stressed the subconscious function that such a vocabulary of images has. One could access the world not of reality but of fantasy through the examination of representations of difference. These were "real" cultural fantasies that could and did impact not only on those who generated these images as part of a means of representing, and thus controlling, the world but those who served as the objects of representation. The patient and the physician were both part of this system of cultural fantasy. Indeed, one could speak of a closed system of representation that shaped and was shaped by the needs of all of the social roles defined by the doctor-patient dyad. Work in this vein has been carried out on psychiatric images by Georges Didi-Huberman (1982) and Elaine

Showalter (1985), and on somatic topics by Michael Fried (1987), Ludmilla Jordanova (1989) and Barbara Stafford (1992). In all cases it is the unseen component of the cultural fantasy that is made visible in these images. We as readers are not shown the reality of daily life through images but rather the internal realities of individual and group experience.

A closely related category is the visual creations by the mentally ill. Following the work of Hans Prinzhorn (1886–1933) in the 1920s, studies of the art of the mentally ill provided images of the painters as well as their works of art. The captions related these images to an internal reality of mental illness made visible through the artistic process. Here the problem of representational versus nonrepresentational images in the history of psychiatry was resolved. For such works always stressed the universal, unconscious processes behind the overt images. One could, therefore, examine nonrepresentational images as a measure of internal states as well as those images that evoked specific themes through some type of overt representation (Prinzhorn, 1972). Individual studies of mentally ill artists tended to replicate such visual structures (Morgenthaler, 1992).

Recent work on the history of the art of the mentally ill has tended to move to a cultural contextualization of these images that stressed the ideological context of the collection and analysis of the works of art within the world of medicine (Meurer-Keldenich, 1979; *The Prinzhorn Collection,* 1984; MacGregor, 1989). In these historical studies, the reality to be captured was the cultural context of the nineteenth- and early twentieth-century fascination with the artistic production of the mentally ill. As in the study of medical themes in high and popular art, the analysis of the history of the art of the mentally ill stressed thematic as well as formal questions: What are the topics addressed in the art of the mentally ill? What are the means by which these topics are represented? These questions are identical to those raised by psychiatrists such as Prinzhorn, but their answers are sought in historical rather than psychological contexts. These studies also address the fascination that the pathological "quality" ascribed to these works of art had in warranting their collection and analysis. In such studies the "pathological" comes to be understood as a purely constructed category, bearing little or no relationship to an autonomous internal reality. These works thus position themselves against the presupposition of the initial works on the subject. The overarching claim of such histories is that there are no specific internal realities to be examined, only the external world internalized and represented in this art. Again and again, these studies of "outsider" art relate this tradition to other traditions (and visual vocabularies) of high art (Tuchman, 1992). Only very rarely has there been an attempt to provide a serious discussion of the art of the mentally ill with both psychological and historical categories of analysis (Sass, 1992).

Each of these approaches to the use of images in the history of medicine needs specific types of images for its purposes. And indeed, each reading can be correct for its specific tradition. What is always avoided is the idea of simultaneous multiple meanings, the very ambiguity that is inherent in visual images no matter what their venue. What is lacking is a comprehensive sense of the function that images can have in the study of the history of health and illness as it is practiced today. Rarely does the historian of psychiatry turn to the wide spectrum of images and draw from their totality. What untold tales can these images spin if they are understood as connecting all of the models above—from the naive attraction that picture books have for the reader, to the notion that the image can give us access to realities and fantasies about the world of the past and the present, to the view that works of art have rules by which they represent the world and that it is important to know what those rules are and how they function.

It is also imperative to understand the historical context that permitted cultural and social history to use visual images as source materials, while medical history consistently avoided them. The illustrated medical history reflects a set of biases limiting the ability of the historian to use fully the multiple meanings inherent in the visual image. This limitation has its roots in the construction of medical history as a professional discourse in the late nineteenth century.

Two academic disciplines, the medical specialty of psychiatry and the academic specialty of the history of medicine, were created within two decades of one another. According to Francis Haskell, it is precisely the period following Jakob Burkhardt's cultural history that the visual became an accepted part of the materials the academic historian could use (Haskell, 1993, 331 ff.). For the new field of psychiatry it is evident even on first glance that there was a need to create a visual epistemology for psychiatry parallel to that existing for the other medical sciences in the age of microscopy, bacteriology, and radiology—all arenas in which the visual image dominated the new science. See it and it is real (Canguilhem, 1989). Nineteenth-century academic psychiatry could and did call upon an older tradition of representing the mentally ill within a broad range of physiognomic traditions. These traditions also appear within the works of the nineteenth-century academic cultural historians like Hippolyte Taine and their appropriation of visual sources to gauge the character of the shapers of history (Haskell, 1993, 346 ff.; Gilman, 1978).

The first practitioners of psychiatry in France were also those who were the first popular historians of psychiatry. They needed to create a genealogy for their new science which was rooted in the status of the visual image as a delineator of "real" scientific medicine as well as in the cultural historical practice of their day. Without a doubt, the most important figure in this tradition was Jean-Martin Charcot, the first Professor of Psychiatry at the University of Paris (1825–93; 1872, Member of the Academy of Medicine and Professor of Pathological Anatomy; 1882, first chair holder as Professor for Mental Illnesses) for whom the visual image had a special and important function. But what is even more important is the link of the epistemology of the new "science" of psychiatry in Paris to the popular history of mental illness, conceived of as proof of the visual categories and nosologies employed by late nineteenth-century psychiatry. This was often but not exclusively linked to the new scientific means of reproducing images, photography and, later, film (Cartwright, 1991).

Charcot conceived the realism of such images to transcend the crudity of the spoken word. In a letter to Sigmund Freud on 23 November 1891 he commented concerning the transcription of his famed Tuesday lectures that "the stenographer is not a photographer" (Gelfand, 1988, 571). It is the photographer who can best capture the "reality" of mental illness; and if not the photographer, then at least the trained physician-artist. For it is the combination of a notion of the positivism of science with the status of the scientific practitioner that gave these images their status. The means of reproduction is therefore of equal importance to the iconographic language used in these images to provide a readable text for the trained interpreter. It is clear that having subconsciously established patterns of description rooted in classic iconographies of insanity, it was relatively easy to find these patterns within the visual record of Western civilization. This became true even to the degree that the patients of such physicians learned an adequate visual vocabulary so as to reproduce the visual traditions from which the description of their illnesses stemmed.

Charcot's audience for his (and his major collaborator, Paul Richer's [1849–1933]) monographs on the visual tradition of mental illness was not merely professional (see Charcot and Richer, 1887; 1889; Richer, 1900, as

well as numerous articles on the relationship between the artistic representation of madness and psychiatric nosologies in Charcot's *Nouvelle
iconographie de la Salpêtrière*). Like the audience of his Tuesday lectures, his
audience was the educated middle class of Paris. Indeed, the professional
audience for psychiatric literature was in the process of being created
during the late nineteenth century. These books were aimed as much at
the educated lay audience as at a professional medical-historical audience.
Such books provided a higher status for the new profession because it
gave it a long history and it showed the lay audience that the technical
knowledge that the new profession had to have to "look at" and "diagnose" various forms of mental illness could be grounded in the high culture which defined the intellectual at the turn of the century.

The sorts of images that Charcot and Richer use in their histories of
mental illness reflect the adaptation of a specific way of using images. It
was in no way subtle. Part of this was undertaken by the parallel use of
identical forms of "outlining." Charcot provided the sort of skeletal outlines of works of art (of the sort that Freud enjoyed producing himself, as
in his study of Moses's Michelangelo [1914]). These outlines stressed precisely the attributes that Charcot wanted the reader to "see." These were
made visually identical in terms of their "proof value" to the images of
the patients undertaking the same types of actions. Paul Richer incorporated similar images in his own work (Richer, 1885). These were presented
as analogous to the visual tradition in art or in other historical sources
that also used such images as "proof." The German response to such a use
of the image in writing a presentist history of psychiatry, with its teleological goals being the truths of the new (in the late nineteenth century)
French psychiatry, can be judged in Freud's own response to this technique. Freud's training with Jean Martin Charcot was a training in seeing
the patient and the signs and symptoms which the patient exhibited as the
central key to diagnosis (Aguayo, 1986). One can argue that Freud's intellectual as well as analytic development in the 1890s was a movement away
from the "meaning" of visual signs (a skill that he ascribes to Charcot in
his obituary of 1893) and to the interpretation of verbal signs, from the
"crudity" of seeing to the subtlety of hearing (Freud 1:17). Freud's rejection of the visual, one might add, precipitated a general response to the
meaning of the visual as "scientific evidence" (Jay, 1993).

Charcot, therefore, established a specific set of assumptions for the use
of images in the writing of the history of illness. (For Charcot, all illness,

mental and physical, had a somatic dimension.) The image and not the word was the real record of the unchangeable visual patterns of neurological disorders over time. For Charcot, older images from high and popular art had validity as proof if their visual structures could be echoed in modern, high-tech media such as photography. This validity was inscribed in the veridicality of the image as it reflected the external reality of the world through the innovations of Western art (from perspective to the photograph). For Charcot, these images provided validity for his own means of diagnosing mental illness. And it was this validity that underwrote his claims for a new medical science, psychiatry, rooted in observable experimental data and based in France. For it was not only science, but French science, the science of Louis Pasteur and Claude Bernard, into which Charcot had to fit his new specialty.

The response to the use of images in the German tradition was different. Karl Friedrich Jakob Sudhoff (1853–1938) was the first Professor of the History of Medicine at Leipzig (1905) and de facto the creator of the modern academic discipline of the History of Medicine in Germany (Rodekirchen, 1992). Sudhoff, trained as a physician, also studied history; in 1878 he was an assistant at the Charite under Rudolf Virchow while at the same time studying history with August Hirsch at the University of Berlin. In 1898, only five years after Charcot's death, he persuaded the German Association of Natural Scientists to add a section on the history of medicine and the natural sciences to their annual meeting. This movement eventually led to the professionalization of the discipline and the creation of the first chair in the history of medicine in Germany, which he then held.

Sudhoff professionalized the history of medicine and in this move toward professionalization he used illustrated materials as the basis for his own idiosyncratic work in the history of syphilis, reproducing images of great interest and complexity. For Sudhoff, his images were often incidental illustrations connected in broadside material on the history of syphilis or the history of anatomy (Sudhoff, 1912a; 1912b; 1920; 1928; 1924; 1925). Certainly there was no attempt to write a history of either syphilis or the body based on the sixteenth-century visual sources that Sudhoff reproduced. Yet Sudhoff was extremely sophisticated in terms of the history of media (Sudhoff, 1911) as well as the function of images for the internal history of medicine (Sudhoff, 1906). One can also add that he was a serious historian of anatomical illustration (Sudhoff, 1909).

Sudhoff employed a version of the Rankean model of history—attempting to document the "way it really was" in the Renaissance, but drawing from the Renaissance meanings for his own time. The Renaissance and the baroque, for German historians of the late nineteenth and early twentieth centuries, from Jacob Burkhardt to Walter Benjamin, were the self-constructed periods that were best able to support such a treatment. They were seen as distanced enough from the existing national cultures of the late nineteenth and early twentieth centuries to provide distinct categories separate from contemporary concerns and yet were, like the nineteenth century, understood as ages of growing secularization. For the idea of the struggle of "theology" with "science" is a central trope of the writing of the history of medicine in the late nineteenth century. It is of little surprise that Sudhoff's cultural hero, the figure to whom he devoted most of his scholarly work and energy, was Paracelsus.

Yet Sudhoff's idea of the writing of history was to use the historical moment as a means of elucidating the present and prognosticating the future. In this he broke with the older view of the history of medicine as advocated, for example, by Theodor Puschmann in 1889 (Puschmann, 1889). Puschmann had given a threefold rationale for the writing of the history of medicine: to add to general education (*Bildung*), to establish professional knowledge, and to aid in the ethical education of the physician. In his inaugural lecture on Puschmann, held on February 4, 1906 in Leipzig, Sudhoff advocated that the historian of medicine stop being mired in multitudes of facts (Sudhoff, 1906). Rather the historian should self-consciously select those facts from the past that are important for the present. Such a process of selection demanded an overview of the entirety of a field, but it was vital to interpret materials as well as present them. Thus Paracelsus, whose work comes to be the centerpiece of Sudhoff's academic activities, becomes not only a figure from the past but a symbol of the ideal physician of the nineteenth century, struggling against a repressive conservative medical tradition. But the only one who can make the leap from fact to interpretation is the trained historian, not the physician. It is the new professional historian who provides meaning to facts and draws them into the present.

Yet the "modern" historical tradition in Germany avoided the illustrated historical text. This set the writing of serious "history" apart from "anthropology," which in the late nineteenth century relied heavily on illustrated volumes. Serious, "scientific" histories of medicine could reproduce illustrations but they could not acknowledge them as "proofs" for any arguments. This view continues the view of older historians of medicine such as Sudhoff's student, Henry Sigerist (1891–1957), who, like his teacher, was quite aware of the relationship between the history of art and the history of medicine (Sigerist, 1943). Only texts from the past could serve as proof. In Germany, "serious" histories of medicine, such as that of Ernst Schwalbe, used in the teaching of the history of medicine to medical students, used illustrations of all types (Schwalbe, 1920).

Indeed, it is only in 1920 that Sudhoff and Theodor Meyer-Steineg, Professor of the History of Medicine at Jena, produced the first illustrated medical history (Meyer-Steineg and Sudhoff, 1921). They intended it to be a replacement for Schwalbe's outline history of medicine. This volume remained in print, up-dated well into the 1960s (Meyer-Steineg and Sudhoff, 1965). In the introduction to the first edition they stress the importance of the 208 images as the central claim to the innovative quality of this book. And they stress that these images are not *merely* illustrations but rather enhance the understanding of the material. Their images are all "factual." They reproduce portraits of the "great men" of medicine, of medical instruments, plates from Vesalius' anatomy and other technical manuals, as well as images of the patient in many contexts. The visual material echoed the use of such visual material in Meyer-Steineg's two books on ancient medicine (Meyer-Steineg, 1912a and 1912b). The assumption behind all of these images is that contemporary photographs of ancient medical instruments have the same epistemological value as do portraits of Hippocrates or Malpighi. This is, for Meyer-Steineg, part of the underlying assumption of the teaching of medicine as a link between past recovered and present experienced (Meyer-Steineg, 1920).

The multiple simultaneous meanings of these images are harnessed to the new professional role of the medical historian. Completely missing from this self-proclaimed first illustrated history of medicine are any references to mental illness, its treatment (with the exception of a portrait of Mesmer), and mental patients. Writing about medicine and its history—at least when illustrated—precluded dealing with the image of mental illness. The emphasis on the physical aspects of medicine in the age of the rise of psychosomatic medicine and psychoanalysis can only be understood as a conscious rejection of the premises of Charcot's popularizing attempt to use the illustration as a visual proof of his own theories of mental illness in a very different academic setting, the creation of modern clinical psychiatry. Indeed, by the time Sudhoff turns to formulating the basis for the history of medicine, Charcot's work (and his sense of his own visual antecedents) had fallen into scientific disrepute. Thus Sudhoff needed to separate medical practice from medical history. History is *Geisteswissenschaft* (humanistic science), according to the philosopher Wilhelm Dilthey, and medicine in terms of its nineteenth-century claims is *Naturwissenschaft* (natural science). This distinction gives the same scholarly status associated with the natural sciences during this period to the humanities. It is also that echoed in Haskell's definition of the role of medical history cited above. But this claim of parity between these two means of organizing knowledge gives equivalent value to two very different means of proof. It raises the role of "interpretation" in *Geisteswissenschaften* to the same level of the "facts" in *Naturwissenschaften*. Charcot elided these two means of proof, disguising his interpretation of history as "facts." And he did so within the realm of the new specialty of psychiatry. In doing so, he polluted the idea of a new professional medical history separate from its professional roots in medical treatment. Sudhoff needed to separate these two models to establish himself as a historian. And interpreting images of madness would bring him (and Meyer-Steineg) back into the professional self-definition of Jean-Martin Charcot, an approach that by the 1920s had totally fallen into disrepute even in Paris.

There is yet one other submerged question that the illustrated history of medicine addresses that had been raised by Charcot. This is the nation as the presumptive reader-viewer. In the 1880s it was necessary to address a more general audience of educated lay readers, such as Marcel Proust, and nonspecialist physicians in the work that he and Richer published. Here it was important to construct the notion that Paris, as the putative cultural center of Europe, was also at the very center of innovation in psychiatry. The view of the time was clearly that French clinical medicine was the best in the world, while German basic medical science was slightly better than the French (Garrison, 1915, 234–35; Haller, 1984). This was linked to notions of the modernization of techniques of analysis, such as the application of photography to the study of the mentally ill. But French academic art of the time was in no way to be challenged by its German equivalent.

The readership of an illustrated history of medicine (in which the history of "French" psychiatry is missing except for a gesture toward its "quack" background through the image of Mesmer) is important. Sudhoff and Meyer-Steineg address the same audience as Charcot and their intent is just as national. It is to "give to German doctors and German medical science the world reputation it deserves" (5). After the defeat in 1919 at the hands of, among others, the French, German science (especially historical science) had to be rescued from the charge of inferiority and partiality. And the "innovation" of the illustrated medical history, with its claim on the epistemology of nineteenth-century historical science, was used to buttress this claim for the "evident" scientific superiority of German natural science. The appeal was to the broadest audience of educated readers, the *Bildungsbürgertum,* that Sudhoff had not understood as his audience prior to World War I.

The reason that Sudhoff could not lay claim to the arena of the illustrated medical history before 1920 was that this arena was already occupied in Germany. Even though Sudhoff and Meyer-Steineg's volume is the first self-proclaimed illustrated history of medicine, this was their own understanding of their project. Popular "cultural" histories using medical imagery existed prior to this medical history. Hermann Peter's illustrated history of doctors and medicine with 153 images appeared in 1900 in a series on German cultural history (Peters, 1900). Focusing on the period from 1500 to 1700, Peters does discuss and represent the history of mental illness in his popular account of the "progress" of medicine. More importantly, Eugen Holländer (1867–1932) had produced a series of illustrated "histories" of medicine as reflected in various visual sources which were mined by many "serious" scholars, such as Meyer-Steineg and Sudhoff (Holländer, 1903, 1905, 1912, 1913, 1921a, 1921b, 1923, 1928). A number of the plates in Sudhoff and Meyer-Steineg's illustrated history came from Holländer. Sudhoff's professional opinion was that they were interesting sources of images but provided no professional insight into the world of medicine in which these images could have been used (Sudhoff, 1912c).

Eugen Holländer was one of the first modern cosmetic surgeons in the 1890s. His medical interest in reconstituting the body aesthetically and his popular interest in how the body was represented in the world of visual culture were reflected in a number of historical studies beginning before World War I. Holländer's work was hugely popular. His "coffee table" books were often reprinted. His audience was clearly the educated lay public as much as the physician. And he saw himself as the natural successor of Charcot and the School of Paris in terms of his interest in visual representations (Holländer, 1921, 3). Thus the representations associated with mental illness play as great a role in Holländer's works as it did in that of

Charcot and Richer. In the second edition of his history of medical caricature (1921), which appeared roughly at the same time as Meyer-Steineg
and Sudhoff's first illustrated history of medicine, one can judge the subtle
differences in the use of images as the basis for analysis. First, Holländer,
like Meyer-Steineg and Sudhoff, use the images as proof of the progress
of medicine. Unlike Meyer-Steineg and Sudhoff, Holländer's reliance on
caricatures would tend to stress the "unreal" qualities of the images. Yet
in his chapter on "mental illness" it is clear that the progressive tone of
the volume is identical to that of Meyer-Steineg and Sudhoff. His text
states—Look how primitive the understanding of this illness is in early
days? And his images repeat this theme. Thus he juxtaposes a contemporary photograph from the Medical-Historical Museum in Amsterdam of
eighteenth-century means of treatment with a Dutch broadside on cutting the fool's stone. (198–99) Here there is an implied visual link between
the caricature of the fool and the world of the treatment of the mentally
ill. But more importantly, there is an assumption that a contemporary
photograph of a museum exhibit would be the equivalent of Holländer's
own project, to create a visual museum of the antiquarian fantasies about
mental illness and its treatment in the past. When Holländer evokes contemporary treatment of illness in his volume, he is much more reticent to
draw the modalities of treatment into question. His final chapter on contemporary medical caricatures stresses the altered social role of the physician, the physician's claim on high social status, not his (and at least one
of the caricatures is aimed against female physicians) ability to cure.

Here the status of the image in the historiography of psychiatry can be
stressed. All of the uses point toward their truthfulness, yet each "truth"
is established in terms of its use in establishing a professional identity. To
quote Foucault in this context, "A proposition must fulfill complex and
heavy requirements to be able to belong to the grouping of a discipline;
before it can be called true or false, it must be 'in the true.'" And why is
it important to belong to a discipline? To gain the power of being "called
true or false" (Foucault, 1984, 199). Images, at least in the early history, are
the field for conflict concerning professionalization and national identity.
Using images placed the author in a specific relationship to the reader and
to the reader's presumed use of such images for enjoyment as well as education. But I would add that the actual power of the visual image made it
the natural space in which such debates could be carried out. For the historical image, especially the image of the mentally ill and those who treat
mental illness, evokes a specific type of anxiety about location and iden-

tification. Each image provides simultaneous multiple meanings that are accessed by the observer immediately and processed in such a way as to attempt to provide a coherent, single meaning. Some of these meanings are found within the image itself, both in terms of an accurate interpretation of the image—an interpretation buttressed by documentation of parallel discourses from the time—or a false reading, a reading through the history of misreadings of an image over the course of its reception. But some of these meanings are embedded in the needs of the historian to shape and delimit the function of the use of images because of the self-definition of the historian's agenda. Such suppressed readings come to be part of the history of missing readings that shape the understanding of the image. They are the "secrets and non-interchangeable roles" that Foucault writes about that exist even in "discourse that is published and free from all ritual" (122). The suppression of the complexity of the visual image, represented by the image of the mentally ill, in the scholarly work on the history of medicine stems from the suppression of such a secret, the politics of creating a historical specialty.

REFERENCE LIST

Aguayo, J. 1989. "Charcot and Freud: Some Implications of Late Nineteenth-Century French Psychiatry and Politics for the Origins of Psychoanalysis." *Psychoanalysis and Contemporary Thought* 9: 223–60.

Bauer, Veit Harold. 1973. *Das Antonius-Feuer in Kunst und Medizin*. Basel.

Baxandall, Michael. 1985. *Patterns of Intention: On the Historical Explanation of Pictures*. New Haven.

Bender, George A. 1961. *Great Moments in Medicine: A Collection of the First Thirty Stories and Paintings in the Continuing Series, a History of Medicine in Pictures*. Paintings by Robert A. Thom. Detroit.

Berger, Ernst. 1970. *Das Basler Arztrelief: Studien zum griechischen Grab- und Votivrelief um 500 v. Chr. und zur vorhippokratischen Medizin*. Basel.

Boeckl, Herbert. 1984. *Herbert Boeckl, die Bilder und Zeichnungen zur Anatomie*. Salzburg.

Canguilhem, Georges. 1989. *The Normal and the Pathological*. Tr. Carolyn R. Fawcett. Boston.

Carmichael, Ann G., and Richard M. Ratzan, eds. 1991. *Medicine: A Treasury of Art and Literature*. New York.

Cartwright, Elizabeth. 1991. "Physiological Modernism: Cinematography as a Medical Research Technology." Diss. Yale.

Charcot, Jean Martin, and Paul Richer. 1887. *Les démoniaques dans l'art*. Paris.

————. 1889. *Les difformes et les malades dans l'art.* Paris.

Charcot, Jean Martin, ed. 1888–1918. *Nouvelle iconographie de la Salpêtrière: clinique des maladies du système nerveux.* Paris.

Cherubini, Arnaldo. 1977. *I Medici Scrittori dal XV al XX secolo.* Rome.

Choulant, Ludwig. 1862. *Geschichte und Bibliographie der anatomischen Abbildung nach ihrer Beziehung auf anatomische Wissenschaft und bildende Kunst.* Leipzig.

Didi-Huberman, Georges. 1982. *Invention de l'hystérie: Charcot et l'iconographie photographique de la Salpêtrière.* Paris.

Dolan, Josephine A., M. Louise Fitzpatrick, and Eleanor Krohn Herrmann. 1983. *Nursing in Society: A Historical Perspective.* Philadelphia.

Donahue, M. Patricia. 1985. *Nursing, the Finest Art: An Illustrated History.* St. Louis.

Duin, Nancy, and Jenny Sutcliffe. 1992. *A History of Medicine: From Prehistory to the Year 2020.* New York.

Foucault, Michel. 1984. "The Order of Discourse." In Michael J. Shapiro, ed., *Language and Politics.* New York. 108–38.

Fox, Daniel M., and Christopher Lawrence. 1988. *Photographing Medicine: Images and Power in Britain and America since 1840.* New York.

Fried, Michael. 1987. *Realism, Writing, Disfiguration: On Thomas Eakins and Stephen Crane.* Chicago.

Garrison, Fielding H. 1915. *John Shaw Billings: A Memoir.* New York.

Gay, Peter. 1976. *Art and Act: On Causes in History—Manet, Gropius, Mondrian.* New York.

Gelfand, Toby. 1988. " 'Mon Cher Docteur Freud': Charcot's Unpublished Correspondence to Freud, 1888–1893." *Bulletin of the History of Medicine* 62: 563–88.

Gerdts, William H. 1981. *The Art of Healing: Medicine and Science in American Art.* Birmingham, Ala.

Gilman, Sander L. 1976. *The Face of Madness: Hugh W. Diamond and the Rise of Psychiatric Photography.* New York.

————. 1978. "On the Use and Abuse of the History of Psychiatry for Literary Studies: Reading a Dickens Text on Insanity." *Deutsche Vierteljahrsschrift für Literaturwissenschaft und Geistesgeschichte* 52: 381–99.

————. 1982. *Seeing the Insane: A Cultural History of Psychiatric Illustration.* New York.

————. 1985. *Difference and Pathology: Stereotypes of Sexuality, Race, and Madness.* Ithaca, N.Y.

————. 1988. *Disease and Representation: Images of Illness from Madness to AIDS.* Ithaca, N.Y.

Grape-Albers, Heide. 1977. *Spatantike Bilder aus der Welt des Arztes: Medizinische Bilderhandschriften der Spatantike und ihre mittelalterliche Uberlieferung.* Wiesbaden.

Hahn, André, and Paule Dumaitre. 1962. *Histoire de la médicine et du livre médical.* Paris.

Harter, Jim. 1991. *Images of Medicine.* New York.

Haskell, Frances. 1993. *History and Its Images: Art and the Interpretation of the Past.* New Haven.

Helfand, William H. 1978. *Medicine and Pharmacy in American Political Prints, 1765–1870.* Madison, Wis.

———. 1991. *The Picture of Health: Images of Medicine and Pharmacy from the William H. Helfand Collection.* Philadelphia.

Herrlinger, Robert. 1967–72. *Geschichte der medizinischen Abbildung.* 2 vols. München.

Holländer, Eugen. 1903. *Die Medizin in der klassischen Malerei.* Stuttgart.

———. 1905. *Die Karikatur und Satire in der Medizin: Mediko-kunsthistorisches Studie.* Mit 10 farbigen Tafeln und 223 Abbildungen im Text. Stuttgart.

———. 1912. *Plastik und Medizine.* Stuttgart.

———. 1913. *Die Medizin in der klassischen Malerei.* 2. Aufl. Stuttgart.

———. 1921a. *Die Karikatur und Satire in der Medizin: Mediko-kunsthistorische Studie.* 2. Aufl. Mit 11 farbigen Tafeln und 251 Abbildungen im Text. Stuttgart.

———. 1921b. *Wunder, Wundergeburt und Wundergestalt in einblattdrucken des fünfzehnten bis achtzehnten Jahrhunderts.* Stuttgart.

———. 1923. *Die Medizin in der klassischen Malerei.* Mit 272 in den Text gedruckten Abbildungen. 3. Aufl. Stuttgart.

———. 1928. *Äskulap und Venus: eine Kultur- und Sittengeschichte im Spiegel des Arztes.* Berlin.

Jay, Martin. 1993. *Downcast Eyes: The Denigration of Vision in Twentieth-Century French Thought.* Berkeley.

Jones, Peter Murray. 1984. *Medieval Medical Miniatures.* London.

Jordanova, Ludmilla. 1989. *Sexual Visions: Images of Gender in Science and Medicine between the Eighteenth and Twentieth Centuries.* Madison, Wis.

Jurina, Kitti. 1985. *Vom Quacksalber zum Doctor Medicinae: Die Heilkunde in der deutschen Graphik des 16. Jahrhunderts.* Köln.

Kaplan, Harold I., and Benjamin J. Sadock. 1989. *Comprehensive Textbook of Psychiatry.* 5th ed. Baltimore.

Karp, Diane R. 1985. *Ars medica, Art, Medicine, and the Human Condition: Prints, Drawings, and Photographs from the Collection of the Philadelphia Museum of Art.* Philadelphia.

Laignel-Lavastine, Maxime. 1936–49. *Histoire générale de la médecine, de la pharmacie, de l'art dentaire et de l'art vétérinaire: Ornée de nombreuses illustrations.* 3 vols. Paris.

Lavin, Irving. 1993. *Past-Present: Essays on Historicism in Art from Donatello to Picasso.* Berkeley.

Lyons, Albert S. 1978. *Medicine: An Illustrated History.* New York.

Lyons, Albert S., and R. Joseph Petrucelli. 1978. *Medicine: An Illustrated History.* New York.

MacGregor, John M. 1989. *The Discovery of the Art of the Insane.* Princeton, N.J.

MacKinney, Loren Carey. 1965. *Medical Illustrations in Medieval Manuscripts.* London.

Marti-Ibañez, Felix, ed. 1962. *The Epic of Medicine.* New York.

Masson, Madeleine. 1985. *A Pictorial History of Nursing.* London.

Meurer-Keldenich, Maria. 1979. *Medizinische Literatur zur Bildnerei von Geisteskranken.* Köln.

Meyer-Steineg, Theodor. 1912a. *Darstellungen normaler und krankhaft veranderter Körper-teile an antiken Weihgaben.* Jena.

———. 1912b. *Chirurgische Instrumente des Altertums: Ein Beitrag zur antiken Akiur-gie.* Jena.

———. 1920. "Geschichte der Medizin als Lehrgegenstand." *Berliner klinische Wochenschrift* 57: 158.

Meyer-Steineg, Theodor, and Karl Sudhoff. 1921. *Geschichte der Medizin im Überblick mit Abbildungen.* Jena.

———. 1965. *Illustrierte Geschichte der Medizin.* 5. durchgesehene und erw. Aufl. hrsg. von Robert Herrlinger und Fridolf Kudlien. Stuttgart.

Momigliano, Arnaldo. 1950. "Ancient History and the Antiquarian." *Journal of the Warburg and Courtauld Institutes* 3/4: 285–315.

Morgenthaler, Walter. 1992. *Madness and Art: The Life and Works of Adolf Wölfli.* Tr. Aaron H. Esman. Lincoln.

Murken, Axel Hinrich. 1979. *Joseph Beuys und die Medizin.* Munster.

Newman, Art. 1988. *The Illustrated Treasury of Medical Curiosa.* New York.

Paret, Peter. 1988. *Art as History: Episodes in The Culture and Politics of Nineteenth-Century Germany.* Princeton, N.J.

Peters, Hermann. 1900. *Der Arzt und die Heilkunst in alten Zeiten.* Leipzig.

Prinzhorn, Hans. 1972. *Artistry of the Mentally Ill: A Contribution to the Psychology and Psychopathology of Configuration.* Tr. Eric von Brockdorff. New York.

Prinzhorn Collection: Selected Work from the Prinzhorn Collection of the Art of the Mentally Ill. 1984.

Puschmann, Theodor. 1889. "Die Bedeutung der Geschichte für die Medicin und die Naturwissenschaften." *Deutsche medizinische Wochenschrift* 15: 817–20.

Rabb, Theodore K. 1975. *The Struggle for Stability in Early Modern Europe.* New York.

Richer, Paul Marie Louis Pierre. 1885. *Etudes cliniques sur la grande hystérie ou hystéro-épilepsie.* 2d ed. rev. Paris.

———. 1900. *L'art et la médicine.* Paris.

Roback, Abraham Aaron, and Thomas Kiernan. 1969. *Pictorial History of Psychology and Psychiatry.* New York.

Rodekirchen, Dirk Friedrich. 1992. *Karl Sudhoff (1853–1938) und die Anfänge der Medizin-Geschichte in Deutschland.* Diss., Cologne.

Rosenberg, Charles, and Janet Godlen, eds. 1992. *Framing Disease: Studies in Cultural History.* New Brunswick, N.J.

Rotberg, Robert I., and Theodore K. Rabb, ed. 1988. *Art and History: Images and Their Meaning.* Cambridge.

Sass, Louis Arnorsson. 1992. *Madness and Modernism: Insanity in the Light of Modern Art, Literature, and Thought.* New York.

Schadewalt, Hans, Léon Binet, Charles Maillant, and Ilza Veith. 1967. *Kunst und Medizin*. Köln.

Schama, Simon. 1987. *The Embarrassment of Riches: An Interpretation of Dutch Culture in the Golden Age*. New York.

Schmidt-Voigt, Jorgen. 1980. *Russische Ikonenmalerei und Medizin*. München.

Schwalbe, Ernst. 1920. *Vorlesungen über Geschichte der Medizin*. 3. Auflage. Jena.

Seidenbusch, Anton. 1975. *Kunst und Medizin in Padua: Beruhrpunkte zwischen Heilkunde u. bildender Kunst, dargest: Anhand von Beispielen aus Paduas Kirchen u.d. Scuola del Santo*. Pattensen.

Showalter, Elaine. 1985. *The Female Malady: Women, Madness, and English Culture, 1830–1980*. New York.

Sigerist, Henry Ernest. 1943. *Civilization and Disease*. Ithaca, N.Y.

Smolan, Rick. 1992. *Medicine's Great Journey: One Hundred Years of Healing*. Boston.

Sournia, Jean-Charles. 1992. *The Illustrated History of Medicine*. Tr. Louise Davies, Graham Cross, and Lilian Hall. London.

Stafford, Barbara Maria. 1992. *Body Criticism: Imaging the Unseen in Enlightenment Art and Medicine*. Cambridge, Mass.

Sudhoff, Karl. 1906a. "Medizin und Kunst: Ein Wort der Einführung und Weihe." In the *Katalog zur Ausstellung der Geschichte der Medizin in Kunst und Kunstwerk: Zur Eröffnung des Kaiserin-Friedrich-Hauses in Berlin 1906*. Stuttgart 21–26.

———. 1906b. "Theodor Puschmann und die Aufgaben der Geschichte der Medizin: Eine akademische Antrittsvorlesung." *Münchner medizinische Wochenschrift* 53: 2270.

———. 1909. "Abermals eine neue Handschrift der anatomischen Fünfbilderserie." *Archiv für Geschichte der Medizin* 3: 353–68.

———. 1911. "Photographie oder Zeichnung?" *Wochenschrift für klassiche Philosophie* 28: 345–51.

———. 1912. *Mal Franzoso in Italien in der ersten Hälfte des 15. Jahrhunderts; ein Blatt aus der Geschichte der Syphilis*. Giessen.

———. 1912–13. "Plastik und Medizin: Eine glossierende Besprechung des gleichnamigen Werkes Eugen Holländers." *Zeitschrift für Balneologie* 5: 461–67.

———, ed. 1912. *Graphische und typographische Erstlinge der Syphilis-Literatur aus den Jahren 1495 und 1496*. München.

Sudhoff, Karl Friedrich Jakob, and Moriz Hall, eds. 1920. *Des Andreas Vesalius sechs anatomische Tafeln vom Jahre 1538 in Lichtdruck, neu herausgegeben und der 86: Versammlung Deutscher Naturforscher und Aerzte zur Feier der 400: Wiederkehr des Jahres seiner Geburt*. Leipzig.

Sudhoff, Karl Friedrich Jakob, ed. 1924. *Zehn Syphilis-Drucke aus den Jahren 1495–1498*. Milan.

———, ed. 1925. *The Earliest Printed Literature on Syphilis; Being Ten Tractates from the*

Years 1495–1498. In complete facsimile with an introduction and other accessory material by Karl Sudhoff; adapted by Charles Singer. Florence.

Sudhoff, Karl Friedrich Jakob, and Max Geisberg, eds. 1928. *Die anatomischen Tafeln des Jost de Negker 1539, mit 6 Tafeln und 2 Abbildungen im Text*. München.

Taureck, Renata. 1980. *Die Bedeutung der Photographie für die medizinische Abbildung im 19. Jahrhundert*. Köln.

Theopold, Wilhelm. 1981. *Votivmalerei und Medizin: Kulturgeschichte und Heilkunst im Spiegel der Votivmalerei*. München.

Thornton, John L., and Carole Reeves. 1983. *Medical Book Illustration: A Short History*. Cambridge.

Tuchman, Maurice, and Carol S. Eliel, ed. 1992. *Parallel Visions: Modern Artists and Outsider Art*. Los Angeles.

Vogt, Helmut. 1984. *Der Arzt am Krankenbett: Eine Charakteristik in Bildern aus fünf Jahrhunderten*. München.

Witkin, Joel-Peter. 1987. *Masterpieces of Medical Photography: Selections for the Burns Archive*. Pasadena.

Zglinicki, Friedrich von. 1982. *Die Uroskopie in der bildenden Kunst: eine kunst- und medizinhistorische Untersuchung über die Harnschau*. Darmstadt.

Zigrosser, Carl. 1959. *Ars Medica: A Collection of Medical Prints Presented to the Laboratories*.

FAMILY, COMMUNITY, POLIS: THE FREUDIAN STRUCTURE OF FEELING

———————➤◦◄———————

John Brenkman

I

PSYCHOANALYSIS SHARES WITH modern literature a penchant for discovering in the forms of personal suffering ciphers of a more general condition. When decked out metaphysically, these ciphers have become, variously, visions of the human condition or mythologies of violence and the sacred, or even allegories of language. I am a partisan of another alternative, where exemplary forms of personal suffering become ciphers of the social relationships in which we wittingly and unwittingly participate. I therefore look to psychoanalysis to contribute to the cultural interpretation of the modern forms of individuality and to help disclose the norms and the pathologies that typically occur in the making of the socialized individual in our society.

Psychoanalysis has generally left its ties to social theory fragmented and largely covert. Moreover, it tends to invert the relation between cultural forms and specifically psychoanalytic concepts, believing the latter to be purely descriptive of the psychic mechanism and then deriving the cultural forms from them. Psychoanalysis also tends to eschew historical questions by casting the historical context of life histories as merely contingent elements in a universal structure.

Nowhere are these intellectual habits more deeply ingrained than in the Freudian theory of the Oedipus complex. The Oedipus complex is also perhaps the most developed figure of exemplary suffering that psychoanalysis has produced. The reference to Greek tragedy, with its ritual reenactments of the actions of ancient royalty, can be misleading. For psychoanalysis tells a very modern and very bourgeois tale. Freud's Oedipal theory was a search for the inner logic of the middle-class male's socialization into heterosexuality, marriage, and vocation.

Freud's own life history and its historical context were at the very origin of Oedipal theory. The basic concepts of psychoanalysis, including the rudiments of the "father-complex," were discovered in the course of the self-analysis whose traces Freud left in *The Interpretation of Dreams*. As Carl E. Schorske showed in his classic essay "Politics and Patricide in Freud's *Interpretation of Dreams*," Freud's autobiographical self-reflection also reveals the "flight from politics" that marked Freud's painful shift from his youthful aspiration to politics as vocation to a safer, more sober decision in favor of science as vocation. He abandoned his plans to study law and eventually entered the medical profession instead.[1]

His dreams are shot through with images of political heroism in which he or his father struggles against the conservatism of the Habsburgs in the name of German, Hungarian, and Italian nationalisms. The dreamed hero also triumphs over anti-Semitism. In the 1890s anti-Semitism was on the rise. Karl Lueger's anti-Semitic party won elections in Vienna, and there was anti-Jewish violence in Galicia. Many Jewish intellectuals, including Freud himself, encountered intensifying obstacles to their advancement in Austrian academic and professional positions. Freud encountered the "blocked ascendence" that Alvin Gouldner has identified as the motive that has historically driven intellectuals to become revolutionaries.[2]

The choice of science over politics changed the scene of his revolutionary ambitions. The phrase Freud chose from the *Aeneid* for the epigraph of *The Interpretation of Dreams* registered the displacement triumphantly: "Flectere si nequeo superos, Acheronta movebo" (If I cannot bend the higher powers, I will stir up the river Acheron [my translation])—that is, I will stir up hell, the demonic, the unconscious.

Unlike many of his contemporaries who witnessed the general breakup of liberalism at the end of the century, the young Freud did not repudiate his liberal father's beliefs. Instead, he sought, Schorske writes, "to overcome his father by realizing the liberal creed his father professed but had failed to defend" (PP 191). Freud's long-unhealed wound at the hand of his father was not some primal paternal castration threat but rather the dismay he felt as a child upon hearing his father tell of being bullied. He recounted the episode, which had figured in his self-analysis, in *The Interpretation of Dreams*:

"A Christian came up to me and with a single blow knocked off my cap into the mud and shouted: 'Jew! Get off the pavement!' " "And what did you do?" I asked. "I went into the roadway and picked up my cap" was his quiet reply. This struck me as unheroic conduct on the part of the big, strong man who was holding the little boy by the hand. I contrasted this situation with another which fitted my feelings better: the scene in which Hannibal's father . . . made his boy swear before the household altar to take vengeance on the Romans.[3]

Karl Lueger, Rome, Austrian aristocracy, the Catholic Church, and the Habsburg regime do not disappear as antagonists to Freud's values and aims, but through his interpretation of his dreams he manages to transform them into merely the setting for the supposedly more fundamental antagonism of son and father. He then completes this intellectual maneuver by making the father the source of political and social power: "The father is the oldest, first, and for children the only authority, and from his autocratic power the other social authorities have developed in the course of the history of human civilization" (*ID* 217n).

The preeminence of the father as a symbol of authority and power takes the place of the real-life father with his unheroic submission to injustice and humiliation. By the same token, in the other register of Freud's imagination, he had transformed his own scientific vocation and his discovery of the unconscious—including the rudiments of the Oedipus complex—into acts of rebellion and retribution. "Patricide replaces politics," according to Schorske (PP 197). "By reducing his own political past and present," writes Schorske, "to an epiphenomenal status in relation to the primal conflict between father and son, Freud gave his fellow liberals an a-historical theory of man and society that could make bearable a political world spun out of orbit and beyond control" (PP 203).

Turning the tables on Freud is never that easy. Schorske himself is caught square in a very Freudian paradox. For he argues his claim that Freud replaced political explanations with psychological ones by advancing, precisely, psychological rather than political explanations. Nevertheless, Schorske's reassessment has the virtue of not refuting the Freudian project so much as disclosing how it aims at something beyond what Freud would, or could, actually articulate. The biographical revisionism points up the need for a theoretical reconstruction as well. Moreover, it would be wrong to conclude that Freud's family, vocation, and politics were merely limitations on his thinking. These concrete circumstances were also its enabling conditions. Ultimately, my aim is to ask: How did Freud use conceptions of the family and the psyche to think out the historical processes that were transforming the forms of *community* and *polis* at the turn of the century? To what extent are Freud's concepts a mere rewriting of social and political processes in psychological terms? To what extent are they a discovery, however partial, of new forms of individuality accompanying new forms of sociality?

II

Carole Pateman has done much to rescue Freud's forays into anthropology and history from the obscurity they might deserve on account of their sheer inaccuracy—*and* from the astounding prestige they have enjoyed on account of structuralism. *Totem and Taboo* (1912–13), *Civilization and Its Discontents* (1930), and *Moses and Monotheism* (1939) focus on ancient and prehistoric societies, but they actually embody, according to Pateman, Freud's very relevant reflection on modern society. He draws the conceptual and narrative resources of this reflection, Pateman argues, from the tradition of social contract theory. His political fiction of origins surpasses other theories of the social contract by revealing what they systematically hide: namely, that a fundamental subordination of women by men lies behind the supposed founding moment of society in an agreement among equals. Male sex-right, in other words, precedes fraternal equality.

The Freudian story of the primal horde—of the rebellious sons who killed the tyrannical father to end his exclusive control over all the women of the horde and then created the rules that outlawed murder, guaranteed the just distribution of women among all the males, and honored the dead father with idealizing symbols—this story may seem infinitely removed from the preoccupations of modernity. But modern society becomes Freud's real referent as soon as he takes up the task of explaining relations of equality established through an agreement upon rules. Like the social contract stories, Freud's primal horde story furnishes the backing for the kinds of equality associated with the economic, the legal, and the political institutions of capitalism and the liberal state. His analysis is really designed to explain present-day society but is projected into the remote past as a narrative of origin.

Pateman credits Freud with giving the story of the emergence of civil society its true starting point. Fraternity is born with the subjugation of women. "The motive for the brothers' collective act," she writes, "is not merely to claim their natural liberty and right of self-government, but *to gain access to women*. . . . No man can be a primal father ever again, but by setting up rules that give all men equal access to women (compare their equality before the laws of the state) they exercise the 'original' political right of dominion over women that was once the prerogative of the father."[4] Even as social contract theorists challenged the justifications of absolute monarchy modeled on paternal authority, they left unchallenged the father-husband's rule. They interpreted it as a natural rather than political power. Contract theorists, like their antagonists the patriarchalists, asserted "first, that women (wives), unlike sons, were born and remained naturally subject to men (husbands); and, second, that the right of men over women was *not political*" (*FSC* 39).

Freud provides Pateman with the needed representation or mapping of the two domains of sociality that contract theory separated: the family and civil society. Pateman points out that what Freud meant by "civilization" is what she means by "civil society": "The fraternal social contract creates a new, modern patriarchal order that is presented as divided into two spheres: civil society or the universal sphere of freedom, equality, individualism, reason, contract and impartial law—the realm of men or 'individuals'; and the private world of particularity, natural subjection, laws of blood, emotion, love and sexual passion—the world of women, in which men also rule" (*FSC* 43). And indeed Freud's conception of "civilization" is at once broad in scope, covering labor and material culture, legal institutions and the state, cultural and ethical ideals; and distinctively modern in that the forms of equality he connects to the fraternal pact are those of the capitalist market, liberal jurisprudence, and the constitutional state.

By the time Freud refined this version of the social contract in *Civilization and Its Discontents,* his Oedipal theory had acquired its achieved form. It was ready for use in those speculative exercises of applied psychoanalysis through which he read out complex historical processes and social institutions as libidinal economy. Like Pateman, I consider these exercises to be attempts by Freud to think out political and social questions in psychoanalytic categories. Such a reading has to begin by following out the movement of Freud's explicit claims regarding archaic societies or civilization in the abstract. His real referent can only be gained through a twist in the more immanent reading. Let us turn, then, to Freud's own terms.

Communal life as such, he postulates, has "a two-fold foundation:

the compulsion to work, which was created by external necessity, and the power of love."[5] He proceeds on the basis of an axiom whose iron-clad gender roles he is at once exposing and naturalizing: "the power of love . . . made the man unwilling to be deprived of his sexual object—the woman—and made the woman unwilling to be deprived of the part of herself which had been separated off from her—her child" (*CD* 101). The elemental form of sociality, therefore, combines the male desire to keep control over a woman for purposes of sexual gratification and the female desire to keep watch over her child.

Men's heterosexual desire and women's maternal love founded the sociality of the family. Civilization then developed not only by proliferating families but also by progressively distinguishing itself from the family. This does not, however, imply that civilization arises solely from the other anthropological foundation Freud identified, that is, the necessity to labor in concert. Love, too, builds civilization, but only in the guise of male desire. Men's sensual love leads them to find a mate and create new families, while their "aim-inhibited love" devotes itself to the whole range of sublimated attachments from friendships to a devotion to cultural or ethical ideals. Male desire divides, to use Eve Kosofsky Sedgwick's terms, into its homosocial and its heterosexual forms.[6] Freud credits both with enhancing civilization. Women's maternal love, however, hardly leads them further into civilization than their participation in the heterosexual couple; maternal love is otherwise what puts the family "in opposition to civilization," since it cements the family attachments that discourage family members from venturing "into the wider circle of life" (*CD* 103). In Freud's view, the evolution of civilization has steadily sharpened the sexual division of labor; men have become ever more extensively and exclusively preoccupied with civilization rather than family. "Thus the woman finds herself," Freud proclaims, "forced into the background by the claims of civilization and she adopts a hostile attitude towards it" (*CD* 104).

Freud's mapping of the differentiation of family and civil society and their interaction is thus complete. He attributes the building of civilization to male homosocial desire; he attributes the civilizing reproduction of families to the combined power of male heterosexual desire and maternal love; and he attributes the conflict between family and civil society to the "retarding and restraining influence" (*CD* 103) of maternal love alone.

The libidinal economy of the family and civil society also turns out to trace the ideal path of male socialization. The son at first lives wholly within "the mode of life which is phylogenetically the older" (*CD* 103) to which he is attached by the bonds of maternal love. Growth will follow a trajectory beyond these bonds, as the little boy, under the pressure of the father's authority within the family circle itself, undergoes the splitting of his love into the homosocial and the heterosexual and, finally, under the impact of his complete individuation, becomes suited for vocation and marriage, that is, the roles which civil society and the family, respectively, demand of him. The cluster of childhood experiences that Freud considered crucial to the realization of this ideal defines the so-called positive Oedipus complex and its dissolution.

From the standpoint of Freud's intellectual career, these various mappings — civil society and family; male socialization; Oedipus — came in a particular chronological order. Oedipal theory emerged first, though fragmentedly and slowly, and with it a tacit model of male socialization, and then later Freud applied the model in works like *Civilization and Its Discontents* to society writ large. But the primacy accorded the psychological concepts is deceiving. As Schorske's interpretation suggests, Freud forged the initial psychoanalytic categories out of the political experiences of his generation as they impinged on his own social aspirations and vocation. And, as Pateman's interpretation suggests, a whole tradition of political thought furnishes the impetus and terms of Freud's conceptualization of the family as well as his distillation of the gender roles that underpin psychoanalytic theory. Freud is caught up in that political discourse's imperatives from the outset, in particular the imperative of explaining and justifying the specifically modern form of patriarchy. It makes some sense, therefore, to consider Freud's thought a social thinking that was always shuttling back and forth between his mappings of civil society and the family and his mappings of the Oedipus complex.

III

These mappings suggest a way of looking at the kind of life history that becomes exemplary for psychoanalysis without, however, taking up the psychoanalyst's own starting point in the clinical picture presented by that life history. Rather than starting with the symptoms, enumerated and categorized through the therapist's medicalized lens, let's use the Freudian map to ask, instead: What are the crises, the stumbling blocks, the sources of suffering, that create this life history's unsolved problems and unfinished tasks? The question is certainly relevant to Freud's self-analysis and his case history of the Rat Man, both of which contributed so crucially to the making of Oedipal theory.

Like Freud, the Rat Man was the son of a businessman who had made the great transition from rural life in a Jewish village to secular, commercial life in the city. The sons did not follow their fathers' footsteps into commerce, but pursued professions. Neither Freud's father nor the Rat Man's reproduced his own religious upbringing in his son's life. Another son who had experienced how this generational divide made it impossible for the shape of his own life to equal his father's wrote: "It was much the same with a large section of this transitional generation of Jews, which had migrated from the still comparatively devout countryside to the cities. It happened automatically; only it added to our relationship, which certainly did not lack in acrimony, one more sufficiently painful source."[7] Like Freud and the Rat Man, this beleaguered son, a contemporary of the Rat Man's, was a child of the Habsburg empire. I have quoted from Franz Kafka's "Letter to His Father." For Kafka, as for Freud and the Rat Man, the watersheds of maturity were marriage and vocation, science for Freud and law for the Rat Man and Kafka. Like the Rat Man, Kafka faltered at both. His sparsely narrated life history discloses the pressures that shape or interrupt or distort the path of male socialization as it traverses and connects the social spaces of family and civil society.

Kafka's "Letter to His Father" was written in 1919 when he was thirty-six. It was never delivered, except to his mother. The letter painfully and painstakingly reveals how the son's response to his father's authority, marriage, and vocation snuffed out his own capacity to value a vocation and ruined his own plans to marry. Kafka had been stopped dead in his tracks on the path of socialization. "I fled everything that even remotely reminded me of you," he writes. "First, the business" (135). He had acquired a double perception of his father's vocation, corresponding to the two-sided role of the dry goods wholesaler: he was an entrepreneur whose "magnificent commercial talents" and decisiveness his son admired, and he was the employer who despised and terrorized his employees, "shouting, cursing, and raging in the shop." Young Kafka acquired a sense of injustice at the store, but at the same moment his impulse to rebel in the name of justice was destroyed: "You called the employees 'paid enemies,' and that is what they were, but even before they became that, you seemed to me to be their 'paying enemy.' There, too, I learned the great lesson you could be unjust; in my own case I would not have noticed it so soon, for there was much accumulated sense of guilt in me ready to admit that you were right. . . . it made the business insufferable to me, reminding me far too much of my relations with you" (136–37). In becoming the imaginary class enemy of his father, he lost his hold on business as vocation; yet, confronted with a tyrant whose paternal recognition he nonetheless craved, he did not rebel but merely became ever more convinced of his own inadequacy: "You must, as I assumed, in the same way be forever dissatisfied with me too" (137).

Cut off from any expectation of his father's approval, he let his schoolwork and then his own choice of vocation become "a matter of indifference to me." "And so it was a matter of finding," he wrote, "a profession that would let me indulge this indifference without injuring my vanity too much. Law was the obvious choice" (154). Kafka's devotion to the law as vocation never got beyond his undistinguished position in the bureaucracy of a workers' insurance company.

While Kafka settled into the bare satisfactions of a vocation that allowed him to balance his indifference to social achievement against his remaining shreds of bourgeois self-esteem, he attained no such heights when it came to his marriage plans. His broken engagements to Felice Bauer, twice, and to Milena Jesenska were catastrophic proof of his failing at life. Marriage possessed a supreme value for Kafka: "Marrying, founding a family, accepting all the children that come, supporting them in this insecure world and perhaps even guiding them a little, is, I am convinced, the utmost a human being can succeed in doing" (156). This valuation led Kafka to desire and fear marriage with equal intensity.

Although his father had undermined the engagements by belittling the women Kafka chose and mocking Kafka's feeling for them, he does not blame his failings on the father's opposition. Instead, he uncovers a paradox in his own desires and aspirations, as they are mediated through his esteem for his father. For when he let himself imagine becoming a husband, it not only gratified a cultural ideal but also held out the utopian prospect of achieving parity with his father: "I picture this equality which would then arise between us . . . as so beautiful because then I could be a free, grateful, guiltless, upright son, and you could be an untroubled, untyrannical, sympathetic, contented father" (162). But "so much cannot be achieved," he laments, and dismisses his vision as a "fairy tale." He does not, however, then cast off this utopian expectation. On the contrary, he lets marriage recede beyond his reach because the equality of father and son seems unattainable. Why should he arrive at this bitter and yet absurd impasse? In part, of course, because of his virtually inexplicable lack of rebelliousness. But his own explanation looks elsewhere.

The uncanny lucidity characteristic of the "Letter to His Father" deserts Kafka when he turns to explain why the aspiration to be like his father has ultimately ruined the marriage plan that would indeed make him like his father: "Marrying is barred to me because it is your very own domain. . . . In your marriage I had before me what was, in many ways, a model marriage, a model in constancy, mutual help, number of children; and even when the children grew up and increasingly disturbed the peace, the marriage as such remained undisturbed. Perhaps I formed my high idea of marriage on this model: the desire for marriage was powerless for other reasons. Those lay in your relation to your children, which is, after all, what this whole letter is about" (163). This passage does not jell with all that one gleans about the marriage from the "Letter to His Father" as well as Kafka's diaries and letters. All these virtues of constancy and help-fulness, as well as the burdens of the family's size and of restoring the peace the children disturbed, were the hallmarks not of the marriage but of Kafka's mother.

His attitude toward *her* adherence to these virtues, however, was hardly affirmative. A few pages earlier he saw in her kindness and desire for harmony the very instrument that destroyed his own ability to rebel against his father. Addressing his father, the harsh disciplinarian, he wrote: "Even if your method of upbringing might in some unlikely case have set me on my own feet by means of producing defiance, dislike, or even hate in me, Mother canceled that out again by kindness, by talking sensibly, . . . by pleading for me; and I was driven back into your orbit" (132). Kafka achieves his idealization of marriage by taking those traits of his parents' marriage that he inadvertently reveals are his mother's contribution and attributing them to his father's power. The basis, therefore, for his identifi-cation with his father and the source of his valorization of the role of hus-band are precisely the father's power. His rule is what makes him, rather than the mother, the author of the marriage. Kafka identifies with his father *in his power.* "When the primal horde gives way to kinship and mar-riage," Pateman remarks, "the father's legacy of sex-right is shared equally among all the brothers."[8] It is this legacy of sex-right that Kafka covets, but he cowers at the thought of exercising it because he fears his real-life

father. Lacan is certainly right to trace Oedipal pathologies to the dissonance the son experiences in apprehending his father as both a real-life
individual like himself (a potential equal) *and* the representative of fatherhood itself. What is missing in Lacan, however, is the sense, so vivid here,
that this very discrepancy feeds on the real-life father's double role as head
of the household, where his sex-right *is* the basis of his tyranny, and as the
bourgeois or citizen whom the son might encounter as an equal. It is his
real-life power in the private sphere that supports his symbolic function.
The patriarchal tyranny Kafka fled in the dry goods store he craves in his
ideal of marriage. There is nothing paradoxical in this. Marriage promises
him a masculinity and power like his father's—until he renounces it as a
fairy tale that his weakness does not permit him to hope for. The pathologies of the Oedipus complex are pathologies of patriarchal power.

I V

Woven into the life histories Freud typically encountered was the dense
web of social relationships in which the family and its members participate. From these social relationships, Freud distilled the Oedipal triangle.
He eschewed the questions of gender, community, and power at play in
the family and its links to civil society and the polis. They became, at most,
the backlighting of the Oedipal scene. Faced with the typical pathologies
of modernity, the stumbling blocks and unsolved problems in men's and
women's life histories, Freud looked through the medical lens to define
symptomotologies solely with reference to the individual as an organism,
never as participant in social and political relations.

Social and political relations are regulated by norms, and they require
justifications and often evoke challenges. Freud's medicalizing, psychologizing stance apparently sidestepped the thorny problem of legitimating
or criticizing norms and practices. Nevertheless, the clinical terrain he
marked out itself still needed some kind of normative order against which
to read the individual psyche's symptoms. What would a nonpathological
outcome of the Oedipus complex really look like? Just as Freud's account
of Oedipal pathologies diverted the elements of social diagnosis and cultural critique into a purely psychological symptomotology, he responded
to the need to imagine a resolution or healing of Oedipal pathologies by
projecting a psychological norm: a dissolution of the Oedipus complex.

This concept was not, however, readily available to Freud. It had to be

wrenched from a confusing array of clinical experiences. Moreover, I am
suggesting that this search for a psychological norm tacitly forced Freud
to register the social and political relationships at play in the formation
of the Oedipus complex. He therefore continued to refine Oedipal theory
until it yielded a coherent conception of the dissolution as well as the formation of the Oedipus complex. The story of the pathogenic family drama
had to be matched with a story of the individual male's resolution of its
conflicts. It was not until *The Ego and the Id* (1923) and "The Dissolution of
the Oedipus Complex" (1924) that Freud found an adequate formulation
for the Oedipus complex's resolution, even though he had steadily pushed
the Oedipus complex to the center of his theory of neurosis for two decades, gradually universalizing its role in psychosexual development.

As it turns out, the dissolution of the Oedipus complex—as opposed
to its merely more or less unsuccessful repression—requires, first, that it
be initially formed along the lines of the "simple positive Oedipus complex," that is, in the heterosexual form where the little boy has an erotic attachment to his mother and a (desexualized) identification with his father.
Freud had in fact come to the conclusion that "a strong innate bisexual
disposition becomes one of the preconditions or reinforcements of neurosis."[9] Lacking a notion of what Adrienne Rich calls "compulsory heterosexuality," Freud misses the political interpretation this hypothesis suggests.[10] The simple positive Oedipus complex enjoys a privilege by virtue
of the fact that it lies on the path to male-dominated heterosexuality: its
every manifestation and nuance is socially validated and rewarded. The
normative outcome it promises is nothing more than the coercive appeal it
holds in an overwhelmingly homophobic and male-dominated life-world.

Once the Oedipus complex is appropriately formed, it can then be
utterly dissolved, without any repressed residue, only if the son's rivalrous
hatred of his father and his erotic attachment to his mother each end in
a particular way. As regards the father, the route for the son to follow is
already laid down by the heterosexual imperative. "What makes hatred of
the father unacceptable is *fear* of the father; castration is terrible, whether
as a punishment or as the price of love. Of the two factors which repress
hatred of the father," Freud writes in "Dostoevsky and Parricide," "the
first, the direct fear of punishment and castration, may be called the normal one; its pathogenic intensification seems to come only with the addition of the second factor, the fear of the feminine attitude" (*DP* 184). As

regards the mother in the simple positive Oedipus complex, the son's fear of castration is the motive for abandoning his erotic attachment. But what then is the fate of this love? "Its place may be filled by one of two things: either an identification with his mother or an intensification of his identification with his father. We are accustomed to regard the latter outcome as the more normal; it permits the affectionate relation to the mother to be in a measure retained. In this way the dissolution of the Oedipus complex would consolidate the masculinity in a boy's character."[11] Here then is Freud's real man. He is required, in sum, to have a weak bisexual disposition; he should abandon his hatred of his father out of fear rather than love; and, when he abandons his love for his mother in the face of the father's castration threats, he should end up identifying less with her than him. The only reassurance here is that, according to Freud, few ever attain this ideal!

The castration complex is the key to each moment of this ideal progress. But it is hard to see exactly how the castration complex can work very well in practice when it is so confused in theory. Lacanianism's elaborate distinction between the penis and phallus notwithstanding, the Freudian castration complex amounts to the notion that children's understanding of sexual difference comes down to their perception — judgment really — of having-a-penis-or-not. Freud's greater stress on bisexuality in the finalized version of Oedipal theory does not ultimately mitigate against this phallocentrism, since it is accompanied by his unwavering reference to the so-called "anatomical difference of the sexes." In fact, bisexuality and having-a-penis-or-not are closely linked concepts in the later Freud.

By bisexuality Freud sometimes meant that children's erotic wishes and love could be directed at men and boys or women and girls, and he sometimes meant that gratification could come through either active or passive aims (seeing/being seen, swallowing/being swallowed, and so forth). In taking these senses of bisexuality into Oedipal theory, Freud introduced two questionable assumptions. First, he regards an "active" sexual aim as *masculine* (or inevitably or completely encoded as *masculine*), while a "passive" sexual aim is *feminine* (or is inevitably or completely encoded as *feminine*). Second, he believes the male child is constrained to picture himself in an *active* and hence *masculine* role with his mother, and a *passive* and hence *feminine* role with his father. Add to this that both *active/passive* and *masculine/feminine* are deemed to straightforwardly correspond to having-a-penis-or-not, and the apparently radical notion of innate bisexuality is completely assimilated to the whole Oedipal regime of compulsory heterosexuality and male dominance.

The phallic equations are in fact all that Freud has to make sense of the simple positive Oedipus complex, its formation, and dissolution. Consider the fear of castration associated with the little boy's erotic attachment to his father, that is, the notion that he discovers that he would have to lose his penis to have intercourse with his father: since *father* = *masculine* = *active,* he himself would therefore become *passive* = *feminine* = *castrated.* Inversely, the consequence of having intercourse with his mother would be a punishment in the form of losing his penis, since *mother* = *passive* = *castrated,* making him *active* = *masculine* = *having-a-penis.*

All the basic equations are anchored in having-a-penis-or-not. But by Freud's own accounts the requisite "recognition" of castration, that is, the judgment that the "one thing" that makes women different from men is that they do not have a penis, is acquired only very late in the socialization process. If that is the case, then the elaborate emotional, libidinal relationships the child has with his mother and father, with other adults male and female, and with other children are obviously webs of passive and active erotic aims that have not been divvied up according to the phallic equations.

In a culture that produces images, symbols, narratives, jokes, and slogans laden with these phallic equations, it is surely safe to assume that their impact will be a crucial part of male socialization, perhaps congealing in a more or less dramatic way in certain experiences or crises. But what is that impact? Freud's emergent ideal of male socialization—that is, the positively formed, completely dissolved Oedipus complex—would suggest that the impact of the phallic equations is mental health itself. This precisely ignores their belatedness and inadequacy in representing the wealth of relationships in which the child has participated. The phallic equations have to recode and recalibrate the intricacies of passive and active sexual aims, the love for same-sex and different-sex playmates, parents, relatives. Wouldn't it make more sense to expect the reign of the phallic equations to be a kind of catastrophe that befalls the layers of uncertain, remembered, ill-named experience? Contrary to Freud's hypothesis, shouldn't we suspect that the acceptance of phallocentrism delivers such a blow to the weave of passivity and activity that you can fall ill?

Freud's definition of health has to be turned upside down. What is pathogenic is the inadequacy of the simple positive Oedipus complex to represent erotic and emotional life. It is not merely a theoretical misrepresentation. When Freud suggests that the simple positive Oedipus complex "represents a simplification or schematization" (33), he inadvertently points up the crucial unsolved question. For this is at once a theoretical and social schematization.

The simple positive Oedipus complex is a social schematization in the sense that it is the distilled form of the models, directives, stories, values, and so on through which our society tells the male child that he must grow up to be masculine and heterosexual in the ways valued by that society. The culture furnishes individuals with a construct for interpreting their relationships in keeping with the norms of compulsory heterosexuality and male dominance. This construct is the Oedipus complex viewed as a social schematization of experience, a disposition, a structure of feeling. The norms embodied in this construct are not the equivalent of the incest taboo; they operate a particular code upon it: I must not want my father, *because* he is a man. I must not want my mother, *because* she *belongs* to my father. I look beyond loving my mother out of fear rather than identification. I identify with my father rather than my mother because I aspire to his power. I identify with him rather than want to love him because I aspire to masculinity.

As a theoretical schematization, the simple positive Oedipus complex simplifies the child's multifarious attachments to this one heterosexual drama in an attempt to explain how the so-called bisexual male child, filled with contradictory ideas about the salient differences between his parents, uncertain of his own or others' gender, and, *pace* Freud, rife with passive and active sexual aims toward both parents, reemerges on the other side of latency and adolescence merely a more or less neurotic heterosexual. The theoretical schematization plainly fails in this task. Even when Freud declared that the ideal was seldom if ever attained, he did not reinterrogate its claim to normativity but simply retreated to his theme that the undifferentiated process of civilization exacts impossible demands on the human organism.

V

Since Freud does not see that the Oedipal structure of feeling derives from specific social practices and cultural forms—compulsory heterosexuality, male dominance, patriarchal symbols, male fantasy—he does not acknowledge that the norms embodied in this structure are in need of moral-political justification. Nor of course does he acknowledge that those norms, particularly the phallic equations, are open to challenge. Even though the Oedipal schematization anchors an entire process of socialization and individuation, it appears to Freud beyond the pale of political reflection. He does, however, tacitly acknowledge that the phallic equations require a theoretical explanation. For they have to come from somewhere. Freud responds by producing another round of origin stories. I refer now not to the primal horde but to the primal scene. Following a pattern we have seen before, Freud's effort to furnish a theoretical explanation for an apparently psychological question will lead him covertly to engage the moral-political justifications used to legitimate specific social and cultural practices.

Freud gave his fullest account of primal scenes in the context of postulating that they most typically were not memories of actual events but rather fantasies whose "psychical reality" was just as decisive as it would be if they also had a "material reality." Freud enumerates the most prominent of these fantasies "in the youthful history of neurotics" as follows: "observation of parental intercourse, seduction by an adult and threat of being castrated." [12] The seduction scenes are most closely associated with Freud's women patients. When he decided to discount the stories he had been told early in his career by young women who had been molested in their childhood, usually by their father, he recast actual manifestations of abusive father-right into the Oedipal fantasy of girls' longing to marry their fathers. Male dominance became a female fantasy, but for that very reason all the more "real" in the sense of "psychical reality," and all the more legitimate and justified in social reality for being no longer an actual father's crime.

The primal scene of parental intercourse and the threat of castration, on the other hand, are the necessary props to the male Oedipus complex. The primal scene presents the child with a view of sexual intercourse in which the *father* is *active* and the *mother* is *passive*. Freud never wavers from his conviction that this is exactly how the child comprehends the sexual act. In fact, it goes beyond *active/passive*. The father performs an act of aggression against the mother. The primal scene is a rape. The phallic equation *father* = *masculine* = *active* is linked to an act of domination. The subjection of women is folded into the culturally validated representation of masculinity and its power.

According to the Freudian scenario, the father's violence next turns threateningly on the male child himself in the primal threats of castration. Because Freud always construcs castration in terms of anatomy, he misses the fact, as feminists as varied as Simone de Beauvoir, Juliet Mitchell, and Luce Irigaray have demonstrated, that having-a-penis acquires its special value because it "stands for" something valuable: prestige, privilege, power, property, and so on. By the same token, the reason these goods get symbolized by having-a-penis is because they are monopolized by men. In having recourse to the anatomical distinction of the sexes, Freud hides and naturalizes this nexus of social relations between men and women.

There is another striking feature of the primal scenes. Unlike the seduction scenes, which were reported as actual events but construed by Freud as fantasies, the primal scenes of parental intercourse and castration threats were seldom remembered at all. In fact, his patients did not advance them as memories *or* as fantasies. Wherever Freud delved into a scene of parental intercourse it was inevitably because he was pressing this vision of the sexual act on his patient as a "construction."[13] The fact that these constructions frequently proved efficacious in the therapy, clarifying the vicissitudes of the patient's symptoms and development, bolstered Freud in his conviction that these "events" were the product of the patient's unconscious memory or fantasy.

There is, I believe, a more viable hypothesis to account for why Freud's constructions were so compelling. The primal scenes provide an origin for the psychic representation of the phallic equations, *masculine = active, feminine = passive.* Masculinity is fused with images of female subordination and male sexual dominance. These representations, I have argued, do not arrive at an appointed hour in the socialization process. They seep into it through the cultural forms the individual takes up to interpret and normalize his desires and his identity. They are certainly not full-blown representations in infantile experience at all. They always arrive belatedly, sometimes catastrophically.

From the standpoint of the therapy's progress, the primal scenes supply the missing representation that links infantile with adult sexuality. From the standpoint of the individual's psychosexual development, they crystallize the cultural forms that have recoded remembered and fantasized experience retrospectively, on the model of the *Nachträglichkeit,* the delayed effect or retrodetermination. From the standpoint of the life-world, the primal scenes are a stylization of the structure of feeling that continually links the individual's life history and the social-symbolic world he inhabits.

Freud's construction of these primal scenes plays the same role for the patient in therapy as the social contract story plays in politics. It represents the several elements of complex social relationships as though they were all created in a single action whose intentions and meanings it renders intelligible. An existing state of affairs is illuminated as though from the inside, aglow with coherence and purposiveness. But just there is the fatal flaw of origin stories and primal scenes. Their extraordinary power to justify—or criticize—some lived set of social and political relationships is purchased at a great cost in historical understanding.

Pateman offers an interpretation of the Freudian primal scene that unveils its social and political significance. The representation of parental intercourse as rape reflects the deep-seated ambiguity that political, legal, and cultural norms have created regarding women's consent in sexual activity and in political activity. The child's fantasy flourishes in the politically significant zone of ambiguity where "there is widespread lack of ability to understand what consensual intercourse is."[14] In the politically structured relations of men and women, coerciveness is blended into ostensibly consensual interactions.

Pateman's critical reassessment of the social contract stories itself runs up against some of the same limits as the Freudian primal scene. The ambiguities and unanswered questions created by her appropriation of origin stories deserve reflection. Pateman's mapping of the family and civil society identifies the salient components in that complex of social and political relationships that she aptly calls modern patriarchal society: (1) private and public spheres are separated according to gender; (2) women are excluded from participation in civil society and are subordinated within its various institutions; and (3) masculine sex-right underlies and sustains the husband-father's real power within the family. The origin story Pateman deconstructs and reconstructs represents these various elements as though they were created by a single set of actions. They thereby become somehow more intelligible, grasped in a bold single stroke, but this newfound intelligibility raises other questions.

When Pateman takes over the Freudian primal scene to represent the origins of male sex-right and paternal power, she ends up having to puzzle out a new mystery. For she is led to ask, Did men subjugate women at the origin for the sake of sexual possession and power, or in order to create and control offspring? Pateman endorses the former position but to make good on her choice she is driven to draw on the speculative excesses of Gregory Zilboorg:

Mother-right was overthrown when, "one day [a man] became sufficiently conscious and sure of his strength to overpower the woman, to rape her." Taking issue with all the stories in which men's discovery of paternity is the driving force that institutes the patriarchal family and civilization. Zilboorg speculates that the primordial deed had nothing to do with paternity; "the act was not that of love and of anticipated fatherhood, nor of tender solicitude. . . . It was an assault. . . . It was a phallic, sadistic act."

Zilboorg argues that the original deed was prompted purely by "the need to possess and master." The subjugation of women provided the example required to enable men to extend their possession and mastery beyond their immediate needs. (107) [15]

Here's the problem: there are no grounds for accepting this interpretation over the alternative. Moreover, like all origin stories, Pateman's has to presuppose one of the things it had to explain. In projecting that men in the beginning took sexual possession of women for the sake of dominance, the story presupposes heterosexuality. But compulsory heterosexuality is another element of our current social order in need of illumination and critique.

And, finally, the origins of the politically structured confusion of consent and coercion are pictured as a purely coercive act performed by a male agent on a female victim; at the origin of the confusions over consent and coercion there is no confusion of consent and coercion, because the origin story expunges all forms of consent. It thereby fails to explain the very thing it was designed to explain. Moreover, women's agency, including their long history of resistance and opposition to male dominance, has no place in the representation itself. There is no female agency on the scene where women are said, primordially, to participate. The supposed scene of political origins is "over there" where female agency does not exist; consequently, women's agency, in the sense of a feminist politics devoted to overcoming coercion and remaking consent, remains unrepresented at the origins.

The radical-feminist gesture Pateman deploys goes insightfully to the root of modern patriarchal society, enumerating the many-sided forms of female subordination in modern social and political institutions. But in simultaneously setting up its critical standpoint outside the structures it criticizes, it loses touch with the actual processes of political change. Pateman sets radical critique against liberal critique, rather than looking to extend the liberal critique in the radical:

> The history of liberal feminism is the history of the attempts to general-
> ize liberal liberties and rights to the whole adult population; but liberal
> feminism does not, and cannot, come to grips with the deeper problem
> of *how* women are to take an equal place in the patriarchal civil order.
>   Now that the feminist struggle has reached the point where women are
> almost formal civil equals, the opposition is highlighted between equality
> made after a male image and the real social position of women *as women*.
> (*FSC* 51)

Such a thesis overstates the completedness of the liberal project and so
underestimates its continuing relevance. Moreover, it does not fully appreciate how radical feminism builds upon the political gains of liberal
feminism. Historically, it has been the panoply of reforms in women's
political rights and economic roles and the penetration of civil and criminal law into the male-dominated household that have enabled a critique of
the gendered division of social and political space. We must be prepared
to radicalize reforms and rights rather than transcending them.

    Pateman is right to open a new path of political criticism by interrogat-
ing the mapping of society derived from social contract theory. Accordingly, the division of public and private on the axis of "civil society" and
the "family" becomes for her the decisive terrain for a critique designed to
cut to the bone of the social structure. However, Pateman too often slides
into the view that the mapping and critique she develops produce the only
politically relevant conception of civil society. While it is the mission of
radical critique to go to the root, as Pateman surely does in showing how
sex oppression pervades modern political life, the inequalities and injus-
tices of contemporary societies have more than one root. Radical critique
always needs to guard against projecting a single explanation of oppression and injustice. Put another way, there are politically relevant criticisms
of our society's institutions that require other mappings, different conceptions of civil society, and other avenues of critique.

                                    V I

When Pateman sets forth the sense of civil society she deems relevant to
feminism, she brushes aside an important alternative. This other mapping
of modern society was developed by Hegel and distinguishes private and
public on the axis of civil society and the state. While the Hegelian mapping may well obscure the path of feminist critique, it has at the same

time illuminated the way for significant critiques of state socialism, on the one hand, and of the impact of imperialism on non-Western societies, on the other.

Should civil society be defined in opposition to the family or in opposition to the state? Pateman has no doubts that the force of the first definition has been in the course of Western political history the more relevant for the issues that concern feminism. In the following passage, she gives a cogent account of the alternatives, while asserting her thesis on behalf of understanding civil society as the public realm set off against the private realm of the family:

> The meaning of "civil society" in the contract stories, and as I am using it here, is constituted through the "original" separation and opposition between the modern, public—civil—world and the modern, private or conjugal and familial sphere: that is, in the new social world created through contract, everything that lies beyond the domestic (private) sphere is public, or "civil," society. Feminists are concerned with *this* division. In contrast, most discussions of civil society and such formulations as "public" regulation versus "private" enterprise presuppose that the politically relevant separation between public and private is drawn *within* "civil society" as constructed in the social contract stories. That is to say, "civil society" has come to be used in a meaning closer to that of Hegel, the social contract theorists' greatest critic, who contrasts the universal, public state with the market, classes and corporations of private, civil society.
>
> Hegel, of course, presents a threefold division between family, civil society, state—but the separation between the family and the rest of social life is invariably "forgotten" in arguments about civil society. The shift in meaning of "civil," "public" and "private" goes unnoticed because the "original" creation of civil society through the social contract is a patriarchal construction which is also a separation of the sexes. (*FSC* 34)

The risks of taking the origin story literally are apparent in the last sentence of this passage. Despite the scare-quotes in the phrase "'original' creation of civil society," the separation of public and private that social contract theory represents at the origin of society is taken by Pateman to really be the basis of modern society. But in fact the many-layered social and political relationships that make up the fabric of modern society were not invented whole cloth from just one set of inequalities.

It is true that social contract theory tells a powerful story about the political equality among men by disguising the political oppression of women, and it is true that it simultaneously tries to map the whole of social and political relationships on the public/private, civil society/family axis. Pateman's immanent critique of this mapping yields a rich vocabulary of feminist political criticism, but the Hegelian model of civil society, family, and state has proved fruitful as well. On the one hand, the threefold distinction points up that the market, the household, and the polis are not ruled by identical norms. And, on the other hand, the Hegelian mapping has itself been the object of immanent critiques that yield yet other valuable political criticisms.

I now want to turn to a recent example of such an immanent critique. It will turn out to bear very directly on Freud and Pateman, even though its own immediate aim is to contest the imposition of Western political thought on non-Western societies. Partha Chatterjee has argued that when Hegel mapped the forms and institutions of social life he was intent on eradicating or subordinating any reference to community in the sense of the various forms of ethnic, religious, or regional belonging that were in fact powerful aspects of social identity in nineteenth-century Europe. The market called for separated individuals who would act in their own self-interest; the modern nation-state called for subjects and citizens whose group loyalty to the state superseded all other group solidarities. "Civil society," writes Chatterjee, "now became the space for the diverse life of individuals in the nation: the state became the nation's singular representative embodiment, the only legitimate form of community"[16] — or, more precisely, I think, the *overriding* form of community.

The imperatives of capitalist development set about to destroy the forms of "pre-capitalist community which, in various forms, had regulated the social unity of laborers with their means of production" (*RTI* 8). What Marx called the "primitive accumulation" of capital set in motion the real destruction of communities and along with it an ideological revaluation that relegated community to the prehistory of capital, indeed, to the prehistory of modern times in general, and identified it "with medievalism in Europe and the stagnant, backward, undeveloped present in the rest of the world" (*RTI* 8). The "particularism" of community and communal identity henceforth appears regressive from the vantage of progressive European social thought.

However, capitalism meanwhile remained, "notwithstanding its universalist scope, . . . parasitic upon the reconstructed particularism of the nation" (*RTI* 8). The nation-state commanded a kind of loyalty that drew on the need for community, while the market gave root to individualistic self-interest. National identity fed on people's subjective capacity for shared feelings and mutual belonging. The market honed their individualism. In Chatterjee's view, nation and capital, polis and market, together set in motion the destruction of community.

Community was never really obliterated, of course, as the upheavals today from Yugoslavia to Central Asia attest. Chatterjee's point is that Western political institutions and forms of political identity are so individualistic and so linked to the "narrative of capital" that they have utterly failed to accommodate communities and forms of communal identity within a meaningful vision of justice, right, and participation. Moreover, imperialism and neoimperialism have imposed this European model on societies the world over under the fraudulent banner of universalism. The potential for "people, living in different, contextually defined, communities [to] coexist peacefully, productively and creatively within large political units" (*RTI* 9) in countries like Nigeria or India cannot be realized, according to Chatterjee, on the Western model of individualism and nationalism.[17]

On its own local terrain European political thought had to struggle with the survival of forms of community that did not readily boil down in the cauldron of the market and the state. Chatterjee suggestively and insightfully reads Hegel as devising a strategy for containing and overcoming the demands of community. Those attributes of community that are not absorbed into the nation-state Hegel sloughs off onto his account of family.

Consider Hegel's reflection on the meaning of family and love in the *Philosophy of Right* at just the point where he is concerned to establish the qualitative and unbridgeable distinction between the family and the state. The family achieves unity through the feeling of love, which is "ethical life in the form of something natural," in contradistinction to the state, in which "we are conscious of unity as law":

> Love means in general terms the consciousness of my unity with another, so that I am not in selfish isolation but win my self-consciousness only as the renunciation of my independence and through knowing myself as the unity of myself with another and of the other with me. . . . The first moment in love is that I do not wish to be a self-subsistent and

independent person and that, if I were, then I would feel defective and incomplete. The second moment is that I find myself in another person, that I count for something in the other, while the other in turn comes to count for something in me. . . . Love is at once the propounding and the resolving of this contradiction. As the resolving of it, love is unity of an ethical type.

The right of the family consists in the fact that its substantiality should have determinate existence. Thus it is a right against externality and against secessions from the family unity.[18]

Chatterjee reads here a deflected narrative of community. "Hegel's arguments on the family remind us," he writes, "of the irreducible immediacy in which human beings are born in society: not as pure unattached individuals free to choose their social affiliations (whether gender, ethnicity or class) but as already-ascribed members of society." He also notes the deep resemblance between Hegel's rhetoric and that "in which, even in this age of the triumph of individualism, all movements which appeal to the 'natural' solidarity of community speak. They claim precisely the right against externality and secession, they seek determinate existence precisely in 'property' and 'representation' through collectively recognized heads, they speak in the language of love and of self-recognition through the free surrender of individual will to others in the community" (*RTI* 5).

Freud's intellectual inheritance includes just this tendency to eradicate community from the mapping of society. The Hegelian topography of civil society, family, and state reduced the relevant sites of social life to the market, the household, and the polis. The values and attributes associated with community had to be absorbed either into the family or the state; failing that, they had simply to be suppressed. This pattern of thinking Freud shared with Hegel and a whole tradition of social thought from Marx to Max Weber and Georg Simmel.

But the deflection of what Chatterjee calls the "narrative of community" into the narrative of family was not merely an intellectual exercise. For it is also true that the bourgeois family inherited many of the norms and habits, feelings and needs, that had previously structured the religious, ethnic, and regional communities that were breaking up, dispersing, and migrating throughout the nineteenth century. The family was in reality as well as ideology a deflected site of communal identities and desires. The bourgeois household was a complex social space. Its inner relationships were determined by its material and symbolic relation to the market and the polis, and also, more covertly, to community.

The liberal ideals of the nineteenth century foresaw a social world in which *men* were offered precise forms of individuality matched to the market, the family, and the polis: namely, the identities of owner, husband-father, and citizen (or citizen-subject). Liberalism envisaged a stable society whose institutions would centrally serve the realization of just these roles. The decades that stretch from Freud's birth to his major intellectual crises and theoretical innovations span the period when Austro-Hungarian liberalism first flourished and triumphed and then floundered and shattered.

In 1857, the year after Freud's birth, Austro-Hungarian liberals unveiled their plan to rebuild Vienna. Streets, buildings, and parks would fill the massive ring that had always separated the walled city of feudal, dynastic, Catholic Vienna from the suburbs, where the lower classes were amassing. As Schorske shows in his study of the Ringstrasse, the liberals projected their ideal self-image into the new architecture and public spaces. The Ringstrasse was a secular city, a large-scale enterprise, a seat of national government, a center of education and the arts. The new Vienna rose up in the very buildings that housed its institutions of democracy, culture, and rational administration.

The liberals built their political identity, including their ideals of citizenship, on their expectation that the male individual would find fulfillment in his roles as owner, father, and citizen. From the 1860s until the 1890s, Austro-Hungarian liberalism thrived on this set of assumptions and expectations. Social and political progress was envisaged as a peaceful process. The liberals, Germanic and bourgeois, believed their own ideals would be the model and beacon for the other nationalities and the other classes whom they expected to adopt this same style of citizenship and this same cultural identity on the way to becoming fuller partners in the civic enterprise.[19]

The expectations proved illusory and shattered in the 1890s. Not only did liberalism never fully liberate the polis from the crown and the church, but its reforms failed to preempt class conflicts, nationalist and ethnic upheavals, or the rise of right-wing Christian Socialism. When Karl Lueger led his Christian Socialist party to victory in Vienna on an anti-Semitic platform in 1895, liberal ideology was left in shambles. The ideological and political program that had progressed so far in remapping society on the model of civil society, the family, and the state was in crisis.

VII

Austro-Hungarian liberals, including Freud, had to face up to the recognition that the polis they had so assiduously helped to construct was in fact distorted and increasingly fragile. They also faced the fear that their vision of inevitable political equality and social harmony was mere illusion. How should they respond to the unhinging of the political identity that had anchored the liberal bourgeoisie's sense of its mission and of the future? Central European intellectuals—writers, social theorists, psychoanalysts —would in the next few decades attempt to comprehend the confusing pattern of change that had overthrown the cherished ideals of progress.

Freud, in my view, had inherited and deeply adhered to the ideal of individual self-realization that was generally the product of liberal and socialist thinking. The training for citizenship was to hinge, as we have already seen, on the achievements of vocation and marriage. Modern liberal political identity enabled, and reciprocally was reinforced by, men's undisturbed participation in their roles in the market and the family, their autonomous freedom in the market-mediated relations of a capitalist economy and their autocratic power within the household they headed. Citizenship, of course, is never merely a question of the individual's qualities or accomplishments; it also requires political foundations. The polis is not, as the ideal image suggests, the open yet protected space in which all the city's dwellers may gather to debate, deliberate, and decide. It is a structurally distorted space of unequal participation.

The crises that threw into doubt the ability of Austro-Hungarian liberals to master this political space challenged Freud to make an intellectual and professional response. I don't disagree with Schorske's conclusion that with Oedipal theory "Freud gave his fellow liberals an a-historical theory of man and society that could make bearable a political world spun out of orbit and beyond control" (PP 203). But psychoanalytic theory and practice more actively sought to relocate an arena of mastery. Freud did not choose the family or the household as this arena; he chose, rather, the individual's *representations* of family relationships. His encounters with the autocratic power of fathers and the traumatic illnesses of their daughters had not only led him into crisis over the seduction theory but also made any kind of intervention in actual families seem impossible. Freud turned the "psyche" into that arena in which the relevant pathologies could be identified and their causes isolated. The psychoanalytic dialogue promised to put those pathologies under the individual's control. The problem, its origin, and its cure became the province, once again, of the individual. Freud waded into the ruins of liberal individualism to rescue the individual, seeking to replace the damaged social and political underpinnings with an unprecedented experience of self-reflection and self-expression.

In order to make such inwardness the consistent reference point of the theoretical language and the therapeutic techniques of psychoanalysis, Freud had to cope with the many social and political experiences that arose within the life histories and the free associations of his patients. Such experiences had to be marginalized, effaced, or absorbed into the Oedipal narrative. Revisionist critics who today want to foreground class or gender or nationality and religion in revaluations of Freud's work have to comb through the detritus of his case histories and his self-analysis, re-accenting the rich testimony of the unconscious to be found there.

Consider the nanny who suddenly reappeared in Freud's dreams during the crucial week he was first tempted to turn from the seduction theory to Oedipal theory. On 3 October 1897, Freud wrote Fliess that "the 'prime originator' [of my troubles] was a woman, ugly, elderly, but clever, who told me a great deal about God Almighty and Hell and who gave me a high opinion of my own capacities."[20] This woman, who was Czech and Catholic, had cared for Freud during his first three years, only to be expelled from the household and sent to prison for stealing from the family. "I asked my mother whether she still recollected the nurse," Freud reported to Fliess on 15 October. " 'Of course,' she said, 'an elderly person, very clever. She was always taking you to church: when you came back afterwards you used to preach sermons and tell us all about God Almighty' " (*EFP* 263).

Religion and nationality are rendered tangential details in Freud's account. Yet, as Schorske shows concerning the crisis Freud was suffering in the midst of his self-analysis, "the Rome of his mature dreams and longings is clearly a love-object" but is fraught with ambivalence because it represents Catholicism and conservatism as well as "pleasure, maternity, assimilation, fulfillment" (*PP* 192–93). The Czech nanny might well be read as a libidinal and symbolic nexus connecting Freud's deepest sense of himself to the historical context in which he was now having to make his life. Schorske rightly questions the tendency of Freud and his followers to identify "the Rome longing with the nanny as mother-substitute and oedipal love-object, reducing the Catholic and Czech attributes of Rome in Freud's dream-pictures to symbols of this primal tie, and interpreting the inhibition preventing travel to Rome as an expression of the incest taboo" (PP 205–6n).

Freud in fact was in the process of transforming the nanny from "originator" into substitute by means of an interpretive trajectory that has been carefully analyzed by Jim Swan and by Peter Stallybrass and Allon White. The self-analysis first disclosed (whether as memory or hypothesis is unclear) that the nanny had initiated him into sexuality: "She was my teacher in sexual matters and scolded me for being clumsy and not being able to do anything." But this history of seduction and the "memory of the old woman who provided me at such an early age with the means for living and going on living" (*EFP* 262) run counter to the Oedipal narrative then emergent in Freud's thinking. The dreams and recollections Freud revealed in his letters to Fliess put the nanny at the very core of his feelings of love and loss, as well as his traumatic sense of inadequacy and guilt. But by the time these childhood scenes are retold in published form, Freud has turned the episode of the nanny's dismissal and imprisonment into a mere happenstance that backgrounded his anxieties connected with a brief separation from his mother and his jealousies toward his newborn sister.[21]

In tracing how "Freud wrote the maid out of the family romance," Stallybrass and White capture the dynamic of social class that is as central to the structuring of Freud's own experience as it is to the structuring of the Rat Man's divided desire for the Poor Woman and the Rich Woman, or Kafka's divided identification with his father and his father's employees: "Paradoxically, to desire one's mother, despite the incestuous implications, is more acceptable than to desire a hired help. And Freud seems to validate his emphasis upon his mother by the conscious adult reconstruction that opposes the 'slim and beautiful' mother to the 'ugly, elderly' nurse. Thus, Freud's grief (he cried 'his heart out' for nurse and mother alike) is split between an acceptable and an unacceptable mother. . . . And in the concept-formation of the Oedipus complex, Freud effaces the 'unacceptable' mother."[22] The nurse was raising him, but she is refused the social recognitions accorded a mother. The place of honor, that is, of esteem, dependence, and desire, had to be reserved for the mother herself. I find it tempting to speculate that here may lie the biographical origins of Freud's promotion of a symbolic mother in the Oedipus complex at the expense of the mother in her real activities and interactions. To the extent that it was the Czech nanny who performed the tasks of caring, teaching, and playing, this "fifth term" of the Oedipus complex gets completely eclipsed by the "second term," that is, the symbolic mother who embodies the requisite social ideals.

The actual functioning of the bourgeois household made this kind of complication of desire a constant feature of everyday life. Yet Freud took such networks of desire and power, subservience and resentment, exploitation and retaliation, and distilled from them the Oedipal triangle of I-mother-father. He brushed out seduction by a servant in his self-analysis, just as he would brush out seductions of servants by the Rat Man, to keep the emotional family portrait free of all these unsightly, uneducated, immoral proletarians. That their actual presence was part and parcel of his patients' and his own experience never found theoretical expression.

Did mere Victorian reticence, or perhaps ruling-class arrogance, form this blind spot? I think it more to the point that Freud carried out the simplification to the nuclear family because it enabled him to contain the larger crisis of political identity in a more manageable form. The splintering of the promised synthesis of vocation, marriage, and citizenship that was disturbing the life-world of liberal Vienna did not have to be confronted as a specific set of deep-seated social and cultural pathologies. The crisis it unleashed in individuals' life histories could be read, instead, as the misadventures of instinct coming into conflict with civilization.

The historically evolved and now threatened norms of male socialization could be rewritten as a psychic norm that could henceforth serve as theoretical and therapeutic benchmark. The puzzle of the individual's integration into market, household, and polis could be solved on an utterly new terrain. Diagnosis could be accomplished by a remembering of family history and a repeating of filial loves and hatreds in the dialogue with the analyst, and the cure could be achieved by the working through of an individual myth and private history.

Freud's intellectual and therapeutic tactics were thus following in the tracks of the social process that had already displaced onto the family the hopes and problems of community. Community, too, is therefore suppressed whenever the clinical picture acquires too much social density. The Czech nanny's importance was also connected to her Catholicism.

The visions of heaven and hell with which she inspired Freud the toddler resonated in his dreams forty years later because of the professional pressures and anti-Semitism that had slowed his career. In the midst of his intellectual doubts, his career crisis, his mourning of his father, and the political crisis in Vienna, Freud was haunted by dreams that questioned his Jewish identity and utopianized complete assimilation and conversion.

The temptation to convert to Christianity tugged at the unconscious and conscious thoughts of Jewish families in the Habsburg empire and in Germany. Schorske shows how Freud's dreams in the critical weeks of 1897 pulled him between two heroic models, both of whom he had often yearned to imitate and who were associated with his own most complex dream symbol, Rome: Hannibal, the Semitic general and politician who had failed to reach Rome; and Johan Joachim Winckelmann, the scholar who conquered Rome intellectually but at the cost of renouncing Judaism for Christianity (see PP 191–93). Politics versus science, Jewishness versus conversion, rebellion versus accommodation.

My point is not to highlight Freud's conflicts of cultural identity. The point to be made is that these kinds of questions of cultural identity, community, belonging, and estrangement are thoroughly a part of the forming of desires and identities. Freud himself always remained very clearheaded about his affiliations, especially in times of greatest political stress and uncertainty. In 1926, for example, he explained in an interview the effect of rising German anti-Semitism on his sense of self: "My language is German. My culture, my attainments are German. I considered myself German intellectually, until I noticed the growth of anti-Semitic prejudice in Germany and German Austria. Since that time, I prefer to call myself a Jew."[23]

In the household in which Freud himself was raised, the visible distinctions between social classes, and the clash of values between rural Catholics and urban secular Jews, were indelible aspects of his earliest, most formative experiences—so much so that when he faced the dangers of anti-Semitism and the doubting of his intellectual achievements at forty, it was the Czech Catholic nanny who came back in his dreams. But Freud's emergent interpretive procedures were destined to subordinate and dispel just this tangle of cultural identities and social relationships. He had made the family his interpretive reference point, that is, the psychic representation of the family simplified to I-mother-father, and forced all else to the wings.

Freud neutralized the many links between history and life history in diagnosing the afflictions that disturbed the bourgeois aspirations of vocation and marriage and the liberal ideals that were to guide young men in becoming owners, citizens, and fathers. He tried, instead, to recover the liberal ideal in his model of an ideal route to the formation and dissolution of the Oedipus complex. A young man had only to overcome his incestuous and aggressive impulses toward his mother and father to step into his roles in civil society, the family, and the state. When Freud then turned to explain why this ideal maturation was typically derailed or complicated or compromised, he set aside the historical dimension altogether. He attributed Oedipal pathologies to nothing more tangible than an insufficient fear of the father and a sexual constitution that failed to be singularly masculine and heterosexual.

The limitations of Freud's view were by no means an intellectual fabrication or a mere error. Pressures within and upon family life do indeed make the I-mother-father relationship into an emotional stencil laid over the individual's relation to the world. It is not therefore a question of examining society and politics instead of family relationships. Rather it is a question of grasping the social and political processes that variously shape or dictate or interrupt family life, or are reflected or refracted or veiled by family relationships.

Freud absented himself from this task by calibrating his theoretical and therapeutic work to an ideal of male socialization that naturalizes compulsory heterosexuality and male dominance as "psychic" norms. As I have also been arguing, this psychic norm was used to ground the mapping of the family, civil society, and the state at the very time that the political underpinnings the liberal mapping really required were collapsing. Historically, a new structure of feeling had crystallized as communal needs and aspirations were shifted onto the family, as public and private were distinguished and encoded anew, and as the male owner-citizen-father role emerged and was valorized. Even as this structure of feeling took root in everyday experience, it was fraught with conflicts and a capacity for pathology. And it was in the midst of a particularly intense crisis at the precise moment of Freud's most significant discoveries.

NOTES

This essay is a revised version of a paper presented at the Commonwealth Center seminar "Sexuality and History: Authors and Institutions."

1. Carl E. Schorske, "Politics and Patricide in Freud's *Interpretation of Dreams*," in his *Fin-de-siècle Vienna: Politics and Culture* (New York, 1981), 181–207; hereafter cited in text as PP.

2. Alvin W. Gouldner, *The Future of Intellectuals and the Rise of the New Class* (New York, 1979), 62–67.

3. Sigmund Freud, *The Interpretation of Dreams* (1900), *The Standard Edition of the Complete Psychological Works of Sigmund Freud,* ed. and tr. James Strachey (London, 1953–74), 4:196; hereafter cited in text as *ID.*

4. Carole Pateman, "The Fraternal Social Contract," in her *The Disorder of Women: Democracy, Feminism and Political Theory* (Stanford, 1989), 43; hereafter cited in text as FSC.

5. Sigmund Freud, *Civilization and Its Discontents* (1929–30), *Standard Edition,* 1:101; hereafter cited in text as *CD.*

6. See Eve Kosofsky Sedgwick, *Between Men: English Literature and Male Homosocial Desire* (New York, 1985).

7. Franz Kafka, "Letter to his father," in *The Sons* (New York, 1989), 148; hereafter cited in text.

8. Carole Pateman, "Genesis, Fathers and the Political Sons of Liberty," in her *The Sexual Contract* (Stanford, 1988), 109.

9. Sigmund Freud, "Dostoevsky and Parricide" (1928), in *Standard Edition,* 21:184; hereafter cited in text as DP.

10. See Adrienne Rich, "Compulsory Heterosexuality and Lesbian Existence," in *Powers of Desire: The Politics of Sexuality,* ed. Ann Snitow, Christine Stansell, and Sharon Thompson (New York, 1983), 177–205.

11. Sigmund Freud, *The Ego and the Id* (1923), *Standard Edition,* 19:32; hereafter cited in text.

12. Sigmund Freud, "The Paths to Symptom-Formation," in *Introductory Lectures on Psycho-Analysis* (1916–17), *Standard Edition,* 16:368–69.

13. The case history of the Wolf Man provides the most detailed discussion of Freud's construction of a primal scene memory. See Sigmund Freud, *From the History of an Infantile Neurosis* (1918), *Standard Edition,* 17:29–47, 89–103.

14. Pateman, "Genesis, Fathers and the Political Sons of Liberty," 106; hereafter cited in text.

15. See also Gregory Zilboorg, "Masculine and Feminine: Some Biological and Cultural Aspects," *Psychiatry* 7 (1944): 257–96.

16. Partha Chatterjee, "A Response to Taylor's Invocation of Civil Society," *Working Papers and Proceedings of the Center for Psychosocial Studies* 39 (1990): 9; hereafter

cited in text as RTI. Chatterjee's response is to Charles Taylor, "Invoking Civil Society," *Working Papers and Proceedings of the Center for Psychosocial Studies* 31 (1990): 1–17.

17. Chatterjee's reflection on the nation and community and on nationalism and the politics of postcolonial societies shares a number of themes with the very important work of Benedict Anderson, *Imagined Communities: Reflections on the Origin and Spread of Nationalism,* rev. ed. (New York, 1991).

18. G. W. F. Hegel, *Philosophy of Right,* tr. T. M. Knox (New York, 1967), 261–62.

19. Carl E. Schorske, "The Ringstrasse, Its Critics, and the Birth of Urban Modernism," in *Fin-de-siècle Vienna,* 24–115.

20. Sigmund Freud, "Extracts from the Fliess Papers" (1892–99), *Standard Edition,* 1:261; hereafter cited in text as EFP.

21. See Sigmund Freud, *The Psychopathology of Everyday Life* (1901), *Standard Edition,* 6: 49–52.

22. Peter Stallybrass and Allon White, *The Politics and Poetics of Transgression* (Ithaca, 1986), 159–60. See also Jim Swan, "Mater and Nannie: Freud's Two Mothers and the Discovery of the Oedipus Complex," *American Imago* 31 (1974): 1–64.

23. Sigmund Freud, Interview with George Sylvester Viereck, in Viereck's *Glimpses of the Great* (1927; rpt. New York, 1930), 34; quoted in Peter Gay, *Freud, Jews and Other Germans: Masters and Victims in Modernist Culture* (New York, 1978), 90.

THE PRODUCTIVE HYPOTHESIS: FOUCAULT, GENDER, AND THE HISTORY OF SEXUALITY

Carolyn J. Dean

In Sade there are no shadows.
—MICHEL FOUCAULT

The sexuality [Foucault] serves us is the rise and deployment of the
desiring subject, sexually as the life and times of desiring man in
bondage and being disciplined and loving every minute of it, and
loving his struggle to get out of it even more.
—CATHARINE A. MACKINNON

WHAT KIND OF historical experience does the concept of sexuality make meaningful? This, of course, is precisely the question historians of modern sexuality are wont to ask of their object of inquiry.[1] Yet Michel Foucault's powerful role in shaping the field has forced historians of sexuality perhaps more than other historians to question their methodological premises in ways that strain the bounds of historical investigation. In this essay, I want to bypass debates about whether Foucault is "really" a historian to address precisely what is at stake for historians of sexuality in the tension Foucault's work produces between two ways of doing history.[2]

The more conventional historicist model in its various liberal and Marxist guises explains and accounts for how the modern sexual self is produced: it interrogates how sexuality (for example, the organization of heterosexual reproduction, the development of sexual identities and desires, and so forth) makes meaning out of specific sociocultural experiences and changes over time. The other—following Foucault's lead—insists that the sexual subject has no intrinsic meaning or agency that might be identified, accounted for, or repressed. The self is no longer the prediscursive Cartesian *cogito,* but is a fiction constructed in the interests of what Foucault termed paradoxically the "intentional" and yet "nonsubjective" power of primarily white upper-class men. However, Foucault and his followers offer no causal account of how the self is constructed.[3] More specifically, they historicize sexuality by describing how sexual subjectivity is created through upper-class men's efforts to stabilize a putatively unstable self. As Domna Stanton has suggested, "The historicization (and the denaturalization) of sexuality can be viewed as part and parcel of the deconstruction of an essential subjectivity that has marked modernity, and more specifically, post-modernity."[4]

As Stanton's essay makes clear in a myriad of ways, most of the recent literature on sexuality is indeed characterized by tension between scholars (mostly historians) who ask properly historical questions about why and how the modern sexual self was first produced in the eighteenth century in medical, legal, and popular texts, and scholars (mostly not historians) who seek to reformulate such questions in new terms. That is, historians, even those most drawn to interdisciplinary methods, still ask how, why, and when sexual selves are produced. The vast interdisciplinary literature now being produced by nonhistorians instead adopts Foucault's critique of functionalist and structuralist models of power and causality. Most of the diverse scholars who adhere to this critique thus reject a theory of history based on the premise that individuals possess presocial inalienable rights or an authentic essence (Marx's "species being," for example) and describe instead how "disciplinary power" constitutes individual subjects. They criticize the humanistic understanding of "man," and claim that the quest for why men did what they did (for causality) begs the question of how "man" (and woman) as a concept was produced in the first place.

Thus many post-Foucauldians—I will refer to them this way for the sake of simplicity, though they differ greatly among themselves—have taken up his antihistoricist, antihumanist bent, paradoxically, in the interests of more rigorously historicizing sexuality.[5] Literary critics and philosophers such as Jonathan Dollimore, David Halperin, Eve Kosofsky Sedgwick, Judith Butler, and others have demonstrated, for example, how historians' reliance on a prediscursive, rational (usually male and heterosexual) subject of history often implicitly excludes or marginalizes women and racial and sexual minorities.[6] Or to put it more simply, historians use normative frameworks that make their role in *producing* the historical subjects whose actions they describe and interpret invisible. Sedgwick has argued that the assumption of normative heterosexuality *as* normative subjectivity has obscured how the homosexual–heterosexual divide was itself historically constructed. Judith Butler argues along similar lines that

heterosexuality depends upon (an excluded, unspoken, invisible) homosexuality for its very meaning. As Sedgwick writes in reference to the
presumed universality of the Western literary canon: "If it is still in important respects the master-canon it nevertheless cannot now escape naming
itself with every syllable also a particular canon, a canon of mastery, in
the case of men's mastery over, and over against, women. Perhaps never
again need women—need, one hopes, anybody,—feel greeted by the Norton Anthology of mostly white men's Literature with the implied insolent
salutation, 'I'm nobody. Who are you?'"[7] The point is that the historical
canon—what events, subjects, and people are important—is particular in
spite of its claims to represent universal "man" and his experiences.[8]

Unlike many historians of women and racial and sexual minorities who
also question such claims to universality within their various specialties,
these scholars are not really interested in why sex has been particularly
subject to normative regulation and its repressive consequences. Instead,
following Foucault's lead, they describe how sexuality is produced by the
practices and exclusions effected by disciplinary power. They describe the
ways in which specific social practices exclude, marginalize, and even
render unthinkable alternative forms of subjectivity and sexuality with the
force and conviction equal to those historians who denounce them for
insufficient attention to "real" political struggles. Nevertheless, in the process of recovering and exposing exclusions, many theorists often sacrifice
meaning and agency in favor of sweeping references to "discourse," "culture," "power," "disciplinary formations," and "undecidability."

Both humanist and Foucauldian modes of investigating and understanding the history of sexuality and sexual cultures more generally are
equally important in all recent scholarship on sexuality. There is really
not a field called the "history of sexuality," but only a vast array of historical interrogations and theoretical questions and critiques bearing on
this tension between older humanist models and newer paradigms whose
intersections have not been fully theorized. That is, is sexuality a discourse
that constitutes experience? Or does it reflect a dominant ideology which
represses sexuality's non-normative manifestations? Or finally, does sexuality express the experiences of diverse individuals and social groups?

Of course, most historians and post-Foucauldian theorists recognize
that to reconstruct sexual narratives and to investigate diverse sexual experiences are inextricable levels of analysis, but that recognition by no
means solves the essentially methodological problem of how to think

these two levels together: of how meaning is always socially constructed, always contingent and yet never arbitrary, how individuals are constituted within discursive systems and yet construct meaning capable of transforming those systems.[9]

The Foucauldian repudiation of conventional historical method helps to explain why many historians, with some exceptions (for example, Judith Walkowitz, Thomas Laqueur, Jeffrey Weeks) invoke him without really grappling with his method.[10] They praise some of his theoretical contributions and empirical insights—his subtle critique of the Marxist paradigm, his attention to everyday social practices neglected by structuralists—while (rightly) scolding him for neglecting agency. Sometimes—in Estelle Freedman's and John D'Emilio's important synthetic work on the history of sexuality in America for example—Foucault warrants an obligatory mention, but has virtually no influence on the structure or argument of the book.[11] For what is to be done with a historian who dispenses with the most fundamental of historical questions, and who is content simply to describe the practices and procedures of institutions that regulate and produce sexuality without explaining why they produce sexuality the way they do? How can historians comprehend a self-professed historian who does not even bother to use representative, empirically sound data?

Foucault purports to be engaged in extending social justice through sociohistorical critique. Yet, as Nancy Fraser argues, in spite of all his "empirical insights" into the everyday workings of sexual oppression, he provides absolutely no grounds on which we might distinguish the powerful from the powerless, and he robs individual actors of agency and hence the power to create meaning.[12] To put it more pointedly, how do we discard epistemic justifications or normative frameworks without also discarding an analysis of power, meaning, and agency? Many historians have already made the argument that if we followed Foucault, we would describe how a social order produces normative categories of sexual subjects without being able to say much about these subjects themselves, without being able, really, to explain why certain social groups and not others profit from the production of sexuality and its meanings.

Most theorists are currently struggling with this question about how Foucault's work effaces experience in one way or another. It is an issue that has been forced on historians by Foucault for quite some time, both because of the demise of certain Marxist and anthropological paradigms, and mostly, at least with respect to historians of sexuality, because of

Foucault's seminal role in conceptualizing our field of inquiry. Because I think theorists have amply used Foucault to attack the grounds or even the epistemological validity of investigating meaning production, I want to address, from the point of view of the feminist historian of sexuality still wedded to questions of meaning, this tension between the necessity of calling into question normative frames and the need to keep them.

In this essay I want to begin to historicize Foucault's work in order to help us move beyond Foucault to other epistemological and historical questions about the link between sexuality and subjectivity. I cannot do justice to the vast literature on sexuality. And obviously I cannot reconcile all the tensions that currently exist between those who criticize a focus on meaning production and those who insist on its centrality, but I can try to address them in ways I hope will prove productive for historians of sexuality.

In order to historicize Foucault's work, I make two points: First, there is a sadomasochistic logic of desire in Foucault's work (interpreted far too literally by Catharine MacKinnon in my epigraph) that is not peculiar to Foucault, sadomasochists, or gay men (as one recent biography would have it).[13] Instead, it might be conceived as an allegory of a historically and culturally specific form of sexual subjectivity that shapes the conceptual and cultural context of Foucault's work. More specifically, it is this logic of desire that marks Foucault's difference from more recognizably historical efforts to account for how sexual subjects are founded on a binary gender division (what Thomas Laqueur calls the "two-sex model").

Second, Foucault's work presumes a construction of men's, but not women's, subjectivity. This presumption represents not just an empirical oversight but grounds his entire antihistoricist method. I will argue that Foucault's own critique of historicism and its "nobodies"—its invisible normative frameworks—his own insistence that the sexual subject is a fiction with no essential meaning, in fact replicates the historicist repression or neutralization of gender as a point of view. Thus, while feminist critics have long made claims about Foucault's neglect of the gendering of sexual subjectivity, I want to move beyond a critique of Foucault on these grounds to demonstrate how that neglect is central to his ability or inability (and now, our own) to theorize resistance to dominant cultural forms (and hence his inability to theorize experience and agency): how the neglect of gender is as important as his other philosophical allegiances in explaining certain of his theoretical contributions *and*, in my view, his most spectacular failure.[14]

Foucault now stands accused both by his detractors and followers (hence the term "post-Foucauldian") of providing no real formulation of how individuals question (or do not question) the socioeconomic, political, and cultural hegemony he describes so well, mostly because he de-emphasizes the power of individual agency and of contested meaning; he does so in favor of monolithic discursive systems that constitute rather than reflect individuals' desires and intentions. The tension between the two ways of conceptualizing history I have discussed bears directly on this question, and it is the central question now confronting all scholars in this field of sexuality studies. Thus, while historians have by and large stood on the sidelines of this debate, ignored it, or borrowed language from other scholars in the field within which to think through questions about the formation and function of sexual culture(s), it is essential that we understand and participate in it.

So, briefly, post-Foucauldians of many varieties, for reasons I have discussed, mostly refuse recourse to historicist frameworks. From their perspective, those frameworks privilege causes (for example, a repressive culture), consciousness ("I have and deserve rights too"), and ideology (such as "how has my difference and hence oppression been naturalized?") as a means of explaining why resistance to dominant sexual systems does or does not occur. Instead, post-Foucauldians have emphasized rhetoric over ideology, and parody, irony, and pastiche over consciousness and pronouncements of "identity," because they believe that to conceptualize resistance requires a more subtle understanding of subcultural codes. Furthermore, as feminist historians have long noted, resistance often takes place in geographic and symbolic locations within and yet hidden from dominant culture. In this vein, Judith Butler, Teresa de Lauretis, and others use Foucault's antihistoricist bent to ask how, for example, gay subcultures self-consciously mock dominant culture or how dominant culture is influenced by subcultures in ways that are not simply reducible to theories of negative cooptation.[15] These are the kinds of questions, in tandem with feminist and "queer theory," that Foucault helped to raise but not to answer.

How can historians of sexuality contribute to this question about how individuals, especially marginalized ones, produce and reinscribe meaning? How has Foucault's work forced us to rethink our own frameworks, and how might our reconsideration of historicism rely on and yet lay the ground for a history of modern sexuality beyond Foucault? In what follows, I hope to explain Foucault's overemphasis on disciplinary power (and hence his de-emphasis on meaning and agency) in terms other than his failure to link his work to rationalist (primarily Marxist) narratives about the unfolding of human history, or to clearly distance it from irrationalist (for example, Nietzschean) narratives whose "dangers" are well known.[16]

I hope to demonstrate persuasively how his neglect of the gendering of subjectivity is central to his neglect of agency, and in so doing, to force us to ask questions about the construction of female sexual subjectivity and how it might be historicized—even if there are no answers yet to those questions.

I begin with Lynn Hunt's recent attempt to historicize Foucault's production of sexual subjectivity, move on to an analysis of the interwar discussion about sexual liberation, and finally turn to the first volume of Foucault's *The History of Sexuality.*[17]

I

In *The History of Sexuality,* Foucault argued that by the eighteenth century, sexual regulation no longer concerned fostering and preserving alliances meant to legitimate and extend paternal sovereignty. Now sex was central to the life and death of nation-states dependent on the regulation and maintenance of healthy populations. Because of capitalist demands for healthy and productive workers, lawmakers and other professionals began to develop medical and statistical norms aimed at defining ideal sexual subjects. Demography, medicine, and pedagogy formed "technologies of sex" to discipline, shape, and regulate bodies in the interest of a "power" Foucault described as a "multiplicity of force relations" (1:92), as "both intentional and nonsubjective" (1:94), and as a "moving substrate" (1:93).

Technologies of sex thus represented the expansion of an omnipresent disciplinary apparatus—of "power"—with no clear point of origin or location such as the state or the law. Most important, technologies of sex did not repress, domesticate, and regulate the intrinsic sexual drives of lazy, pleasure-bound, inefficient bodies, but produced them in the interests of the power whose aims they served. The sexual subject thus has no cause or origin because it is always the regulatory effect of a "power" that cannot be located—it has no intrinsic, essential meaning or "drive." As is well known, Foucault thus repudiated a narrative of origins (an account of why power shapes and transforms the world the way it does) in favor of a description of how power works, of how, in this case, technologies of sex produced a new kind of individual.

In her recent pathbreaking essay on Foucault, Lynn Hunt offers a suggestive alternative to Foucault's description of how sexual selves were produced. She seeks to explain in historical rather than purely theoretical terms why Foucault refused to account for that process of production, thereby moving beyond a discussion of his method.

First, she reverses his terms. She claims that technologies of sex did not produce the modern self but emerged as a result of its invention.[18] As Hunt sees it, in eighteenth-century materialism, identity became an active process of self-formation in which individuals were "figured as separate beings with separate selves who are able to act upon themselves and even transform themselves" (85). Technologies of sex did not give birth to the modern subject, but developed as a means to control this new and egotistical self: "The materialist view of the individual was responsible for that central characteristic of the new technology of sex, which Foucault defined as the demand that the social body as a whole and virtually all its individuals place themselves under surveillance. Surveillance was necessary because the new desiring individual, imagined as fundamentally egotistical, threatened constantly to undermine the requirements of the social" (91). Modern forms of discipline thus arose as an effort to manage a social world now populated by "like bodies in motion" (91), in which "deference, birthright, monarchy," and (theoretically speaking) the grounds of gender inequality "were gone," and in which desiring man was thus the new and problematic "basis for social relationships" (92). In short, this implied moral relativism led to the need for new forms of older mechanisms of social and moral enforcement—the prison, the school, the family.

Hunt thus argues that Foucault's concept of how power produces the subject represents a more recent unfolding of the problems inherent in Enlightenment materialism—the difficulties both in locating and legitimating lines of social division in a new democratic order comprised of equal desiring bodies. To make this argument more forcefully, Hunt links Foucault to the Marquis de Sade, whose work is "a precursor of Foucault in a way that Foucault himself fails to recognize"[19] (88). In the

History of Sexuality, Foucault distanced himself from the "divine marquis" whose work he believed manifested an older form of disciplinary power grounded in paternal sovereignty instead of technologies of sex (148–49). But Hunt claims to the contrary that Foucault replicates the problems exposed by Sade in this eighteenth-century figuration of the sexual subject.

In this article and elsewhere, Hunt brilliantly conceives Sade's pornographic work as a reductio ad absurdum of the problems implicit in the construction of a new, secular political order in which sovereignty is no longer vested in the king (the "Sovereign Father" of whom Foucault speaks) but in a social contract between fundamentally equal and "egotistical" bodies who determine what they desire and whom they desire to be.[20]

Briefly, Sade offers a parody of the social contract in which all acts of cruelty are represented as coextensive with rather than in contradiction to the laws of nature. Our common humanity—our presumed likeness and equality—does not necessarily bind us together. In a world in which all have equal desires, every "man" is for himself, and crime is justified as the natural propensity of every man to get what he desires. The dissolution of divinely sanctioned inequalities does not become the basis for increased freedom and equality but for the affirmation of inequality—indeed, of tyranny. For in this world there can no longer be morally grounded defenses of the weak against the strong, no normative framework within which to distinguish acceptable from unacceptable conduct: individual desires are conceptually indistinguishable from socially appropriate ones because each individual who follows his or her desire adheres to the "rules" of the contract. Rousseau's world of virtue and harmony thus turns into Sade's nightmare: democracy turns into the absolute rule of tyranny.

In both Sade and Foucault, then, the absence of a stable metaphysical and hence moral foundation for social discipline and division transforms social order into what Foucault, speaking of Sade, calls an "all-powerful monstrosity" (1:149). In Sade, as we have seen, a new and presumably freer social order based on equal desiring bodies becomes indistinguishable from despotism, and in Foucault, the progressive expansion of educational, work, and other opportunities to which Enlightenment materialism leads is indistinguishable from power's absolute regulation and production of sexual subjects. Rousseau's "moralizing of the individual through the social" (90) does not liberate "men" but binds them to their chains. In short, power is monstrous precisely because it can no longer be anchored, located, or contained: it now infuses, occupies, and produces everything. In other words, Foucault's refusal to assign a location to power in the state or the law, to explain why it forms lines of social and gender division and hence produces new selves, is not merely a methodological refusal or oversight but the sign of Foucault's inability to "imagine a self other than the one newly deployed in the eighteenth century" (87).

The eighteenth century is thus "at once the pivotal moment of [Foucault's] analysis and the great hole in it" (85) because Foucault presumed the self whose production he purports to explain. Foucault could not and does not feel the need to account for the process by which sexual subjects are produced by technologies of sex because he does not historicize subjectivity, because his effort to describe the historical production of selves paradoxically already presumes a specific sort of subject: "The practices and techniques of the deployment of the self presumably vary over time, but subjectivity itself does not" (84).

Second, because Foucault does not account for how subjectivity is gendered, he cannot account for one of the most important social processes by which individuals "recognize themselves" (93), by which individuals are constructed as individuals, and hence the ways in which power makes us who we are. When Foucault speaks of non-gendered selves, Hunt claims, he really assumes a male self, since "upper class adult men are the only ones who possess selves, but no history is offered of how this came to be"[21] (85).

Hunt persuasively demonstrates that Foucault presumes a historically specific form of male subjectivity even though he claims to destabilize subjectivity itself. She demonstrates how Foucault conflates subjectivity with the integral, egotistical, desiring male self of Enlightenment materialism and so how he presumes rather than explains the historical process by which subjectivity is gendered. Hunt's analysis provides the framework for my own question about the centrality of gender in the construction of subjectivity in Foucault's history of sexuality. But in what follows, I will argue implicitly that in her formidable critique of Foucault, subjectivity has a history, but male subjectivity does not. That is—and I hope to make this argument more persuasively in what follows—she does not historicize the relationship between gender and subjectivity and so replicates Foucault's gendered framework even as she seeks to dismantle it.

I will argue that Foucault's work is in fact very distant from Sade's, and that distance marks Foucault's historical location, originality, and above all, explains his neglect of the gendering of subjects. That distance must be understood in terms of how subjectivity is gendered differently at different historical moments, and, in this case, in terms of different historical crises around the question of the male self.

II

As I mentioned earlier, Foucault's work supplements a more recognizable though hardly conventional historical emphasis on gender—most recently discussed in terms of how, in whose interest and by what means masculinity and femininity were produced at different times—with what I called a "logic of desire." [22] In order to define what I mean by this, I will discuss Foucault's work in relation to the historical transformation of sexual subjectivity that crystallized in the early twentieth century. To cut this discussion down to manageable size, I address broader historical conditions— the rise of consumer culture, shifting models of scarcity and abundance, antifeminism, the crisis around reproduction and the preservation of the French "race"—only insofar as they were expressed in the vocabulary of liberal, early twentieth-century heirs of the Enlightenment who, like Sade, took the pedagogical purpose of sex education seriously. [23] These cultural critics often had diverse agendas. They were primarily British, French, and German, and included luminaries such as sex reformers Magnus Hirschfeld and Havelock Ellis. Foucault explicitly counts Wilhelm Reich among them, but they included as well a wide range of progressive thinkers, medical professionals, journalists, and others. For our purposes, they articulated one crucial moment in the unfolding of what Foucault was famously to call the "repressive hypothesis."

In *The History of Sexuality* Foucault criticized our conventional assumption that the history of sexuality was the history of increasing repression from which "liberation" was desirable. That assumption, he argued, was born of the nineteenth-century middle-class's effort to nurture and create a specific symbolic "sexual body" in their own image, and given intellectual and cultural respectability by medical professionals, social workers, psychoanalysts, and others since then, especially during the interwar years. Most of Foucault's seminal work on sexuality is devoted to dismantling this narrative about the so-called history of sexuality to which he claims we are still beholden.

"This whole 'sexual revolution,' this whole 'antirepressive' struggle,'" he argued, "represents nothing more but nothing less . . . than a tactical shift and reversal in the great deployment of sexuality" (1:131). Foucault described it this way:

> Around [psychoanalysis] the great requirement of confession that had taken form so long ago assumed the new meaning of an injunction to lift psychical repression. The task of truth was now linked to the challenging of taboos.
>
> This same development, moreover, opened up the possibility of a substantial shift in tactics, consisting in: reinterpreting the deployment of sexuality in terms of a generalized repression. . . . Thus between the two world wars there was formed, around [Wilhelm] Reich, the historico-political critique of sexual repression. . . . But the very possibility of its success was tied to the fact that it always unfolded within the deployment of sexuality, and not outside or against it. (1:131)

He goes on to say that "it is . . . apparent why one could not expect this critique to be the grid for a history of that very deployment. Nor the basis for a movement to dismantle it."

In other words, Foucault insisted that this concept of sexual liberation was itself a ruse of power since there is no escape from power, since power produces all sexual subjects, all sexuality in its "intentional and nonsubjective" interests. All promises of liberation thus do not oppose power but extend its grasp. By claiming that the emphasis on sexual liberation could not "dismantle" the "deployment of sexuality," Foucault meant that liberationists conceived sexuality as a natural, essential drive instead of the product and expression of power itself—of the normative production and regulation of bodies. In contrast, Foucault insisted that we—including and especially our sexuality—are never outside of power and thus can never be liberated from it. Foucault's main, counterintuitive argument is thus that derepression does not represent the lifting of taboos but the extension of power, and that any description of power as well as resistance to it must proceed from the understanding that "power is everywhere."

Foucault's own counterintuitive logic—and hence his scathing critique of this discourse on derepression—does have a history. To borrow Hunt's term, Foucault's logic might be conceived as a reductio ad absurdum of the so-called progressive discourse of sexual liberation (that first articulation of the "repressive hypothesis" in the interwar years) and hence its extension as well as its critique.

In a reversal of the discourse of "degeneration" prevalent in different

forms through the fin-de-siècle, many European cultural critics after the
Great War attributed a so-called decline of manhood to overzealous repression. Indeed, before the war, European politicians and medical men
sought to control perceived threats to social order—among them political
radicals, criminals, prostitutes, and homosexuals—by passing repressive
measures designed to keep them in check. The passage of tough criminal
legislation was facilitated by expert assurances that criminals of all sorts
were beyond help because innately pathological, and this pathology was
most often represented in gendered terms as a sign of the nation's increasing emasculation. The purported slackening of social discipline on which
feminism, the rise of consumerism, and a slow birth rate were blamed,
signaled the "feminizing" of the nation, the loss of its vital moral fiber.[24]

But by the mid-1920s (though the discourse was underway before then),
cultural critics demonized the forces of repression because, as one writer
put it, they constrained instinctive currents which made nations and races
great. Rather than acting as a constraint that guaranteed the freedom of
all—and hence balancing individual and social needs—repression in a
secular state sapped morale and reduced "man" to nothing other than a
"lowly cog" in a "gigantic machine . . . less and less free to do what he will
with his activity and his body."[25] After all, had not thousands of men become the disposable material parts of a war machine whose rationale was
proved false? Had they not been seduced by a "grand illusion" that blinded
them to their real spiritual degradation? Was not the repression of so-
called obscene material in the name of social order and the war effort only
a surreptitious means by which politicians emasculated young men while
feeding them delusions of virility? In short, didn't repression encourage
rather than inhibit moral degeneration, now conceived as the bankruptcy
of the political system, as the hypocrisy and tyranny of established elites?

Progressive advocates of derepression often made such analogies between war, pornography, and consumer capitalism and insisted they were
synonymous with the dissolution of masculinity and hence with the dissolution of the fragile moral fiber that held the social body together. In
regulating men's "genital activity" in the name of the national interest,
the state robbed them of their individuality and hence of their virility, so
that, for example, censorship laws did not preserve the nation from emasculation—as the authors of such legislation in France, England, and Germany in particular had hoped—but instead encouraged it. Most critics
now stressed the beauty and naturalness of sexuality, no longer conceived

as base and repulsive or overwrought and undisciplined — feminine — but as an uplifting spiritual force. In France, one opponent of censorship and a staunch anti-Catholic argued that "perversion" was born of the repression of "natural" instincts by a puritanical culture.[26] And Wilhelm Reich believed that homosexuality and pornography would disappear once sexuality was freed of constraints.[27]

This rather paradoxical insistence that the liberation of sexuality would lead to the end of "perversion" meant that sexual liberation was not really about freeing so-called instincts but about socializing them in the name of helping men to remain men. Understood in this way, sexual liberation did not refer to the dissolution of corporeal boundaries, the loss of discipline and hence to the acting out of dangerous longings, but to the restoration of an expressive, integral male self that had been commodified and hence reified in pornography, in consumerism, and in war.[28]

This regenerative impulse becomes especially clear in defenses of so-called obscene literature: Emile Zola was considered a smutty writer by conservatives and literary purists, but his defenders, Havelock Ellis among them, asserted that his work was not the "raw material" of pornography, but represented the "rawness of truth and indignation."[29] The French surrealist Robert Desnos claimed that in contrast to pornography (which was writing confined to the "inferior faculties"), erotic literature from Baudelaire to Apollinaire was great because it was both liberated and manly: Baudelaire's work was "male" and "virile"; Apollinaire was too cerebral but did manifest "a liberty of spirit and especially a masculine quality without which a man cannot produce an erotic work whatever the form in which he expresses his passion."[30]

Nature and sexuality were thus no longer equated with the female body and degeneration as they had been around the turn of the century but with regeneration, and hence with masculinity and cultural grandeur.[31] In short, sexuality was now conceived as continuous with, rather than distinct from, the phallic, boundaried self that thinkers sought to recover. In 1914 Havelock Ellis, the influential British sexologist, argued for a rational approach to sexual matters because, he insisted, it was only through sex education that young people could be taught a proper "reverence for the body." Frank talk about adulterous, homosexual, and other longings would "help to steady the individual and prove a check against disrespect to his body."[32] Ellis thus equated the achievement of monogamous, heterosexual, reproductive — that is to say "healthy" — sexuality with a phantasmatic corporeal integrity and impermeability that guaranteed psychological as well as social stability. He thus figured the body's sexual drives as necessarily continuous with the purity, smoothness, and impermeability of its surfaces.

Derepression in this formulation guaranteed sexual health. As Ellis put it: "Secrecy and repression" are "against nature."[33] The liberation of nature served to regulate it, and the abolition of censorship ensured the preservation of moral order. The State at once retained social equilibrium—kept men virtuous—and liberated nature—kept men potent. While this paradoxical assertion played itself out in multifaceted and complex ways in practice—it served in many instances to legitimate the liberalization of censorship laws and to encourage programs of sex education and health reform in England, France, and Germany—in rhetorical terms it represents an entirely new construction of the relationship between masculinity and moral order. I cannot possibly offer a fuller historical account of this complicated shift here. Rather, my point is to suggest that when critics brought sex out in the open, they sought, paradoxically, not to tell all but to sanitize or purify it. When they liberated sex, they at the same time insisted that some pleasures remain in the dark, unspoken and unseen, confined to realms where cultural conservatives had long sought to banish them. They assumed those pleasures would disappear entirely, because pleasure would now only ever express what was in the best interests of social order. As late as 1964, the British critic Montgomery Hyde wrote that "Obscenity and pornography are ugly phantoms which will disappear in the morning light when we rehabilitate sex and eroticism."[34] Even Herbert Marcuse, whose position was quite different from the interwar writers, defined sexual liberation in terms of a "nonrepressive sublimation" and a "rationality of gratification." He thus did not advocate permissiveness, but rather sought to remake integral selves out of the remains of alienated "man."[35]

In conclusion, when Havelock Ellis announced that today's obscenity is the future's propriety, he meant that all pleasures must eventually become permissible—that is, all pleasures must conform to the requirements of social order. In this vision, pleasure only ever furthered the aims of reason. Masculinity no longer symbolized the darkness and secrecy of repression, but the glare of the morning light, the glorious hardness of reason. It no longer neutralized threats to the social body by repressing libidinal excess—its diseased and presumably feminized components. Instead masculinity sustained virtue by sustaining sexual potency, regulated moral order by removing repressive constraints on nature. When the morning light bleached pleasure of its impurities, all sexuality would be "natural" and hence beautiful.

When these critics sought to restore masculinity they sought to stabilize the meaning of manhood (as phallic, boundaried, and impermeable). In a reversal of Sade, the history of self-possessed desiring man was no longer continuous with the unrestrained, tyrannical desire of omnipotent criminal subjectivity, but with the restraint of desire. Or rather, the history of desiring man was now the history of desire fulfilled—restored to its potency—when properly socialized. In other words, the self-congratulatory discourse of derepression from the interwar years through the 1960s does not really pretend that we have broken "free of a long period of harsh repression, a protracted Christian asceticism, greedily and fastidiously adapted to the imperatives of bourgeois economy," as Foucault argued (1:158); it does not take issue with the so-called virtues of repression, to which it is committed, but with the anarchic, undesirable consequences of too much repression.

I want to suggest, then, that Foucault's argument was already implicit in the critique of sexual repression between the wars (and replicated later, in a different fashion, in the work of Herbert Marcuse and now, Anthony Giddens)—albeit in a different form. In the interwar years, derepression, as I have argued, did not lead to what Maurice Blanchot, in reference to Sade, called "the ruin of moral conscience" but to the intensification of moral restraints.[36] In other words, the explicit purpose of derepression was not to liberate man from the prison of his body and the institutions that discipline it, but, paradoxically, to restore social discipline by restoring manhood. The history of the sexual subject was continuous with an attempt to socialize the self-possessed, self-transforming, and expressive individual through an effort to heal *men's* wounds, seal their divisions, purge them of excesses, and restore their moral purity.

While Foucault offered a powerful critique of this process of socialization, I want to argue that he too was concerned to restore equality, desire, and wholeness to men's bodies, albeit by rethinking the image of the integral male body itself. In contrast to Hunt's claim, Foucault's history of sexual subjectivity is derived from a history of male lack rather than male potency, and the historicity of Foucault's work is inextricable from this perception of male lack. His concept of sexual subjectivity emerged out of the "historico-political critique of sexual repression" rather than out of the materialist critique of monarchical despotism.

If this argument is correct, then perhaps Hunt's claim that Foucault "cannot imagine a self other than the one newly deployed in the eighteenth century" must yield to another possibility: Foucault's work emerged in relation to a different logic of desire articulated one hundred years after Sade's death. Foucault's subject would then not be founded on the exclusion of women from a social contract based on self-possessed, self-transforming bodies (and hence on the need to discipline equal desiring bodies) but on a necessarily futile effort to restore a male self perceived as lost.

III

In Foucault's account, as I noted earlier, the bourgeoisie constructed its sexuality as having been repressed in order better to regulate and hence protect it. Advocates of derepression, for example, conceived what Foucault calls the modern confessional (talking to psychoanalysts, psychologists, lawyers, doctors, all variety of "experts") as a means of bringing sex and its dangers to light. For Foucault, the confessional exemplified the bourgeoisie's nurturing of their own phantasmatic, impermeable, and smooth "sexual body"—a "body to be cared for, protected, cultivated and preserved from many dangers and contacts" (1:123).

He argued that at the end of the eighteenth century a new discourse was thus constructed around bourgeois sexuality which said: "Our sexuality, unlike that of others, is subjected to a regime of repression so intense as to present a constant danger; not only is sex a formidable secret . . . not only must we search it out for the truth it conceals, but if it carries with it so many dangers, this is because . . . we have too long reduced it to silence." Henceforth social differentiation would be affirmed, not by the "sexual" quality of the body, but by the intensity of its repression" (1:128–29). The pleasure of confession serves not to liberate sex from repression but to subject it to increasing restraint. The confession does not release tension and ease guilt, but *produces* the so-called truths it reveals:

> The pleasure that comes from exercising a power that questions, monitors, watches, spies, searches out, palpates, brings to light; and on the other hand, the pleasure that kindles at having to evade this power, flee

from it, fool it, or travesty it. The power that lets itself be invaded by the pleasure it is pursuing; and opposite it, power asserting itself in the pleasure of showing off, scandalizing, or resisting. Capture and seduction, confrontation and mutual reinforcement: parents and children, adults and adolescents, educator and students, doctors and patients, the psychiatrist with his hysteric and his perverts, all have played this game continually since the nineteenth century. These attractions, these evasions, these circular incitements have traced around bodies and sexes, not boundaries not to be crossed, but *perpetual spirals of power and pleasure.* (1:45)

Sex is thus not something repressed and so something that might also be liberated. The production of sexual subjectivity is not therefore a "boundary-crossing" (the transgression of or submission to cultural customs and taboos) but a circular incitement in which power must endlessly produce new pleasures in order to guarantee its own expansion, in order to justify its own existence. The confession in this sense is an allegory for the production of a sexual subject at once revealed (brought into the light) and perpetually in formation, never fully itself (always partially in the dark). As Foucault conceived it, after all, power is "the hidden and yet generative principle of meaning" that defines our intelligibility (1:155). It permeates all discourse, but its origins cannot be ferreted out. "Power is tolerable only on condition it masks a substantial part of itself" (1:85). Or: "Its success is proportional to its ability to hide its own mechanisms" (1:86).[37] In short, power is hidden; in contrast to Sade's ostentatious displays of mastery, it doesn't show itself off.

Thus if the subject were to move fully into the light, if power were to cease its endless pursuit of pleasure and reveal the mysteries of its ways, the self would become transparent. According to Foucault—and in marked contrast to Hunt's own assertions—this is precisely what happens in Sade and what marks the distance between the two men. In Foucault's reading, the Sadean self's form and desires are singular, transparent, and self-evident. For in Sade, as Foucault put it, "there are no shadows."[38] There is only "total night" or "absolute day." In Sade, he went on, the so-called light of reason, grounded in our natural propensity for goodness, is finally indistinguishable from the "total night" of tyranny. Similarly, Sade's fictional sisters, the virtuous Justine and the immoral Juliette, are no longer opposed visions of social order but represent the singular, logical unfolding of reason: "The lightning flash which nature drew from herself in order to strike Justine [who is struck by lightning at the end of the book named after her] was identical with the long [and dark] existence of Juliett." Nature herself becomes "criminal subjectivity."[39]

In Sade, then, totalitarianism is continuous with freedom, night with day, Sade's tyrants with the preachers of virtue (Sade's most cunning criminals almost always occupy the most prestigious and influential social positions—they are judges, lawyers, politicians, priests, bishops, even the Pope). This sovereign reign of subjectivity constitutes the "unique and naked sovereignty" of which Foucault spoke with reference to Sade in *The History of Sexuality*—a law which casts no shadows because it is self-same, because it "knows no other law than its own," because transgression (vice) is conceptually inseparable from the (presumably virtuous) law.

According to Foucault, in Sade's work the self could not be other than what those in power claim it has always been. The self is not the site of meaning production, where "other" pleasures might be imagined, but symbolizes the end of disputes about meaning, the establishment of meaning once and for all. In short, the Sadean self represents the end of history, or rather, the restoration of history "as it has always been."

Foucault's theory of power on the other hand—at least as he states it—is quite distant from all theories of subjectivity that cast no shadows. We can never know how technologies of sex produce sexual subjects because their motives are at once hidden and yet immanent in all discourses. Foucault argued that "the logic [of power] is perfectly clear, the aims decipherable, and yet it is often the case that no one is there to have invented them, and few who can be said to have formulated them: an implicit characteristic of the great anonymous, almost unspoken strategies which coordinate the loquacious tactics whose 'inventors' or decisionmakers are often without hypocrisy" (1:95). So the logic of power is clear, but there is no one who can make sense of it; the logic of power is decipherable and yet it is exercised by no one—or by no one who can be identified. This is the kind of reasoning that drives historians crazy: For how can the aims of power be clear if no one understands why it works the way it does? How can power exercised by no one extend its own reach? How can power be absolutely hidden and yet absolutely everywhere?

But this logic does, as it were, have a reason. In Foucault the self is always a regulatory effect whose cause (whose desire) can never be identified except in terms of the cultural norms that give it form. His history is thus one of a sexual subject that can never be revealed, of a self-possession that is simultaneously a self loss. It is a history that can never get to the bottom of things, one in which a crucial part of the story must always remain beyond the historian's grasp. Sade's libertine casts no shadows because the world is merely an extension of himself. Foucault's subject is instead anxiety-ridden, guilty, knowing without knowing he can never fully be himself. In Sade's parody the individual becomes the social because his desire is at one with the Law that governs all people—the authoritarian rule of the powerful is founded on the "right" to fulfill one's desires. Thus whereas in Sade the end of deference, birthright, and monarchy consolidates and legitimates the laws of despots, in Foucault the simultaneous revelation and inaccessibility of the self (it is both in light and shadows) wrenches the social world from its moorings, since the origin of power can never finally be traced. In Foucault's world, everyone can be anything (as Hunt claims of Sade's libertines) not because they are free, self-possessed, and self-transforming, but because at the core of our being there is nothing identifiable, nothing solid or immutable, nothing that can be known for sure (1:93).

In this reductio ad absurdum of sexual liberation theory, desiring man is no longer transparent but is never what he appears to be. In a reversal of that discourse, Foucault does not rescue man by restoring his manhood but restores manhood by eroding the traditional foundations of masculinity. That is, sexual liberationists sought to repress men through derepression. Foucault unraveled this paradox by demonstrating how derepression does not effect the restoration of traditional manhood, but the dissolution of a knowable truth on which manhood is purportedly founded. He demonstrated how derepression does not necessarily restore history as it has always been but reveals that manhood has a "history"—that there is nothing transcendent, immutable, or unchanging about masculinity.

But Foucault, as I have already noted, did not simply have satirical intentions (if he had them at all). He sought to rewrite history. So how exactly does this reductio ad absurdum of sexual liberation theory represent the restructuring of sexual subjectivity? In other words, how exactly does derepression reveal the history of masculinity (if we follow Foucault) it is meant to repress?

IV

It has been objected that Foucault exaggerated the tyranny of power precisely because he left it in the shadows, unknowable except in its manifestations and hence impervious, ultimately, to change. In this view, which I think is Hunt's, Foucault's work, like Sade's, leads to the legitimation of a tyrannical law. Because if power's origins can never be known, what is to prevent anyone from claiming that tyranny is just as valid as democracy—and more efficient too?

This insistence on leaving power's origins in shadows also, as Hunt notes, marks Foucault's lack of interest in questions of gender and his insensitivity to the differential effects of power on women and men. Furthermore, it helps place his work in the poststructuralist (anti) canon, with its effort to find shadows in every text, its suspicion of all clarity, knowledge—all "light"—and its consequent refusal to accord authority to what people say they experience, feel, or "are," regardless of the position from which they speak.

Of course, Foucault *did* theorize resistance and, by implication, change, in his now famous notion of "reverse discourse," whereby power produces terms to label threats that are then appropriated to challenge power itself (for example, the construction of the homosexual becomes the grounds for demanding homosexual rights). But in the end, it is not a very satisfying concept, since, as I implied earlier and many critics have pointed out, it too weds resistance entirely to dominant cultural formations.

Notwithstanding the possibility that Foucault's concept of power functions as a transcendental principle, as a "bottom line," it nonetheless engenders a formulation of resistance that is far more nuanced and troubled than most critics have allowed. In spite of Foucault's political work for prisoner's rights, among other activities, he does not advocate "openness"—grand declarations of who you are and what rights must therefore accrue to you. In Foucault's work, the "old mole" (Karl Marx characterized revolution as an "old mole" that works away in the dark) never comes to the surface but continues its efforts underground.[40] Perhaps Foucault sees power everywhere (though it does not "embrace everything") in order to increase the significance of what shadow is left—to increase the importance of hiding places that become the unseen, inaccessible repositories of history, of what makes us who we are. Perhaps Foucault is a truth seeker, albeit of an entirely other order than Marx—a man bound by a truth he knows he will never know, bound to write never knowing what it will amount to, driven as it were, not by the confidence of eventual discovery, but by the trauma produced by a crisis of confidence.

Of course, Foucault worked very much in the light—at Berkeley and the Collège de France at the end of his career. And as his biographers have told us, he spent a lot of time in leather bars and bathhouses. This opposition between the famous bourgeois professor and the gay leather man already points to a problem with such oppositions between light and dark: Foucault was most "out" (as a gay man) when (at least metaphorically speaking) in the dark, and most concealed in the light of the lecture hall. He was most in when out and most out when in. (As Eve Sedgwick has demonstrated, the "closet" is not a place but represents a structural relation that marks and upholds binary divisions between being "in" and "out").[41]

It is precisely this kind of ultimately untenable opposition between light and dark, out and in, that the logic of desire in Foucault's *History* repudiates. The sexual subject is not formed when he is subjected to the law—not when he crosses forbidden borders. There is no inside or outside to legality. Instead, the sexual subject is perpetually in formation, because power is perpetually unsatisfied, forever in search of more pleasures to regulate. Power is thus never fully in control, never totalitarian, and it is in the pleasure of always being one step ahead of power that Foucault locates resistance—in the invisible but felt, tangible relation of power and pleasure. Because in his world, like Freud's, everyone's thoughts are revealed even as they hide them, the subject is at once in the light and inaccessible.

However, Foucault warns us not to interpret this relation as an opposition between a true self (that is, the unconscious or the "real" self) and another false one. He urges us instead to turn that conflict between truth and falsehood (say, gay reality, straight appearance) itself into an identity and hence to turn identity into an exhilarating "game."[42] Foucault used the game playing implicit in sadomasochistic desire to describe the structure of the subject: "[In sadomasochistic practice] this mixture of rules and openness has the effect of intensifying sexual relations by introducing a perpetual novelty, a perpetual tension which the simple consummation of the act lacks."[43] It is in this sense that sadomasochistic desire allegorizes the structure of the Foucauldian subject: subjectivity is never "consummated," as it were, never closed. It is never the expression of a deep, expressive inner core but the performance of a perpetually shifting, mobile self: "Relations of knowledge are not static forms of distribution, they are 'matrices of transformation'" (1:99).

This essentially poststructuralist alternative to humanism is often criticized: the fragmented, performative, lacking subject merely replicates the status historians and others have always attributed to racial and sexual minorities and women through neglect and distortion. Henry Louis Gates, for example, has argued that poststructuralist arguments are not particularly radical or helpful when analyzing the diverse experience of African-Americans, whose subjectivity has always been defined as somehow "lacking." Many feminists have made the same point.[44] In short, for this kind of "game" to empower rather than disempower individuals, they have to have something to draw on—some socially valued qualities that can be put into play. One must already have been endowed with an integral subjectivity, with a universally recognized tradition, culture, and canon.

This criticism, however valid, nevertheless reduces the complexity of Foucault's position, not only as a gay man, but in relation to the history of masculinity itself. For Foucault, like Sade in his own time, demonstrates the problems implicit in a new identity formation—here, not newly self-contained, reasonable, and desiring individuals who always say what they mean, but men who must learn to mean what they say, whose self-confidence and vigor must be restored. This image of the male subject— the one assumed by interwar cultural critics—thus already presumes a self rooted not in masculinity, but in its erosion, not in reason, but in its disruption. Remember interwar critics rejected the constant vigilance assured by repression in favor of a vigilance paradoxically maintained through the removal of repressive restraints; they conceived manhood as so sapped of egotistical, self-preserving instincts, so shorn of rational decision-making power, that repression could no longer be an effective deterrent.

Foucault insisted that sexual liberationists accounted for and legitimated that restoration of manhood only by covering up the power that produced it—that is, he argued that the "antirepressive struggle" was merely a "tactical shift" in the deployment of sexuality and hence in the deployment of power. He did not believe that derepression represented the natural expression of manhood, but the production and regulation of manhood in the interest of power. Although Foucault insists that interwar critics naturalized the history of manhood and so covered it up, he offers no theory of power within which to frame an investigation. Renegade historian, Foucault's testimonial leaves the trace of a crime (here, a cover-up) that can never be detected.

In so doing, he simply made explicit the history of manhood implicit in interwar critics' very effort to restore a traditional male self, one that had presumably always been. He defined "real" (that is, changing, mutable, foundationless) manhood as the "trace" that forever eludes the historian (the would-be detective). Foucault is both the product and producer of a new normative sexual subjectivity anchored not by reference to an integral male self but by reference to a male subject at once self-possessed and (unspeakably) fragmented. As I have argued, Foucault's work on sexuality—in which the sexual self is produced paradoxically through a self-loss—constitutes a recent effort to shatter the reified, instrumental structures of (now late) capitalist culture by recourse to what Foucault called "bodies and pleasures": that is, by recourse to a self-loss that might be experienced as an exhilarating self-renewal, an exhilarating "game" that would never end. (Isn't this, to some extent, how Western cultures now conceive the very experience and purpose of sexuality: as a loss of boundaries that enables relationships in which the "true," most intimate self struggling in an atomized instrumental culture is finally revealed, restored, renewed only to be lost again? In which plenitude is necessarily illusory? Has there not been a shift, replicated and effected by Foucault, from a self whose individuality is defined in terms of its sexuality or sexual identity to a self for whom sexuality represents the dissolution of individuality, the effort to lose the self?)

My central argument thus links Foucault specifically to a historical context in order to explore his limitations. Following Foucault, what we now consider natural does not just represent "sexual modernism," to paraphrase Paul Robinson—an increasing respect for sexuality and tolerance of sexual diversity—but a new ideological context in which men's bodies and psyches had to be reconstructed in the interests of the dominant social order.[45] Simply put, what was "perverted" in the nineteenth century became "natural" by the early twentieth as elites reconfigured masculinity in the hopes of sustaining its normative qualities.

Though Foucault shows how the discourse of sexual liberation is really a discourse of sexual discipline (hence his reductio ad absurdum of liberation theory), he already presumes the disciplined (because lost, eroded) male self that "technologies of sex" are supposed to produce. Foucault's concept of power in this way presumes and extends the paradoxical logic sexual liberationists' used in their effort to liberate male desire from mechanization and atomization by disciplining it in new ways. He presumed that the most rigid kind of discipline and masculinity were perfectly and perhaps necessarily inextricable so that individuals inevitably mimicked the very power they resisted. In so doing, he conceived sexual subjectivity—indeed subjectivity and agency in general—in terms of the mimicry of power, in terms of an unrepresentable location within power itself.[46] He thus moved beyond Sade's parody of Enlightenment reason, for he does not simply demonstrate the dark underbelly of its optimism but sought through mimicry to conceive subjectivity itself in new terms.

Foucault's love of shadows marks his attempt not to undermine but to restore the male self in entirely new terms, to give unspeakable selves power by theorizing power as a "game" in which self loss is always a means of self-renewal, in which one must lose one's self in order to possess one. I have claimed that Foucault locates resistance in the unspeakable but exhilarating pleasures of bodies formed, paradoxically, through self loss (repressed through derepression); his reductio ad absurdum of the discourse of derepression shows how the self is at once possessed and lost, shaped in the image of a perpetually unsatisfied power always in search of what it lacks. Foucault calls the self entirely into question in order to provide it with an (albeit unrepresentable) reason to go on living, to persevere in what must always be an unsatisfied quest for its "truth." He implicitly turns the discourse of wounded manliness—of emasculation, hidden weakness, of secret, unspeakable thoughts—into the equally *unspeakable* power of men. This structuring of the subject as an oscillation between light and dark (as structurally undecidable) describes the subjectivity of the "passing" gay man and turns his identity into a joke on dominant culture.[47]

But under what conditions can self loss function as the grounds of agency; under what conditions can participating in power's ruse give one power? How, in other words, does mimicry become empowering, how does self loss understood as an a priori condition of selfhood renew rather than simply reiterate the self's emptiness? How does self loss finally guarantee an albeit always compromised self possession? How, finally, does this construction of male desire also account for female desire, for women's sexual agency?

Because Foucault uses his unraveling of the paradoxical refiguration of "healthy" masculinity after the Great War as the normative model within which to figure all sexual subjectivity, self loss is always simultaneously a self possession. As we have seen, Foucault turns performance—here meant as "passing"—into a game rather than into a painful site of powerlessness, of physical and psychic trauma and immobility; he turns performance into an exhilarating joke on power rather than into a strategy by which powerless people learn to survive.

In defining self loss as the condition of self possession, he makes all kinds of agency meaningful, especially those which cannot pronounce their intentions loudly. But the structural oscillation — between pain and pleasure, light and dark, professorships and bathhouses — that defines male subjectivity can also be understood as a new, historically specific normative construction of sexual subjectivity that can only conceive female subjects in terms of that "trace" of "real" manhood which always remains unarticulated. Like sexual liberationists — and, as I've noted, as many feminist critics of Foucault have long pointed out — Foucault ends up assimilating women's desire to men's desire — although in a new way.[48] Insofar as self loss is a condition of self possession, Foucault replicates a normative and recent framework of male subjectivity within which a female subject's agency is limited to a choice between reiterating women's absence (since self loss really does not describe a radical or deviant cultural condition for women), or theorizing women's presence as the unsymbolizable rift in patriarchal cultural formations — as the unarticulated presupposition that stabilizes even as it destabilizes male subjectivity, as an (often unconscious) signifier of anxiety.[49] These alternatives have again been replicated in recent scholarship: either we use Foucault to help understand more effectively how women's sexuality was constructed, regulated, or even rendered unthinkable; or we use him to demonstrate the real instability of patriarchal and heterosexual meaning systems.

But if we take the historical framework within which Foucault conceptualized the "power" that defines modern sexual subjectivity and refigured it for women the way he does for men, why would we necessarily only have these options? Rather than reject or defend Foucault's position for feminist analysis, I have sought to understand how and why he constructs the paradoxical claim that self-loss is essential to having a subject position, or to put it differently, that self-possession is not essential to having one. As Ian Hacking aptly noted, "Foucault said the concept of Man is a fraud, not that you and I are nothing."[50] If "man" is a fraud, and yet something is there, it may be possible to get at what might be there by doing what Foucault did to sexual liberationists: to deconstruct the way in which his work is and is not beholden to the culturally and historically specific premises he challenged.

I can only speculate here about how to begin imagining other historical possibilities, other methods, which would not assume a prediscursive concept of the subject.[51] This is the challenge now before most theorists and historians of sexuality compelled by Foucault's demonstration of the way humanism replicates dominant cultural norms. I have sought to begin such speculation by understanding not just the theoretical but the historical limitations of Foucault's work, and to emphasize from a historical point of view why Foucault's concept of power is perhaps less monolithic—or at least subject to more diverse uses—than many historians have imagined. By considering how Foucault was the product of a historically specific link between modern subjectivity and sexuality, we might begin to analyze how that cultural formation both constrains and opens new possibilities for scholarship, and thus, presumably, how it shapes and produces sexuality as well.

NOTES

I would like to thank the participants of the History Workshop and the Graduate Women's American History workshop at Brown University for their helpful comments. I am especially indebted to Mary Gluck, Martin Jay, Naomi Lamoreaux, Amy Remensnyder, Michael Roth, and Elizabeth Weed. Lynn Hunt read and criticized this as acutely as she has read and criticized nearly everything I have asked her to since I was her student now several years ago. For this reason, and others too numerous to mention, I dedicate this to her.

　　1. I limit this discussion to the analysis of works dealing with the history of modern sexuality—that is, sexuality since the eighteenth century. There is, of course, much literature in the early modern period—especially on family history—but it does not engage Foucault specifically.

　　2. On this debate, see especially Patricia O'Brien, "Michel Foucault's History of Culture," in *The New Cultural History,* ed. Lynn Hunt (Berkeley, 1989), 25–46. O'Brien provides ample references for those interested in pursuing the nature of this debate among historians.

　　3. Michel Foucault, *The History of Sexuality, vol. 1, Introduction,* tr. Robert Hurley (New York, 1980), 94. All further references will be cited within the text. Since I am focusing on scholarship on modern sexuality and since Foucault's later work on Greece and Rome complicates the analysis beyond what I can cover here, I have chosen to exclude this work from my discussion. I do not think this choice changes the argument I make here in any substantial manner.

　　4. *Discourses of Sexuality from Aristotle to AIDS,* ed. Domna C. Stanton (Ann Arbor, Mich., 1992), 4. This is perhaps the first real effort to assess the state of "sexuality studies" since Martha Vicinus wrote her review essay of "Sexuality and Power: A Review of Current Work in the History of Sexuality" in *Feminist Studies* 8 (Spring, 1982): 134–156, and B. Ruby Rich published her review of "Feminism and Sexuality

in the 1980's," *Feminist Studies* 12 (1986): 525–61. These two essays reflect struggles within academic feminism as well as the relationship between work on sexuality within the academy and political fights within feminism itself about issues concerning sexuality. Stanton's essay not only demonstrates to what extent those struggles are still alive in different ways, but how much academic work has proliferated because of them. My focus here is on that by now vast body of work, of which my account will be necessarily reductive.

5. I thus use the term *post-Foucauldian* to refer to a wide variety of scholars who have in one way or another taken up Foucault's antihumanist premises. They fall under a number of different categories, including new historicists (often referred to as post-Foucauldian historicists), and queer theorists. Since the term *poststructuralist* is a contested one with many different adherents (including post-Foucauldians), I have preferred to call these theorists post-Foucauldians, since all are engaged with Foucault's ideas and more specifically are engaged in rethinking "history" as a concept and a discipline in the aftermath of Foucault's work. However, many of them might even refuse such an appellation—hence I use this term for the sake of coherence only. I cannot possibly cover all the different camps and the debates between them, any more than I can clarify the still contested meaning of the various terms they employ (say, *poststructuralism*). I have sought merely to provide a synthetic survey of what they do have in common as a means of evaluating the history of sexuality as it is now practiced.

6. Judith Butler, *Gender Trouble: Feminism and the Subversion of Identity* (New York, 1990); David Halperin, *One Hundred Years of Homosexuality and Other Essays on Greek Love* (New York, 1990); Eve Kosofsky Sedgwick, *Epistemology of the Closet* (Berkeley, 1990); Jonathan Dollimore, *Sexual Dissidence: Augustine to Wilde, Freud to Foucault* (Oxford, 1991). There is now a vast literature addressing these questions. I cite only some of the most influential works.

7. Sedgwick, *Epistemology of the Closet*, 50. Sedgwick is quoting the inimitable wit of Emily Dickinson. For an interesting critique of historicism in this vein (but one that does not engage with historians themselves), see Elizabeth Deeds Ermarth, *Sequel to History: Postmodernism and the Crisis of Representational Time* (Princeton, 1992). Finally, Robert Nye has recently noted how historians have often taken sexual science at face value even while doubting the field's objectivity (*Masculinity and Male Codes of Honor in Modern France* [Oxford, 1993], 103).

8. One of the few historians to address historical work specifically from this point of view is Joan Scott, most recently in her "The Evidence of Experience," *Critical Inquiry* 17: 773–97 (1991). Martin Jay examines the poststructuralist critique of experience in the context of Foucault's work in "The Limits of Limit-Experience: Bataille and Foucault," *Working Paper 3.11* (Center for German and European Studies at the University of California at Berkeley), October 1993.

9. One historian who has sought to integrate both approaches is Judith Walko-

witz, *City of Dreadful Delight: Narratives of Sexual Danger in Late-Victorian London* (Chicago, 1992).

10. *Ibid.;* Thomas Laqueur, *Making Sex: Body and Gender from the Greeks to Freud* (Cambridge, Mass., 1990); and Jeffrey Weeks's pioneering *Sex, Politics, and Society: The Regulation of Sexuality since 1800* (London, 1981), among his other works. See also the essays by John Boswell, David Halperin, Robert Padgug, George Chauncey, and Carroll Smith-Rosenberg, in *Hidden from History: Reclaiming the Gay and Lesbian Past,* ed. Martin Duberman, Martha Vicinus, and George Chauncey (New York, 1989; and essays by Jennifer Terry, "Theorizing Deviant Historiography," *Differences* 3 (1991): 54–74; and Lisa Duggan, "The Trials of Alice Mitchell: Sensationalism, Sexology, and the Lesbian Subject in Turn-of-the-Century America," forthcoming in *Signs.* Of course there are many othe works that mention Foucault, but few of them directly address his method except to take issue with his neglect of agency. I don't want to suggest the above works solve the problems presented by Foucault, but they do engage him in more than a superficial manner.

11. John D'Emilio and Estelle Freedman, *Intimate Matters: The History of Sexuality in America* (New York, 1988), xiii. This is one prominent example.

12. Nancy Fraser, *Unruly Practices: Power, Discourse and Gender in Contemporary Social Theory* (Minneapolis, 1989), 17–34. As feminists have noted again and again, many poststructuralists and more generally postmodernists, who turn everyone into a creator-actor and privilege no point of view, often replicate patriarchal structures of domination in their own work and so in fact do privilege a point of view, in spite of their claims to the contrary.

13. James Miller, *The Passion of Michel Foucault* (New York, 1993). Though this biography has met with acclaim from all sorts of people—the blurbs on the book are from Edward Said, Richard Rorty, Roger Shattuck, and Edmund White—very few have taken on Miller's replication of pernicious cultural associations between AIDS, sadomasochism, sexual promiscuity, and homosexuality (Foucault was a gay man, a sadomasochist, and died of AIDS in 1984). The lack of critical attention to this issue is especially troubling since Miller purports to stand above such prejudice while encouraging and subtly confirming it. Lisa Duggan's review in the *Village Voice* (May 4, 1993) does an excellent job of exposing Miller's presumptions: she points out, for example, that Miller writes the biography with the intention of getting to the bottom of rumors about how Foucault eagerly sought "suicide by sex" in gay bathhouses in San Francisco rather than to examine why such rumors would circulate in the first place. She also points out that Foucault was probably infected with HIV many years before anyone had heard of AIDS, and remarks that Miller's description of gay male bathhouses as "suicide orgies" may reflect Miller's own fantasy (itself replicating cultural associations between male homosexuality, sadomasochism, disease, and pitiful manliness) rather than the reality of gay bathhouses. Martin Jay notes that Miller's desperate effort to be tolerant in the best tradition of lib-

eral politics makes sadomasochism "almost as untransgressive as stamp-collecting" (*Limits of Limit-Experience,* 15, n. 29). See also the various perspectives on Miller's book in *Salmagundi* 97 (Winter 1993).

14. See, in particular, *Feminism and Foucault: Reflections on Resistance,* ed. Irene Diamond and Lee Quinby (Boston, 1988); and Jana Sawicki, *Disciplining Foucault: Feminism, Power, and the Body* (New York, 1991). Sawicki makes an admirable effort to put Foucault in the service of feminism, to demonstrate how Foucauldian insights are indeed compatible with theorizing female sexual subjectivity. I agree generally with this argument, but I want to address it historically rather than theoretically.

15. See Butler, *Gender Trouble;* and Teresa de Lauretis, *Technologies of Gender: Essays on Theory, Film, and Fiction* (Bloomington, Ind., 1987).

16. The list of works on Foucault in this vein is virtually endless. See, among others, Jean Baudrillard, *Oublier Foucault* (Paris, 1977); Hubert L. Dreyfus and Paul Rabinow, *Michel Foucault: Beyond Structuralism and Hermeneutics* (Chicago, 1982); Allan Megill, *Prophets of Extremity: Nietzsche, Heidegger, Foucault, Derrida* (Berkeley, 1987); John Rajchman, *Truth and Eros: Foucault, Lacan, and the Question of Ethics* (New York, 1991). For other interesting readings, see Hayden White, "Michel Foucault," in *Structuralism and Since: From Lévi-Strauss to Derrida,* ed. John Sturrock (Oxford, 1979), 81–115; and Geoffrey Galt Harpham, *The Ascetic Imperative in Culture and Criticism* (Chicago, 1987), esp. 231.

17. Lynn Hunt, "Foucault's Subject in the *History of Sexuality*" in Stanton, ed. *Discourses of Sexuality,* 78–93. All further references will be cited in the text.

18. Since here the invention of modern subjectivity is coextensive with sexual subjectivity, when I refer to the self or subjectivity I am always referring to a sexual subject. Occasionally, I will use the word *sexual* for emphasis.

19. The way in which Hunt forges this link between Sade and Foucault is original, but the link itself is not. Because Sade was a relentless critic of humanist presumptions, he was a privileged figure in Foucault's corpus, an emblem of human tragedy whose extreme fantasies relentlessly strip humanity of all the illusions it has about itself—its integrity, its reason, its moral laws, in short, its humanism. Other French intellectuals also privileged Sade for this reason.

20. See Lynn Hunt, *The Family Romance of the French Revolution* (Berkeley, 1992), 124–50.

21. Hunt points out that even Sade, the man who so radically inverted and challenged gender norms, assumed the male body as the normative body ("Foucault's Subject," 92).

22. I am referring to Thomas Laqueur's book *Making Sex* which has inspired wide commentary. Robert Nye has recently written a rich book on the production of masculinity in modern France. In different ways, such work takes up Joan Scott's insistence that historians must demonstrate how gender roles were historically produced rather than focusing on how women were or were not included in already

gendered frameworks. See Laqueur, *Making Sex;* Nye, *Masculinity and Male Codes of Honor;* Joan Scott, *Gender and the Politics of History* (New York, 1989); Joan Landes, *The Public Sphere and the French Revolution* (Ithaca, N.Y., 1990); Carole Pateman, *The Sexual Contract* (Stanford, 1988), among others. The relationship of femininity and masculinity to sexuality is of course a complex question that historians have only begun to consider.

23. On shifting models of scarcity and abundance and their relationship to sexology, see Lawrence Birken, *Consuming Desire: Sexual Science and the Emergence of a Culture of Abundance, 1871–1914* (Ithaca, N.Y., 1988). Birken makes an interesting argument about the transition away from sexual difference but does not analyze to what extent sexual sameness takes male sexuality as normative.

24. The following few pages are a condensed version of one section in Carolyn Dean, "Pornography, Literature, and Virility in France, 1880–1930," *Differences* 5 (Summer 1993): 62–91.

25. Paul Lapeire, *Essai juridique et historique sur l'outrage aux bonnes moeurs par le livre, l'écrit, et l'imprimé* (Lille, 1931), 23.

26. Armand Charpentier, cited in Lionel d'Autrec, *L'Outrage aux moeurs* (Paris, 1923), 247.

27. See Anthony Giddens, *The Transformation of Intimacy: Sexuality, Love and Eroticism in Modern Societies* (Stanford, 1992), 163. Giddens also notes that Reich believed sexual "freedom and sexual health [were] the same thing."

28. On this point in particular, see Ian Hunter, David Saunders, and Dugald Williamson, *On Pornography: Literature, Sexuality, and Obscenity Law* (New York, 1993), especially the chapter on "Literary Erotics," 92–134.

29. Henry Marchand, *Sex Life in France* (New York, 1933), 265–67.

30. Robert Desnos, *De l'érotisme considéré dans ses manifestations écrites et du point de vue de l'esprit moderne* [1923] (Paris, 1952), 67, 76, 112.

31. I should note that many of the texts I use discuss sexual liberation in nongendered terms. Nevertheless, the language they use almost always indicates that they are speaking about male sexuality. Almost all the sexual purity campaigns of the mid- to late-nineteenth century sought to regulate prostitutes and male homosexuals, indicating that the danger to social order came from uncontrolled male lust (for which women were often assumed responsible). This is very confusing because uncontrolled male lust was most often gendered feminine—conceived as emasculating and hence dangerous. I want to argue that by the early twentieth century, sexuality could be celebrated because conditions existed in which its so-called excesses could now be gendered masculine—that is, they could be expressed and contained at once.

32. Havelock Ellis, *The Task of Social Hygiene* (New York, 1914), 212–16; 254–57.

33. Ellis, *More Essays of Love and Virtue* (London, 1931), 124, 137.

34. Montgomery Hyde, *A History of Pornography* (New York, 1964), 204.

35. See Giddens, *The Transformation of Intimacy,* 164–68.

36. Maurice Blanchot, "Sade," preface to D. A. F. de Sade, *Justine, Philosophy in the Bedroom, Eugenie de Franval, and Other Writings* (New York, 1965), 52.

37. In the most famous example from *Discipline and Punish,* Bentham's Panopticon maps space so that disciplinary power sees without being seen; power is itself in shadow (Michel Foucault, *Discipline and Punish* [New York, 1975]).

38. Michel Foucault, *Madness and Civilization: A History of Insanity in the Age of Reason* (New York, 1965), 285.

39. Ibid., 284–85.

40. This is also a reference to George Bataille's critique of surrealism using the same term. See Georges Bataille, "The 'Old Mole' and the Prefix *sur* in the Words *Surhomme* [Superman] and *Surrealist,*" *Visions of Excess,* ed. and transl. Allan Stockl (Minneapolis, 1985), 32–44.

41. Sedgwick, *Epistemology of the Closet.*

42. On social formations and identities as games see Pierre Bourdieu, *The Logic of Practice* (Stanford, 1990), especially 66–68. I thank Elisa Glick for reminding me of Bourdieu's work.

43. Michel Foucault, *Foucault Live* (New York, 1989), 226.

44. Henry Louis Gates, "The Master's Pieces: On Canon Formation and the African-American Tradition," *The Politics of Liberal Education,* ed. Barbara Herrnstein Smith and David Gless (Durham, N.C., 1992), 111. For some feminist discussions around this issue, see Louise Newman, "Critical Theory and the History of Women: What's at Stake in Deconstructing Women's History," *Journal of Women's History* 3 (Winter 1991): 58–68; and the exchange between Joan Scott and Linda Gordon in *Signs* 4 (1990): 348–60.

45. Paul Robinson, *The Modernization of Sex: Havelock Ellis, Alfred Kinsey, William Masters and Virginia Johnson* (Ithaca, N.Y., 1989). In a way I have been following up Robinson's sense that Foucault treats discourses of sexuality as "Olympian abstraction[s]" (xi) hardly connected to the way "most of us experience our sexuality." For Foucault, as his biographers make clear, his sexuality was not at all an abstraction, but a site of both tremendous social pain as well as pleasure. In this paper I am trying on one level to connect that experience to the "Olympian abstractions" of his work.

46. Judith Butler has pointed out how even Foucault could not sustain this notion of resistance as mimicry: she demonstrates how he celebrated a prediscursive, utopian notion of "bodies and pleasures" in spite of himself (Butler, *Gender Trouble,* 106).

47. Interestingly enough, as Robert Nye has shown, in 1898 a book by Ludovic Dugas on timidity defined the absence of manliness this way: " 'Timid individuals

are *naturally shameful [honteuse].*' They lead lives of 'complicated dissimulation, full of subtleties and detours . . .,' which are lacking in 'cordiality, spontaneity, and frankness'" (Nye, *Masculinity and Male Codes of Honor,* 223).

48. Both Paul Robinson and Janice Irvine have pointed out how sexologists assumed men and women were sexual equals but defined sexuality itself in terms of male desire (Robinson, *The Modernization of Sex,* especially 17–18); Janice Irvine, *Disorders of Desire: Sex and Gender in Modern American Sexology* (Philadelphia, 1990), 87.

49. Even those theorists (for example, Butler) who theorize gender roles as sites of instability theorize female subjectivity as the lack it has always been assumed to be, although they do provide a critique of normative femininity because they demonstrate that it is always constructed rather than natural.

50. Ian Hacking quoted in Sawicki, *Disciplining Foucault,* 63.

51. Imagining female self loss in a way that is not paralyzed by fear of replicating dominant cultural norms whereby woman's integrity is defined paradoxically in terms of self-denial might be a place to start. The challenge here would be to imagine it while sustaining some concept of agency in self loss that is not unrepresentable (as in masochism). This would require trying to reconceptualize the relationship of gender and sexuality in ways that both disrupt the normative continuity between the two (as Butler and others such as Gayle Rubin do) and keep the power relations that maintain that continuity in constant focus.

FILM AND HISTORY:
SPECTATORSHIP,
TRANSFERENCE, AND RACE

E. Ann Kaplan

THE *and* BETWEEN the terms *film* and *history* allows for differing sorts of exploration. Is it a question of how American film has represented historical events? Is the relationship between a particular film and its historical context—events ongoing at the moment of its production and exhibition—at issue? Is the history of film itself at stake—how film arose, under what contexts, film as institution, histories of specific genres, directors, stars, studios? Is the historicity of the film *spectator,* as this changes over time, involved? Or yet again specific representations in American film, as they have evolved historically?

While my project touches on some of these perspectives, its main focus is, first, cinema's historical formation along with imperialism and psychoanalysis, and second, issues of history and spectatorship. Cinema's relationship to power and knowledge emerges in its enmeshment with imperialism and psychoanalysis; spectatorship, on the other hand, offers possibilities for agency/resistance, even if such possibilities have to be struggled for against processes of domination.

Gender and race are important sites for exploring how both power/knowledge and agency function in cinema, but since most theorizing has focused on white (ethnic) and gender constructions, I look at African-American problematics. Within that context, I first explore Hollywood's use of psychoanalytic transference because it shows how power/knowledge functions on the intersubjective level. I will argue that intersubjective transference functions as a metaphor for larger social institutions through which knowledge becomes power. Second, I am interested in how spectator positions may become a space for agency.

CINEMA, IMPERIALISM, PSYCHOANALYSIS

The intricate historical enmeshment of cinema with both imperialism and psychoanalysis explains much about how cinematic forms and images developed historically. The history of film is complicit with the history of imperialism, and not only through strong analogy or metaphor. Cinema may act as a tool of colonial domination (e.g., *Tarzan* [1932]; *King Kong* [1932]; *Birds of Paradise* [1933]; *South Pacific* [1954]). The camera is used to gaze upon, and in so doing to distance, the gazing (white, male) subject behind and in front of the camera from Others constructed as "different" through the process of the gaze (Haraway, 1989; Shohat, 1991; Doane, 1992). The camera's global gaze equals that of colonial domination: like the virgin land Edward Said describes awaiting the colonialist's touch to awaken it to fertility, productivity (Shohat, 1991), or the "mapping" of knowledges by European travelers into universalized systems (Pratt, 1992), so the camera becomes the ethnographic tool through which cultures are "otherized" and brought to Western populations without their needing to move physically from their cinema or, more recently, TV, spectator positions (Shohat, 1991; Stam, 1983, 1988). Cinema is complicit, then, in justifying and abetting colonialism through its penetration of other cultures, its production and "freezing" of "otherized" images, and its worldwide proliferation of them. Comparison between the mechanisms of cinema and the mechanisms (or technologies) of colonial government are metaphorically suggestive.

The imperial gaze of cinema also works within the United States context to dominate others and to distance the white patriarchal subject from "otherized" subjects it produces (Trinh T. Minh Ha, 1990).[1] At the same time, it constructs the United States as an "imagined Nation" (Anderson, 1983)—a concept intricately bound up with the binary it opposes, namely, savagery, noncivilization. The historical process of interpenetration between racial constructs and the constitution of nation in America was manifest in the Revolutionary War and again in the Civil War. Cinema has colluded in linking concepts of the country as *nation* to race. As Clyde Taylor has suggested, some affinity exists in the United States "between breakthrough (cinematic) productions and national allegories in which the definition of national character simultaneously involves a co-defining anti-type" (Taylor, 1991, 13). Taylor notes that "landmarks in American (film) culture for technical innovation and/or popular success have often importantly involved the portrayal of African Americans" (Taylor, 1991, 13). He goes on to discuss how the western aesthetic system used in *Birth of a Nation* may be seen to elevate whites and denigrate blacks.

Joel Kovel, writer and psychoanalyst, has pointed out that after the Revolution, "when the time came to structure the new nation . . . propertied interests reasserted themselves and further etched the slave-race complex into our national culture" (Kovel, 1970, 22). Kovel argues that "the height of racism was reached with the consolidation and expansion of white America" into a new historical entity, the nation-state (Kovel, 1979, 24). The state, according to Kovel, maintains underlying assumptions about fundamental concepts, like property, and he argues that it has "entered the arena of racial struggle as a third party, along with white and black peoples," who are themselves changing rapidly in the modern world. He notes that "just as skin is a kind of boundary between an organism and the world, so too does racism provide boundaries within a culture. . . . Racism can be considered a kind of bounding process that goes on in American culture as it grows" (Kovel, 26).

Hollywood is one of the sites where racial boundaries are delineated, codified, and marked. Cinema has traditionally enabled the white male subject to secure his imaginary dominance—a dominance associated with the United States as an "imagined community" of white peoples of European descent dominating Native and African Americans. The imperialism underlying the invention and production of classical cinema also underlies the invention and practice of psychoanalysis.[2] The invention of cinema at the same historical moment as that when Freud was developing psychoanalysis as a "talking cure" has been discussed by film theorists in relation to constructs of gender and white female and male spectators. The psychoanalytic discovery of the location of subjective desire in dream imagery— dreams as a vehicle for the release and expression of repressed (perhaps inarticulable) wishes and desires—arrived at the same time that humans were developing a technology for the reproduction and relay of moving images on a screen. The operation of imagery in the production and circulation of desire is similar in both psychoanalytic dream theory and film, although in the case of film, the interfaces of consumption, normalizing, and cultural construction of desire are also involved (Heath, 1981; Metz, 1971/84; Baudry, 1974/75).

While sophisticated 1970s and 1980s analyses explored ways in which the figure of *woman* (really "white" woman) was circulated to accommodate specific unconscious (white) male desires, fears and fantasies, little has even now been done in relation to psychoanalysis, cinema, and race. Research on the nature of ethnic images in Hollywood has advanced (Cripps, 1978; Bogle, 1989; Wallace, 1990; Diawara, 1991, 1992), but few have studied what unconscious fears and fantasies the circulation of Hollywood ethnic "others" in cinema alleviated for white spectators; the psychoanalytic impact of such images on black or other ethnic spectators; or Hollywood's use of psychoanalytic transference in relation to normalizing African Americans, namely transference as a model/metaphor for mechanisms of larger institutional domestication and control.

FILM, HISTORY, AND SPECTATORSHIP

Addressing spectatorship is one way to tease out resistances to institutional control and to illuminate how agency may subtly assert itself despite cinematic processes of domination. Looking for agency in spectatorship avoids reproducing victims when analyzing the attempts of the American cinematic institution to dominate the "others" it first constructs; such study also opens up space to address the often unconscious negative impact on spectators of ethnic images. Theoretically, spectatorship offers a space not controlled by the knowledge/power axis of cinema as institution. In the mid-1980s, I distinguished at least three levels or kinds of spectator that may be useful in this connection (Kaplan, 1984, 1985): first, the so-called hypothetical spectator of film theory—that is, the psychoanalytic spectator produced through cinematic strategies of editing, suture, montage, as well as camera angles, lighting, and mis-en-scène. An "absent" spectator is constructed through cinematic mechanisms as a *theoretical position* rather than a living, warm body. The hypothetical spectator refers to processes that offer specific unconscious identifications, with their attendant emotions/meanings, to the "warm body." That "warm body" is asked to merge psychically with the abstract gaze constructed in the processes of filming and editing, and reproduced in the secondary processes of projection and exhibition. The spectator is encouraged to comply through complex mobilizing of unconscious libidinal desires via the narrative.

Second, I isolated the contemporary spectator (the "warm body" in the cinema) that I labeled perhaps misleadingly the *historical* spectator to distinguish her from the *abstract* or *hypothetical* spectator. The contemporary spectator brings to the viewing context a whole range of broad, discursive, historically produced formations, such as gender, class, race; and more specific discursive formations, such as profession, marital/familial situation; sexual orientation; political/religious beliefs, and so on. Such specific discursive formations will impact on the readiness or not of the spectator to *become* the abstract gaze she is invited to become through the filmic processes. This is the spectator that much so-called British "cultural studies" audience research has investigated.

Finally, I isolated an often forgotten spectator, namely, the different *historical spectator*—the one who watched the film at the moment of its emergence, or at any time in between. At each historical moment that a film is viewed, the construction of the historical spectator will be different because discursive formations differ: therefore the relationship to the hypothetical position, the abstract subject, will be different. Research on the historical spectator in this sense is difficult, for obvious reasons. Studying the discursive formations (the Foucaultian "episteme") of a particular period may, however, produce some generalities that one can assume apply to a broad section of spectators. Research can attempt to recreate discursive formations, at least those operating at the moment of a film's production.

Perhaps because of film theory's now notorious lack of attention to issues of racial difference (hooks, 1992, 122–26), I did not give special attention to spectatorship and race. Already alerted to this absence, I was struck by parenthetical comments about film, advertising, comics (usually relegated to footnotes) in Frantz Fanon's *Black Skin, White Masks* (1967) because the comments open up important issues about black spectatorship.[3]

Fanon's historical location and moment of writing—1950s, postcolonial Antilles—needs noting before referring to his remarks because this context partly explains the form of his concerns. The comments have relevance today because they address still-undeveloped theoretical issues. Fanon's specific colonial-postcolonial context—in which racial divisions were explicit—stimulated his comments on race and spectatorship. In an America striving to mask racial discrimination and white supremacy, such divisions are only reluctantly acknowledged.

"In the Antilles," Fanon says, the "view of the world is white because no black voice exists." He notes that "there is . . . a series of propositions that slowly and subtly—with the help of books, newspapers, schools and their texts, advertisements, films, radio—work their way into one's mind and shape one's view of the world of the group to which one belongs" (Fanon, 1967, 152) Fanon offers the first parenthetical comment in this discussion as a kind of challenge to "those who are unconvinced" about the eradication of black voice, black subjectivity. Fanon recommends that people "experiment" by attending a showing of a Tarzan film in the Antilles and in Europe. When watching *Tarzan* with and without whites in the audience, Fanon notes how when no whites are present, African audiences identify with Tarzan. When whites are present, Africans feel awkward and compelled to identify with the "savages" (152–53). Fanon notes also that when watching any American film (presumably when whites are present, although this is not clear), he is nervous, dreading the moment when "he" will appear on screen in the guise of butler, doorman, janitor, driver. Such images embarrass him because he feels a compulsion to adopt the white gaze at him—and therefore to identify with these images. Having made this identification, he feels less than the whites present in the audience.

Fanon's comments attracted my attention because they complicate theories of spectator identification with "like" on screen that film theorists have discussed in relation to white spectators by showing that cinematic identification *changes with the context of the viewing, and specifically with the racial composition of the audience.* This is not something that white theorists have discussed, as far as I know. Fanon's anecdotal comments problematize theories of spectator identification and the unconscious desire that is presumably at work along with obvious narrative positionings. As a black spectator, Fanon obviously desires to identify with—and thus to "be"— the superior white characters who fulfill the heroic roles in a film. As one would expect, he rejects identification with the ignorant and simple Hollywood "natives" that Tarzan lives amongst or the lowly, silent, marginal roles of blacks in Hollywood melodramas. While Fanon anticipates white and African-American theorists' notions regarding the fluidity of identifications—the ways that identification is produced through narrative rather than essentializing gendered or racial processes—he inserts a dimension little dealt with by white theorists, namely, that of the *disruption* of identificatory flow in specific audience contexts: for if white people are present in the audience, as noted, Fanon fears that they identify him with the black filmic "others" and that he ought to so identify himself. His normal identification processes are disrupted because of other people in the audience— because, specifically, of what he expects whites to expect of him. It is impossible for him psychically to adopt the hypothetical/psychoanalytic spectator position when whites are present because their presence brutally calls him from that suturing process by active self-consciousness of his skin color.

I was struck by the way these comments highlighted processes that female spectatorship theories had perhaps overlooked. Surely women's identification processes similarly change when they are seeing a movie only with male or with female friends. Perhaps the process takes place on a different level than it does in relation to race. In any event, Fanon suggests that identificatory processes function in relation to skin likeness only given certain audience contexts: a black person must identify with a black person only when whites are there. The racism of the images is there in either case, of course: if black viewers identify with Tarzan, they presumably deride the "Hollywood" natives, as Fanon has argued Antilleans in real life deride other black groups because of white hierarchies they have adopted. (Fanon sees the conditioned nature of such responses in real life but does not note them in relation to *Tarzan*.) White spectators' presence evidently reproduces in the black spectator the processes of needing to identify with the oppressed images of people "like" him on a superficial (skin) level.

Fanon's conception that he must identify with blacks in certain contexts is surely socially and historically produced: it arises within the particular discursive racist formations of his time and place. But clearly more research needs doing in relation to white identifications with black Hollywood characters, and indeed, even with figures like King Kong.[4] Bernard Wolfe evidently inspired some of Fanon's analyses of generalized white identification with black subjects, but neither author explicitly discusses white audience response to film figures.[5]

Fanon's comments open up questions of how he might have identified in a nonracist situation: the contradiction in his comments belies the complexity of the issues he is dealing with. His comments also deepen contemporary feminist and other spectator film theories: if race power relations were equal, presumably a white spectator would also only identify with white figures and experience prohibition in relation to black figures when blacks were present in the audience. This would conflict with feminist theories arguing that identification processes are fluid, varied, and nonessentializing. But I assume that white spectators, given their privileged power position, are freer to identify with whatever the powerful figures may be, not needing to be troubled by doubt as to whom they are supposed to identify with or by pressure from minorities not to identify with them. I assume that white spectators do not identify with Hollywood racial caricatures but do identify with strong, powerful, and admirable black figures in recent Hollywood films, such as Spike Lee's *Malcolm X.*

Some recent African-American theorists have built from Fanon's concepts as in the late 1980s and 1990s they have begun to theorize black spectatorship in new and important ways. Manthia Diawara has theorized both the hypothetical, psychoanalytic spectator (Diawara, 1991), and a resisting black male spectatorship (Diawara, 1988)—the latter in contrast to Fanon's notion that black spectators must identify with black figures, no matter what narrative position the figures occupy, at least if whites are present. Diawara's time and context of writing in part account for his ability to make different kinds of argument than those available to Fanon. Against the background of 1970s feminist and other film theories, Diawara is able to construct new theories of black male spectatorship. On the one hand, he argues that dominant cinema "situates black characters primarily for the pleasure of white spectators (male or female)" (Diawara, 1988, 71); on the other, he shows that the black spectator may have agency and the space within which to resist identification with Hollywood's negative black stereotypes. He argues that the black spectator of *Forty-Eight Hours,* for example, is preempted from identification with Eddie Murphy "because ultimately his [Murphy's] 'transgressions' are subject to the same process of disciplines and punishment" (72). While the degree to which different black spectators might respond differently to Eddie Murphy is glossed over here (and does need examination), in discussing *Birth of a Nation* Diawara notes complexities of black male and female spectatorship identifications. The complexities of hypothetical spectatorship (as against the *historical* one) are possibly in some ways easier to theorize at a historical distance than in the contemporary situation.

Later, Diawara usefully explored how cinema's suturing process and construction of a psychoanalytic spectator-position might be mobilized within an avant-garde tradition to construct a black imaginary hitherto denied in film. In analyzing Isaac Julien's *Looking for Langston,* Diawara argues that the film "invites the spectator to enter [the] black imaginary, to perform a new identity for him/herself by stepping into the void left by his/her predecessors in Blackness, and thereby to carry on the eternal search for freedom" (Diawara, 1991, 108).

Bell hooks, meanwhile, argues that African-American spectators have long resisted the images Hollywood and television propagated: "When most black people in the United States first had the opportunity to look at film and television, they did so fully aware that mass media was a system of knowledge and power reproducing and maintaining white supremacy" (hooks, 1992, 117). She sees such spectator resistance as crucial to the process of social change and liberation: "To stare at the television, or mainstream movies, to engage its images, was to engage its negation of black representation" (hooks, 1992, 117). She argues that the very production and proliferation of stereotypes became an agent for mobilizing resistance, or at least a rallying point for resistance, a means through which those "otherized" understood the enemy and its strategies. The TV or movie screen, according to hooks, provided the space of unfettered, uncontrolled gaze at white people, "black looks," as hooks calls the oppositional gaze. And it was the oppositional gaze "that responded to these looking relations by developing independent black cinema" (hooks, 1992, 117). Hooks would no doubt agree with Diawara's comment that "one of the roles of black independent cinema . . . must be to increase spectator awareness of the impossibility of an uncritical acceptance of Hollywood products" (Diawara, 1988, 76).

Hooks complements Diawara's research by focusing explicitly on black female spectatorship. Having deplored how white feminist film theory mirrored "the erasure of black womanhood that occurs in films" through eliding difference beneath the monolithic category "women" (really white women), Hooks argues that those black female spectators not duped by Hollywood "actively chose not to identify with the film's imaginary project because such identification was disabling" (hooks, 1992, 122). Once again, theory posits agency in the spectator, challenging Hollywood's knowledge/power institution.

Developing models of spectatorship as agency is crucial in the 1990s as full awareness of the oppressive mechanisms of dominant cinema as an institution in which knowledge functions as power emerge.[6] But it is also important to fully understand the processes through which such power is mobilized, and the difficulty of adopting or assuming a resisting spectator position. Adrienne Kennedy is only one of many African-American writers who has noted identification with famous white Hollywood stars.[7] The force of the hypothetical spectator position is seen in such comments. Michele Wallace, meanwhile, is reluctant "to cede the psychoanalytic framing of spectatorship" and argues that "a psychoanalytic approach to black forms of spectatorship is much needed" (Wallace, 1993, 2). Like Diawara,

Wallace is aware of different levels and kinds of spectatorship, and she
is reluctant to stop at the second, contemporary/embodied black female
spectator (the one hooks is concerned with), for whom discursive race formations have large import. It is the black female spectator's unconscious
processes that Wallace aims to explore in relation to whether on that level
race difference makes a difference.

It is significant for my project on film and history that work on the
resisting and psychoanalytic black spectator has only recently been made
possible by discursive changes in the United States. The research is part
of the same epistemic shift that is producing my own new perspectives
in this and other scholarly activities. Diawara's, hooks's, and Wallace's
important contributions emerge as part of the new black/spectator subjectivities made possible by epistemic shifts, themselves partly produced
through political processes. These historical shifts, in turn, make possible
the kinds of film analyses I now turn to.

Hollywood's own unconscious appears in its use of the psychoanalytic transference, which has historically offered a model of mechanisms
of domination that may have nothing to do with psychoanalysis outside
Hollywood! In the films discussed below, I aim to explore the intersections of history, spectatorship, race, and gender first, through a focus on
the uses Hollywood makes of psychoanalytic transference to normalize
American male race relations; second through analysis of a rare film that
uses psychoanalytic transference to *problematize* (also male) race relations
and psychoanalysis itself; finally, I show how an independent film by a
black female filmmaker problematizes and illuminates black female looking relations, while also educating audiences against uncritical acceptance
of Hollywood products. In all these I locate my own position as a white
female spectator in the course of setting up analyses, loosely, according to
the tripartite spectatorship series noted above, namely, the position of the
"hypothetical" (psychoanalytic) spectator the film constructs; that of the
contemporary spectator (the "warm body" in the cinema today); and that
of the *historical* spectator, watching a past film at the time of its making or
any time in between then and now.

HOLLYWOOD, RACE, AND TRANSFERENCE

American racism could not be denied after the experiences of GIs in
World War II. Having witnessed such racism as well as having personally

been a victim of anti-Semitism right after World War II, Stanley Kramer directed a crucial film, *Home of the Brave* (1947). Donald Spoto exemplifies a critic who has tried to recreate the discursive formation for the film's production, and select spectator-response to the film, in 1947. I thus begin with my third spectator position, that of the *historical* viewer. In 1947, according to Spoto, the film was considered "ground-breaking." *Home of the Brave* was "the first picture to deal with the nasty problem of discrimination against the black man, and, bluntly and unprettily, to detail the psychological scarring caused in both blacks and whites by hatred and prejudice" (Spoto, 1978, 44). Spoto notes that Kramer changed the original anti-Semitism in the play version to racial prejudice, presumably because, according to Spoto, anti-Semitism was by this time no longer a new Hollywood theme, and Kramer wanted to be the first to make a film about racial prejudice and stereotyping. For me, however, the series of slippages amongst differences in Hollywood films of this era—anti-Semitism, homosexuality, race—reveals how the dominant thought difference in 1947 from the perspective of a white, male center.

Spoto claims that Kramer knew the film would be controversial, so his team made it in a mere three months in near-total secrecy. He found evidence for fears of rioting at the film's opening, something that may evidence the depth of racial hatred in the country even after World War II.[8] Significant, too, is Spoto's statement that "blacks turned out in great numbers for Houston's 'separate-for-blacks' midnight showings and for seats in the segregated section of Dallas' Majestic Theatre by Day" (Spoto, 46).

I value Spoto's attempt to reconstruct some historical spectator response, and to provide evidence that the film was seen as "breakthrough" and "progressive." For me as a white contemporary spectator, however, the film's representation of Moss, the African-American, is extremely problematic. I am interested in the film's use of a psychoanalytic transference between a black male patient and a white analyst as this might unconsciously express mechanisms for domination—the knowledge/power axis institutionalized in psychoanalysis—and accompanying normalization of race relations.[9]

Surely, Kramer could not help but be part of the discourses regarding race pervasive in his historical moment. The slippages noted above are part of those discourses: the unconscious structure of a white, male-dominant norm around which congeal "differences" all made equal, the same, dominates the film. It is particularly evident in the psychoanalysis that constitutes the film's framing narrative. This analysis concerns a black soldier, Moss, being analyzed by a white army psychiatrist. The refusal of the analyst to deal honestly with issues of race, and his own form of racism, are quite clear to a contemporary spectator, but obviously something that Kramer could not see, given the pervasive discourse on difference. The psychiatrist's bullying of his black patient is partly accounted for narratively by his having little time in which to undertake a proper analysis—his patient is paralyzed but just about to be shipped home. The analyst wants to make sure that his patient, Moss, is "cured" before he leaves the base. His aim is to make Moss understand that the real reason he became paralyzed in the heat of battle was *not* that his best friend had called him "nigger" when under stress but that he felt guilty about surviving the mission while his friend died.

Before looking more closely at the process of the analysis and the way it exemplifies knowledge/power as domination, I want to comment on the first, hypothetical spectator position the film constructs. *Home of the Brave* is unusual in the plurality of positions it foregrounds and in its not establishing any very obvious hero to the film. In this sense, Kramer's progressive agenda emerges, albeit unconsciously. The camera stands back from the characters, as is evident in the pervasive use of long and medium shots, and the interest in group discussion, in which a plurality of positions is voiced.

The "hero" of the film, to the degree that he can be called one, is Moss, the African-American engineer called in to participate in an otherwise all-white dangerous war mission. But if Moss's position is the hypothetical one the spectator is asked to occupy, this poses a problem for spectators of many different discursive constructions, at least today (which I begin with). In fact, Moss poses the same problems that the passive female victim in many melodramas poses: namely, the unconscious conflict such narrative identifications produce for spectators. Unconsciously, any spectator (black or white) yearns (oedipally) for heroism or love; a brave leader or an erotic object. *Home of the Brave* has neither. The psyche is reluctant to identify with a passive, undynamic victim. The narrative tells the story from Moss's perspective—he is the narrating voice behind the flashbacks—but his position is paradoxically often as the one silenced, the one who cannot speak. In this sense, he is feminized. He stands in awe of the white psychiatrist, and his transferential position is similar to that of the female patient. His awe of the psychiatrist mimics that toward Finch, the white friend from his high school whom he refinds by coincidence on this mission. But neither position is analyzed by the psychiatrist, as would presumably happen in any actual clinical situation. The spectator, thus, is also left the choice of identification with subordination or distancing from the narrative process.

Arguably, Kramer's didactic concerns encourage such Brechtian alienation from the story in the hopes of promoting awareness of the "message" deemed progressive in 1947. The film's overriding aim is to educate audiences about discrimination—albeit that Hollywood insists on taming, domesticating, for commercial reasons, the message about discrimination.

As a contemporary spectator, I resist identifying with Moss and rather focus on the way the film moderates what might originally have been a progressive message. Since the psychoanalytic process in the film is central to its method of normalizing race relations, it warrants focus. The analyst is determined to cure Moss of his paralysis, which means, actually, to cure him of his oversensitivity to racial slurs. The paralysis, thus, is equated with such oversensitivity. To achieve this end, the psychiatrist uses every method to hand, including hypnosis. The hypnosis provides the flashbacks that become the film's main narrative. The patient on the couch recalls the scenes in which he was chosen for and engaged in the mission, undertaken in distressing heat, to survey the terrain on a Japanese-occupied island. Several scenes indicate Moss's sensitivity to the unthinking racism of most men in the group—a racism that takes obnoxious forms. Only Finch, his friend, defends him openly. The educated lieutenant is sympathetic but already overwhelmed by his responsibility for the mission. (Note, by the way, the stereotypical binary—educated equals racially tolerant; uneducated and working class equals racist.)

To a contemporary spectator now discursively positioned to recognize race, the white psychiatrist is clearly constituted by the racist codes and norms of his World War II period, which, at that time, took the form of denying that there was any real racism and finding other reasons to account for reactions to racial difference. Only once does the psychiatrist allude to the generations of slavery that have their legacies, and then it is more or less to excuse the whites who call blacks names. Nowhere does the psychiatrist appear in the least self-reflective or self-questioning. On the contrary, he is condescending, bullying, and impatient. This is no psychiatrist who would even think about any countertransference. His bullying tactics evidently succeed, and the patient walks again (because of the film's narrative needs, the tactics had to work), but the film's cosy solution represses actualities about racial relations. Moss's blackness is seen to be a handicap or difference equal to that of mate's loss of an arm. The two agree that together they can make it by setting up a restaurant. It is the typical Hollywood individualist solution — and the male bonding so common to them — eschewing all analysis of the larger contexts within which individuals grow, develop, and learn. The racism the spectator has witnessed in the course of the film is not cured by the bonding of the two men, any more than Moss was really cured by the psychoanalysis. *Home of the Brave* obviously displaces race issues functioning in the public sphere into individual psychic conflict, where they can be apparently resolved without addressing social oppressions at all.

Kramer's interest in difference continued, however. By 1962 new awareness about the nature of difference began to emerge as the country prepared for a major resistance to racial exploitation and oppression in the Civil Rights movements. With the first film surely in mind, Kramer produced *Pressure Point,* directed by Cornfield, which has a black liberal psychiatrist treating a white, working-class neo-Nazi, who is obviously racist and anti-Semitic. Interestingly, once again Kramer has changed a narrative with a Jewish protagonist to one with an African-American protagonist.[10] The film is remarkable for its deliberate linking of the psychoanalytic process — of the beliefs and ideas of both analyst and patient — to the larger social-political sphere. Fanon had claimed, as we saw, that such linkage was essential if psychoanalysis was to avoid being merely normalizing, as it is in *Home of the Brave. Pressure Point* investigates the knowledge/power axis of psychoanalysis as an institution by having the analysis take place within a state prison and, within the prison, the psychiatric unit. The institutional level of the film is overdetermined, deliberately, since in the framing story we have yet another prison psychiatric hospital in which a parallel interracial analysis is taking place.

The framing story is significantly set in the present (1962). In terms of spectatorship and history, there are three different periods whose tensions need noting: the period when most of the film is set, provided in the prolonged flashback, 1942; the period of the film's making and of the framing story within the film, 1962; and there is my own reading and research on the film roughly thirty years later, 1992. I do not think the three crucial years are arbitrary: in 1962, Kramer is motivated to make a film about a black psychiatrist and a neo-Nazi because race issues were uppermost in his mind in the context of early 1960s Civil Rights movements, and the entire new political awakening of the United States in the 1960s. The recurrence of right-wing populism, in the form now of the John Birch Society, correctly recalled the proliferation of neo-Nazi groups during World War II in America (Janson and Eismann, 1963; Herzstein, 1989). The film's replaying of the ideas and practices of such groups through the analysis of the white male patient has import for what was going on in 1962. Meanwhile, my own interest in this film—which has hardly been written about at all during the past thirty years—is, in turn, sparked by urgent 1992 awarenesses of oppressive racial and postcolonial relations in this country—new naming of relations as "white supremacist"—and by increased African-American and other ethnic activisms.

The film opens in a state psychiatric hospital in 1962, with Peter Falk storming into Poitier's office and declaiming that he can no longer work with his disturbed black patient. Falk is at the limit of his endurance: the patient refuses contact after months of sessions, and Falk cannot bear his impotence or the hatred the boy exudes towards him.[11] He demands that Poitier put one of the black analysts in the hospital on the case.

Poitier disagrees, and claims that it would be disastrous for Falk to quit now. He suggests that Falk can actually help his patient just because he is white. It is in the context of persuading Falk to continue the analysis that Poitier begins the long flashback to 1942 to the case that nearly broke him and that provides the main body of the film's narrative. The film returns to this opening framing story at the end: Poitier notes that while he lost, he did not quit the case, and Falk actually has a chance of winning. Interestingly, Falk responds by saying: "I'm getting some burnt-out cork, and going into the next session in black face," and the film ends.

The two cases are not parallel, but it is interesting that they are linked across the divide of the years: Falk is confronting black hatred in 1962, on the verge of the Civil Rights movements that will begin the slow process of integrating African-Americans into American society; Poitier confronts white hatred in 1942 in the context of a Nazi theory of deliberate genocide.

Pressure Point is important because it actually addresses the intersection of intrapsychic oedipal drama and oppressive social (political, economic) conditions. Poitier is torn between pursuing the psychoanalytic processes of cure and outrage at the political danger his patient manifests as a neo-Nazi organizer in the public sphere. Poitier has to endure, repeatedly, the racist verbal assaults of his patient.[12] The reduction of the patient's political activity to the oedipal drama is ultimately refused, even if during the process it seems that film is at times reductive, as was the story it was made from.[13] The analyst's countertransference sometimes threatens to harm the process of cure, but it is a countertransference that the contemporary spectator experiences as justified (see note 7). The patient at once complies with the therapeutic process—he hopes to be rid of his terrible nightmares and hallucinations—and indeed, he is so relieved. His telling of his child-hood deprivations and traumas, his loneliness, his hateful drunken father and sickly, incestual mother—all this frees him of his symptoms. In the course of this narrative, the patient's obscene hatred of sexual women and his sentimentality for the one "pure" (paradoxically Jewish) woman who takes any notice of him are exposed but not dwelt upon. There's a scene in which he leads a cruel, sadistic attack on a female bar woman that is nearly unbearable for me to watch, but the analyst has no time to explore it.

Despite the relief of symptoms, the patient in the film is not cured of his psychotic hatred of blacks and Jews or his determination to elimi-nate them through political work, as he is in the story. It is here that Cornfield and Kramer show their sophistication and awareness of the im-possibility of reducing the political to the psyche. Specific social, eco-nomic, and power relations in certain societies at certain times produce fascism. If psychopaths are particularly drawn to fascism, the reason for fascism is not psychopathy but complex intersecting and often contradic-tory material and symbolic forces. Poitier, playing the film psychoanalyst, has to take a moral stand and refuse the patient's release from prison, although apparently cured of his symptoms. And it is here that the bor-der between psychoanalysis and political responsibility is probed. It is precisely because Poitier refuses to ignore larger social responsibilities—because he puts such responsibilities before the immediate good of his patient (namely, leaving the prison where he is being treated)—that Poi-tier himself is forced to give up his position as psychiatrist. In the pro-cess, the limitation of the other ordinary (white) prison psychoanalysts is made clear: they do not care about or respond to Poitier's fears about the harm that his patient would do in mobilizing hate and racist violence outside prison. They focus narrowly on the immediate surface health of the patient and his apparent cure, and they are not willing to believe the black analyst about his patient's cunning duplicity. In other words, they are racist in their choice to believe the white patient over the black ana-lyst.[14] Didn't they know that psychotics like the patient in the film lack a moral sense and are thus not really amenable to cure by the psychoanalytic process? Could they not imagine how brilliant many psychotics are—brilliant enough to try to delude even them?

The film's use of psychoanalysis allows one to see the danger of such psychotics for democratic and liberal societies, without, as noted, being reductive. The links between psychosis and reactionary politics are marked. To a contemporary spectator, the film may be faulted for dealing only with the extremist form of racism, such as psychotics manifest: it must have been possible for 1962 spectators to disidentify with the white patient and his political aspirations just because of his extremism and his personal unpleasantness.

But how did white spectators in 1962 feel about identifying with the black liberal psychiatrist, whose point of view dominates the film? If my earlier thesis is correct, there should have been no problem, even then. The film assures that the spectator will identify with Poitier since this narrative, unlike *Home of the Brave,* has a black hero in a position of power and moral authority with which most spectators then and now would want to identify. I imagine that the discursive formation of 1962 and the urgent need to end discrimination provided a fitting moment for such a representation. But I am interested in what the film would have been like had it taken up Falk's 1962 case: Is the film trying to equate black hatred of whites in 1962, with white hatred of blacks in 1942, in a kind of liberal/pluralist equalizing move?

However that may be, *Pressure Point* is remarkably challenging for a Hollywood film. It raises in fact, some of the cultural and racial issues that would have interested Mignon, the heroine of Julie Dash's short film *Illusions,* made ten years before Dash's recent, highly successful *Daughters of the Dust.* Dash's film also involves a series of overlapping historical moments, since, like *Pressure Point,* it is set in 1942. This time, however, it is made in 1982 and is being read in 1992. Like Kramer's year 1962, 1982 was important for renewed political concern about racial discrimination and emerging awareness about popular culture's oppressive role in derogatory racial images.

That the film is made by an African-American woman director, is partly about Hollywood's silencing of minorities, and raises issues of spectatorship directly within the text makes it central to my project. The film both anticipates *and* illuminates black female spectatorship, not only raising interesting spectatorship issues within the text of the film itself but also those that result from 1992 spectators watching a 1982 film set in 1942 in a Hollywood studio.

Illusions produces complex cross-identifications for the 1990s spectator in its explicit 1942 narrative about a light-skinned African-American, Mignon, an executive at a fictional National Studios during World War II, who has to negotiate the sensitive issue of dubbing in a young black woman's beautiful voice (in fact, that of Ella Fitzgerald) for the absent voice of the hapless white female star. But accepted identifications are also challenged in the film's dialogue with the well-known Hollywood story *Imitation of Life* (1934, 1959), about a young black woman who wants to pass, but whose passing is forbidden by her black domestic mother. A complex set of intertextual intersections doubles or triples the already complex historical spectator situations. The 1992 spectator has to negotiate not only the gap between 1982 and now but also the gap in perceptions about race relations between 1934 and 1959 (the *Imitation of Life* dates) and those relations in 1942—in the midst of World War II.

Illusions exposes complex interconnections among white and black, women in America in 1942, 1982, and 1992, within the context of a story about Hollywood itself—one of the significant "machines" for the imaginary construction and repetition of social identities. The film supports Toni Morrison's, Hazel Carby's, and others' theses about the complex interdependencies of black and white American identities: for instance, in *Playing in the Dark,* Morrison movingly uncovers the unconscious shaping force of what she calls "American Africanism" (Morrison, 1992, 6). Morrison's empathic project of exploring "the impact of racism on those who perpetuate it . . . [of] what racial ideology does to the mind, imagination, and behavior of masters" is crucial for understanding race in America (11–12). But it also illuminates the theories of many (including Hooks, 1991) that media's impact on self-constitution can be powerful.

While in *Illusions* there is no literal transference scene, psychoanalytic mechanisms of projection, displacement, transference, and oedipality are played out, quite self-consciously, in the structure of the film and the relationships. Part of the film's project is to illuminate the transference and oedipal mechanisms at work amongst the studio personnel, and the part that race plays in them. It is no accident that Hartman and Griffin's first quotation in the opening of their useful essay on the film is from Fanon's *Black Skin, White Masks:* "I took myself far from my own presence, far indeed, and made myself an object. What else could it be for me but an amputation, an excision, a hemorrhage that splattered my whole body with black blood" (Hartman and Griffin, 1991, 362).

The quotation from Fanon's chapter "The Fact of Blackness" returns me usefully to Fanon. There he exemplifies through first-person narration the excruciating experience of being the amazed, feared, and scorned object of the white child's gaze—a gaze that mimics the hidden adult gaze behind it. The result is the black subject's fragmentation into parts, his dislocation: "I was responsible at the same time for my body, for my race, for my ancestors. I subjected myself to an objective examination, I discovered my blackness, my ethnic characteristics; and I was battered down by tomtoms, cannibalism, intellectual deficiency, fetishism, racial defects, slaveships, and above all else, above all: 'Sho' good eatin'.' " There has rarely been a more concise and graphic statement of the black subject's constitution by and through the white imaginary—an imaginary permitted blunt articulation through a white child's innocent playing out of it. Hartman and Griffin rightly see the links between this painful imaginary constitution brought home to Fanon and the Hollywood machine Dash is critiquing.

A thread running throughout *Black Skin, White Masks,* as already noted, is that of black self-alienation—a self-alienation brought about through negative white reactions to black skin and blackness generally. Fanon argues that the black man desires to be white, and that, growing up middle class in the Antilles, the black child imagines he *is* white because his education has been European and no one has troubled to break the illusion. Like Europeans, Antillean blacks may laugh at the "niggers" they find in their comic books or see ridiculously imaged in Western films, including documentaries (Fanon, 1967; 49n, 162n). Upon contact with white culture, a severe neurosis (if not psychosis) can set in with the discovery that skin color is of paramount, negative importance.

Fanon's theories are precisely the ones that pertain to the complex psychoanalytic processes Dash shows at work in studio race relations. Although made in the United States and far from Antillean culture, Julie Dash's film evidences similar insights to those of Fanon. The film deals not only with the ways in which Hollywood narratives promote black female spectator identification with white female stars but also with the bitter paradox that the image of the white blonde beauty being fetishized relies for its perfection on the dubbed-in voice of a young black singer— a reliance erased by the film's processes. As Hartman and Griffin note in

commenting on Dash's film and what it says about Hollywood's production of identity: "The problem of synchronization in the film-within-the-
film demonstrates how racial and sexual differences are produced. . . . The
projection room scene unveils the role of the cinema's technological mastery in creating identities; and, in doing so, the film foregrounds the role
of the gaze and the voice in producing subjects" (Hartman and Griffin,
1991, 365). Esther is quite simply erased by the filmic process.

The paradox of Esther's voice being dubbed into the white star's image
enables Dash to symbolize the much larger general dependency of white
women upon black women. But it also shows how Hollywood produces
a certain identity through technological manipulation, cinematic domination. The black woman is erased in the process of producing the white
woman with a sexy voice as central subject. She is obliterated, physically,
in order to bolster and enable the white woman's perfected image.

Indeed, the scene exemplifies the puzzling paradoxical difference between white and black women's oppression. White women, the scene
shows, are objects of the "male gaze," voyeuristically specularized, and
either adored or debased. They endure, one could say, *too much visibility*.
Black women, however, are oppressed by being rendered *invisible* or, at
any rate, *despecularized* in a way analagous to Mary Ann Doane's analysis of
the despecularization of women by the medical gaze in the woman's film
(Doane, 1987). Just as the white woman could not be an object of desire for
the female spectator, and so was despecularized through being rendered
sick, so the black woman, even when literally present (as in *Imitation of Life*
[1934, 1959] or in *Pinky* [1949]), is despecularized through marginalization
or through reduction to the "Mammy" figure, whose deliberately large,
dark body is made to fill the cinematic frame and to offset the svelt, fashionable white bodies.[15] As I have argued elsewhere, the "Mammy" figure
is paradoxically somewhat redeemed through her narrative function as a
sort of Winnicottian "holding" environment or "transitional object" *for
white children and even white female adults* (Kaplan, 1993), but the full dimensions of this function remain to be explored in future research.

Julie Dash broaches the dangerous terrain of complex white-black
interdependency in *Illusions*. She explores the complexities of a double-
desire through focus on the light-skinned heroine's guilt about passing
for white and refusing the "Mammy" body in her svelt figure and fashionable clothes. Mignon's guilt arises when she participates in permitting the
young black singer's stirring voice to animate the pallid, disturbed white

female star's performance on the screen. Guilt about colluding in the marginalization of the black woman leads Mignon to seek out the comforting voice of her traditional black mother—a scene with explicit reference to *Imitation of Life*—which follows the recording scene in an abrupt cut, which is not narratively anticipated. Mignon's mother's anxiety regarding Mignon's "passing" (and thereby rejecting black culture) is implied in this scene.

But *Illusions* deliberately rewrites the story of the woman who passes. Mignon resists her mother's desire for her to "keep with her own" and not strive for more. She does not give up being a studio executive or passing for white but vows to try and make stories about blacks. Her resistance parallels that possible in spectatorship: she refuses the scenarios prepared for her and takes responsibility for constructing her own scenario. The scene in which Mignon talks to her mother is structured so that she is confined in the phone box (symbolizing her psychic confinement), and the spectator does not see the mother or hear her voice. The spectator is given the conversation through Mignon's questions and responses. The refusal of the countershot suggests the powerlessness of the mother figure, or perhaps that time has passed her by. Her world is not the world of the future. Mignon seeks the comfort of the mother's voice, but it is clear that the mother can no longer help her. Mignon must take on the battles of her 1942 historical moment, which have to do with seeking to end discrimination and functioning within the realm of the Father—the Law, white patriarchy.

In this connection, Mignon's inspiration by the American Indian code, which the enemy are unable to break, is important. She tries to convince her boss, DJ, to make a film about the code resisters, which, she thinks, should interest many people. DJ rejects it immediately as not the stuff of entertainment. The patriarchal Law is clearly represented in DJ here as elsewhere (as in the scene with Esther's agent, where Mignon challenges him). Significantly, the possibly white *literal* father is absent (as was the case in *Imitation of Life*, and as is often also the case in alternate films— something I explore elsewhere). Mignon must leave the mother behind precisely so that she can battle the white Name of the Father.

In this sense, *Illusions* refuses to repeat the white constructions in *Imitation of Life* (both versions), which freeze time for African-Americans through white constructs of the all-encompassing maternal. Rendered much like Winnicott's holding environment, or his transitional object phase, the black "Mammy" function is the only viable one for the "good" black woman. Mignon's psychic individuation is made specific through her position as a woman passing for white and as a woman who takes on the Father. The film situates Mignon in time and within change: her personal change (such as leaving her mother's idea of what she should be, and challenging the Father) is linked to the social change she wants to help bring about, perhaps paradoxically through "passing," by providing positive images of blacks in Hollywood film.

I say paradoxically because of Hartmann and Griffin's critique of the passing-story, following Ralph Ellison and others, as a story meant to stimulate empathy for blacks on the part of white audiences. They criticize Dash for asking 1992 black spectators to identify with the mulatto heroine because "to do so we would have to perform the trick of mimicry employed by Esther. We should have to close our eyes and pretend it's us up there. Under what conditions can we identify with a heroine of the passing melodrama, particularly when her mulatta [*sic*] visibility depend upon the erasure or marginalization of black women?" (Hartman and Griffin, 1991, 371).

The critique is interesting in my context because the authors do not mark the historical distance between 1982 and their reading of the film in 1991 — something that might have signficance. Mignon has arguably countered black Hollywood female stereotypes in her own body language and speech: the theoretical problem is whether this is "subversion" or "co-optation, accommodation."

Secondly, the theory of spectatorship underlying Hartmann and Griffin's critique does not distinguish the three types of spectators with which I began my discussion and which might have been useful. Their critique *seems* to suggest that spectators can only identify with their absolute likeness on the screen. While some early feminist scholarship supported such a view, more recent research, as noted above, has successfully argued for spectators occupying multiple spectator-positions when participating in narrative cinema. If it were true that spectators could only literally identify with their likeness (in terms of race, gender, and class) on the screen, Hollywood's entire multinational, indeed global, popularity—a popularity whose mechanisms Fanon perhaps unintentionally revealed—would have been impossible. And equally impossible would be asking European white audiences to begin to identify with African-American and other subjectivities on the screen in an effort to decentralize white cultures. While there is a danger of a naive humanism/pluralism in a desire for cross-cultural identification, in a fuller version of this project I will explore how far the concept of transference may provide a theoretical analysis of useful, as well as negative, processes in cross-race identifications.

In the end, I do not think Hartman and Griffin mean that spectators can only identify with their "likes" on screen. Rather, their comments need linking to the concept of the resisting spectator explored earlier in the work of Manthia Diawara, bell hooks and Michele Wallace. Hartman and Griffin choose, for political reasons, to resist the spectator-position offered vis-à-vis Mignon. In this sense, they are mobilizing the spectator-agency that is their prerogative and that alternate cinema encourages.

Illusions does not follow classical Hollywood codes strictly and invites multiple identifications that may be more or less acceptable to spectators depending on prior identities. As a contemporary white spectator, I identify with both Mignon and Esther, and to a small extent with the Lieu-tenant and Mignon's (absent) mother. My relationship to the politics of gradations of black skin color is obviously complex, difficult, but differ-ent from that of Hartman and Griffin because white privilege ensures that "white" is not a color. Because of the cinematic strategies employed, it is impossible for me to identify with the white female star, her white secre-tary or assistant, or any of the other males in the film. I am shocked by the projection-room sequence and what it unveils about the hidden labor of the black woman, which "must be hidden in order that the white woman's status be maintained," and about the way in which, "like capital feeding off the body of labour, Leila's corpse is resuscitated by Esther's voice" (Hartman and Griffin, 1991, 365). Ultimately, I identify most strongly with Esther. If such cross-identifications were impossible, the point of con-structing alternate images with new, counterhegemonic, countermythic subjectivities would be important but limited to impact on any specific group's alternate images.

At this historical moment, models for exploring and negotiating ethnic conflict are needed. Subjects must learn to accept and understand differ-ence (of whatever kinds, but race and sex are key), and then negotiate such difference through democratic processes. Alternate film surely has a major role to play in producing and disseminating such models. Meanwhile, more awareness about cinema's knowledge/power axis and its dominance, as well as about spectatorship's possibilities for agency, should help miti-gate classical cinema's negative roles in furthering white supremacy.

NOTES

1. Such strategies are explicitly attacked by a brilliant counterhegemonic film-maker like Trinh T. Minh Ha, who, in attempting to avoid the oppressive mechanisms of Hollywood and classical cinema generally, exposes the violence of those mechanisms vis-à-vis peoples who are not white, male, and dominant.

2. Indeed, the historical racism inevitable in imperialism cannot help but also affect psychoanalysis. However, neither imperialism nor psychoanalysis *need* be applied in racist ways: Europeans of similar ethnic origins dominated (and still dominate, as in the case of Ireland) each other for religious, class, or territorial reasons. Arguably, psychoanalytic processes can illuminate psychic traumas in cultures other than white, Western ones (Kaplan, 1993; Kurtz, 1993). Hollywood's ideological uses of transference and psychoanalysis have little to do with actual clinical practices.

3. I do not have room here to analyze all the comments about popular culture that appear parenthetically in Fanon's volume, but these details will be taken up in future research.

4. This issue is too complex and little researched for me to discuss authoritatively here. I understand that some critics have argued that blacks identify in complex ways with the Kong figure, for instance. Despite white critics' assumptions that Kong is a negative image, standing in for how whites see/construct African Americans in a displaced, derogatory way, some African-Americans may see Kong as symbolizing a heroic revolt against white domination. Kong could challenge prohibition against miscegenation by falling in love with, and carrying off, the beautiful white blond woman. Meanwhile, Fay Wray's—the aging white female star's—1993 comments about her own fascination with Kong may give one pause: Wray is quoted as saying that "Kong has become a spiritual thing to many people, including me. . . . Although he had tremendous strength and power to destroy, some kind of instinct made him appreciate what he saw as beautiful. Just before he dies, he reaches toward me but can't quite reach. Men are gratified by something Kong represented. The movie affects males of all ages" (*New York Times,* February 28, 1993, 13). Here the white blonde female expresses her also prohibited desire for blackness, but in so doing condescendingly humanizes Kong by seeing something tender in him. Doesn't she repeat stereotypes of the Uncle Tom or the strong but kindly "savage"?

5. Fanon quotes Bernard Wolfe, who noted that in the United States in particular the white man's admiration "corresponds to a certain identification of the white man with the black. . . . There is a quest for the Negro, the Negro is in demand . . . but only if he is made palatable in a certain way" (Fanon, 1967, 174–76). Fanon has interesting, if problematic, things to say about the black man as the repository for white aggression, psychoanalytically, especially in relation to white women's fear/desire to be raped by a Negro. But this is too complex a matter to discuss here.

6. Jacqueline Bobo's important research into how studios and Hollywood film producers misunderstood, underestimated, and in general show complete ignorance about black audiences throws crucial light on some of these issues. Of particular interest is her study of the specific case of *The Color Purple* and how the dominant studio miscalculated black audiences.

7. For instance, in *People Who Led to My Plays* (New York, 1987) in a section titled "Elizabeth Taylor," Kennedy writes: "We saw Elizabeth Taylor in *A Place in the Sun*. We all wanted a formal dress like the one she wore when she danced with Montgomery Clift. "He loved her so much," I'd think, "he murdered" (71). In *Funnyhouse of a Negro,* Kennedy uses a central scene with Betty Davis from Irving Rapper's 1942 film *Now Voyager* as a theme running throughout the play having to do with ideal love.

8. However, Spoto remains vague about exactly who it was thought might riot against the film or what exactly about the film was so provocative in 1949. Was merely the idea of a sympathetic African American figure so threatening to whites?

9. It is surely significant that, to my knowledge, there is no film whose narrative includes a prolonged psychoanalysis, including transference phenomena, with a black woman as either analyst or patient. Contemporary films, like *She's Gotta Have It* (Lee, 1986) include brief scenes with a black female therapist talking to the African American heroine, but in general black women as patients and analysts are few and far between in Hollywood. Why this is so needs in-depth research, which I hope to undertake in the future. Obviously, the phenomenon is linked to larger issues to do with the erasure of black women in dominant culture and the painfully limited roles accorded them in dominant fictions, even when better roles were being developed for black males. Hansberry's *A Raisin in the Sun* was a landmark for black female roles (hooks, 1990) but did not immediately produce general change. Possibly, Hollywood, like dominant culture, unconsciously saw black males as more threatening than black females and therefore more in need of normalizing/domesticating through transference processes and metaphors. Perhaps the absence has to do with culture not according black women psychic interiors, depth? Much still needs to be uncovered here.

10. Robert Lindner's 1954 story "Destiny's Tot" has a Jewish psychiatrist as narrator. While the opening dialogue between patient and Poitier follows Lindner's text closely, as do details of the patient's oedipal traumas, the story has no framing narrative like that in the film. Most important, as will be clear later, Kramer alters the ending in ways crucial to my argument.

11. The dialogue here runs roughly as follows: *Falk:* "I've been treating the boy for seven and a half months. I keep running up against a wall. Time and again I bring him to the point of contact, and I run into his hate: he hates me." *Poitier:* "That's his problem." *Falk:* "Look, he's 13 years old, his mother was a prostitute; his father was killed by one of the white men. . . . You have several Negro psychia-

trists here. Why don't you put one of them on the case?" *Poitier:* "I thought about putting one of the Negro psychiatrists on the case. They are good, but not as good as you." *Falk:* "Then I'm washed up: I quit." *Poitier:* "I know how you feel. I had a case like that 20 years ago. A 29-year-old caucasian, on 3 years for sedition. I had 40 or 50 cases at the time, but I remember this one as if it were yesterday."

The flashback begins with one patient leaving Poitier's prison office and Bobby Darin, the neo-Nazi, being brought in. The camera catches a picture of Roosevelt on Poitier's wall. Darin bursts out laughing when he comes in and sees Poitier. Poitier ignores this for a while, then says: "You've been saying strange things. Do you really believe those things?" *Darin:* "Of course I do. But I don't care what you think." *Poitier:* "Why?" *Darin:* "Because you're a Negro. Look, ask your questions and let me get out of here." *Poitier:* "You can go at any time." (Darin moves to the door) "But, before you go, tell me what have you got against us Negroes?" *Darin* (leaning over Poitier's desk): "What have you got against us whites? Now that the Jews have put that cripple (pointing to picture of Roosevelt) in the White House, you guys think you've got it made." *Poitier:* "It would only take a couple of Jew psychiatrists to certify you insane!" *Darin:* "You're just trying to needle me." *Poitier:* "I'm just trying to get to know you. Do you really feel what you say? Do you believe your politics? How do you expect to win?" *Darin:* "We've had a couple of predictable setbacks. Hitler had his. He wrote *Mein Kampf* in prison."

Poitier's voice-over from 1962 (still in the meeting with Falk) takes over the narrative at this point with reflections on his performance as analyst in this intake interview, and fully aware of his countertransference: "I didn't feel I had been objective. I was disappointed that he had been confined for a short time, since all that he stood for alienated me. I could be objective with the most hardened criminals, who had murdered, but this paranoid psychotic could be a force for evil with the other prisoners. I requested that he be isolated to prevent him from spreading his ideas." At this point, the camera focuses in on Darin having hallucinations and nightmares in his isolated cell—dream and fantasy images which will be repeated in the analysis and used to relieve the prisoner of his psychic trauma; this is not, however, a process that cures him of his hateful public, paranoid political stance.

I have spent so long on this initial scene because it provides the flavor of following dialogues between analyst and patient. It shows Poitier to be a self-reflective analyst, who, even at the time, as noted, was aware of the intense countertransference with this patient. The dialogue also shows the evil canniness of the patient, who precisely knows how to needle Poitier. Later on, I will note just one more important scene where Poitier's countertransference perhaps prevents him from getting through to the patient, although, by the end, it's clear that Darin's psychopathic structure is beyond the psychoanalytic "cure."

12. At one point Poitier tries to coax Darin into letting him help him. Darin says, scornfully, "That's like the kettle calling the pot black. Whoever heard of a

black psychiatrist? Don't you people have enough troubles? You must be a masochist. Psychiatry is expensive. Your people can't afford it. This isn't the place for you, trying to be white, being doctors, lawyers. Why don't you go back to Africa?" A bit later on, he notes that Negroes aren't inferior in Africa although they are in America. Poitier keeps on with the analysis, and asks Darin if he knew any Negroes or Jews when he was a child, and then if he had many friends at all. Darin begins to talk about his childhood and youth, and when describing a particularly hard time as a construction worker, he says it was work "not fit for white men." He pauses, looks at Poitier, and says: "Sorry; what I meant to say was . . ." Poitier keeps looking down and does not respond. It is here that a possible link to the patient might have taken place: Darin gets uncomfortable and says: "Look, can't you appreciate the fact that I apologized?" But Poitier really is offended, as is clear when he says, defensively: "You think I'm hypersensitive about my color. You are also thinking you can hurt me by such comments. But I'm a doctor. Continue on." After this, Poitier, in a manner not unlike that in which Falk came to him, goes to his (white) supervisor and asks to be taken off the case. He admits that he cannot take the patient's needling. The white doctor notes that of course such needling is one of the patient's symptoms. He tells Poitier that he has surpassed his expectations since he came to the hospital, and follows this with: "Don't tell me you're going to let me down just because you're a Negro."

13. Significantly, the Lindner short story referred to above on which the film script relies, at times quite closely, does end up reducing the patient's fascism to his terrible oedipal traumas. "In Anton's case," the psychiatrist narrator in the story says, "The adjustment he had made through Fascism was destroyed when he came to prison. Under conditions of confinement there, the old conflicts were mobilized; symptoms that had been held in abeyance overwhelmed him. The festering evil, hidden beneath the pretense of fascist faith, showed through, proving his faith to be shallow and false." When treatment terminated, the narrator continues, "His symptoms had disappeared and his personality was altered." The psychiatrist later learns that the patient died in battle against the Nazis (Lindner, 1954, 154–55).

14. Fanon's observations about the plight of "the Negro teacher, the Negro doctor" seem apt here: "I knew, for instance, that if the physician made a mistake it would be the end of him and of all those who came after him. What could one expect, after all, from a Negro physician? As long as everything went well, he was praised to the skies, but look out, no nonsense, under any conditions! The black physician can never be sure how close he is to disgrace" (Fanon, 1967, 117). The 1950s Hollywood film, also starring Poitier as an intern, *No Way Out,* makes similar points. In that film Fanon's comment that "brittle as I was becoming, I shivered at the slightest pretext" fits even more firmly than in the case of *Pressure Point,* where the physician is remarkably patient and tolerant, given the violence of the attacks from the patient.

15. Donald Bogle found evidence that Stahl and his producers insisted that Louise Beavers in the 1934 version of *Imitation of Life* maintain her original weight. Beavers usually lost weight in making a film!

WORKS CITED

Abel, Elizabeth. "Black Writing, White Reading: Race and the Politics of Feminist Interpretation." *Critical Inquiry* 19 (1993): 470–98.

Anderson, Benedict R. *Imagined Communities: Reflections on the Origin and Spread of Nationalism.* London, 1983.

Baudry, Jean. "Ideological Effects of the Basic Cinematographic Apparatus," *Film Quarterly* 28, no. 2 (1974/75): 39–47.

Bobo, Jacqueline. "'The Subject Is Money': Reconsidering the Black Film Audience as a Theoretical Paradigm." In Valerie Smith, ed., *Black Literature Forum,* Summer 1991, 421–32.

Bogle, Donald. *Toms, Coons, Mulattoes, Mammies and Bucks: An Interpretive History of Blacks in American Film.* New exp. ed. New York, 1989.

Carby, Hazel. *Reconstructing Womanhood.* New York, 1987.

Cripps, Thomas. *Black Film as Genre.* Bloomington, 1978.

Manthia Diawara. "Black Spectatorship: Problems of Identification and Resistance." *Screen* 29, no. 4 (1988): 66–76.

————, ed. *Wide Angle: Black Cinema* 13, nos. 3 & 4 (1991).

————. "The Absent One: The Avant-Garde and the Black Imaginary in *Looking for Langston.*" *Wide Angle: Black Cinema* 13, nos. 3 & 4 (1991): 96–109.

————, ed. *Black American Cinema.* New York, 1993.

Doane, Mary Ann. "The Dark Continent: Epistemologies of Racial and Sexual Difference in Psychoanalysis and the Cinema." In *Femmes Fatales.* New York, 1991.

Fanon, Frantz. *Black Skins, White Masks.* Tr. Charles Lam Markmann. New York, 1967.

Freud, Sigmund. *Civilization and Its Discontents.* Tr. and ed. James Strachey. New York, 1961.

————. *Totem and Taboo: Some Points of Agreement between the Mental Lives of Savages and Neurotics.* Tr. James Strachey. New York, 1950.

————. *Moses and Monotheism.* Tr. Katherine Jones. New York, 1955.

Gaines, Jane. "White Privilege and Looking Relations: Race and Gender in Feminist Film Theory," *Screen* 29, no. 4 (1988): 12–27.

Gilman, Sander. *Difference and Pathology: Stereotypes of Sexuality, Race, and Madness.* Ithaca, 1985.

Hall, Stuart. "New Ethnicities." *ICA Documents* (1978): 27–30.

Haraway, Donna. "Teddy Bear Patriarchy: Taxidermy in the Garden of Eden, New

York City, 1908–55." In Haraway, *Primate Visions: Gender, Race and Nature in the World of Modern Science.* New York, 1989.

Hartman, S. V., and Farah Jasmine Griffin. "Are You as Colored as That Negro?: The Politics of Being Seen in Julie Dash's *Illusions.*" *Black American Literature Forum* (1991): 361–73.

Heath, Stephen. *Questions of Cinema.* Bloomington, 1981.

Herztein, Robert Edwin. *Roosevelt and Hitler: Prelude to War.* New York, 1989.

Hooks, bell. *Yearning: Race, Gender, and Cultural Politics.* Boston, 1990.

———. *Black Looks: Race and Representation.* Boston, 1992.

Janson, Donald, and Bernard Eismann. *The Far Right.* New York, 1963.

Kaplan, E. Ann. "Dialogue" (*Stella Dallas* debates). *Cinema Journal* 34, no. 2 (1985): 40–43.

———. "Dialogue" (continued). *Cinema Journal* 25, no. 1 (1985): 52–54.

———. *Motherhood and Representation: The Mother in Popular Culture and Melodrama.* London, 1992.

———. "Re-Visioning White Feminist Film Theory: Black Maternality in Hollywood and Alternate Film." Seminar Paper, Humanities Research Institute, UC Irvine, January 1993.

———. "The Couch-Affair: Gender and Race in the Hollywood Transference." *American Imago* (Winter 1993): 481–514.

Kovel, Joel. *White Racism: A Psychohistory.* 2d ed. New York, 1984.

Lindner, Robert. *The Fifty-Minute Hour: A Collection of True Psychoanalytic Tales.* New York, 1954.

———. *Prescription for Rebellion.* New York, 1952.

Mannoni, Octave. *Prospero and Caliban: The Psychology of Colonization.* Tr. Pamela Powesland. Rev. ed. Intro. Maurice Bloch. New York, 1991.

McCulloch, Jock. *Black Soul White Artifact: Fannon's Clinical Psychology and Social Theory.* Cambridge, 1983.

Metz, Christian. *Langage et Cinema.* Paris: Larousse, 1971; tr. as *Language and Cinema.* The Hague, 1974.

———. "The Imaginary Signifier," *Screen* 16, no. 2 (1975): 14–76.

Morrison, Toni. *Playing in the Dark: Whiteness and the Literary Imagination.* Cambridge, Mass, 1992.

Poussaint, Alvin F. *Why Blacks Kill Blacks.* New York, 1972.

Pratt, Mary Louise. *Travellers: Imperial Eyes.* New York, 1992.

Shohat, Ella. "Ethnicities-in-Relation: Toward a Multicultural Reading of American Cinema." In *Unspeakable Images,* ed. Lester Friedman. Urbana/Champaign, 1990.

———. "Imaging Terra Incognita: The Disciplinary Gaze of Empire." *Public Culture* 3.2 (1991): 41–70.

Simpson, Donald. "Black Images in Film: The 1940s to the Early 1960s." *Black Scholar* 21, no. 2 (1991): 20–29.

Smith, Valerie, Camille Billops, and Ada Griffin, eds. *Black American Literature Forum,* Summer 1991.

———. "Introduction." *Black American Literature Forum* 13 (1991): 217–19.

———. "Black Feminist Theory." In Cherly A. Wall, ed., *Changing Our Own Words: Essays on Criticism, Theory, and Writing by Black Women.* New Brunswick, N.J., 1989.

Spillers, Hortense J. "Mama's Baby, Papa's Maybe: An American Grammar Book." *Diacritics* 17, no. 2 (1987): 65–81.

Spoto, Donald. *Stanley Kramer Filmmaker.* Hollywood, 1978.

Stam, Robert, and Louise Spence. "Colonialism, Racism and Representation." *Screen* 24, no. 2 (1983): 2–20.

Taylor, Clyde. "The Re-Birth of the Aesthetic in Cinema." *Wide Angle: Black Cinema* 13, no. 3 (1991): 12–31.

Trinh T. Minh Ha. *Woman, Native, Other. Writing Postcoloniality and Feminism.* New York, 1989.

———. *When the Moon Waxes Red: Representation, Gender, and Cultural Politics.* New York, 1991.

Wallace, Michele. *Invisibility Blues: From Pop to Theory.* London, 1990.

———. "Multiculturalism and Oppositionality." *Afterimage,* October 1991, 6–9.

———. "Race, Gender and Psychoanalysis in 40s Film: *Lost Boundaries, Home of the Brave,* and *The Quiet One.*" In Manthia Diawara, ed. *Black American Cinema.* New York, 1993.

———. "Black Female Spectatorship." Unpublished, 1993.

HISTORY AND MUSIC

Leo Treitler

I WILL HAVE two main topics: (1) thinking about music historically and (2) the relations between history and the composition and performance of music. Both topics entail the effort to work out something about the tricky relationship between past and present in our understanding and in the way things happen.

Thinking about music historically is a task that we are currently concerned with in the field of musicology as we try to wrestle ourselves free of some historiographical dogmas by which the field has been constrained since its beginnings early in this century. A principal condition of that task, from which perhaps all the other aspects follow, will be the *presence* of music in the historian's consciousness. For the central premise of historical and even of critical studies in music has been the *exclusion* of music from the historian's consciousness. Music has been out there, and bringing it in will mean a reversal of styles of knowing and telling, from an epistemology based on the distance of the knower from the known to one based on the interaction of the two. That's asking a lot, and it brings up the question encased in a famous punch line: "What you mean, 'we . . .'?" I shall want to say something about who is "we," about why it's asking a lot—a question that will lead me to some reflections about the conditions of knowing in our culture—and about factors in the visible field of musical studies that can help to move us toward such a reversal.

I shall begin at the end of this agenda and address one of the questions that our host, Michael Roth, has put to me in a very good list, a question that I must address in order to identify myself and my field to you: "Can we translate some of the critical styles we use with texts for use with scores?" That is, can we expect help from the theory and metatheory of literary criticism?

Musicology has always been a parasitic discipline of sorts, dependent from the beginning on art history for its historiographic paradigms and on literary studies for its paleographic and philological principles. That is ironic, considering how much the other arts have aspired to be music, or claimed to be music, throughout history. Our borrowing from other disciplines certainly helped to get us going, but it has tended to keep musicology the least reflective of the three fields, the most resistant to theory. I can illustrate quickly with a problem in medieval studies, one that became chronic for the entire field because of the propaedeutic role that medieval studies have played in the development of musicology. From the beginning musicologists have approached medieval texts with principles of text criticism and stemmatics that were appropriated whole cloth from classical philology. But we have yet to conduct a serious discussion about how the generation of a musical text in a time when music still circulated in an oral tradition might have been like the generation of a canonical literary text with a written tradition of many centuries behind it. The products of this graft are still highly questionable.

We have not yet aired the question, "What is a text?" in relation to composition, transmission, notation, and performance. Following our parasitic habits, we could again borrow: from the domain of Stanley Fish, in one direction, or that of Nelson Goodman, in another. I hope that we will not, because their formulations have not been informed by an awareness of the problematics of music. If we were to do so we would again be making a short circuit: leaping to take on a ready-made methodology that has not been grounded in musical experience and in reflection on the nature of the material and the problems that we have to deal with. That is my general answer to Professor Roth's question.

On the whole it is a little difficult for me to locate myself in the vocabulary of this conference as it has been set out; I think it would be for any musicologist. In a certain sense that I shall shortly illustrate, the synchronic is the dimension in which music has been almost exclusively viewed in musical scholarship, but structuralism and functionalism are words that will hardly be found in our literature (although you *will* find a book by Arnold Schoenberg with the title *The Structural Functions of Harmony*).[1] Musicology has not enjoyed deconstructionism's playfulness or suffered its destructiveness. Anglophone musicologists, at least, have not seriously questioned the significance or worth of historical knowing, and so no one in the field has yet spoken of a new historicism. But I shall propose in the final section of this paper that we regard a major recent development in musical study and practice in just such a sense. (In Germany the story is somewhat different; doubts were raised in the sixties, the field grew a sociological wing, and the rest sailed on down, or up, the mainstream of history. That has always been characteristic of this very conservative field: it casts off deviant limbs, or they separate off on their own. In this country we have a Society for Ethnomusicology and another for Music Theory, both representing subdisciplines that can absorb scholars with structuralist leanings.)

That provides a short answer to another of Professor Roth's questions: Is historical thinking for the musicologist more akin to that of the anthropologist or the art historian? The short answer is that musicologists who think like anthropologists generally function as ethnomusicologists. Historical musicology has traditionally been conducted on the model of art history. But this question is like being asked to triangulate three moving images; I see all three disciplines as being in some sort of dance together in which each approaches the others. But it isn't possible to tell whether they will meet.

If I am catching the drifts of change in anthropology aright, there are similar currents in musicology: the tendency of some younger scholars to abandon their distant and omniscient stance vis-à-vis their objects and to take their experience of music as a point of departure for historical knowing; and to recognize that it is representations of their objects that they are writing, not reports on them. What is entailed is a gamble on letting the scholar's self back into the game. I say this with all due caution, for it would be an exaggeration for me to characterize the present state of musicology in this way. And there is the grumbling of disapproval to be heard from among the guardians of the profession (most recently the president of the American Musicology Society, worrying ex cathedra about the "reliance on ephemeral and subjective verbal formulations to describe musical contents").[2]

As for art history, I've already said that we borrowed our first historiographical paradigms from that discipline. But the "revisionism" that I hear about there, under the dual influences of Marxism on one side, and feminism on the other, has no parallel in Anglophone musicology.

I am going to take the liberty of quoting myself as another way of trying to circle around this question—from a contribution to a publication on *Musicology in the 80's* that was published in 1982. We need to depart freely and imaginatively from traditional causal and evolutionary models of historical discourse toward "a hermeneutic sense, in which [music] is viewed as a meaningful item within a wider context of practices, conventions, assumptions, transmissions, receptions, social relations—in short, a musical culture, which serves to endow its constituent aspects with meaning while attaining its own meaning from the combination of its constituents."[3] I would think that such an attitude constitutes an accommodation with recent thought in both of those other fields.

Those of us who work with medieval sources—and with an open mind —understand that our interests provoke some aspects of a deconstructionist stance and that the questions that are raised by our sources about textuality probably ought to be raised about music on a much broader front. Whether that will happen remains to be seen. But on the whole these winds have mainly blown over the heads of musicologists, the old historicism has not blown away, and there is no talk of a new historicism. So the sense of crisis that Professor Roth evokes in his letter is not in the present experience of my field. But you will understand that I do not say this in the sense of "I'm all right, Jack." I say it, rather, with something of the bewilderment of an Eastern European immigrant arriving for the first time in New York City.

But now let me put out another instance of the way that a problem is focused from inside musical studies, provoking an approach that comes to look like a literary-critical style. Here is the score of a very familiar little piece by Chopin (fig. 1). Not long ago the president of the Society for Music Theory gave a public account of this piece by way of an analytical notation that has become the predominant mode of analysis in the United States for music from Bach to Brahms.[4] It is a leading paradigm in the field of music theory. As its main characteristic it aims to display the "essential" structure of the piece as a stepwise descent in the melody through the degrees of the lower segment of the scale of A major to A, the tonic, in conjunction with a descent in the bass from the "dominant" tone E to the tonic (see fig. 2). All surface details of the piece are interpreted as elaborations of that structure and are subordinated to it. The advantage that is claimed for such analyses is that they demonstrate the coherence and organic unity of the work by virtue of the very fact that they can present a synoptic view of it. That view is sometimes compared to

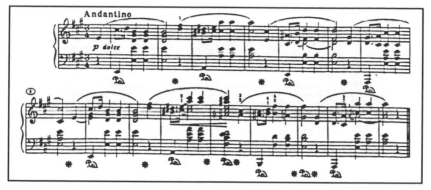

Fig. 1 Chopin Prelude, Op. 28, No. 7.

linear perspective. It is no small part of the affirmed value of this type of analysis that it exemplifies a universal principle of the musical language of the period from Bach to Brahms, namely, that all of it can be reduced to just such coordinated soprano-bass descents to the tonic of whatever key a piece may be in and that all details of such music result from transformations, projections, elaborations at successive levels of a resulting hierarchical structure. The claimed value of this kind of analysis, then, is in its capacity to produce generalized knowledge in the historical and theoretical domains, knowledge can therefore be regarded as objective. But it can serve the historical domain only in a restricted sense, as we shall see.

The conception of unity and coherence behind this method can be expressed something like this. The work of the artist is an instantaneous creative act, and its product cannot but be unified by the single impulse that informs every cell of it. That informs the work concept. A work is conceived as a thing, not an event or a process. Things can be represented as structures, and in representing the structure we represent the thing. The musical thing, or work, can be represented by a score or by an analytical notation that amounts to a reduction of the score to its essential structure. We have come by this conception in two historical stages: a shift of emphasis in the conception of what music is, from process to structure, that we can recognize in the late Middle Ages;[5] and the conception of work as architectonic structure, that we have had only since the late nineteenth century. You will recognize the structuralist center in this whole notion, but it is a structuralism that grew out of the history of musical thought, independently of Saussure and Lévi-Strauss. It is significant that this ana-

Fig. 2.

lytical methodology has been highly developed for representing pitch-structures, which have a spatiality about them that can be represented synchronically, whereas it has concerned itself but little with patterns of durations, that is, the temporal dimension. The performance act (I mean that in the sense of speech act) has hardly been a factor in the analysis or in the work concept at all. And the qualities of sound have been equally disregarded, except insofar as details of instrumentation help to articulate pitch structures.

Now the respondent to Berry's talk in which this account of Chopin's Prelude was presented raised a disruptive question: If the sketch is supposed to show the essential structure of the piece, why does it not include the F♯ in mm. 13 and 14? For she claimed that this note is an essential element in the expressive program of the piece, as indeed it is. In itself it creates, with the bass, an exposed and unresolved dissonance. And in context it is involved in the gathering extravagance of the sweep of the melody in the second half that determines the character of the piece as a whole. It is that character that is an entrance to the understanding of the piece as an item that participates in and contributes to the culture of Romanticism. The formalist analysis fails to provide such an opening, and its mode of approach has in fact been an obstacle to historical understanding in musical studies altogether.

The orthodox response to the respondent's question would be, "Your question shows that you don't understand the nature of the analysis, which is meant to reveal the structure against which the F♯, or any other detail, becomes expressive." But the counterresponse would be, "But you didn't say so, in fact you wouldn't be caught dead talking about the expressive or the beautiful in music." (Perhaps you have caught that this exchange could be translated into a colloquy about a poem: someone gives a syntactical analysis of its sentences and represents that as an analysis of the poem. Someone else says, "You haven't accounted for its expressiveness." The response is, "I have shown you the structure or the system against whose background the poem can be expressive," and so on. The musical analysis I showed you has the status of the syntactical analysis that is presented as an account of the poem. And it is quite representative.) My belief is that we have no access to music as a historical item, we have no possibility of historical knowledge of music, unless we take account of its beauty, its expressiveness, its power to move people, in its time, in the present, and in between.

But expressiveness functions in a historical context of meaning. Beethoven's Overture to Goethe's *Egmont,* to cite another familiar piece, begins with a dark and ponderous motif that sets the atmosphere for the play's beginning (fig. 3). The character speaks to us immediately. But there is something more precise about its meaning. In the rhythm of this motif it makes reference to a Spanish dance genre called sarabande, but you will never hear the sarabande movement of a Bach suite, say, presented in such somber colors. "Ah," we think, "the Spanish Oppressors." But we must incorporate in our understanding that in the context of Beethoven's culture the sarabande would have been identified as an archaism, like the religiosity of the sudden reversion to something like a Palestrina style in the midst of the reveries in the slow movement of Beethoven's Ninth Symphony. These momentary archaisms achieved through the transformation of a conventional sign were relished as such, and that itself is a Romantic phenomenon.

With this brief excursion into the historical-critical interpretation of music behind us, we can appreciate how complex must be any answer to the central question that Professor Roth has asked: "What is the status of the object we are investigating when we do music history? Is it a past performance, or a text presented to us in notation or in contemporary performance?"

It is natural for someone trying to take a comparative view of the intersection of history with the arts to ask this question. But in fact during nearly the entire life of historical studies in music (that is, since the turn of this century) it is the autonomous work that has been the object of study, conceptualized as a structure that is inferable from a score.[6] The

Fig. 3.

music-historical paradigm has been a blend of style history—appropriated from art history—with the attitude of the New Criticism toward the literary work.

It is within the confines of this paradigm that the mode of analysis that I showed before has been functional. And it is in the security of it that musicology was able to evade questions that have been occupying students of the history of art and literature about the presentness and pastness of its objects, and questions unique to music about the relations among works, scores, the notational medium, and performances. But these questions have lately been forcing themselves upon us from within by investigations and activities that begin as perfectly normal historical problems. Questions about the presentness and pastness of our objects are raised in a new way by the Historical Performance movement, about which I have already promised to speak in the last section. Questions about works, scores, notation, and performance have become newly activated through our awareness that the medieval music culture, in which we locate the roots of our Western tradition, lacked all the conditions that have been for us the premises for the possibility of a history of music: a transmission founded on the written score, a work concept, the idea of musical structure, the idea that the musical work is autonomous. Recognizing that these are not universals, we are, in effect, challenged to understand why we have thought them to be. And that engages us in an evaluation of their meaning for all of the history of learned music in the West. Once the questions about textuality and the work have planted themselves on medieval soil, they spread to the present.

In reverse motion to such a flow of questions and conceptions from the past to the present is the opposite tendency to let the conceptions we hold in the present spread to the past. (Walter Ong put this problem in a nutshell by supposing that one would characterize a horse as a wheelless carriage.) The resolution of that conflict is not always a simple matter. We can issue caveats about the old habits of historians of thinking from their present into the past, especially about the tendency toward teleological thinking with which that habit is associated. For example the current tendency to think of a score as a blueprint for a performance, when projected upon scores from the ninth through the sixteenth centuries, produces the evaluation of the notation of those scores as defective, not yet fully developed. But for musicians in those centuries their scores were perfectly adequate given the reliance on unwritten traditions, except at certain critical moments that produced change in notational principles. We are in the present, and the practices we understand best are present practices. That understanding can be taken as an entry into the past. I am thinking here of everything that is brought to mind by Malraux's remark that it isn't research that has taught us to understand El Greco, it is modern art; and

Eliot's notion that what happens with the composition of a new poem happens to all the poems composed before. That is something of what I mean about the trickiness of the past-present relation. In historical understanding, past and present are like the two sides of a tennis court. The object does not move once and for all from one side to the other, it is volleyed back and forth. If it stops for a time in one court, it is eventually picked up and sent back to the other—unless it is lost, as sometimes happens (we have lost the music of ancient Greece).

The questions about the status of the object of study—especially with respect to scores and works—could have taken shape in connection with one of the most heavily cultivated fields in musicology today, the study of the sketches of composers; but they have not, and it is instructive to consider why.

When it is said, for example, that a certain leaf contains a "sketch for the second movement" of Beethoven's String Quartet opus 134 in C♯ minor, it is worth considering what is meant by that, and what is the status of the notational markings on that page. The statement is made with the full score of that movement as a backdrop, although of course there was not yet any such thing as "the second movement of Beethoven's String Quartet" and so on when that sketch was being produced.

This tendency reflects a predisposition to teleological thinking, but it reflects, too, the history of sketch studies. They were undertaken initially in the nineteenth century, under the dominion of an aesthetic idea—about the nature of creativity and genius. This whole type of investigation—which now counts as a major industry in musicology and is one of the main places to which students turn in their search for dissertation topics—was focused on the sketches of Beethoven, which were famous for the way they sometimes begin with pedestrian ideas and then suddenly take a radical leap and all at once show the essential idea of the final version. An easily accessible case is the beginning of the fourth Piano Concerto (fig. 4). The opening statement by the solo piano in the final version is shown at *a*. Beethoven's sketch for the orchestral response is shown at *b*. It is nearly identical to the piano's statement, the main difference being the full close on the tonic, in contrast with the piano's inconclusive pause on the dominant. This kind of binary phrase structure is generally referred to as an antecedent-consequent pair. The final version of the orchestral response is shown at *c*. It entails a wholly different rhetoric, an insistence on reformulating the opening in its own way—at once a different key, a more ex-

Fig. 4.

tended, more expressive, *cantabile* phrase. That sets up a dramatic confrontation between the two characters that is a commanding idea of the piece.

Under the aesthetic ideas of the nineteenth century, and as I remember explaining it myself as a young Beethoven enthusiast, that leap is energized by the spark of genius. Beethoven's sketches exemplified the theory of creativity that entails as its central idea the spontaneity and instantaneousness of the creative act and attributes to that characteristic the unity of the work—the theory presented, among others, by Croce circa 1900.[7] The topic itself is still generally known by the phrase "compositional process," a phrase that legitimates the enormous research energies that have been invested in the study of the sketches and drafts of composers.

A different sort of explanation of such changes might follow E. H. Gombrich's idea, in *Art and Illusion*, of "making and matching."[8] The binary, symmetrical, balanced, open-closed phrase structure of the first version is one of the transmitted schemata or norms of the style. The fact that Beethoven wrote it down initially does not necessarily mean that he actually contemplated at that moment that the piece would go that way, any more than does the fact that an artist begins the drawing of a head by making an egg-shaped figure mean that he or she actually contemplated at that stage that the head would look like an egg.

The human mind forms images—in words, music, visual figures—that are more or less evanescent. The artist, writer, composer clutches at them, trying to catch them before they vanish, using words, phrases, figures that are most readily at hand, then comparing what has been put down with the mental image, adjusting what does not seem right, thus changing the mental image itself, and so a process of mutual accommodation takes place and the sketch becomes more like a work. In the course of such a process the graphic text evolves, not only through different states but through different statuses.

Taking the musical notation of the sketch "literally" reveals a habitual belief in the tight, compliant, one-on-one relationship between the notation and something that is denoted. That conception belongs to a powerful complex of concepts that controls musical studies on a broad front: the composer, through the creative process, producing closed, fixed works that display the attributes of organic unity and originality by virtue of their origin in the creative impulse and that are uniquely represented by scores which are written in a notation that unambiguously denotes the essential details of the work so that performers can read them to make performances that are compliant with them. The score, in that conception, is the blueprint for the performance and the touchstone for the work, but what the work is, is not clear.

From this brief paragraph can be deduced virtually all of the projects that have occupied musicologists and the conceptions by which they are controlled. The example as a whole exhibits the historicity of such concepts as a topic that demands a place in music-historical studies.

I turn now to the relationship between history and the composition of music in the present, which I would like to introduce with two metaphors.

First: there is a composition by John Cage called *Imaginary Landscapes #4* for twelve radios. Two performers sit at each radio, one controlling the volume, the other the station dial. The score is literally a blueprint for performance. There are bar lines and tempo markings. Each performer has specific instructions concerning what to do at each moment with the knob (or buttons) he or she controls — louder or softer, higher or lower Kilohertz. The conductor is admonished to be very strict. There is a story in circulation about a performance in Town Hall, New York City, in which one of the radios caught strains of Mendelssohn's Violin Concerto and someone in the audience yelled, "Leave it on."

Nowadays you can turn on the radio and hear what sounds like a Beethoven String Quartet, but you know the quartets and you know it isn't one. The announcer tells you that you have just heard a quartet by George Rochberg, once a serialist composer. Another time you might hear what you think is a waltz by Johann Strauss, but the announcer tells you it is by a young Polish composer named Kotkowicz, who had previously been working in Cologne in the studio of Karlheinz Stockhausen. Yet another time you might hear what you think is a newly discovered tone poem by Richard Strauss, but it turns out to be by David del Tredici. The morning of this writing I read through a sonata for cello and piano composed in 1987 by Easley Blackwood, which sounded as though it had been composed by Frank Bridge, the teacher of Benjamin Britten. It is a common phenomenon in art music since the 1970s (historians and critics usually fail to notice that it happened earlier in pop music — for example, the Beatles' "White Album," Janis Joplin doing Bessie Smith).

There are all sorts of labels for this. Rochberg speaks of "a music of remembering." Most commonly it is called "New Romanticism." I don't much care about labels as such, but I worry about the focus on "Romanticism," for it leaves out other familiar stuff you might hear if you switch on the radio. For example, I would like to persuade you that so-called minimalist music has an aspect that could suggest the label "Stretched Neo-Baroque music." (Peter Schickele demonstrated this recently with a newly discovered opera by P. D. Q. Bach called *Einstein on the Fritz,* based on the first Prelude of the First Book of J. S. Bach's *Well-Tempered Clavier.*)

I would like to call this phenomenon "Radio Music," and in doing so I think of the radio as a kind of stage, or frame, in which these things are presented. Or perhaps I want to say represented.

The second metaphor: the *New York Times* for Sunday, 21 February 1988 carried an article about recent findings that Charles Ives had falsified dates for some of his early "modernist" compositions (those polytonal, polytextural, polycharacter compositions for which he is known), evidently to create the impression that he anticipated the modernist innovations of Stravinsky and Schoenberg.[9]

Ives was preoccupied with music's character, and particularly with respect to its gender characteristics. The music of Mozart, Mendelssohn, early Beethoven, Haydn, Tchaikovsky, Gounod, Wagner, and Massanet was for him "emasculated." The three B's produced "too much sugar plum for the soft ears." "One just naturally thinks of [Chopin] as wearing a skirt." Debussy's music is labeled "sensual sensuousness." Sibelius's music is "yellow sap flowing from a stomach that had never had an idea." The music of Franck, D'Indy, and Elgar, on the other hand, is "manly and wholesome." And Ives's own music, together with that of Carl Ruggles, is "strong and masculine."

"Masculine," for Ives, was identified with "rational." "The genius," he said, must exercise that "self restraint which can control the emotional . . . impulses" (like Reason, the charioteer in Plato's myth in the *Phaedrus,* who struggles to control the twin steeds of Passion and Desire). Sensuality is associated with the loss of masculine identity. It seems that Ives's "modernism" came about as a way of covering over the "atmospheric, lyrical, yielding" character of his first ideas.[10]

In fact, "modernism," so far as the history of music in the twentieth century is concerned, has always been associated with rationality and control, and with an ambivalence about sensuality and emotionalism, which could run to extremes in both directions. Therein it displays, despite its new means, an ancient polarity of thought and feeling in Western culture. Ives's manifestation of it sets in the foreground the gender associations that are always in the background of that polarity. To the extent that rationality was given priority, it was associated with a claim for objectivity and for its own historical necessity. There is a famous story about Arnold Schoenberg's being introduced to an army doctor in the First World War. The doctor said, "Not *the* Arnold Schoenberg!" And Schoenberg answered, "Someone had to be, so I volunteered." This quintessential Hegelian bon mot reflects Schoenberg's deep conviction that he carried the future of German music on his shoulders. But the general idea of the necessity of the progress of advanced music as a premise of the continuation of a musical culture represents the historicist nature of modernism from the inside, throughout its history. It could be heard through the 1960s from composers of nearly every cast. And it is exactly parallel with the historicism of the descriptions of historians, from the outside, of modern music, and of music in general.

Saying it, in this case, made it so. To a degree that was rarely matched in the history of Western music, the composition of the music rode in tandem with a theory that deliberately forged ahead, mainly articulated by the composers themselves and was as rationalistic as the analytical theory that I described in connection with the Chopin Prelude.

There is a characterization of musicology by Nino Pirrotta, an octogenerian Sicilian who is the most graceful writer in English in the field, that captures the spirit, not only of musicology, but as well of musical composition and theory during the period of modernism that coincided with the formative years of musicology:

> Musicology is a recent word . . . one many people are not too happy with. It is modeled, as others are, after the old and glorious name of philology. But whoever invented the older name set the accent on love—love of beauty in speech; every subsequent derivation has emphasized instead the logos component, with inelegant verbosity and, in the name of objectivity, with a detached, almost aggressive attitude toward its purported subject. Lovely and loving Philology was deemed by a poet the worthy bride of Mercury; I can think of Musicology only as a maiden, whose secret love for no lesser deity than Apollo will never have a chance until she gets rid of her heavy glasses, technical jargon, and businesslike approach and assumes a gentler, more humanistic manner.[11]

I read the splitting of the word *philology* as a metaphor for the consciousness divided between reason and sensibility, under which modernism increasingly ran its course. Ives was a casualty of this deeply rooted cultural condition of knowing.

As tightly as musical modernism was locked in with history, so the phenomenon of "radio music" shows a new liberation of musical composition from the imperatives of a driving historicism. In that sense it is postmodernism in music. There is a parable of this history composed by Kafka in 1920, which Hannah Arendt cited in her book *Between Past and Future*. It is called "He."

> He has two antagonists: the first presses him from behind, from the origin. The second blocks the road ahead. He gives battle to both. To be sure, the first supports him in his fight with the second, for he wants to push him forward, and in the same way the second supports him in his fight with the first, since he drives him back. But it is only theoretically so. For it is not only the two antagonists who are there, but he himself as well, and who really knows his intentions? His dream, though, is that some time in an unguarded moment—and this would require a night darker than any night has ever been yet—he will jump out of the fighting line and be promoted, on account of his experience in fighting, to the position of umpire over his antagonists in their fight with each other.[12]

This new freedom is admirably displayed and exploited in a set of piano pieces by William Bolcom, "Three Ghost Rags for Piano" (1979), that we may take as emblematic.[13] What goes on there is a kind of representation, and re-presentation, in which the composer's voice is heard against the background of tradition. He is present as both principal player and director and the whole is both graced and haunted by ghosts of different shades that play all around him.

Just at this point in the writing I was about to drift off into reveries about the concept of "appropriation," about its appropriation almost the minute it was uttered in the discourse about recent art, about how on the mark it is if one takes it literally, in the sense of making something one's own, about how it represents the reversal in direction of the concept of influence, about how all such terms seem to belong to a discourse of critics who need something to do—except, perhaps, for the progenitor of "appropriation," "rip-off," which was uttered with a certain urgency by black musicians about the appropriation of their music by white musicians. And then I wondered, is it really musical postmodernism I am talking about here or a matter of "tradition and the individual talent,"[14] a sense of the whole available history of music as an order that is reordered with each new work of note? An irony about "radio music" is that, despite its flirtations with the musical past, it represents a relief, a relaxation of modernism's drive to continue the line from Beethoven, to keep musical progress at that intensity, to compete with Beethoven, in effect. As long as that drive was under way it was impossible to continue using Beethoven's sounds and his musical grammar and aesthetic. Numerous composers said as much early in the century. Once that tension snapped, once the ambition was given up, composers could give up their scruples against engaging the past, without feeling threatened. But this is an irony only from the vantage point of history regarded as an orthogenic procession.

My discomfort with the list of "isms" that is on the agenda of this conference is just with the way that they imply a notion of the history of thought about art also as a procession, one that, like the other, ends up being circular because it succeeds only in reaffirming its premises. If we could think of history less as though it were an advancing central point that cleans up all around itself as it goes and more in accordance with Darwin's revolutionary attempt—not yet fully successful—to reorient the historian's focus from the modal properties of groups to the actual variation among actual things, the present would not seem such a problem.[15]

Still, there *is* a kind of new historicism in the study and practice of music. It is sui generis, and it is evolving a new paradigm for itself, which it offers to musical studies in general. I refer to the phenomenon of "historical performance practice," which I had announced as my last subject.

The investigations and practical experiments in historically accurate performance began in the 1950s. The goal was to achieve "authenticity" in the performance of the music of Bach and—increasingly—his predecessors. I have put that word in quotation marks because, while its meaning and appropriateness as a goal were regarded as self-evident at the beginning, both came to be increasingly questioned in a process that was the vanguard of a major shift in the epistemology of musical studies. The unspoken premise of the authenticity concept was the concept of the autonomous work as I have described it. Within the boundaries of the "work" construct there was assumed to be enfolded a performance that would be as authentic as the "correct" text of the work, and that would be established by scholarly methods, just as would the text itself. The authentic performance and text would represent the authoritative work—

taking *authoritative* in the literal sense deriving from "authorial." In the context of this tradition, as in others, the word *historical* gave off a penumbra of "authoritative" and "authentic." To claim that something was "historical" was to claim also that it was "authentic" and "authoritative." Once that claim was established, especially with the support of the claim that it was established by "objective" means, there could be no arguing with it. (As it turned out, the sharpest arguments were staged between those who made just such claims.) Through an astonishingly rapid historical development that cannot be sketched in detail here, the situation has been radically transformed.[16] One factor in that history should be mentioned: the spread of the historical performance movement over an ever wider domain in both directions, resulting in its encounter on the earlier side with traditions for which the work concept was increasingly questionable, and on the later side with traditions that have a continuity to the present—the March tradition of John Philip Sousa, for example. But it must be recognized, too, that the transformation has been to an unusual degree conscious and deliberate on the part of the participants.

The best and briefest way to give an impression of what that transformation has been is to sketch the attitudes that have replaced those earlier ones, and in doing so I shall call upon three informants, two of whom are also participants: Joseph Kerman, Laurence Dreyfus, and Richard Taruskin (the latter two are active as performers and conductors of early music).

Historical performance, or as Dreyfus prefers to call it, "Early Music," is no longer an antiquarian attempt to return to the past but a reconstruction of the musical object in the here and now, "enabling a new and hitherto silenced subject to speak."[17] It is a "blend of old and new," "a play of the contemporary creative sensibility upon the past."[18] The products of Early Music are acts of the performer-historian faced with a text, they are not autonomous objects. "Early Music signifies first of all people and only secondarily things. . . . [It is] a late twentieth-century ensemble of social practices."[19] As Verdi wrote, "It's fine to reproduce reality, but how much better to create it," so Taruskin writes, "It's fine to assemble the shards of a lost performance tradition, but how much better to reinvent it."[20]

The radical shift of focus, from the objects of Early Music to the agents in the process of making it in the present, shows the ideal of "authenticity" to be, not so much false for lack of good and sufficient evidence, but meaningless for its dependence on the maintenance of a strict separation between subject and object. The stubborn insistence on that separation does not survive a dedicated performance practice that has its own authenticity, now in the sense of conviction, of genuineness, of presentness (in the sense of both "here" and "now"), of a lack of falseness or ostensibleness, the sense in which a "Three Choirs Festival" performance of *Messiah* may be more authentic than a "historical reconstructionist" one.[21] This has implications for a different sense of history than the authoritative sense associated with the earlier sense of "authentic."

But why specifically *Early* Music, why not musical performance altogether? Because Early Music, freed of the burden of "authenticity," nevertheless confronts its text in view of its historicity. The very ambiguity of the designation itself is apt: it points to the historicity of both text and interpreter. The Mozart performances of Bruno Walter were concretizations of an Apollonian Mozart image that was widely held in Walter's culture—by scholars as well as performers. The Bach performances of Stokowski, like the one in Disney's *Fantasia,* were concretizations of a monumental Bach image that was likewise widely shared. Each of those styles had its own history and its own historicity, yet each was practiced without consciousness of its historicity; there was no sense of its being chosen from among other options; there was no questioning that such performances reflected the true Bach, the true Mozart. Paradoxically such performance traditions could thrive on an objectivist work concept; the concept of "interpretation" provided the dialectical bridge between subject and object, but it seemed to function without violating the hard boundaries between the two. Ironically, the "interpretation" concept shielded the doctrine of the subject/object split from its inevitable exposure as illusory. It required no great conceptual reorientation, then, for the first wave of the Historical Performance movement in the fifties to throw over those traditions, first of all with respect to Bach, for not being faithful to the works.

In the end, Dreyfus refers the operations of Early Music to the epistemology of hermeneutics—the strategies of interpretation in confronting a text, as they are described by Paul Ricoeur. The interpreter moves between two poles, aiming at one for the restoration of meaning from a primary attitude of respect for the text, and at the other for a critique of the text from the standpoint of the interpreter's own hermeneutic position, that is, for a demystification of the text. It is not a matter of choosing between these two stances but of recognizing the necessity of interpreting the text from both stances, which are inextricably linked. At one pole the text is granted authority and the goal is the restoration of its content. At the other pole we criticize the text. We ask why it says what it seems to say, in what context and tradition it seems to say it, for whose attention it is written, with what biases, on the grounds of what reasoning habits. In raising these questions we question its authority and we stage the reasoning process in our own minds, as though we were its author. We ask what might we have meant if we had uttered those words, just as we try to understand a person with whom we are in conversation. We demystify the text in that we ask, in a very broad sense, what its intention is.

But how does one criticize a musical text? Well, for one thing all musical texts are evasive, they hold out. They never tell you everything you need to know. (But I hasten to add that they almost always have told the people for whose eyes they were intended what they needed to know.) In the extreme, the oldest Gregorian chant texts tell about nothing but the contours of melodies, how melodic figures are grouped with syllables of language, and certain details about voice production and other qualitative aspects of performance. The texts of the masterpieces of sixteenth-century vocal polyphony are sufficiently evasive so that one can read out of one of them a performance in two different tonalities. The texts of Mozart's symphonies are sufficiently evasive so that you can find two recordings of the same *andante* with tempi in the ratio of nearly 2:1. On the other hand, all musical texts distort in relation to performance. The quickest way that I can think of to convey that to you is to refer to the sorts of transcriptions of jazz pieces for piano that you can buy for home use. If you play them as written they sound square and unlike what you hear in live performance by people in the tradition. It is easy to overlook what an extraordinary ambition it always has been to capture sound patterns in graphic signs, and we expect and assume that the signs will be right on the mark in doing so. But they might instead over- or underdetermine their objects in trying to approximate them; they might develop their own identities and histories that run parallel to the performing traditions to which they refer, without being identical with them. And finally, because they evade and distort, different musical texts that are supposed to depict the same items can contradict one another, they can distort and evade in different ways—not only the texts of medieval and sixteenth-century masterpieces but also the texts of operas by Handel and Verdi, the texts of cantatas and passions by Bach, and the texts of mazurkas by Chopin and symphonies by Bruckner. So we must put ourselves in the same critical and demystifying stance vis-à-vis musical texts as we do vis-à-vis literary texts or, indeed, paintings and sculptures, where similar kinds of questions arise. We must ask what intentions they embody, and that is a question of history.

There is something satisfying, to this musician at least, in the fact that a living performance tradition just now represents the most enlightened and enlightening thinking about the relation between music and history. Virtually everything that has been said here about historical performance has its counterpart in historical thinking about music which, too, must have an authenticity that balances the two senses of that word.

NOTES

1. See Arnold Schoenberg, *The Structural Functions of Harmony* (New York, 1969).

2. Lewis Lockwood, Presidential Address to the American Musicological Society, New Orleans 1987, *College Music Society Symposium* 28 (1988):1–9.

3. Leo Treitler, "Structural and Critical Analysis," in *Musicology in the 80's*, ed. D. Kern Holoman and Claude V. Palisca (New York, 1982), 69.

4. See Wallace Berry, "Sense and Sensibility: What Can We Know about Music?" in *Fact and Value in Contemporary Musical Scholarship* (Boulder, 1986), 9–14.

5. In the time of the oral tradition of the early Middle Ages music was conceived only as process, not as work or structure; I shall return to that.

6. Carl Dahlhaus, the most prominent musicologist working in Germany today, has written in his *Foundations of Music History* (Cambridge, 1983): "The concept 'work' and not 'event' is the cornerstone of music history. Or, to put it in Aristotelian terms, the material of music history resides not in praxis or social action, but in poiesis, the creation of forms" (4). In the last section of this paper, I will talk of one domain of music history, at least, where the case is precisely the reverse.

7. See Benedetto Croce, *Estetica come scienza dell'espressione e linguistica generale* (Milan, 1902).

8. See E. H. Gombrich, *Art and Illusion* (Princeton, 1960).

9. See Donal Henahan, "Did Charles Ives Fiddle with the Truth?" *New York Times,* 21 Feb. 1988, sec. 2, pp. 1, 25. The story was based on Maynard Solomon's article "Charles Ives: Some Questions of Veracity," *Journal of the American Musicological Society* 40 (1987): 443–70.

10. Solomon, p. 467.

11. Nino Pirrotta, "Ars Nova and Stil Novo," in *Music and Culture in Italy from the Middle Ages to the Baroque* (Cambridge, Mass., 1984), 26.

12. Franz Kafka, " 'He': Notes from the Year 1920," in *The Great Wall of China,* tr. Willa and Edwin Muir (New York, 1946); cited in Hannah Arendt, *Between Past and Future* (New York, 1968), 7.

13. William Bolcom, "Three Ghost Rags for Piano," in Paul Jacobs, *Paul Jacobs Plays Blues, Ballads, and Rags,* Nonesuch Records, 79006, 1979.

14. I refer here to T. S. Eliot's essay with that title, published, among other places, in *Selected Prose of T. S. Eliot,* ed. Frank Kermode (New York, 1975).

15. See the chapter "What Kind of Story Is History?" in my *Music and the Historical Imagination* (Cambridge, Mass., 1989).

16. The story is well told by Joseph Kerman in *Contemplating Music* (Cambridge, Mass., 1985). See also my essay "The Power of Positivist Thinking," *Journal of the American Musicological Society* 42 (1989): 375–402.

17. Laurence Dreyfus, "Early Music Defended against its Devotees: A Theory of Historical Performance in the Twentieth Century," *Musical Quarterly* 69 (1983): 304.

18. Kerman, p. 200.

19. Dreyfus, p. 298.

20. Richard Taruskin, "On Letting the Music Speak for Itself: Some Reflections on Musicology and Performance," *Journal of Musicology* 1 (1982): 343.

21. Ibid., 343.

HISTORY AND THEATER:
REWEAVING THE AFTERPIECE

━━━━◆━◆━◆━━━━

W. D. King

It is late to be late.
—John Ashbery

Lately, theater history has discovered its adverbial quality. Or is it belatedly? Ten years ago, fifteen hundred or so people watched as *A Chorus Line* surpassed *Grease* as the longest-running show in Broadway history. A special performance was arranged so that 332 of its past and present cast members could perform the work together, then go on to a big party. At this time a promotional poster declared to the world: "It's theater! It's history! It's theater history that's happening RIGHT NOW!" [1] Some two thousand agents of theater history were on hand for this event, both on stage and off, there to mark a transition and have a good time. A dozen or so books and countless articles have appeared to account for and establish the place of the phenomenon that was *A Chorus Line* in history. It has now closed. The afterpiece will show that its run stretched to 6,137 performances, that six and a half million people had the experience of watching it on Broadway and millions more elsewhere, but theater history will always, ever after, arrive too late for the ideal adverbial state (an advertiser's fantasy) of "RIGHT NOW." A curtain—or several thousand—came between—and always will. Personally, I never saw it. Unfortunately.

How does an adverb participate in the action of the verb or adjective it modifies? How does history manifest its participation in the steady fall of time, crossed with the sudden "do" of performance? Some sort of linguistic tendril crosses to the prepositive verb and juices it—or sucks its blood. The adverb calls to the already receding verb or adjective, out of a deep desire to become not modifier but action or object—the horse or the gallop, not the dusty echoes. Too late for the show, theater history nevertheless wants to be there amid the doings, not in the bone-heap of words that could be cut—"quite," "rather," "definitely," "enough."

The point of theater history is sharp—a project of separating what

231

is happening from what *has* happened when some closure has come between, call it a curtain, for old times' sake (since they are not always seen
these days). The point of traditional theater history is to stand upon that
curtain line, telling production from reception, the past from the present,
the manifest from the latent, and articulating other classic dualisms. That
curtain comes down, time and again, and enacts the *différance* of what will
be the history—distinguishing one playbill from another, one moment
from the next, and the next from the last. Each division jostles the terms,
so that the past in focus unsettles the present. Theater history modifies—
adverbially—that displaced term, which is the iterative death of theater
within each final curtain. Oh, how "theater history" would love to be
there, for once, on the scene, before the curtain came down. Theater history does not, by any means, always show up, but when it does, it typically
shows up too late.

I

Theater (of whatever sort) as an object for historical study (of whatever
sort) has a (surely not singular?) status (if plural, how static?) somewhere
between event and text. A piece of theater is neither so unique or unpre-
dicted as a car crash, nor is it so determined as a book. A casting call for
dancers in a new musical is an event that becomes part of the musical's
history, as do the texts of the songs that are sung on opening night. When
those songs speak for, of, and by the dancers who were there at the casting
call, as in *A Chorus Line,* then theater history, in its meshed form, seems
especially apparent. And yet what is the historical object called *A Chorus
Line?* Is it the book and score? The staging and choreography? Is it the
workshop evolution of the piece from concept to "finished" form? Is it
the original cast or the original dancers upon whose lives it was based (not
in all cases the same)? Or is it the performance of any one of the over five
hundred or so performers who replaced the originals through the years in
the assorted professional companies, not to mention the stock, amateur,
and school companies? Is it, as some have supposed, the life and life's
work of Michael Bennett? Is it the experience of any one of the one to
three percent of Americans who saw it on Broadway? Or all of them? Is
it the opening night off-Broadway, or on Broadway, or the closing night?
Does it include the inevitable Broadway revival five years from now or any
of the countless faithful reconstructions by members of the original cast

or understudies of the originals or understudies in the international company? Is it the performance of any one night, or the ideal performance that never happens, or the faulty performance that somehow illuminates?

Perhaps the only repeated term to be found in this complex series of questions is the action of a sort of curtain, although *A Chorus Line,* of course, as a backstage musical, did not use a curtain. But in whichever form it has taken, *A Chorus Line* apparently cannot be conceived as a historical object without a metaphorical curtain opening, creating an open event that is tonight's show, with its various events and texts, ending with a metaphorical curtain closing, creating a closed text that was and *is* (in a transhistorical fantasy) *A Chorus Line.* As an open event, it engages with its time—it speaks, it develops, it lives—whereas after the curtain falls, it becomes silent, frozen, memorial. The closed "text" of that performance can then be cited, by means of the program, because it has achieved its telos, or proper end, which is a death, a subsidence into fondly remembered insubstantiality. The repeated action of the metaphorical curtain is what makes this intersection of events and texts into an object for theater historical study. As the curtain is a metaphor for theatrical production, it might also be posed as a metaphor for historical production, and for theater historical production it is the inescapable metaphor. What is this curtain?

Theater curtains, as such, were found in Roman theaters, but the doors of the *skene* in Greek theaters had earlier functioned as a sort of curtain. Some sort of "reveal" was arguably evident in the Elizabethan stage, for certain scenes, and could be found in medieval pageant wagons, as well, but the modern theater curtain, closed to change the scene and lifted or lowered or parted to reveal the new, dates from the late seventeenth century in France, Italy, England, and elsewhere. Western European theater has manipulated the mechanics of this metaphor ever since, whether by the diversity of curtaining devices that were introduced or by the engineering of darkness within the spectacle, in the blackout and other manipulations of the limit of human vision. Since the late seventeenth century, Western European theater curtains have had the function of concealing scenery changes, if nothing else. As the trend in stage and scenic design shifted through the eighteenth and nineteenth centuries to a setting of the play behind the picture-frame proscenium arch, the curtain, as the device that sealed off that famous "window" on the reality of the play, has become more and more closely associated with the demarcating of reality and illusion. The curtain, *by its absence,* stands for the fourth wall, and the trick-or-truth of this illusion defines the very essence of theatricality. Stage vocabulary reflects this. For example, nineteenth-century English playwrights usually aimed to end a scene with a "good curtain," meaning a sensational line to leave the audience thrilled when restored to its own reality in the interval. These strong dramatic moments might then spur the audience to demand a "curtain call," summoning the actors out of their recessed world for a "curtain speech." These pronunciations and adornments of the closure of the performance—indeed, this fetishizing of the curtain— should be understood within the context of the parental family of metaphors associating the stage with life and the fall of the curtain with death. Within this symbolism, the deathly curtain seals the stage in order that life might be recreated within, and so the curtain can be seen as a generative agency or opener, as well. The stage gives birth to life by this opening.

Furthermore, as a paradoxical sign of both life and death, the curtain can be read as a metonymy of the whole range of dualisms that define the theater. The word derives from the Latin for enclosure, and is related to "court," as in the inn courtyards where theaters were often situated during the sixteenth century in England, Spain, and probably elsewhere. The flat "pit" area with a temporary trestle stage or perhaps porch or loading dock at one end, and the balconies of the inn surrounding it all, like galleries, perhaps gave the basic structure. All that remained was to seal or curtain off the open end of the courtyard in order to control entry to the performance. Elizabethan theaters had no front curtain but perhaps did have an inner stage, closed off by a traverse, for certain scenes of the play. However, one might suppose that the association of the curtain and the sixteenth-century playhouse was far more fundamental than that, since the operation of a professional theater had much to do with screening (or curtaining) off the courtyard so as to exclude those who had not paid for admission.

Thus, the curtain is both what defines the theater and what must be removed so that the theater can function; its presence and absence are required, alternately, and as a metaphor of presence-absence it is required constantly. The curtain is a device that might *open* onto the life, a device that might *deny* access to the life and iterate death, and a *screen* upon which the foundational dualisms of theater are projected. I wish now to introduce three gross conceptual models for the discourse known as theater history in terms of the relation of this discourse to the curtain.

    1. Theater history happens to happen. That says a lot of it. Only what

happens in the theater makes (theater) history, and even then, only what happens to *make* theater (history) makes (theater) history. There's this accident of attendance, being there, then of attention, registration, then of attenuation, refinement of the gross effect into a thin line, which is "the" history. The history is what comes across. It is what carries beyond the curtain, which is a filter—a permeable and selective membrane. This variety of curtain is a barrier most valued for its capacity to allow certain matter to pass into history. Theater history is always a series of closed curtains, but certain documents, stories, trends do come across to stand for the history of a particular moment or era, nation or people, author or director or actor or "tradition."

Some supposed factuality or materiality of what-makes-theater-history is called forth from behind the curtain in order to have a sustained life in theater history. Theater history thus depends on some kind of crossing, some kind of curtain call or encore. Theater history "lives" in a time beyond the closure of the curtain when the curtain seems to be rung up again, or when it comes to be accepted that, in effect, the curtain never had come down. Then the player, who is the historical subject, comes forward still in costume but not in character, to give thanks to the hundreds or thousands of heads of the house (the status and static, the ones who afford), who are dimly seen beyond the floats, as well as the handful of movers and shakers (the mobile and emotive, who indulge). (And in sad cases only ten or twelve of either sort will remain for this end, though rarely fewer.) A deep bow or curtsey. Theater makes, then meets, its reception into history. The movers and shakers carry on the event into textuality and history on behalf of the heads of house. The assumption of this sort of historicism is that an unbroken, though perhaps sadly diluted, contact with the original has been maintained. The afterpiece complements the curtain raiser.

2. Theater history does *not* get written. That says a lot of it. In this view, the apparent permeability of the curtain is a deception. The curtain is a barrier or obstacle, as any close examination will show. It obstructs the passage of light and sound; it interrupts the continuity of time. What happens or is seen after the curtain is down has no necessary or reliable relation to what went before. What does get written as theater history has essentially the status of disjunctive afterpiece. In place of permeability, the curtain has reflectivity, and all efforts to tell the story become iterations of the conditions of the writer, ghosted onto the skeleton of the object.

In a radical sense, the historian becomes in this view as much a performer behind the curtain, awaiting the illusory appearance of opening, as the actor. History arrives in the form of ideological predisposition to be intoned with "authenticity" into the record. Where number 1 presumes an empirical linkage between theater as performance and theater as history, this skeptical view proposes that that linkage is at best a rhetorical feat, a matter of capitalizing on the opportunity. Those texts which do seem to have emerged from the textual-eventual phenomenon known as the performance or from the textual-eventual phenomenon known as the theater (as an institution or art) become the occasion for another sort of textual-eventual phenomenon known as theater history, but the curtain seals off these phenomena from one another.

3. Theater history is already written, as the Word. That says a lot of it. In this view, the curtain is the means by which the past speaks without mediation to the presnt. This defiance of radical skepticism (no. 2) also rejects materialistic-mechanistic rationalizations (no. 1) by positing a higher level of intentionality in history, beyond rational formulation, which the historian might nevertheless appeal to by mystical means. There is in ancient Jewish mystical writings an image of a curtain that surrounds the throne of God in order to conceal its glory from the host of angels.[2] On this curtain a complete image of creation is depicted—all of history, including the present and what is to come—in some sort of archetypal form. Metatron, the highest of all angels and chief confidant of the Lord, the so-called prince of the presence, is the only angel who can read here the secret of future Messianic redemption. This angel was once a pious man named Enoch, taken up after death into Heaven to watch over the throne and its curtain. He was also to operate as guide and mediator to human beings, bringing knowledge from the curtain to the righteous and recording the sins of the wicked onto it. Thus, some passage back and forth through the curtain is figured; the past is sufficiently recorded in history, and history has some necessary effect on the present. On the other hand, other early writings about this supernal curtain emphasize the shadow that was cast by the radiance of the throne (and of Metatron himself, who was conceived as an embodiment of fire in various forms). Out of the "Darkness" of this shadow matter itself was conceived, matter which is the negation of divinity. Thus, in this view, the curtain utterly separates the antithetical realms. Both the translucence and opacity, the openness and the closure, of the curtain are thus figured. Through the curtain was to be found an

opening or access to eventuality—the true event structure of existence, including the events of the past—as well as an *impermeability,* or the inscribed closure implicit in the apparent textuality of a prescribed teleology.

Thus, in this composite myth, the curtain takes on both of the functions described above in numbers 1 and 2. What is added, here (no. 3), is that the curtain itself is seen as the bearer of significance, a figuring of all existence. Just as the potter comes to *know* in shaping the form of a traditional pot the lineage of its earlier creators, supposedly effecting a mystical passage into the history of the form, so the creator or historian of theater might come to believe that a direct access to the history of the form can be attained by an awareness of the mystery underlying its inherited elements. The curtain, as an actualization of the principle of opening and closure, might be thought to afford knowledge of the essential nature of theatrical presentation itself. And yet, of course, this view presupposes access to mystical knowledge—that a certain passage into the past (or from the past) is possible. How is this so?

A playbill, say of the Broadway opening of *A Chorus Line,* supplies certain information that might be thought to "tell" you of the event, as if a window had opened onto the past. What is supplied is mainly a certain set of names and terms, arranged in predetermined patterns, in order to complete what might be called the citationality of the event. The program seems to culminate the development of the production by giving it a textual status. It transmits one sort of history (the workshop) into another (the work and its pathway to reception). This particular work pushed the limits of what is known as authorship, since its contents derived in unprecedented ways from the lives of many of the performers in the original cast, and so each of those names points to a vital locus for further historical inquiry. The prominent, though not unprecedented, use of an alphabetical cast listing "tells" of a work that became famous for its idea that stardom is latent in the desires of even the journeymen dancers, even when bare association, at the lowest level of employment, with the institution that sponsors stardom has become the only option. While these details of the playbill might seem to transport a reality of the past into the present, they in fact pertain more directly to the customs of crediting and the citation. They are effects of a mechanism, and as such attest to that mechanism, as this show made especially clear.

This particular program in this particular autobiographical show contained an unusual collective "bio" of the performers: "Prior to the first

performance of *A Chorus Line* at the Public Theater, the original company
had collectively appeared in 72 B'way shows, 17 national companies and
9 bus and truck tours in which they gave a total of 37,095 performances.
Collectively, they had 612 years of dance training with 748 teachers—
counting duplications. They spent approximately $894 a month on dance
lessons. While performing they sustained 30 back, 26 knee and 36 ankle injuries. . . . The characters portrayed in *A Chorus Line* are, for the most part,
based upon the lives and experiences of Broadway dancers."[3] The message
here—that the lives or "bios" you see before you after the "curtain" goes
up and you put your program down, are the substance of the show—becomes progressively obsolete as soon as that "curtain" goes down on the
"One Singular Sensation" (the chorus line now made uniform and faceless
for the finale) and those dancers go on to take more lessons and sustain
more injuries and so on. The program always tells the spectator of the
achieved record, the history that is here inscribed and nightly reiterated.
The program memorializes a death, which is the curtain on that first performance, when ever after the lives of the people onstage need bear only
a general relation to the characters portrayed. This program note mimics
the structure of the show, which is a relation of the history of what has
been (in *these* performers' lives) to the archetypal patterns of what eter-
nally will be (in the lives of "performers" of all varieties). This structure
is parallel to that of the supernal curtain around the throne; it records experience even as it reveals fate.

If the afterpiece—the inscribed history—of Curtain number 1 is a logical outcome of the work, and of Curtain number 2 it is a disjunctive consequence, then of Curtain number 3 it is no afterpiece at all. Instead, it
might irrationally aim *to inhabit the form of the past,* tracing its contours with
an exact line, so that the inscription speaks directly of the historical object
even though the logic of its mediation cannot be expressed. The skep-
tic might declare this a mystification, discounting such an inscription as a
shadow play upon the ever-closed curtain of the past, while the historicist
might tend to agree, given the lack of connective material with which to
make rational contact through such openings as are available into the past.
But the theater historian might be forgiven for taking Curtain number 3
in this game show, since it is largely by repetition and reiteration and re-
seeing that theater becomes historical at all. How rarely does the isolated
event in theater register in history! How does the notable, but unnoted,
brilliant debut of the fourth replacement for Cassie, one night in 198_(?),

or the injury of same, two months later, enter into the history of *A Chorus Line?* How often has the catastrophic first performance of Chekhov's *Seagull* been elided by the incautious historian in favor of Stanislavsky's production, opening a few years later, which was to be in repertoire for over half a century? That earlier event was a misfire, an exception, and left little trace of itself to be felt in the thousands of repetitions and imitations and reinterpretations that echo the latter event. Each performance of Chekhov's *Seagull* might be said to effect a historical passage because, in effect, a potter's fingertips are sensing the history of this form in shaping a new instance of it.

This superstitious notion of performance as a means of historical understanding, and even of mystical transport, is widespread in the theater and other performing arts. In other respects, the theater has not been served well by the historians, who have not generally come to terms with either its essential ephemerality or its variform institutional persistence. There have been the time-servers, the laborious chroniclers, the afterthinking critics and the historians of critical afterthought, whose casual comments veer wildly from the complex event-text of the theatrical creation. A concerted effort has been made, especially in recent years, to deduce by scientific means certain propositions about the history of theater, but there are few, I think, even in the world of theater history, who feel satisfied that the historians of theater have touched regularly or to any profound degree on the experience of theater. Nietzsche, in his invaluable admonition against the abusers of history, calls this sort of writing, "secondhand thought, secondhand learning, secondhand action." He at one point uses the metaphor of a drama as a way of ridiculing the historicists: "If the value of a drama lay merely in its final scene, the drama itself would be a very long, crooked, and laborious road to the goal; and I hope history will not find its whole significance in general propositions, and regard them as its blossom and fruit. On the contrary, its real value lies in inventing ingenious variations on a probably commonplace theme, in raising the popular melody to a universal symbol and showing what a world of depth, power and beauty exists in it."[4] These "general propositions" are a function of the final scene or curtain that appears to define the historical object, taking the outgrowing conclusion to be its summation. In this way the historicist fixates excessively on the curtain, on what manages to squeeze through the aperture and make its mark on the historical slate. Then again, there are those who fixate excessively on the curtain as an instrument of forgetting, a producer of discontinuity, and these exult (or despair) in the freedom from historical sense, since the object seems hopelessly inaccessible. Finally, however, one might discern within the theater a species of historical apprehension that amounts to "ingenious variations on a probably commonplace theme," even a theme so commonplace by artistic standards as *A Chorus Line.*

Nietzsche's concern is that excessive dwelling on remembrance will lead to inaction, and so it is by denial of the historicist's impulse to "secondhand action" and embrace of the final curtain of forgetfulness that action might be attained. But Nietzsche does not suggest that this sort of acting exists independently of an awareness of the past. Indeed, his project for the historian is to abide by the third curtain—closed and yet legible, definitive and yet subject to elaboration—where, by a power that I cannot resist calling Metatronic, a passage from the experience of the past, such as it was lived fully by a man named Enoch, comes in direct contact with the creation of the future: "Thus history is to be written by the man of experience and character. He who has not lived through something greater and nobler than others will not be able to explain anything great and noble in the past. The language of the past is always oracular: you will only understand it as builders of the future who know the present." The curtains that might seem to separate one time from another—past from present from future—do not obstruct an oracular enunciation, which might be compared to angelic translation through the supernal curtain. But is this not profoundly superstitious? Indeed, Nietzsche attributes the power to effect such a translation to "a great artistic faculty, a creative vision from a height," in the latter phrase more or less paraphrasing the root sense of "superstition."[5] Perhaps a sort of over-standing, derived from a performer's knowledge of the "very long, crooked, and laborious road," and quite different from the propositional understanding that is situated among the audience, might be just what is required to "rais[e] the popular melody to a universal symbol." Perhaps, indeed, it is in the experience of the performer, who has the sublime experience of making, in the present moment, historical contact with the past, that Nietzsche might locate the woman or man "of experience and character" who would be fit to "write" history. Is this as much as to say that only actors should write theater history? Of course not, but it is to say that theater history demands a writing one might call performative, and in keeping with the mysterious nature of the actor's art, I would suggest that what is called for is the "whatever works" attitude of a bootstrap pragmatism, conditioned to the peculiar temporal rhythm of an art that works both in and beyond time.

The four books that came out about *A Chorus Line* in 1989–90 provide a fortuitous illustration of this. They range from a show-biz biography of Michael Bennett (who took credit for conceiving, directing, and choreographing the show) to a well-researched and reasonably balanced study of this and other musicals by Bennett. One other was an insider's look at the show by a member of the international cast, and that was followed by a collective insider's story of the show by most of the members of the original cast.[6] The well-researched study of Bennett, by Ken Mandelbaum, comes closest to being a theater history of the show, and it is premised on Bennett's centrality to the event, giving his point of view authority in the construction of the history. But an interesting and valuable thing happened in the making of this show, which is that the subjects (the "originals," as they called themselves), upon whose lives the work was based, retained some authorial control over the unfolding text, and they even shared a portion of the author's royalties. It follows that they also maintained *some* authority over the construction of its history, though only as a collection of minority voices, expressing contradictory opinions, and so mainly lost in the shadow of Bennett. Still, Mandelbaum encountered enough dissidence in the preparation of his study, including contradictions of the often unreliable Bennett, that he had to evolve a rather unusual form for his book, in which he includes long quotations from "other" voices, organized in what resembles a dramatic format. The testifying company of "others," under the direction of Mandelbaum, Bennett's surrogate, thus perform a history of an event that is in many ways a reiteration of *A Chorus Line* itself. Mandelbaum does his best to train these disparate voices into a "chorus line" unity, but in the very act of auditioning his sources, the process of recreating the history of *A Chorus Line* mixes with the process of creating the show in the first place. Mandelbaum's book demonstrates that the elements of *A Chorus Line* are always radically anterior to any authorship.

The historical moment of all of these books is the time just following Bennett's death in 1987, when a reauthorization of the show's history became possible. Most of the original cast, with the assistance of a writer, Robert Viagas, collaborated on another unusual history of the show in a book that openly seeks to take back the stories that had been taken from them by Bennett and others. This book is even more dialogical than

Mandelbaum's, but it has the further quality of reactivating the same sort of competition among the performers as in the story of the show, both its plot and the history of its making. At its most serious moment, *A Chorus Line* showed its characters considering the question "What do you do when you can't dance anymore?" This book, by answering that question in terms of the lives of the "originals," becomes a remarkable recurrence of the form of *A Chorus Line,* tracing without indicating its manifold history. With the master dead, the original cast become (the) subject(s) once again and counteract the appropriation of their histories. They open again the question of what they were said to have done for love, as the most popular lyric had it:

> Kiss today good-bye,
> And point me t'ward tomorrow.
> Wish me luck: the same to you.
> Won't forget, can't regret
> What I did for love.[7]

Ultimately, though, their presence in this cycle of desire and self-fulfill-ment has proved a fiction, as they are now willing to testify, and their places were taken by others, who auditioned in other places, in other times, with other histories, in order to become the same. And even now, when the "original" is no more, *A Chorus Line* remains suspended in its iteration, every stock or dinner theater production a citation that extends and reactivates its history. These four books show that this musical de-mands a radical readjustment in the discourse to account for a work that is especially challenging to both formalist and historicist expectations. The univocality of the always already written musical for which the dancers audition, symbolized by the final song they sing, called "One," decon-structs when the line, the uniform chorus line, breaks into the infinite number of points that make it up—the multiple repetitions of the mul-tiple subjects proclaiming the sameness and difference of their steps in this determinate and not free-floating historical dance.

The peculiar circumstances of this show seem to call out peculiar *and important* pragmatist histories. Even Kevin Kelly's show-biz biog of Michael Bennett seems to speak as much about the longing to know someone for whom stardom was mainly a longing as it does to tell it "the way it really was" with Bennett. Given Kelly's own evident longing for stardom, his book becomes a remarkable resonator for *A Chorus Line* and the complex mechanism of acceptance-rejection that extended even to the miscellaneous aspirations of the audience. The point is, under these special circumstances, a set of histories has emerged that reflect the *unresolved* questions of the past, rather than the bare citationality. It does not seem unreasonable to suggest that these special circumstances might be extended more generally in the writing of theater history.

I I

The curtain is to be seen in that negative, differential space between "theater" and "history," creating a false dualism between the two categories, as if the art could remain detached from its history, or the history could exist apart from the art. The dualism is not unlike that within post-Darwinian natural history, where a temporal rhythm that is dominated by cyclic repetition is seen to be intersected by an apparent historical evolution—two opposite relations to time. The German montage-term *Naturgeschichte* leaves undefined the grammar that must connect the two apparently incongruous terms, until Walter Benjamin, in his unfinished Arcades project, proposed a radically dialectical usage of the term and a sense of historical analysis that undermined old categories. In this sort of analysis, according to Theodor Adorno, in his exploration of Benjamin's work, "the moments of nature and history do not disappear into each other, but break simultaneously out of each other and cross each other in such a way that what is natural emerges as a sign for history, and history, where it appears most historical, appears as a sign for nature."[8] If one were to replace the term *natural* in this quotation with the word *theater,* does not a similarly radical dialectic begin to occupy what we might just as well call "theaterhistory." In the search for a pragmatist access to the theater of the past, perhaps no better model might be found than in Benjamin's antihistoricist project, where, indeed, in the spirit of Metatron, Benjamin seeks redemption of the past. The time for redemption on the supernal curtain is fixed and precise, and the moments for redemption of theaterhistory need not be less so. How are these moments to be determined pragmatically?

The evolutionary model for the discussion of theater history (conventional spelling) is all too evident in historicist writings, where the conclusive proposition is privileged over the "very long, crooked, and laborious road." But this model, favoring the "history" side of the term, should be conflated with a sort of natural rhythm that favors the cyclical repetitions within "theater." The curtain operates as a demarcator of theatrical time in at least two different ways. First, within the performance the curtain routinely, mechanically opens a "new time," an originative moment, and by its tempo (slow, medium, or fast) and by its interruption of the time, including its closure of the time, it frames the amplitude of time. It gives measure and shape and orientation. Second, on the institutional and even global level, night after night, or weekly, or seasonally, or sporadically, the theater carries on its history by opening and closing its curtains in an eternal recurrence. The curtain suggests the capability that exists within virtually any moment for the metaphorical opening of a new time, the time of performance, and the history of the theater takes something of its structure from the utilization of this capability.

The intersection of the first, the encompassing time that is interrupted, and the second, the framed time that is opened, has historical significance according to the fittingness of the one for the other. The classical Greek word for this felicitous agreement was *kairos,* which has been translated as "the opportune" and "the right time." In the context of rhetoric, the term refers to the propriety of a particular speech (rhetorical action) for a particular context (audience, time, place, etc.), and vice versa. The circumstances that, for example, make the same speech succeed with one audience and fail with another, or that make the same audience respond differently at two different times, or that make one speech effective and another ineffective with the same audience cannot be described by any simple formula but must always be seen in terms of the unfolding opportunities opened through time. Eric Charles White calls *kairos* "a radical principle of occasionality," which "discovers in every new occasion a unique opportunity to confer meaning on the world."[9] The Greeks even conceived of this quality of "the fitting" as a divine force, associated with the power of Persuasion (*Peitho*) herself. A similar mystique seems to pervade the coordination of theatrical performance with theater history. The ancient rhetorician Gorgias specifically associated this formidable capacity of the logos to (mis)lead the minds of the audience with the capacity, vested in language, to deceive them by the timely use of paradox, that is, opinion that is counter to belief or public opinion (*doxa*). A speaker might construct, by a clear reading of the *kairos,* a clever fiction in order to suit the audience's capacity to be deceived for a certain purpose. In other words, the concept of *kairos* pointed to a gross sort of theatricality (in the sense of timely illusions) that was inherent in speech performances.

Mario Untersteiner, in his thorough analysis of this and other concepts in sophistic thought, has persuasively argued the importance of *kairos* for the tragic drama (later Sophocles and Euripides), but I would push further for a pervasive applicability of the concept to the placement of performance in history.[10] The theatrical work must first (and usually repeatedly) register itself in its moment, at the time when the curtain is open and the material transmission of the play is underway; then the play must reregister itself after the curtain is closed, when access to the object, the performance in its time, is impossible. But this dichotomy is far too simple, as the time of openness bears obstruction within its moment, and the time of closure is not so radically distinct from the performance as might be supposed. The notion of material transmission is misleadingly mechanistic about the way performance is received, and the notion of absolute closure misleadingly privileges the time of performance as the historical object. The third image, that of the curtain as a site of the preinscription *and* recording of history, a predicative *and* susceptible medium, helps put the static, dualizing image of the curtain into the flux of time, or more precisely into the changing socio-spatio-temporal configuration of *kairos*.

The concept of *kairos* seems to have derived from two separate root senses.[11] One has to do with a device through which an archer must shoot an arrow toward a target; the winning shot is proved by the accuracy of the aim, to enter the *kairos,* and sufficient force to carry the arrow through the length of it. The other sense pertains more directly to the project of theaterhistory. In the process of weaving, an aperture is repeatedly opened in the warp through which the shuttle must pass with the woof before the weave is closed; *kairos* referred to the gap and the moment in the process when the shuttle must be passed. As in the term from archery, this sense of *kairos* refers to a long, narrow passageway through which a moving object must pass, but here the physical limitation is compounded with a temporal constraint, since the opening will close following the action. Hence, the notion of "critical time" comes to be associated with *kairos*. In the rhythmic repetitions of the theater, the time repeatedly arises for the maker to pass the shuttle with accuracy and force through the uncurtained aperture in order for an historical thread to become permanently a part of the text(ile). The weaving process is taken up necessarily by the historian whose opening up of the textile in order to recover evidence of the event is a reentry into the *kairos*. The weave of theaterhistory is never complete on its fringe, rarely sound at its center. Nietzsche gives one image of how the historian enters into this weaving process as an artist, a maker of metaphor, in order to give unity to the textile: "To think objectively . . . of history is the work of the dramatist: to think one thing with another, and weave the elements into a single whole, with the presumption that the unity of plan must be put into the objects if it is not already there. So man veils and subdues the past."[12] For Nietzsche this veiling is part of the necessary task of forgetting without which action in the present would be impossible. The past should remain under concealment so as not to paralyze the actor with a sense of belatedness. Walter Benjamin points to a quite different imperative motive toward the past, one that sees the historian's rhetorical performance as shaped and vehemently prompted by a sense of *kairos:* "The past can be seized only as an image which flashes up at the instant when it can be recognized and is never seen again."[13] The past presents itself as a torn curtain, and it is the historian's task to reweave the tears in the curtain ("tears" pronounced either way). As an art that continually produces fragments, opening great wounds in time, the theater speaks eloquently of the rending process, and the historian who recognizes and speaks to the gaps that are opened when performance goes unacknowledged or is subsumed in textuality takes up the piece—wherever and whenever and however—for reweaving in the afterpiece.

NOTES

My epigraph is from John Ashbery's "Answering a Question in the Mountains," *Some Trees* (New Haven: Yale Univ. Press, 1956), 80.

1. Advertising poster (1983) for *A Chorus Line,* New York Shakespeare Festival. My information on *A Chorus Line* comes mainly from: Ken Mandelbaum, *"A Chorus Line" and the Musicals of Michael Bennett* (New York, 1989). See also Robert Viagas, Baayork Lee, Thommie Walsh with the entire original cast, *On the Line: The Creation of "A Chorus Line"* (New York, 1990); Kevin Kelly, *One Singular Sensation: The Michael Bennett Story* (New York, 1990); Denny Martin Flinn, *What They Did for Love: The Untold Story Behind the Making of "A Chorus Line"* (New York, 1989). Also Natalie Crohn Schmitt's discussion of the work's postmodernism in *Actors and Onlookers: Theater and Twentieth-Century Scientific Views of Nature* (Evanston, Ill., 1990), 77–91.

2. See Gershom G. Scholem, *Major Trends in Jewish Mysticism* (New York, 1961), 72. Also see the Gnostic variation on this image in Hans Jonas, *The Gnostic Religion,* 2d ed. (Boston, 1963), 299.

3. Quoted in Schmitt, p. 85.

4. Friedrich Nietzsche, *The Use and Abuse of History,* 2d ed., trans. Adrian Collins, introd. Julius Kraft (New York, 1957), 72, 39.

5. Nietzsche, pp. 41, 39.

6. See above, note 3.

7. Edward Kleban and Marvin Hamlisch, "What I Did for Love," *A Chorus Line: Vocal Selections* (N.p.: MPL Communications, 1975), 74–77.

8. Quoted in Susan Buck-Morss, *The Dialectics of Seeing: Walter Benjamin and the Arcades Project* (Cambridge, Mass., 1991), 59.

9. Eric Charles White, *Kaironomia: On the Will-to-Invent* (Ithaca, N.Y., 1987), 14.

10. Mario Untersteiner, *The Sophists,* trans. Kathleen Freeman (Oxford, 1954), 92–205. On *kairos,* see also Marcel Detienne and Jean-Pierre Vernant, *Cunning Intelligence in Greek Culture and Society,* trans. Janet Lloyd (Chicago, 1991).

11. See Richard Broxton Onians, *The Origins of European Thought about the Body, the Mind, the Soul, the World, Time, and Fate* (Cambridge, 1951), 343–48.

12. Nietzsche, pp. 37–38.

13. Walter Benjamin, "Theses on the Philosophy of History," *Illuminations,* ed. and introd. Hannah Arendt, trans. Harry Zohn (New York, 1969), 255.

HISTORY AND ANTHROPOLOGY

Clifford Geertz

I

ONE HEARS A fair amount these days, some of it hopeful, much of it skeptical, and almost all of it nervous, about the supposed impact of Anthropology, the Science, upon History, the Discipline. Papers in learned journals survey the problem with a certain useless judiciousness: on the one hand yes, on the other no; you should sup with the devil with a long spoon. Articles in the public press dramatize it as the latest news from the academic front: "hot" departments and "cold"; are dates out of date? Outraged traditionalists (there seems to be no other kind) write books saying it means the end of political history as we have known it, and thus of reason, freedom, footnotes, and civilization. Symposia are convened, classes taught, talks—like this one—given, to try to sort the matter out. There seems to be a quarrel going on. But a shouting in the street, it's rather hard to make out just what it is about.

One of the things it may be about is Space and Time. There seem to be some historians, their anthropological educations having ended with Malinowski or begun with Lévi-Strauss, who think that anthropologists, mindless of change or hostile to it, present static pictures of immobile societies scattered about in remote corners of the inhabited world, and some anthropologists, whose idea of history is roughly that of Barbara Tuchman, who think that what historians do is tell admonitory, and-then, and-then stories about one or another episode in Western civilization: "true novels" (in Paul Veyne's phrase) designed to get us to face—or outface—facts.

Another thing the quarrel may be about is Big and Little. The penchant of historians for broad sweeps of thought and action, the Rise of Capitalism, The Decline of Rome, and of anthropologists for studies of small, well-bounded communities, the Tewa World (*which?*), The People of Alor (*who?*), leads to historians accusing anthropologists of nuancemanship, of wallowing in the details of the obscure and unimportant, and to anthropologists accusing historians of schematicism, of being out of touch with the immediacies and intricacies, "the feel," as they like to put it, considering themselves to have it, of actual life. Muralists and miniaturists, they have a certain difficulty seeing what the other sees in contained perfections or in grand designs.

Or perhaps it is about High and Low, Dead and Living, Written and Oral, Particular and General, Description and Explanation, or Art and Science.

History is threatened (one hears it said) by the anthropological stress on the mundane, the ordinary, the everyday, which turns it away from the powers that really move the world—Kings, Thinkers, Ideologies, Prices, Classes, and Revolutions—and toward bottom-up obsessions with charivaris, dowries, cat massacres, cockfights, and millers' tales, that move only readers, and them to relativism. The study of living societies, it is held, leads to presentism, snapshots of the past as ourselves when young ("The World We Have Lost," "The Fall of Public Man"), as well as to the illegitimate reading of contemporaries as ancestors (*kula* exchanges in Homeric Greece, ritual kingship in Versailles). Anthropologists complain that the historian's reliance on written documents leaves us prey to elitist accounts and literary conventionalisms. Historians complain that the anthropologist's reliance on oral testimony leaves us prey to invented tradition and the frailties of memory. Historians are supposed to be swept up in "the thrill of learning singular things," anthropologists in the delights of system building, the one swamping the acting individual in the onrush of surface events, the other dissolving individuality altogether in the deep structures of collective existence. Sociology, Veyne says, meaning by this any effort to discern constant principles in human life, is a science of which the first line has not been written and never will be. History, Lévi-Strauss says, meaning by this any attempt to understand such life sequentially, is an excellent career so long as one eventually gets out of it.

If this is what the argument is really about, this methodological thrashing around amid the grand dichotomies of Western metaphysics, Being and Becoming revisited, it is hardly worth pursuing. It has been quite some time now since the stereotypes of the historian as mankind's memorialist or the anthropologist as the explorer of the elementary forms of the

elemental have had very much purchase. Examples of each doubtless re-
main; but in both fields the real action (and the real divide) is elsewhere.
There is as much that separates, say, Michel Foucault and Lawrence Stone,
Carl Schorske and Richard Cobb, as connects them; as much that con-
nects, say, Keith Thomas and Mary Douglas, Fernand Braudel and Eric
Wolf, as separates them.

The centrifugal movement—any time but now, any place but here—
that still marks both enterprises, their concern with what has recently
come to be called, with postmodern capital letters, and poststructuralist
shudder quotes, "The Other," assures a certain elective affinity between
them. Trying to understand people quite differently placed than ourselves,
encased in different material conditions, driven by different ambitions,
possessed of different notions as to what life is all about, poses very similar problems, whether the conditions, ambitions, and notions be those of
the Hanseatic League, the Solomon Islands, the Count-duke of Olivares,
or the Children of Sanchez. Dealing with a world elsewhere comes to
much the same thing when elsewhere is long ago as when it is far away.

Yet, as the irreversibility of the slogan that is commonly used to express
this view, L. P. Hartley's "the past is another country" (another country is
quite definitely *not* the past), shows, the question is rather more complex:
the equivalence of cultural distance between, say, us and the Franks and
us and the Nigerians is a good deal less than perfect, particularly as there
may be, these days, a Nigerian living around the corner. Indeed, not even
the "us," "The Self" that is seeking that comprehension of "The Other,"
is exactly the same thing here, and it is that, I think, which accounts
both for the interest of historians and anthropologists in one another's
work and for the misgivings that arise when that interest is pursued. "We"
means something different, and so does "they," to those looking back
than it does to those looking sideways, a problem hardly eased when, as is
increasingly the case, one tries to do both.

The main difference is that when "We" look back "The Other" appears
to us as ancestral. It is what somehow led on, however vagrantly, to the
way we live now. But when we look sideways that is not the case. China's
bureaucracy, pragmatism, or science may remind us forcibly of our own,
but it really is another country, in a way even Homeric Greece, with adulterous gods, personal wars, and declamatory deaths, which remind us
mainly of how our minds have changed, is not. To the historical imagination, "we" is a juncture in a cultural genealogy, and "here" is heritage. To

the anthropological imagination, "we" is an entry in a cultural gazetteer, and "here" is home.

These at least have been the professional ideals, and until fairly recently reasonable approximations of the actualities as well. What has progressively undermined them, both as ideals and actualities, and stirred up all the anguish, is not mere intellectual confusion, a weakening of disciplinary loyalty, or a decline of scholarship. Nor, for the most part, has "trendiness," that voluminous sin academic Tories attribute to anything that suggests to them that they might think thoughts other than those they have already thought, played much of a role. What has undermined them has been a change in the ecology of learning that has driven historians and anthropologists, like so many migrant geese, onto one another's territories: a collapse of the natural dispersion of feeding grounds that left France to the one and Samoa to the other.

This can be seen, these days, on all sides: in the greater attention paid by Western historians to non-Western history, and not only of Egypt, China, India, and Japan, but of the Congo, the Iroquois, and Madagascar, as autonomous developments, not mere episodes in the expansion of Europe; in anthropological concern with English villages, French markets, Russian collectives, or American high schools, and with minorities in all of them; in studies of the evolution of colonial architecture in India, Indonesia, or North Africa as representations of power; in analyses of the construction of a sense of the past (or senses of it) in the Caribbean, the Himalayas, Sri Lanka, or the Hawaiian Islands. American anthropologists write the history of Fijian wars, English historians write the ethnography of Roman emperor cults. Books called *The Historical Anthropology of Early Modern Italy* (by a historian) or *Islands of History* (by an anthropologist), *Europe and the People without History* (by an anthropologist) or *Primitive Rebels* (by a historian) seem quite normal. So does one called *Anthropologie der Erkenntnis,* whose subject is the intellectual evolution of Western science.[1] Everybody seems to be minding everybody else's business.

As usual, what such shifts in the direction of interest come to practically can be more securely grasped by looking at some work in fact going on — real geese, really feeding. In the human sciences, methodological discussions conducted in terms of general positions and abstracted principles are largely bootless. A few possible exceptions possibly apart (perhaps Durkheim, perhaps Collingwood), such discussions mainly lead to intramural bickering about the proper way to do things and the dreadful results ("relativism," "reductionism," "positivism," "nihilism") that ensue when, perversely or in ignorance, they aren't done that way. The significant methodological works in both history and anthropology— *The King's Two Bodies, The Making of the English Working Class,* or *The Structure of Scientific Revolutions; The Social Organization of the Western Pueblos, Trade and Markets in Early Empires,* or *The Forest of Symbols*—tend at the same time to be significant empirical works, which is perhaps one of the deeper characteristics that, across whatever divides of aim and topic, most connects the two fields.[2]

I shall take as my cases in point, then, two moderately sized bodies of work. The first is that of a small, fairly definable clutch of social historians who, involving themselves with anthropological ideas and anthropological materials, have found themselves drawn more and more deeply into the darknesses that plague that discipline. The second is that of a rather larger number of historians and anthropologists, who, having discovered an interest in common they did not know they had, have produced a series of unstandard writings suffused with uncertain debate. The one, which I shall refer to as the Melbourne Group, mainly because its protagonists are from Melbourne and form a group, provides a nice progression of examples of the continuum between anthropologized history and historicized anthropology; the other, which I shall refer to as the Symbolic Construction of the State, because that is what its wranglers are wrangling about, provides a well-bounded instance of what happens when historians and anthropologists explicitly try to coordinate their efforts with respect to a topic traditional to them both. These are but samples, partial and quite arbitrary, and schematized at that, of what is going on right now in looking backwards/looking sideways sorts of study. But they do reveal something of the promise offered, the difficulties encountered, and the achievements already in place.

II

The members of the Melbourne Group with whom I will be concerned (there are apparently some others, whose work I do not know) are: Rhys Isaac, whose *The Transformation of Virginia* is a study of the vicissitudes of colonial culture on the way to the Revolution; Inga Clendinnen, whose *Ambivalent Conquests* is an analysis of the encounter of Spanish and Indian forms of life in the Yucatan peninsula during the middle of the sixteenth century; and Greg Dening, whose *Islands and Beaches* seeks to trace the destruction of Marquesan society under the impact of Western intrusions into it after the 1770s.[3] Three places, three times, one problem: the disequilibration of established ways of being in the world.

This paradigm, if that is what it is, is most bluntly apparent in Isaac's book, because he divides his work into two more or less equal halves, one static, one dynamic. The first, called "Traditional Ways of Life," presents the outlines of planter-dominated culture up to around 1750 or 1760 in a synchronic, snapshot manner—a social order not without interior strains or endogenous directions of change, but essentially in balance. The second, called "Movements and Events," traces the disruption of this settled order by the appearance of elements—most especially evangelical Christianity and, toward 1776, American nationalism—that its simple hierarchies could not contain. An image, thus, of a social cosmos—Planter Life, and all that went with it (country houses, horse races, court day, patriarch slavery, formal dancing, and the muster field)—coming apart along the fissures induced in it by "stern faced [Northern] preachers," New Lights and others, exciting the populace, and "factious [Southern] republicans," Patrick Henry and others, haranguing the elite: "[The] great men [set] up fine brick courthouses and churches as emblems of the rule they sought to exercise and of the divinity legitimizing that rule. . . . Within half a century of its apparent consolidation the system [was] overturned" (ix).

This picture of the ragged Forces of History shattering the crystal Patterns of Culture, consensus first, dissensus after, makes possible a quite straightforward approach toward sorting the gazetteer from the genealogy as frameworks for placing a distant society in relation to one's own. The first goes in the first part, constructing the image, the second goes in the second, accounting for its transience. Anthropology gets the tableau, History gets the drama; Anthropology the forms, History the causes.

At least partly out of the same impulse—the desire to distinguish the events that arise from differences in outlook from the differences in outlook that arise from events—Clendinnen, too, divides her book into more or less equal, dialectical halves. But in her case the division is not between what is moved and what moves it; it is between two peoples, one a cultural scouting party a long way from home, one a cultural fortress deeply *in situ,* locked in an encounter neither of them can really understand.

The two parts of her book are thus called simply "Spaniards" and "Indians," and the same sort of distribution, though rather less radical, of historical narrative to the one half and ethnographic portraiture to the other, takes place. Here, however, the order is reversed; the drama comes before the tableau, the disruption before what was disrupted. In the first, "Spanish," section, the historical actors—"explorers," "conquerors," "settlers," "missionaries"—are set out and their exploits, and exploitations, chronicled, as are the conflicts among them, the crisis through which their enterprises passed, the mental world within which they operated, and the final outcome, the consolidation of Spanish power. In the second, "Indian," section, an image of Mayan society and the passions that animated it—stoicism, cosmography, human sacrifice—is delicately reconstructed out of what is admittedly a fragile and fragmentary native record.

The story the book has to tell (or the picture it has to present) is consequently not one of a consensual social order forced into disarray by the entrance onto its public stages of obstreperous men with contrarious ideas but one of a profound cultural discontinuity between intruder and intruded upon, a discontinuity that grows only more profound as their relations intensify. Familiarity breeds incomprehension: to the Spanish, possessed of "that extraordinary European conviction of their right to appropriate the world" (xi), the Maya appear less and less reachable the closer the Spanish come to them; to the Maya, "the objects and the victims of Spanish world-making" (128), the Spanish appear less and less assimilable the more they become entrenched. Everything ends in a terrible and blood-drenched "hall of mirrors"—clerical floggings and folk crucifixions: "The product of the miserable confusion which besets men when they do not understand the speech of others, and find it easier to make of them familiar monsters than to acknowledge them to be different" (188). An Anthropological tragedy with a Historical plot.

Dening, too, divides his book in half, putting what historians would call the story in the one part and what anthropologists would call the analysis in the other. Only he does it, so to speak, lengthwise. To each substantive chapter on one or another phase in the 160-year European-Marquesan encounter ("Ships and Men," "Beachcombers," "Priests and Prophets," "Captains and Kings") he appends a topically oriented interchapter called a "Reflection" ("On Model and Metaphor," "On Rites of Passage," "On Boundaries," "On Religious Change," "On Dominance," "On Civilizing"), which sets forth a more or less systematic array of ideas for interpreting what has just been related. The textual movement here is less between what was and what happened to it, as in Isaac, or between incommensurable sensibilities, as in Clendinnen, as between alternative styles of rendering such matters—cultural mutation and cultural mis-connection—generally intelligible. Though he started as a historian and ended as one, Dening took a doctorate in anthropology along the way, and he is engaged in an enterprise somewhat eccentric to both fields: the writing, as he puts it, of a "discourse on a silent land."

It is silent, because unlike the Virginia Planters, echoes of whose out-look persist today, if only as social claims and ancestral fantasies, or the Mayan Indians, segments of whose civilization continue as folk tradition beneath the Hispanic personality of modern Mexico, the Marquesans, as Marquesans, simply are no more: "Death [carried them] off . . . before they had the time or the will to make any cultural adaptation to their changed environment" (287). There are people living in the Marquesas, of course, at least some of them physical descendants of those who lived there before the Captains, Priests, and Beachcombers arrived; but they are "dispossessed," their history ruptured, themselves turned into gener-alized, indefinite "Pacific Islanders":

> Everybody's past is dead, [the Europeans' and the Marquesans'] together. Events happen only once. Actions are gone with their doing. Only the his-tory of the past has some permanence, in the ways consciousness gets pre-served in writing or in memory or in the presumptions of every social act. But for [the Marquesans] even their history is dead. All the history that is left to them . . . binds them to those whose intrusion on their Land caused them to die. Events, actions, institutions, roles become history by being translated into words. In [the Marquesans'] case, these are [the Euro-peans'] words in their description of the Land. Even [the Marquesans'] own words about their lives, collected in legends or even in dictionaries, cannot escape this fundamental reality. There is not a legend or a geneal-ogy that has survived that was not collected many years after [the Euro-peans'] intrusion. They belong to the time of their writing down. (273)

The behindhand collectors, the appropriating writers-down, were, these being "primitives," mainly anthropologists, though a few originals, like that expansive beachcomber Herman Melville, were also involved. The classic ethnographers of the place, those from whom we know most of whatever we know about Marquesan society in that *illo tempore,* "the ethnographic present"—Karl von Steinem, E. S. C. Handy, Ralph Linton —all came to the islands well after the Western mariners, traders, missionaries, and vagabonds had done their civilizing, or decivilizing, work. (Handy's *The Native Culture in the Marquesas,* upon which "virtually all models of [indigenous Marquesan society that] have been constructed" are founded, was published only in 1923.)[4] The result is that "Marquesan Culture" has become a Western reality, no longer a Marquesan one.

> At one time [the Marquesans'] legends, their genealogies, the very conti-
> nuity of their living culture kept them conscious of their past, told them
> the way their world should be. They were dispossessed even of these. Like
> their material artefacts, their customs and their ways were transformed
> into [European] cultural artefacts. Their living culture died and was res-
> urrected as a curiosity and a problem about such things as cannibalism or
> polyandry. . . . All [their] words, [their] consciousness, [their] knowledge,
> were extracted from [the islands] and put in the service not of continuity
> or identity for the [Marquesans], but of entertainment, education and edi-
> fication for the Outsiders. The [Marquesans'] lives ceased to be part of
> their discourse with themselves [which, unlike that of the Virginians and
> the Mayans, was of course wholly unwritten] and became instead part of
> [European] discourse. (274–75)

We have moved (logically, not chronologically—Dening's book is the earliest of the three, Clendinnen's the most recent) from Anthropology as the state of affairs upon which History acts, through Anthropology as the jungle through which History stumbles, to Anthropology as the grave in which History is buried.

Taken together, these three works suggest that the conjoining of History and Anthropology is not a matter of fusing two academic fields into a new Something-or-Other but of redefining them in terms of one another by managing their relations within the bounds of a particular study: textual tactics. That sorting things into what moves and what moves it, what victimizes and what is victimized, or what happened and what we can say about what happened, will not, in the end, really do, is hardly the point. In the end, nothing will really do, and believing otherwise will but bring forth monsters. It is in efforts such as these, and in others employing other rhythms and other distinctions, that what, beside polemic and mimicry, this kind of work has to offer (not least, I suspect, a critique of both fields) will be discovered.

III

My second example of history-anthropology relations in action is of a rather different sort—not a deliberate tacking between variant modes of discourse but an unintended, almost happenstance convergence of them upon a common concern: the enmeshment of meaning in power. Since at least the time Burkhardt called the Renaissance state "a work of art," Kantorowicz began to talk about "medieval political theology," or Bagehot noted that Britain was ruled by "an elderly widow and an unemployed youth," historians have become more and more interested in the role of symbolic forms in the development and operation—the construction, if you will—of the state. And since at least the time Frazer began to talk about royal immolation, Eliade about sacred centers, or Evans-Pritchard about divine kings on the upper Nile, anthropologists have become so as well. An odd reference now and then aside, the two interests developed more or less independently until rather recently, when they began, with some force, to break in upon one another. The results have been as one would expect: a burst of work, a bigger burst of questions.

The burst of work is apparent on both sides. A classical historian has written on the celebration of Roman emperors in the Greek towns of Asia Minor; a modern historian has written on Victoria's Diamond Jubilee. There have been studies on the meaning of Constantine's coronation, on imperial funerals in Rome, on "models of rulership in French royal ceremonial," on "rituals of the early modern popes," and someone has brought Kantorowicz forward to Elizabethan times in a work called *The Queen's Two Bodies*.[5]

On the other, the anthropological, hand, where I have myself been a witting, or half-witting, conspirator with my work on "the theatre state" in Java and Bali, there have been studies of the ritual royal bath in Madagascar, a book on *Le roi ivre; ou l'Origine de l'état*,[6] another on "the ritual context of [contemporary] British royalty," in which Princess Di, Elizabeth's handbag ("perhaps the most intriguing royal accessory"), fox hunting, and the emir of Qatar all figure, as well as more standard ethnographies of the histrionics of sovereignty in Chad, Nepal, Malaysia, and Hawaii. Royal marriage, royal death, royal tombs, and royal succession have all come in for the sort of attention that used to be reserved for kinship terminology, as have regicide, deposition, and whatever the technical term may be for royal incest. A recent, quite partial, bibliographic review lists over fifty titles, from "The Queen Mother in Africa" to "The Stranger King, Dumézil among the Fijians," in the last ten years alone, and "symbolic domination" has become, even if no one is entirely certain just what it means, a standard term of art and invective.

It is from the interplay of the two lines of thought as they have discovered one another that the burst of questions has come. Most of this interplay remains citational in nature; historians of Renaissance Italy mentioning ethnographers of Central Africa, ethnographers of Southeast Asia mentioning historians of Renaissance France. But recently there have been some more intimate conjunctions in the form of symposia collections containing both sorts of study and setting them off against one another in the interests of some more general overview. In two of the best of these, *Rites of Power: Symbols, Ritual, and Politics since the Middle Ages,* emerging from the Davis Center for Historical Studies at Princeton a couple of years ago, and *Rituals of Royalty, Power and Ceremonial in Traditional Societies,* emerging from the Past and Present group in Britain last year, the problems that have arrived with the advances are as apparent as they are unresolved.[7]

The most vexed of these, and the most fundamental, is simply: How much does the symbolic apparatus through which state power forms and presents itself, what we are used to calling its trappings, as though it were so much gaud and decoration, really matter? To do this sort of work at all involves the abandonment of a radically "smoke and blue mirrors" view of the issue and of the simpler forms of reductionism—military, economic, structural, biological—that go with it. The signs of power and the substance of it are not so easily pried apart. The Wizard of Oz or How Many Battalions has the Pope won't do, and neither will mutterings about swindles and mystifications. But the question nonetheless remains, and indeed grows more pointed, as to what precisely, and how important, the effects of these royal baths and lordly tooth-filings, majestic effigies, and imperial progresses (or, for that matter, television summits and congressional impeachment hearings) are. How are they come by? How are they not? What sort of force does spectacle have?

Sean Wilentz, in the introduction to the Princeton volume, focuses the issue as having to do with "the limitations . . . of symbolic interpretation . . . the limits of *verstehen* in any scholarly enterprise":

> If . . . all political orders are governed by master fictions [as anthropologists have claimed], is there any point in trying to find out where histori-

cal rhetoric and historical reality diverge? Can historians of the symbolic
even speak of objective "reality" except as it was perceived by those being
studied, and thereby transformed into yet another fiction? Once we respect political mystifications as both inevitable and worthy of study in
their own right—once we abandon crude and arrogant explanations of the
origins of "false consciousness" and vaunt the study of perception and experience—is there any convincing way to connect them to the social and
material characteristics of any hierarchical order without lapsing into one
form or another of mechanistic functionalism? Some historians [he cites
E. P. Thompson, Eugene Genovese, and Felix Gilbert] insist that it is still
possible—indeed imperative—to make these connections, and they warn
of the rise of an "anthropologized" idealism, disrespectful of historical
contexts, in which a new fetish of elegant presentation replaces the old
fetish of sociological abstraction and cumbersome prose. Others [he cites
Natalie Davis, Carlo Ginsburg, and Bernard Cohn] respond that such
fears, although justified, need not block the historical study of perception
and political culture in ways influenced by the anthropologists' insights.[8]

Cumbersome Prose and Elegant Presentation aside, dire crimes that
they doubtless are, the general anxiety that if meaning is too much at-
tended to, reality will tend to disappear (meaning by "meaning" mere
ideas and by "reality" munitions and the lash), does haunt this sort of
work. The anthropological desire to see how things fit together sits un-
easily with the historical desire to see how they are brought about, and
the old nineteenth-century insults, "idealist!"—"empiricist!"—get trotted
out for one more turn around the track. "A world wholly demystified is
a world wholly depoliticised," an anthropologist contributor feels called
upon to proclaim, as though it were some sort of revelation;[9] "power is,
after all, something more than the manipulation of images," a historian
contributor is moved to assure us, as though there were people around
who thought otherwise.[10]

This question—how can we bring the articulations of power and the
conditions of it into some comprehensible relation?—continues to trouble
the discussions, in some ways even more internally torn, in the Past and
Present collection.

David Cannadine, who introduces the volume with an essay that seems
to change direction with every paragraph, sees the problem as arising from
the combination of a general recognition, on the part of both anthropologists and historians, that "the whole notion of power as a narrow,

separate and discreet [*sic*] category [is] inappropriate . . . the idea that splendour and spectacle is but . . . window-dressing . . . ill-conceived," with the absence in either field of anything in the way of a more adequate conception."[11] "If conventional notions of power seem to be unsatisfactory, what if anything may better be put in their place?" (15). We need, he says, and his contributors for the most part follow him, to ask such questions as: "Why exactly is it that ceremonies impress?" (15). "What are the building bricks from which [such ceremonies] are actually constructed?" (15). "Does ceremonial convert systems of belief about celestial hierarchies into statements of fact about earthly hierarchies . . . [or] does ceremonial convert statements of fact about power on earth into statements of belief about power in heaven?" (16–17). "Why . . . do some societies . . . seem to need more ceremonial than others?" (17). "How does pomp appear to the alienated or the dispossessed?" (18). "What is the connection between the overthrow of royalty and the overthrow of rituals?" (18). "Why does some pageantry take root and 'work,' and some dwindle and die?" (18).

Except for the fact that the problem may lie less in a too narrow conception of power than in a too simple conception of meaning, a philosophical mistake not a definitional one, these are indeed the sort of questions this odd coupling of semiotical anthropologists and institutional historians has cast up. And if navigating in strange waters doesn't induce fears of going overboard so intense as to inhibit motion altogether, some of them may even come to be, in some degree, and however rephrased to make them less flat-footed, answered.

Certainly they seem likely to go on being asked. I have before me as I write an announcement of a new book (by an anthropologist, but it could these days be as easily by a historian) on *Ritual, Politics, and Power,* which treats, apparently, among other things, of Ronald Reagan's visit to Bitburg, the funeral rites for Indira Gandhi, the arms-control meetings between Soviet and American leaders, the cannibal rites of the Aztec state, the inauguration of American presidents, a parade of Ku Klux Klan members in the 1940s, the activities of contemporary terrorist groups, the "healing" ceremonies of seventeenth-century French and British kings, and May Day march-bys in Moscow.[12] What looked like a nice little problem now looks like a nice little mess—which is perhaps what one should expect when the two most multifarious enterprises in the human sciences, however opportunistically, however nervously, combine forces.

IV

The recent surge of anthropologists' interest in not just the past (we have always been interested in that) but in historians' ways of making present sense of it, and of historians' interest not just in cultural strangeness (Herodotus had that) but in anthropologists' ways of bringing it near, is no mere fashion; it will survive the enthusiasms it generates, the fears it induces, and the confusions it causes. What it will lead to, in surviving, is distinctly less clear.

Almost certainly, however, it won't lead much further than it already has either to the amalgamation of the two fields into some new third thing or to one of them swallowing up the other. That being the case, a good deal of the anxiety on either hand concerning the dissipation of proper scholarly character (usually referred to, limply, as "rigor"), and the defensive polemics it gives rise to, are, to say the least, misplaced. Most particularly, the concern on the History side (which seems the greater, perhaps because there are more Personages there) that trafficking with anthropologists will lead to soul loss is, given the enormous discrepancy in the size of the two fields, to say nothing of their cultural weight, ludicrous. Any conjunction, whether as a mixture of discourses or as a convergence of attention, is bound to be an elephant and rabbit stew ("take one elephant, one rabbit . . ."), about which the elephant need not unduly worry as to its savor coming through. As for the rabbit, it is used to such arrangements.

If work of the originality, force, and fine subversiveness as that I have reviewed, and an enormous lot, reaching out from all parts of both fields toward all parts of the other, that I have not, is to prosper (to get through a discussion like this without mentioning the *Annales,* structuralism, Marxism, *The Life and Death of the Senecas,* or Phillipe Ariès is a bit of a tour de force in itself), a sharper sensitivity to the conditions—practical, cultural, political, institutional—under which it is taking place would seem to be necessary. The meeting, collusively or otherwise, of a scholarly tradition, vast, venerable and culturally central, closely connected to the West's effort to construct its collective self, and a much smaller, much younger, culturally rather marginal one, closely connected to the West's effort to extend its reach, has a structure of its own. In the end, it may be in a deeper understanding of the "and" in the "History and Anthropology" *accouplement* that progress lies. Take care of the conjunctions and the nouns will take care of themselves.

NOTES

1. Peter Burke, *The Historical Anthropology of Early Modern Italy* (New York, 1987); Marshall Sahlins, *Islands of History* (Chicago, 1985); Eric R. Wolf, *Europe and the People without History* (Berkeley, 1982); E. J. Hobsbawm, *Primitive Rebels: Studies in Archaic Forms of Social Movement in the Nineteenth and Twentieth Centuries,* 2d rev. ed. (New York, 1963); Yehuda Elkana, *Anthropologie der Erkenntnis* (Übers. v. Achlama, Ruth., 1988).

2. E. H. Kantorowicz, *The King's Two Bodies* (Princeton, 1957); E. P. Thompson, *The Making of the English Working Class* (New York, 1963); Thomas S. Kuhn, *The Structure of Scientific Revolutions* (Chicago, 1962); Fred Eggan, *The Social Organization of the Western Pueblos* (Chicago, 1962); *Trade and Markets in the Early Empires,* ed. Karl Polanyi, Conrad M. Arensberg, and Harry W. Pearson (Glencoe, Ill., 1957); Victor Turner, *The Forest of Symbols* (Ithaca, N.Y., 1967).

3. Rhys Isaac, *The Transformation of Virginia, 1740–1790* (Chapel Hill, N.C., 1982); Inga Clendinnen, *Ambivalent Conquests: Maya and Spaniard in Yucatan, 1517–1570* (Cambridge, 1987); Greg Dening, *Islands and Beaches, Discourse on a Silent Land: Marquesas 1774–1880* (Melbourne, 1980); hereafter cited in text.

4. See E. S. Craighill Handy, *The Native Culture in the Marquesas* (Honolulu, 1923). The quote is from Dening, p. 279.

5. Marie Axton, *The Queen's Two Bodies: Drama and the Elizabethan Succession* (London, 1977).

6. Luc de Heusch, *Le roi ivre; ou l'Origine de l'Etat* (Paris, 1972).

7. *Rites of Power: Symbols, Rituals and Politics since the Middle Ages,* ed. Sean Wilentz (Philadelphia, 1985); *Rituals of Royalty, Power and Ceremonial in Traditional Societies,* ed. David Cannadine and Simon Price (Cambridge, 1987).

8. Sean Wilentz, Introduction, in Wilentz, 7–8.

9. Clifford Geertz, "Centers, Kings, and Charisma: Reflections on the Symbolics of Power," in Wilentz, 30.

10. J. H. Elliott, "Power and Propaganda in the Spain of Philip IV," in Wilentz, 147.

11. David Cannadine, Introduction, in Cannadine, 15; hereafter cited in text.

12. The book, an interesting one, has now appeared: David I. Kertzer, *Ritual, Politics, and Power* (New Haven, 1988).

RESPONSE TO CLIFFORD GEERTZ

Renato Rosaldo

CLIFFORD GEERTZ'S PROSE can at times dazzle the reader into missing its critical edges and its humor. His essays fairly bristle with wit, irony, and critique. In reading "History and Anthropology" I laughed out loud at the tale of the rabbit stew. On reflection, I wondered how a historian might react to the essay, so I used anthropological method and asked a native (a historian) to read the paper and tell me what he thought. The historian did so and reported that he found the essay comforting. He in fact had worried, much as Geertz anticipated, about being devoured by the anthropological rabbit, but he now felt much more secure in the knowledge that he lived in the belly of the historical elephant. He felt better and I felt worse.

If Geertz's essay comforts the reader, it has failed to do its job. My brief comments will argue that Geertz's essay should produce a certain anxiety about the consequences of deepening relations between the disciplines. The relationship between history and anthropology has been productive and it has brought changes to both partners. Yet such changes usually require, as motive and consequence, a certain degree of discomfort and anxiety on both sides.

What are plausible reasons for fretful concern about the relations of history and anthropology? The likelihood that the anthropological David will slay the historical Goliath appears, as Geertz says, to be quite low. One should not expect, however, that no changes will result from the blessed union of history and anthropology. Both partners seem unlikely to live happily ever after precisely as they were before they met. Certain changes, less than catastrophic and more than superficial, seem both inevitable and desirable.

Let me from the outset review Geertz's characterization of history and

anthropology as they were just a few years ago. Not so long ago, it sometimes helps to think, matters were ever so much clearer than they are
today. Historians used to tell stories about who we are and how we got to
be that way; their job was to preserve our heritage (who, I wonder, does
this "we" include and exclude?). Anthropologists, on the other hand, used
to move sideways, rather than back in time, to study other cultures that
differed from our own (again, the magical "we"). If the cardinal sin of history was presentism, that of anthropology was ethnocentrism, and both
involved similar failures to appreciate the cultural differences separating
us from them.

In depicting the relations between history and anthropology Geertz
invokes three recent books from the Melbourne school. One explores
a patterned past, more or less frozen, homogeneous, and anthropological, which is disrupted by historical events. Another studies the conquest
of Spaniards over Indians, telling tales of both the intruders and the intruded upon and delineating the cultural incomprehension on both sides.
A third divides each chapter between the story and analysis, history and
anthropology. In all three books history and anthropology stand quite
apart from one another, marked off as Part One and Part Two or distinguished by subtitles within chapters. The moral of Geertz's story up to
this point appears to be that each discipline remains fully intact yet is im-
proved upon because of the presence of the other. Diachronic analysis,
the anthropologist might say, nicely complements our synchronic analysis. The historian might say that one can profitably add a cultural totality
at a slice in time to our study of processes of change through time. The
interaction between the disciplines allow each a separate but equal status
in which one specializes in moving backward in time and the other devotes itself to moving sideward in space. These examples do appear to
promote a certain comfort.

Geertz goes on, however, to discuss the symbolic construction of the
state. Here he blurs the boundaries between the disciplines. Anthropology
folds into history and vice versa. Meaning is enmeshed in power and
power is saturated with meaning. One thinks of Michel Foucault's notion
that all human relations are saturated with power or his gift for reversing
the usual relation of past and present so that, for example, the present age
of prison reform appears barbaric and the past epoch of corporal punishment seems humane. Foucault's narrative uses the classic before-and-after
technique, two slices in time juxtaposed, and it almost compels his reader

to plead, "Please, please cut off my hand, but don't give me the Panopticon, don't subject me to your disciplining gaze." This technique for making the familiar strange and the strange familiar helps readers see the stark cultural and historical contrasts between epochs. Viewed from this perspective, even the most brute of brute facts requires cultural analysis. To say that an execution results in death and that is that (a brute fact, nothing more and nothing less) clearly will not do. Is an execution enacted, for example, as a morality tale in which the victim confesses in public, or is it a private act designed to be as humane as possible?

Geertz's discussion about the symbolic construction of the state should produce a measure of anxiety on both sides. How can one proceed? Where does one discipline end and the other begin? And how will the rabbit-elephant stew taste after all this simmering anyway? I should now like to further increase the reader's anxiety by recasting Geertz's argument from another perspective.

To begin, there are two disciplines, history and anthropology. They enjoy overlapping research programs; in certain respects they are the same, and in others they differ. Books aside, they mark their differences through mass rallies and brutal initiation rituals. In their mass rallies, called national meetings, historians vastly outnumber anthropologists; in their initiation rites, called oral exams, historians demand the recitation of lists of dates and anthropologists require the drawing of linguistic maps. Each discipline has its own separate arenas and social mechanisms for creating an imagined community of professionals. Only individuals endowed with enormous stamina can subject themselves to the obligatory ritual cycles of both disciplines. Both disciplines work hard to maintain their boundaries and they by and large succeed in keeping insiders in and outsiders out.

Those of us (another magical "we") who inhabit borders, whether by birth or by choice, tend to go beyond official culture by asking about informal groupings and social relations. Who hangs out with whom, who talks together, and who listens to whom? Such groups often appear less visible than more official organizations, but their influence in producing change can nonetheless run quite deep. They may espouse innovative research programs that raise questions that not only provide a new look at old topics but also bring new topics into view. Elizabethan self-fashioning, the Moroccan market, the early modern French charivari, Hawaiian historical metaphors, and European fairy tales all have emerged as significant subjects for study within recent years. In fact, informal networks do connect the authors of the studies just invoked. The characteristic institutional forms of such networks include the visit, the phone call, and the conference. If more formal disciplinary allegiances derive from initiation rituals and mass rallies, informal ones grow out of conversations and the processions and demonstrations called conferences.

The aftermath of decolonization has stimulated further changes in the disciplines. Changes in the postcolonial world have become increasingly evident in metropolitan centers throughout the world. The hinterlands have engulfed urban centers and the Third World has imploded into the First. Different races, ethnicities, languages, and cultures now live side by side in Jakarta, Paris, Lima, London, Bombay, and Manhattan. In the state of California, demographers estimate that twenty years from now the state's population will be 60 percent minority (and 40 percent of Mexican ancestry). Already today in California the kindergarten through high school population is over 50 percent minority (as is the undergraduate student body at the University of California at Berkeley). In this context it should probably come as no surprise that when ethnographers and "natives" meet it is difficult to predict who will pick up the pencil and who will put on the loincloth. A number of scholars in history and anthropology now write as academics and as members of minority communities based on race, class, gender, and sexual orientation.

In such contexts yesterday's solid truth now appears to be a partial truth or the dominant ideology. More importantly, and this should cause anxiety, the possibility of synthesis between divergent perspectives seems less easy to achieve than it once did. The intruders and the intruded upon, to return to the Melbourne school, may disagree not only about who was at fault but also about what happened, when it began and ended, and who was involved. If an earlier generation gave voice to the voiceless and became their advocates, their successors now speak as members of relatively disenfranchised groups.

Such scholars occupy the borderlands between the two disciplines and between their academic colleagues and their minority lay communities. Their research encompasses classic notions of historical periods and whole cultures as well as a sense of inconsistencies and interactions within and between cultures. Their worlds are more polyglot than monolingual.

If an imagined predecessor sees the nuclear family as a social building block, the polyglot scholars view it as both unified and cross-cut by boundaries of generation, age, gender, and legitimate sexual relations. If Alexis de Tocqueville finds increasing prosperity to be one among many factors that caused the French Revolution, one hastens to add that the Haitian slave economy produced much of that wealth and that one could productively study the mutual relations between the Haitian slave revolt and the French revolution.

If traditional American historians restrict the colonial period to the thirteen colonies, scholars from the borderlands contest the exclusion of other areas at the time, including what is now the southwestern United States. Who is included in that magical "we" which excludes a number of historical heritages from its dominant narrative? Why should I not see my heritage reflected in the mirror of American history? For us Chicanos such blindspots comprise more than intellectual errors. They wound, they offend. They grow out of largely unconscious patterns of white supremacy. The disciplines are undergoing change in part because once-sovereign scholars must now engage in dialogue with natives who are both objects of analysis and analyzing subjects. Such challenges do not make scholarly life more comfortable, but they do pose complex and compelling problems for research and teaching. In our present circumstances scholarly life may not get easier but it could expand its range and become more engaged and significant.

HISTORY AND FOLKLORE:
LUCK-VISITS, HOUSE-ATTACKS,
AND PLAYING INDIAN
IN EARLY AMERICA

———⊱•◦•⊰———

Roger D. Abrahams

BETWEEN THE PRODIGAL pageantry of the theater-state and the topsy-turvy inventions of Carnival lie a great number of less extravagant display events.[1] These expansive festivities, celebrations, and entertainments provide a source of deeper understanding of how collective memory comes together with traditional practices to produce experiences in common at particular times and places. In these customary activities the vocabulary of public display emerges as a congeries of forms and routines in use in a wide variety of settings. Conventional display events such as parades and pageants, processions and marches, are receiving a good deal of notice by a wide range of scholars, notably folklorists and historians of society and culture. Along with the more unruly kinds of conventional group disturbances, like riots, marches, lynchings, and other mobbings, display events have come to provide some basic insights into the ways in which power is manifested and projected in symbolic formulations.

In the late nineteenth and early twentieth century, traditional displays of this sort were an important feature of folklore study. Throughout Europe the various seasonal festivities stood at the center of the study of traditions. Around these points of passage accumulated the arguments that claimed the interest of local historians and antiquarians, producing a scholarship aimed at synthesizing these homages to the seasons as they were practiced "for time immemorial," masterworks such as Sir James George Frazer's *The Golden Bough* and Arnold van Gennep's *The Rites of Passage*.[2] The globalizing arguments of these men have been eclipsed in the face of the more tightly circumscribed ethnographic and distributional analyses that have come into fashion. The Frazerian perspective has been eschewed because of its perceived Eurocentric bias. On the other hand, van Gennep's work, based after all on his field observations in France and elsewhere, has maintained its viability in further ethnographic analyses, as elaborated by Victor W. Turner.[3] Here it has not only influenced ethnographic analysis, but for a few moments such Turnerian ritual analysis attracted a great deal of notice in the areas of religious studies, literary criticism, and social and cultural historians.

Until the development of a New Cultural History strongly informed by these ethnographic reports, historians had foresworn the use of traditional materials of this sort because of their perceived ephemeral character. These are events in which costumes and other devices of display are endowed with power and meaning for the day and then thrown away, or put back in the storeroom for use next year. They therefore seem transitory, using disposable devices to seize the moment and produce an intense if fleeting experience. And yet as enactments drawing on collective memory, in festive and ritual format, the past is put at the service of present needs. Indeed, many pasts are contained in the intensity of the festive moment, only some of which invoke traditions and relate to the folkness of the community. Others refer to particulars of the historic experience of those parading. Little wonder that folklorists and historians have each found their way to this body of traditions, conducting their own archaeological investigations of these sedimented cultural performances.

These public displays often spring from those times out of time associated with life passage or calendar customs. But they are constantly adapted to new social, political, economic, and cultural conditions, changes that are often spelled out explicitly as part of the program of the celebration. Moreover, the devices drawn upon even in the most technologically sophisticated metropolitan displays consistently show their origins in the most archaic vocabularies of festive elaboration. Seasonal celebrations call for hypertrophied and amplified performances, even at the level of village economies with their limited resources. In these timeless moments of celebration, objects and identities are pulled out of shape as well. These activities always contain the motives by which the social structure is celebrated at the same time as license is given to make fun of all official representations.

In the recent drift toward interdisciplinary study, public display events are receiving extensive attention from folklorists and, more recently, by historians. In this they are joined by scholars in other disciplines; literary and art historians and anthropologists have cast light on these collective

forms by which a community celebrates itself and proclaims its ideal values
to the spectators. In the programmatic working out of the procession, the
pageant, or the parade, in its combination of ceremonial elaboration in
speeches, in musical performances and in dance, these scholars find lapi-
dary representations of community rendered in such self-conscious and
highly spelled out formulations that they reap a harvest of understandings.
The licensed play of the festival moment encourages both the ceremonial
elevation of those in power and the inversion of the social order through
a stylized set of activities that involve both dressing up and cutting up.

In the 1960s and 1970s, carrying out ethnographic fieldwork with advanced technological apparatus made it possible to record such events in
a manner that these complex forms and vital experiences might receive
appropriately rich rendering. Under the impact of structuralist thinking,
symbolic anthropologists such as Victor Turner and Clifford Geertz wrote
a series of profound works on the symbolic processes contained with specific rituals and festivals.[4] They demonstrated that the cultural productions
of all groups, if approached sensitively, could reveal complexities as great
as any of the masterworks of written literature.

In the wake of the work in symbolic anthropology, historians as well as
folklorists rethought how display activities such as parading or mobbing
might provide ways of understanding the thinking and acting that animate the everyday life of a people. The displays themselves promise quick
and firm insights into the symbolic system of a community. The intensity
of the occasion and the power of invoking meaningful pasts within the
confines of the events encourage a hermetic idealization of festive forms
of the group that has chosen to represent itself from within. The mirrors
that reflect inwardly within the event must be made into windows if the
outside world is to understand the meaning of the experience of celebration to those involved.

These public displays commonly are not so heavily programmed or so
fully rehearsed. Some of the most effective public displays are contrived
to seem improvised at that moment. They derive their attractiveness by
their apparent spontaneity and their rag-tag costumes and willy-nilly (and
often confrontative) behaviors. These traditional outbreaks, while considerably smaller in scale, embody many of the same socially inversive
motives as Carnival. In this they contrast with the ceremonially stylized
power pageantry of the theater-state. Indeed, the two kinds of display are
often found juxtaposed even within the same community, as in the various

"Doo-Dah Parades" that have sprung up in the United States as inversions of more official civic pageants. That this has been an American tradition for some time is shown in Susan G. Davis's study of parades and counterparades in nineteenth-century Philadelphia.[5] Through such a mixture of forms and motives any community is capable of operating on a number of symbolic levels at the same time, and in such a vocabulary that players and audience are able to respond on many levels at the same time.

Certain conventional figures emerge at the heart of these events involving serious play. Leaders are elevated along with their court, even when they are anointed only for the festive times. Clowns, fools, people dressed as animals and animals dressed as people are also commonly found, to say nothing of the wildmen dressed in leaves and birds' nests, and the various other masked figures representing the half-world of the spirits. Of these, none is more important for the proceedings than the exotic figures who represent significant outsiders. Often clothed in the garb of an ancient enemy of the people (such as the Moors after the Crusades throughout Europe), these figures are both enormously attractive and fearsome. In parades and pageants, they are among the most attractive of the figures, and among the most dreadful.

In each domain, either in homelands or hinterlands, uncivilized figures emerge as distinct from those living with good manners and civic responsibility. Cast as being backward, tradition-bound, behind the times, they are old-fashioned and less refined. At home, the resident aliens were called *peasants* in Early Modern Europe, later taking the more honorific term *folk*. In the outposts of civilization, of course, the strangers were called *savage* or *primitive*.[6]

In more informal revels, these scare figures become mischief makers. These entertainments are widely reported under a variety of names that announce their helter-skelter organization and tactics: as *callithumpian bands* or *skimmington riders* the players mumble their lines and rush their speeches, often delivered in distorted voices and through a voice-altering mask.[7] This role-playing occurs most commonly in the form of bands of luck-visit *mummers* who carouse during holiday times. License is given then to beg, coerce, trick, entertain, and on rare occasions, to heal sick individuals or the community as a whole.[8] These groups announce themselves as they come to the door or gate through making noise or formal speech-making which proclaim their purpose in coming. Commonly they stage a fight, stylized around speeches or a dances, an activity that brings the proceedings close to mayhem. They take a formal leave and are recompensed in a symbolic way for their visit.

Historians, drawing on court records and other official documents, have uncovered many scenes of such mummery throughout Europe. Folklorists have returned, once again, to these materials, now informed by ethnographic details drawn from both observation and from local memorial traditions. That the two disciplines have not joined forces in casting light on these materials indicates that the interdisciplinary movement has some distance yet to travel. Historians have recovered some of the political and social messages contained in certain of the mobbing practices as they were employed at particular times and places, finding in them clues to movements of resistance within specific polities. In the wake of E. P. Thompson's studies on how such organized bands play *rough music*,[9] a great number of historical studies have been produced charting the activities of a nonofficial group concerned with dispensing a local form of justice, while clad in blankets or some other such simple disguise.[10]

Folklorists, of course, see in these figures a thread leading to a very ancient past, and to a kind of society in which the community provided its own entertainment. In this, they share the sense of nostalgia of the community itself, of the players and the audience who well know themselves that this is the old way of playing. This sentiment commonly accompanies traditional revelries when they have been maintained self-consciously. That this nostalgic note resonates through the work of social historians as well may not be so self-evident. By casting these scenes in terms of the moral economy of the populace, historians have idealized the notion of "the crowd," seeing in these gatherings evidences of a protorevolutionary group formation. For historians wishing to construct a success story for the development of class consciousness among workers, this essentializing move has proved to be too tempting, especially in searching for the place of the worker in a successful resistance movement, like the American Revolution.[11]

Neither folklorists nor historians have addressed the largest question involved in these representations—getting at the horizon of possible meanings when masking of this sort takes place. In these traditional displays, repeatedly, the figures that are played (and the singing, dancing, and speech-making that are simulated) are not simply the product of the imagination. They are based on figures who have entered into the historical experience of the group doing the playing, as when the play of "The

Moors and the Christians" is replayed at Corpus Christi throughout Iberia and the Hispanic New World. In such cases, playing the role of the Other can also mean becoming the enemy. But more than this, in such imitation these Others are represented in distinctly ambivalent and ambiguous ways. They are endowed with the power of the uncivilized outsider as they are rendered in a positively attractive manner. That addressing such questions takes us beyond the usual domains of both folkloristics and social history and into semiotics is evident.

I

The ongoing project of resuscitating the materials of tradition, then, has involved the efforts of many disciplines working in a number of different geographic areas and cultural traditions. In the process, riddles, proverbs, traditional systems of belief, as well as these folk mobbings no longer are seen to be simply the unaccountable fragments of past traditional practices. In this the serious address by historians of materials of this sort emerged as the New Cultural History developed. Discussing this change, one of those most deeply involved, Robert Darnton, noted that "after generations of struggle to discover 'what actually happened,'" during specific historical times, "historians have learned to cope with documentary problems. And if they want to understand what a happening actually meant" to those who participated or looked on, historians "can take advantage of the very elements" that in the past have distorted our reading of reports derived from hearsay or from journalistic accounts. The aims of historical writing have been altered in an attempt to arrive at greater understandings not of what happened when but of how people acted and reacted in the quotidian world. As a result, today "we can read a text . . . not to nail down all the whos, whats, wheres, and whens of an event but rather to see what the event meant to the people who participated in it." [12] And as Darnton and others of this persuasion have shown, the chance records of traditional performance and celebration are prime resources for this historical reconstruction. [13]

This intellectual enterprise extends far beyond the confines of any one profession to that interdisciplinary cohort sometimes referred to as "the cultural critique." Those language and cultural philosophers, anthropologists, folklorists, and social, literary, and art historians have all joined in describing specific cultural formations with regard to how they come to be produced or "invented"[14] in response to historical conditions. The very idea of culture is addressed by this group as a manifestation of the rationalization of bourgeois nation-states through bureaucratic consolidation at home and through colonial expansion abroad.

By problematizing the basic premises of all disciplines and, in the process, recognizing the contingent character of their practices, folklorists and historians now find common ground in these everyday display events. As overtly constructed worlds, public displays make no claims for veracity. They deal only in pomp and in play. They are complicated cultural operations that most interest scholars concerned with detailing the pervasiveness of the notion of deconstructed worlds.

With other human sciences, the writing of folklore and history had come to be studied as a cultural accomplishment rather than a revelation of truth. Both disciplines have acknowledged that they emerged as part of larger sociopolitical and intellectual situations and are equally affected by Western biases. Perhaps even more important, a number of historians have begun to address their materials in terms that are especially conducive to a fruitful conversation between the disciplines. One such historian, Greg Dening, pursues a situation in which different peoples confront each other across a cultural divide. He discusses the reactions of as many of those involved as he can discover, his special insights deriving from the interactions between Tahitians and Europeans. At the center of his response to the variations in perspective is the insight that historians are like other people who tell stories to each other, seizing upon the fragments of the past for whatever the present purposes may call for. "Storytellers, mythmakers, gossipers, sculpt events with choice words and fine dramatics and pass them on by word of mouth so that their histories are embellished by each occasion of their telling," Dening keenly observes. Describing the writing of history in this manner is to cast it into the terms usually drawn on by folklorists. Says Dening, glossing further this metaphor: "Participants in the event choose a genre—a diary, a letter, a poem, a newspaper to clothe their interpretation of what has happened. . . . These relics of experience—always interpretations of the experience, never the experience itself—are all that there is of the past. Historians never confront the Past, only the inscriptions that the Past has left. History is always interpretation of interpretation, always a reading of a given text."[15]

The materials of folklore are also derived from chance recordings made of relics of the past that wander into the present through the power of memorial apparatus. Owning up to the contingent and sometimes arbitrary character of these fragments constitutes the most important move in understanding lived experiences. Perhaps we might say that much of folklore and social history, then, involves the discovery of these fragments and a consequent move that makes relics of them—that is, endows them with preternatural meanings. Acknowledging the process by which the fragment is made the relic then becomes an important step in developing more reflexive procedures in the mutual attempt by historians and folklorists of making some sense of the past.

To demonstrate what I am getting at, I describe a series of cases that involve public-display activity of a special sort—maskings and mobbings. While these scenes are not so profoundly programmed as the more elaborate pageants or festive parades, they nonetheless reveal a great deal concerning the groups coming together in the activity. As with other public-display events, they achieve a congeries of meanings, even while they comment on each other as related occasions performed in America around the period of the American Revolution. These cases draw upon traditional techniques for organizing and mounting house-attack mobbings—maskers dressed in exotic garb and acting in an openly confrontative manner.

The reports come from works by historians who report them as if the cases were *sui generis*. They are immediately recognizable to the folklorist, however, as something quite ordinary, if noisy and disruptive. They draw upon some extraordinarily archaic vocabularies of aggressive display, but ones that appear to be uniquely American because the costumes, emblems, ways of walking, talking, dancing, and fighting were derived from American Indian models.

II

In 1761 a group of Maine farmers staged an attack harassing the home of Dr. Silvester Gardiner, the principal figure of the Kennebeck Proprietors, the group owning title to the land the men were cultivating. Squatters or settlers, depending on one's perspective, they represented their interest in the land by enlivening the night with their clamor. Garbed as Indians, they howled outside of Gardiner's lodging and forced him to take precipitous flight out of his back door, indeed out of the valley.[16]

The house-attack by a masked band was far from unusual in the American settlements in the volatile circumstances before the Revolution.[17]

More than a *posse comitatus* converging to settle a local grievance quickly, these squatters set up a formal organization and had badges of membership as well as customary ways of dressing, holding meetings, and ordering their attacks.[18] As Alan Taylor has revealed, these self-named *White Indians* staged attacks from 1761 well into the 1820s.[19]

In communications with each other their leaders made allusions to Indian things to establish a sense of membership in a freedom-loving agrarian brotherhood: "we all won [*sic*] brother" united against "lordships and slaveourey."[20] They identified themselves by wearing "a Capp and blanket and a gun and tommahawk."[21] They wore hideous masks, "caps about three feet high" and moccasins. The masks altered their voice production, making their speech sound strange.

A witness-participant in one scene in 1808, Pitt Dillingham, described the band in detail as they advanced "in ominous silence" toward a tavern, going in Indian file "behind an elegant standard," and "with military precision" they fired a volley into the air, deafening those inside. Forming themselves into a semicircle, they summoned the deputy, who addressed them with great trepidation. As Dillingham reported, "The frantic imagination of a lunatic in the depth of desperation could not conceive of more horrid or ghastly specters. Their savage appearance would strike terror in the boldest heart."[22] Groups of masked men on a mission like this commonly developed a routine, a ritual, establishing dread in their prey by being at one and the same time well organized and yet at the edge of anarchy.

Choosing Dillingham himself as the spokesman for those gathered within, they had him carry their ultimatum and bring back the reply. When Dillingham gave them the proposal, the Indians had him leave for their discussion, and then carry back their acceptance of the offer. Their "chief" made a speech in which he indicated that "all injum like very much your talk, all injum agree as you say."[23]

Such masquerading carousers have provided the stock in trade of folklore study for some time. As traditional maskers or mummers, young men in villages and towns have dressed and acted in this riotous manner going from house-to-house during holiday seasons in many parts of the West and elsewhere. Masking to disguise their identity, they led the seasonal play. They learned a traditional dialogue and set of actions which they took from house to house as a way of eliciting the largesse of those living there. They made their way to the cross-road, the inn, the pub; they

performed to even larger and more serendipitous audiences, receiving the
agreed-upon seasonal refreshment and perhaps a few coins as well.[24]

When these exotic roles were played during festive times they became especially charged with symbolic meaning. The costuming, masking, noise-making and inversive behavior of the Maine house-attack drew
upon the same set of roles and the same kinds of energies that are commonly found among holiday carousers. At points of passage in the year,
the maskers intensify the sense of community through licensing the approach to the house and its mock-attack. Such grotesquery is commonly
found in the form of holiday house-visits. For these are the times when
the family dwelling place is, by custom, most available to this kind of
comic attack.

The seasonal maskers were commonly young men of indefinite social
standing within the community. Often, they were called *strangers*. While
everyone within the community knew that local boys were involved, the
fun was in the disguise and the guessing of who was playing that year.
Performances were often prepared ahead of time and brought to the gate
or the doorway throughout a settlement offering the gift of luck to the in-
dwellers in the form of a trick (a play, a comic routine, a song, or simply
recited speeches telling of the season, the meaning of the costume, and
the comic threat posed by having a grotesque or malignant figure at the
door). This was customarily responded to with the largesse of the house,
a treat of food, drink, or money. As grotesque disguisers, they brought
both laughter and the potential of mischief with them.

Far from being restricted to countryside performances, this older style
of mumming was and is found in towns and cities as well, just as caroling
and serenading have been widespread. In fact, the clearest contemporary
retention of the carousing mummers is found as groups of old-style mas-
queraders in cosmopolitan celebrations of Christmas, New Year's Day,
or Carnival. In the more cosmopolitan centers, these groups of maskers
more commonly rehearse their performances far ahead of time, develop
more elaborate costumes and masks, and enter into competition with each
other as they encounter each other on the streets. As these festivals become
tourist events, the competitions are more formalized and prizes awarded
to the best warriors in each category.

These house visits may seem a world apart from the house-attacks of
the White Indians. Through rehearsal and customary understandings, the
mummers are given special license to invade the house and yard to enliven

it with their performance. Yet studies of these groups have shown that the mummers often saw this as an opportunity to carry out some mischief, often upsetting the order of the household and even reenacting locally notorious upsets. Hangings and burnings in effigy and other such local outbreaks of social commentary drawing on the masking traditions invoke the same festival vocabulary of breaking the calm of the night through scare tactics.

Here, rather than focusing on a particular instance of the historical deployment of traditional devices, I look at the range of ways in which playing Indian operated during one epoch at the beginning of American life, the period immediately before and after the Revolution, to see how traditional ways of playing and masquerading were constantly reinvented for a variety of related purposes.

III

Not all White Indian mobbing was so politically pointed, nor so organized, as the Maine case. As early as the Mast Tree Riots in Massachusetts in 1734, men costumed as Indians committed acts of spontaneous mayhem in the face of the perception of unjust laws.[25] There are innumerable reports of these more unrehearsed maskings, *whitecaps, shivarees, lynching parties,* and, most characteristically American, the *tarring, feathering, and riding the rail.*[26] One group of revellers more playfully garbed as Indians became a part of May Day activities in Annapolis by 1771. An English visitor attending a ball, William Eddis, exclaimed that it was seemingly a customary practice for the affair to be assaulted by young bucks. "During the course of the evening and generally in the midst of the dance," Eddis noticed, "the company are interrupted by the sudden intrusion of a number of persons habited like Indians, who rush violently into the room, singing the war song, giving the whoop and dancing in the style of these people; after which ceremony a collection is made and they retire well satisfied with their reception and entertainment."[27]

But the same cultural display devices were employed on less-than-fun occasions at many points in American history, moments in which white people were discovered drawing on the fearsome qualities of Indians to make more serious fun of individuals at whom the masking play was directed. Throughout the colonies, whites dressed and acted as Indians at those moments when they most wanted to take liberties. Seizing on Old

World techniques for achieving license, and taking on the disguise of Indians, the colonists found themselves asserting local and colonywide rights which, they argued, derived from natural law, thus the resort to playing these "native naturals," carrying the emblems that they had decided were characteristic of all Indians, mounting the attacks in what they had decided was Indian style. This involved a simple substitution of emblems of Indianness for the grotesque figures of the Old World. Clearly these figures are a part of the traditional apparatus by which orientalism of the most stereotypical sort was practiced. Exotic and grotesque figures had become part of the familiar landscape under festive conditions. Thus does stereotyping enter into the dynamic of everyday life in a rather different way than is commonly noticed.

In fact, the most celebrated masquerading as Indians to carry out extralegal actions, the Boston Tea Party, may have derived the name Mohawks from a similarly named group in London, the Mohocks, who represented themselves as *East* Indians. A famed band of "bucks and blades," one of many such carousing groups in the early part of the century terrorizing parts of the city, they deployed the masking and the mockery of traditional festival mumming. They deployed it in a more reckless manner and in connection with no known holiday. Presumed to be renegade members of the beau monde, they were operating rather like street brawlers for the thrill of the experience. Mentioned in the *Spectator* as well as by the writers Jonathan Swift and John Gay, they were widely feared as marauders: "a set of men who have borrowed their name from a sort of cannibals, in India, who subsist by plundering and devouring all the nations about them." The Spectator continues: The president is "styled 'Emperor of the Mohocks;' and his arms are a Turkish crescent, which his imperial majesty bears . . . engraven on his forehead." Members carried tatoos of the crescent on them, and went about marking people's faces with their strange daggers.[28]

Of course, the use of exotic garb differed considerably in the colonies at a time when Indians were still in evidence—and often feared as enemies. Yet at the point at which the colonists needed to pronounce themselves different from the British in their fighting tactics, they "became" Indians of a sort of rag-tag fashion. As Benjamin Labaree summarizes the remembrances of those dressing as Mohawks in Boston, they were "small groups of men roughly disguised as Indians, in most cases with no more than a dab of paint and with an old blanket wrapped about them. . . . others had dabbed soot or dirt on their faces to conceal their identities."[29]

This technique was not unique to New Englanders. When Virginians needed to raise a militia in the face of hardening official policies in 1775, as Rhys Isaac has shown, they projected a voluntary militia distinguished by their dress of "painted Hunting-Shirts and Indian Boots."[30]

These troops, under the name of "the shirtmen," evidenced the Indian character of their uniform by wearing their shirts belted outside their trousers, and tucking into the belt a tomahawk or scalping knife for display. The "heroes in huntingshirts" thus became the men of the hour as the revolutionary conflict was launched.[31]

Ironically, as the war was in progress, a tory in Upstate New York organized a band of marauders, perhaps known as "False Faces" in imitation of Iroquois practice. They launched attacks against the households in the neighborhood that had supported the revolutionary cause, using the wooden Indian masks for disguise to cast blame elsewhere when they engaged in the raid on these farmsteads.[32]

IV

Imitation may mean a great many things, especially in public display activities. When imitation is carried out at public holidays, it may embody motives as various as veneration and mockery, sometimes at the same moment. Indeed with White Indians wherever they were found, it is difficult to ascertain from the records how much was tomfoolery and how much was deadly serious. Motives are seldom unmixed or unmitigated, especially when people imitate styles of dress, talk, eating, singing, and dancing. Even the most mocking performance carries with it tones of attractive contamination. And when a moment is socially defined as licentious or playful, the mixture of motives is all the more complicated and explosive.

The playfulness of masquerading, emerging as a way of practicing political resistance, confounds common understandings of the ways in which political and social changes are brought about. Nonetheless, it is clear that in all of these festival activities serious cultural business is being transacted. In festivities a community comes together to experience life intensely. All symbolic forms at such moments are endowed with specially powerful meanings. Festivals are commonly held at those points of passage in the year when a group undergoes release most fully. Insofar as the masks that are put on and the roles that are played are often derived from the figures regarded as the enemies of culture at all other times, the social motives being played out are made all the more complex.

In a commercial culture these holiday techniques of masking and of display have spilled over into popular entertainments and into devices of displayed resistance to the official worlds. Indeed, it is precisely through festive entertainments like parades and civic pageantry, that one can begin to posit the existence of a culture developed within a market-driven polity in the towns and cities which might be studied in the same manner as both folk and elites groups, through the development of their own traditional modes of self-representation. Especially interesting are those circumstances in American history when peoples who ostensibly are allied with officialdom and power take on the appearance and some of the actions of an otherwise stigmatized and dispossessed group.[33]

One of the most extreme forms of this identification with the Indian as Other occurred as early as 1705, when Robert Beverley began his description of Virginia as the New Eden by claiming "I am an Indian."[34] The indigenous peoples that he encountered there impressed him with a naturalness that he intended to emulate. "In a state of Nature" without the benefits or the constraints of written law, Beverley argued (along with many others of his time), Indians were guided by "their own convenience." He saw them as "perfect in their outward frame" and governed by natural passions but guided by peaceful dispositions.[35] The earliest images of the New World developed pictorial versions of a stereotype Indian in masculine ideal form derived from classical representations of warrior princes. The Indian warrior departed from these figurations only in terms of superficial details, such as the paraphernalia of dress. As a symbol of America itself, Indians in blankets or some other toga-inspired wrapping, and carrying a tomahawk, a peace pipe or a string of wampum came to epitomize America in European representations.[36]

Even as the French and Indian War was coming to an end in the 1760s, an Indian was chosen as American's patron saint, St. Tammany, and a national holiday, May 1, was designated to honor his name. In towns throughout the colonies, Tammany came to be so celebrated, and in the formation of the organization the Sons of St. Tammany, one can see just how the devices of masking and mumming so widely associated with country pastimes and house-attacks were also deployed by the mercantile elite. Indeed, through an understanding of the inventing of traditions among these fraternal orders one can begin to see the lineaments of a commercial community that was able to invent its own traditions around which they could come together to celebrate at a particularly momentous time in American history.

In Philadelphia in the middle of the eighteenth century, the opening of the fishing season was May 1. A local organization, the Schuylkill Fishing Company, celebrated the day, by having its member to go to the country for their own enjoyment. The wags in the group seem to have dressed as Indians for the occasion and developed an elaborate explanation why this would be appropriate. They traced the ancestry of the organization to the doings of one Tammany (given in many variant spellings in the earliest documents), the Indian chief credited with signing the peace pact with William Penn under the treaty elm.

As the membership increased, a hierarchy emerged: thirteen Sachems representing the thirteen states, each symbolizing a different lodge and given a separate tribal designation. Members developed a set of arcane practices that gave them the sense of belonging to a secret society. They paraded regularly with other such organizations, displaying themselves hierarchically, and always marching single file. They devised their own calendar, referred to the months as "moons" and carried on their meetings in a mock-Indian oratorical style derived from the stock descriptions of Indian peacemaking ceremonies. Indeed, they saw themselves as following in Tammany's footsteps as a peace-bringer and treaty-maker, a role they were to actively play in the late 1780s and early 1790s when it became necessary for the new nation to make treaties with some of the contiguous east coast groups.

As with other White Indians, their Indianness came to reside in the emblems of the tomahawk and blanket, though the devices that were even more characteristic of the Sons of St. Tammany were the calumet (peace pipe) and the buck's tail — in fact, they were popularly known as the bucktail crew. They had a motto, "Kwanio Che Keeteru," meaning "This is my right: I will take it."[37] This was emblazoned on the buck flag that was to be found in their meeting rooms, and seems to have been used by the members as a sign to each other of membership.

The organization was one social group among the many fraternal groups that sprang up throughout Europe, especially in England and its colonies. Like the Freemasons, the most successful and widespread of these lodges, the Sons of St. Tammany developed out of the male sociability that emerged as the coffee house and the club began to provide a place in which Enlightenment ideas might be discussed and put into practice. The same political principles and social ideals of the Masons certainly permeated those discussions of the Sons of St. Tammany that were recorded. Beginning as a social society, along with so many such organizations, they were politicized after 1765, rallying around the Liberty Pole, thus making common cause with the Sons of Liberty—indeed, in some documents the organizations are confused.[38]

Chief Tammany was early spoken of as "King," the customary honorific term used by Europeans to refer to the leaders of Indian groups. However, he was soon elevated to a position as the American patron saint.[39] Ebenezer Hazard in 1784 recalled of his childhood twenty-five or thirty years before that May 1 had already been consecrated to the memory of Tammany and that he would wear in his hat a gilded buck's tail and a picture of an Indian (Tammany no doubt), shooting a deer with a bow. "We used to talk of King Tammany then but it seems he has been canonized since the Declaration of Independence and has now become a saint. He will make as good a one as any in the Calendar."[40]

As one of their anthems had it:

> Of Andrew, of Patrick, of David, & George,
> What mighty achievements we hear!
> While noone relates great Tammany's feats,
> Although more heroic by far, brave boys,
> Although more heroic by far.[41]

The symbolic importance of Tammany in analogy to the other saints was evidenced in the first notice of the spread of this society, given by William Eddis in his notice of the ball in Annapolis referred to above. This report from 1771 indicates that by that date the fraternal group had already spawned other *wigwams* outside of Pennsylvania. "The Americans on this part of the continent have . . . a saint" who shares legendary status with St. George, St. Patrick, St. Andrew, and St. David," a status "lost in fable and uncertainty." May Day is dedicated "to the memory of Saint Tamina on which occasion the natives wear a piece of the buck's tail in their hats or in some conspicuous situation."[42]

Detailed descriptions of their meetings carried in newspapers before, during, and after the Revolution indicate how their status had been elevated, for many of the most powerful Philadelphia political figures were members. With the Sons of St. Tammany, as with the Mohawks and the Maine whitecapping, playing Indian provided a way in which men could organize themselves in amity and common purpose. If the mobbing began in the spirit of fun early in the history of the organization, the players would prove to be involved in a controversy that extended far beyond local affairs.

These reports indicate, through the printing of toasts and songs, that by the early 1770s, the Sons of St. Tammany were already positioned to comment on affairs extending beyond their own interests to those of "the country" (at that point, the colony of Pennsylvania), their use of Indian paraphernalia and practice served the ends of promoting unity in the face of a perceived threat to the common interests, a threat that emerged from across the Atlantic. As merchants and artisans, they entered into public displays on public occasions at the heart of a commercial center like Phila-delphia. They dramatized social and political perspectives openly in a way that extended beyond even the more clandestine doings of the Mohawks of Boston Harbor. They had an open and ongoing organization.

The speeches and other display activities reported for the Sons of St. Tammany articulate their philosophic aims clearly. As the inheritors of the tradition of treaty-making, they represented both the Quaker and Lenni Lenape perspectives on making and keeping peace and underscoring sac-rifice in the service of social harmony.[43] Tammany's story was elaborated in such a way that he was described as living a life in service to the main-tenance of both peace and liberty, and then, having grown old, he died in flames, in his own wigwam, still proclaiming these virtues.

> At length growing old and quite worn out with years,
> As history doth truly proclaim,
> His wigwam was fired, he nobly expired,
> And flew to the skies in a flame, my brave boys,
> And flew to the skies in a flame.[44]

With the organizing of the Sons of St. Tammany, as with the rise of the Mohawks for the Boston Tea Party, voluntary associations of both a formal and informal sort availed themselves of this widespread way of dramatizing resistance. Putting on this garb played an important part in developing a symbolic vocabulary of what came to be national identity.[45] Playing Indian must be understood in the context of festive form and the historical experience of the colonies as devices were developed that carried both global and local meanings.

The nation was built on the promises of independent landholding and the development of a middle way of civilization through agricultural cultivation. Such a vision called for farmers to regard it in their interest to produce surplus crops, but in the context of an otherwise self-sufficient agricultural unit. As the land to be used for this agricultural development was seized from the Indians, the farmers came into repeated confrontations with Indians over proprietary use of the lands. Thus, Indians held an especially complicated place in the symbolic imagination of the European settlers in America. The primary foods on which the settlers had come to rely were Indian foods, the cultivation of which, it was strongly remembered, was learned from the Indians. Yet, as savages, they were more identified with the forests than the fields, and thus the Indian foods themselves were marked as being cultivated in a different style from European crops. The planting of Indian corn, squash, pumpkins, and gourds carried messages of the same kind of freely and naturally arrived at organization as Indian treaty-making, peace-keeping, and fighting. Growing and eating Indian stuff at the frontier, then, provided a constant reminder of living at the edge of the cultivated—and civilized—world.

This provided the major theme in the writings by Europeans about American frontier life, a theme known best in the work of J. Hector St. John de Crèvecoeur, especially his *Letters from an American Farmer.*[46] This living on the edge was certainly not regarded as a license to return to nature in any way. Indeed the earliest settlers in the North argued that the acts of agricultural production carried out in the cooperative American style would most fully confront the potential evils of "wilderness temptations" as John Eliot put it.[47]

Many have pointed out this theme in which regulated agriculture was equated with the civilizing process.[48] A number of settlers themselves, like Crèvecoeur, feared that the encounter with the wilderness and with savages would lead to a retreat from the recent European achievements of civility and refinement.[49] On the other hand, necessity called for compromise with the demands of the land, and with their "natural" neighbors, the Indians. Crèvecoeur recognized that this presents more difficulties for his wife and children than himself, for he "can plough, sow, and hunt" while she must, "like other squaws, . . . cook for us the nasaump, the ninchicke. . . . she must learn to bake squashes and pumpkins under the ashes" all the while cheerfully adopting the foods and "the manners and customs of her neighbors," including their ways of dressing and comporting themselves.[50]

Crèvecoeur admitted to an even greater fear, that of capture, for he, and others understood, that those captured never were willing to return to their white communities. "By what power does it come to pass," asks the troubled Crèvecoeur, "that children who have been adopted when young among these people . . . can never be prevailed on to re-adopt European manners?" [51]

Crèvecoeur was far from alone in voicing these concerns and in attaching notions of savagery to the Indians. Benjamin Rush, for instance, described the process of settlement in similar terms. He noted that there were three different "species" of settlers who represent "regular stages which mark the progress from the savage to civilized life" specifically with regard to how "Indian" they are in manner and practices. "The first settler," Rush points out, "is nearly related to an Indian in his manners— In the second, the Indian manners are more diluted: It is in the third species of settlers only, that we behold civilization completed." [52] Crèvecoeur saw irony in the fact that the civilizing process was constructed from the domestic practices learned from the indigenous peoples they were displacing. The lessons absorbed were so various and self-evident that to catalog them is simply to rehearse the ubiquitous symbolic presence of Indians long after they had been made savages and put into sylvan retreat.

In terms of food of both the animal and vegetable sorts, frontier technology rested on Indian practices: in the way in which fields were to be quickly and easily cleared, by girdling the trees and planting between the resulting stumps; in the planting of Indian crops like squash, pumpkin, gourds, and maize, in the Indian manner, in hills, so that the corn stalks could be used to support the gourd and squash vines as they emerged; and by preparing these crops in Indian style, as did Crèvecoeur's wife.

Moreover, when speaking of the plenitude to be found in the New Eden, this indigenous element was to be regarded as part of nature, to be seized upon and made orderly. In fact, Crèvecoeur and many others feared that this natural plenitude would become the enemy of civilization, for settlers too often found it too easy to live off of the land and therefore did not engage in the agricultural practices that seemed essential for maintaining the proper order of family and community. Through the surplus production of crops and the orderly way in which agriculture was carried out in the settlements, Indians would learn the benefits of the civilizing process, Crèvecoeur and others argued. "As long as we keep ourselves busy in tilling the earth, there is no fear of any of us becoming wild." [53]

This was said in response to his fears, and those of his European readers, that somehow the frontier experience, and the disporting with Indians would contaminate his children. "I have been for several years an expert marksman" he notes, "but I dread lest the imperceptible charm of Indian education, may seize my younger children, and give them such a propensity to that mode of life, as may preclude their returning to the manners and customs of their parents."[54] The central feature of these manners and customs derived from acts of rational agriculture itself; Indians were ignoble to the extent that they were rootless hunters and foragers, ones who did not know the sense of divine order inherent in the passage of the seasons and the cultivation of the land in an orderly fashion.[55]

Adopting the manners and the style of Indians to make a social and political fraternity involved a complex and ambiguous licensing arrangement. This became all the more complicated after the Revolution when other kinds of self-conscious cultural invention was called for. This was registered in the doings of the Sons of St. Tammany after the war. They discovered that they might use their club in parades as a way of illustrating their sense of symbolic involvement in the war; they also found a new use for their rituals and speechmaking. The Indian chief Cornplanter and five other chiefs of the Seneca nation were called to Philadelphia in 1786 to assist the Sons of St. Tammany in their annual celebration. In the account given in the Philadelphia *Independent* of April 22, it is clear that both the real and the play Indians took each other and their ceremonies very seriously, indeed. All of the paraphernalia of serious civic celebration was called for, the trooping of the colors, the array of flags and the ceremonial firing of cannons. Then both groups formed one large circle and passed the "great calumet of peace," the chief poured a libation upon the ground, making appropriate note of what he was doing. The two groups, now joined by the leaders of the local militia, proceeded to dance both a dance of war and one of peace. From the speeches which were reported, it seems clear that this was an occasion for explaining to Cornplanter how the British had misled the Indians during the war.[56]

At the time of the War for Independence, and ever since, these characteristics have maintained the stereotypical Indian warrior in the repertoire of figures to be admired and imitated. Depicted as independent, strong, well-spoken, capable of adapting to the environment, full of pride in manly achievement, with the capacity to sacrifice self for the sake of higher principles, all of these have served whites who would imitate Indians in good stead. This was especially true at historical periods in which the vigor of the manly estate was questioned; at these points it was supposed that the moral fiber of the nation's youth would be restored through the toughening wilderness experience. Playing Indian came to operate like playing Pioneer or Cowboy or Mountain Man, ways of connecting the putative past with the present. Thus have manly groups like the Rough Riders, the rugged Maine Woodsmen, the Boy Scouts have played an important part in projecting the values of hardiness and moral vigor.

In playing Indian, the Sons of St. Tammany portrayed themselves as representing the party of peace with honor, in messages conveyed through the calumet, the council fire, the burying of the hatchet, all of the devices used by the Sons of St. Tammany as a way of extolling themselves as men of vigorous honor and peace. Such groups serve as a gauge to the tensions of particular times and places. Through their endeavors a clear relationship emerges between these sources of conflict and the self-representational enactments of these voluntary associations, as men band together to assert their sense of liberty.

V

Surveying the impact of the strange and marvelous creatures discovered by Europeans in the New World, Howard Mumford Jones describes the attractions and the terrors of the images that were sent back: "The New World was filled with monsters animal and animals human; it was a region of terrifying natural forces, of gigantic catastrophes, of unbearable heat and cold, an area where the laws of nature tidily governing Europe were transmogrified into something new and strange. Terror and gigantism have their attractiveness. . . . the Renaissance image of the New World was compounded of both the positive and negative elements which attract and repel."[57] This terror and gigantism became socially useful as Americans developed the details of their own style and social organization. The attractive features began to outweigh the fears, at least as far as the invention of useful roles to take on in early display activities.

In Indian life was discovered a sense of social unity, at least on the level of the achieved community. As the White Indians had announced, "We all won brother" as they dressed up and acted as Indians in resistance to what they regarded as the introduction of class attitudes in their lives. In the face of a perceived foe, then, they engaged in a good deal of inventing of traditions, suggesting that they were availing themselves of an already well-known and customary means by which adopted practices might be endowed with the sense of being "as old as time." If the settlers saw themselves as rejecting the old European decadent traditions, they found materials in the New World which they could draw upon that seemed to be even earlier and closer to the earth, "older than the flood."

That this invention was both a historic process and a folkloric one is manifest. Cases like this sort demonstrate the usefulness of bringing the insights of historians and folklorists together as they bear on occasions in which public display events are invented. Folklorists, studying these activities in terms of their continuity with a kind of timeless past, hone in upon the vocabulary and the motives of traditional practices. Historians encountering these materials find in them techniques of cultural invention that are central to understanding how social forces manifest themselves in organizations of volunteers as they invent themselves, even as they enter into mobbing activities. Bringing these perspectives together with the insights of the cultural critique one can recognize the immense amount of cultural production accomplished in the most mundane social activities. By understanding the display events as highly intensified political activities as well as heated-up semiotic constructions, a deeper understanding of the uses and reuses of traditional practices may be derived. In addition, we might find ourselves closer to a usable theory of cultural imitation across boundaries.[58]

NOTES

1. For the theater-state see Clifford Geertz, *Negara: The Theatre State in Nineteenth Century Bali* (Princeton, 1980). An extensive literature on Early Modern European state processions and royal progresses underscores the theatrical character of royal and civic ceremony. See, for instance, Sydney Anglo, *Spectacle, Pageantry, and Early Tudor Policy* (Oxford, 1969); Natalie Zemon Davis, "The Social and the Body Sacred in Sixteenth-Century Lyon," *Past and Present* 90 (1981): 40–71; Richard C. Trexler, *Public Life in Renaissance Florence* (New York, 1980); David Bergeron, *English Civic Pageantry, 1558–1642* (London, 1972). For Carnival and its related form, carnivalization, the most important literature seems to derive from the impact of the Russian language philosopher M. M. Bakhtin. See his *Rabelais and His World,* tr. Helen Iswoldsky (Cambridge, 1969). For an overview of the concept in relation to other of Bakhtin's notions, see Katerina Clark and Michael Holquist, *M. M. Bakhtin* (Cambridge, 1984), esp. 299–320. For further discussions of the usefulness and the limitations of the term, see Peter Stallybrass and Allon White, *The Politics and Poetics of Transgres-*

sion (Ithaca, 1986); Roger D. Abrahams, "The Discovery of Marketplace Culture," *Intellectual History Newsletter,* 1988. Roger D. Abrahams, "Review Article: Bakhtin, the Critics and Folklore," *Journal of American Folklore,* 102 (1989): 202–6. See also a number of the articles in *The Reversible World: Symbolic Inversion in Art and Society,* ed. B. A. Babcock (Ithaca, 1978); and Alessandro Falassi, ed. *Time out of Time: Essays on the Festival* (Albuquerque, 1987).

2. Sir James George Frazer, *The Golden Bough,* 3d ed., 12 vols. (London, 1908); Arnold van Gennep, *The Rites of Passage,* tr. Monika B. Vizedom and Gabrielle L. Caffee (Chicago, 1960).

3. See especially Victor W. Turner, *The Ritual Process* (Ithaca, 1969).

4. The books which had the greatest impact during this period included Victor W. Turner's *The Forest of Symbols* (Ithaca, 1967); *The Ritual Process: Structure and Anti-Structure* (Chicago, 1969); and *Dramas, Fields and Metaphors: Symbolic Action in Human Society* (Ithaca, 1974); and Clifford Geertz's series of articles included in the two collections, *The Interpretation of Cultures* (New York, 1973) and *Local Knowledge* (New York, 1983).

5. Davis, especially pp. 73–112.

6. The foundational arguments here arise from the reading of the literature of travel resulting in the perception (and creation) of the Other. Important arguments here are Margaret T. Hodgen, *Early Anthropology in the Sixteenth and Seventeenth Centuries* (Philadelphia, 1964); Ronald L. Meek, *Social Science and the Ignoble Savage* (Cambridge, 1976); Johannes Fabian, *Time and the Other: How Anthropology Makes Its Object* (New York, 1983); James Boon, *Other Tribes, Other Scribes* (Cambridge, 1982). An especially useful overview of the subject written from the perspective of the cultural critique is Arjun Appadurai, Afterword, in *Gender, Genre and Power in South Asian Expressive Traditions,* ed. Appadurai, Frank J. Korom, and Margaret A. Mills (Philadelphia, 1991).

7. For the range of use of *callithumpian* in the United States, see *Dictionary of American Regional English.* See also Hans Kurath's *A Word-Geography of the Eastern United States,* fig. 182, "Serenading." Kurath includes other terms, mapping their deployment: horning (horning bee); chivaree; calathump or calathumpian band; skimerton or skimelton; belling; bull banding and tin panning. For a brilliant study of a local callithumpian tradition used for political commentary, see Susan G. Davis, *Parades and Power: Street Theatre in Nineteenth Century Philadelphia* (Philadelphia, 1986).

8. This healing function is described in detail in Gail Kligman, *Calus: Symbolic Transformations in Romanian Ritual* (Chicago, 1977). For the role of luck in healing the sense of community, see Martin J. Lovelace, "Christmas Mumming in England: The House-Visit," in *Folklore Studies in Honour of Herbert Halpert: A Festschrift,* ed. K. S. Goldstein and N. V. Rosenberg (St. Johns, Newfoundland, 1980); and Henry Glassie, *All Silver and No Brass: An Irish Christmas Mumming* (Philadelphia, 1975).

9. Following Thompson, such scenes are commonplace illustrations of what he

called "the moral economy of the crowd"—that is, the inherited technique for organizing and dramatizing forms of resistance. See his "The Moral Economy of the English Crowd in the Eighteenth Century," *Past and Present* 50 (1971): 76–136. Central here for the recent effusion of studies is his "Rough Music: Le Charivari Anglais," *Annales* 27 (1972): 285–312; and Natalie Zemon Davis, *Society and Culture in Early Modern France* (Stanford, 1975), esp. chaps. 3–5. Thompson and other historians mention the earlier work of the English folklorist Violet Alford, "Rough Music or Charivari," *Folklore* 70 (1959): 505–18, as well as the work by the French folklorist Arnold Van Gennep. A survey of North American practices is Bryan Palmer, "Discordant Music: Charivaris and Whitecapping in Nineteenth Century North America," *Labor/Le Travailleur* 1 (1978): 6–62. Susan Desan provides a historiographic survey of the development of these ideas in "Crowds, Community, and Ritual in the Work of E. P. Thompson and Natalie Davis," in *The New Cultural History*, ed. Lynn Hunt (Berkeley, 1989), 47–71.

10. Key works here include, in addition to the above, Emmanuel LeRoi Ladurie, especially, *Carnival in Romans*, tr. Mary Feeney (New York, 1979); *Le Charivari: Actes de la Table Ronde Organisee a Paris (25–27 Avril, 1977),* ed. Jacques Le Goff and Jean-Claude Schmitt (Paris, 1981); Charles Tilly, "Charivaris, Repertoires, and Politics" (working paper), Ann Arbor, 1980.

11. See especially Young in this regard.

12. Robert Darnton, *The Kiss of Lamourette: Reflections on Cultural History* (New York, 1990), 342–43.

13. Here the work of Natalie Zemon Davis and E. P. Thompson, mentioned above, and the studies included in Robert Darnton, *The Great Cat Massacre* (New York, 1984), illustrate both the usefulness and the restrictiveness of this kind of historical writing dealing with the materials of tradition.

14. *Tradition* and *authenticity* in this critical literature have been shown to be anchoring terms in bourgeois ideology. Many studies have recently emerged detailing the *invention* of traditions. See here *The Invention of Tradition*, ed. Eric Hobsbawm and Terence Ranger (Cambridge, 1983). Ranger himself has pointed to the strange reception of the work by folklorists and historians in "The Invention of Tradition Revisited: The Case of Colonial Africa," in *Legitimacy and the State in Twentieth Century Africa,* ed. Terence Ranger and Ofumeli Vaughan (London, in press). In a related argument, homelands have been described as *imagined* as communities. See here Benedict Anderson, *Imagined Communities: Reflections on the Origin and Spread of Nationalism* (London, 1983). Both terms, *inventing* and *imagining,* at first glance make the process of national culture-building seem imposed, unnatural, propagandistic, spurious by its very character; the construction of a history based on the power of such inventions does not conform to "the facts." No matter how much intellectual pleasure the demystification attending the revelation that these are inventions may produce, one can not ignore that these social constructions were successful in

bringing about a sense of shared culture and community sufficient to rationalize politically the idea of the nation.

15. Greg Dening, *History's Anthropology: The Death of William Gooch* (Lanham, 1988), 27.

16. [Gershom Flagg], *A Strange Account of the Rising and Breaking of a Great Bubble* (Boston, 1767), 11, cited in Peter Taylor, *Liberty Men and Great Proprietors: The Revolutionary Settlement of the Maine Frontier, 1760–1820* (Chapel Hill, 1990), 264.

17. Here Robert St. George's discussions of the house-attack in pre-Revolutionary North America has informed and deepened my argument, as have the arguments waged by Alfred Young: Robert Blair St. George, *Fictions of the Soul,* forthcoming. See also Alfred F. Young, "English Plebeian Culture and Eighteenth-Century American Radicalism" in *The Origins of Anglo-American Radicalism* (Atlantic Highlands, N.J., 1991).

18. For a survey of voluntary male organizations and their impact on American life, see Mary Ann Clawson, *Constructing Brotherhood: Class, Gender and Fraternalism* (Princeton, 1989); somewhat less useful is Mark C. Carnes, *Secret Ritual and Manhood in Victorian America* (New Haven, 1989).

19. Taylor provides a list of the primary disturbances, 264–79.

20. From a recruiting notice written by Daniel Brackett, a veteran of the Revolution and a leader of the backwoods rebels, reprinted in Taylor, 186.

21. Brackett, in Taylor, 186.

22. Taylor, 184.

23. Taylor, 184–85.

24. There have been a great many studies of both the St. George and the Turk play and the Morris Dance, conveniently surveyed in Alex Helm, *The English Mummers' Play* (Suffolk, 1981) and Violet Alford, *Sword Dance and Drama* (London, 1962). See also the special issue of *Journal of American Folklore* 94 (1981) on folk drama, edited by Thomas A. Green. For a description of the range of these festive entertainments in village entertainments, see Herbert Halpert, "A Typology of Mumming," in *Mumming in Newfoundland,* ed. Halpert and G. M. Story (Toronto, 1969).

25. Calvin Martin and Steven Crain, "The Indian behind the Mask at the Boston Tea Party," *Indian Historian,* 7–8 (1974–75): 45–47.

26. Young argues that tarring and feathering came to be associated as an American practice in England, a frontier amusement as a political action. For the relationship of this kind of activity to lynching in the American South, see Bertrand Wyatt-Brown, *Southern Honor* (New York, 1982), 435–61.

27. William Eddis, *Letters from America* (London, 1792), 114–15.

28. See here John Timbs, *Clubs and Club Life in London* (London, 1872), 33–38.

29. Benjamin Woods Labaree, *The Boston Tea Party* (London, 1966), 143.

30. Rhys Isaac, *The Transformation of Virginia, 1740–1790* (Chapel Hill, 1982), 256.

31. Isaac, 258.

32. See the Jacobus Kuydall Diary, Kimble Papers, reported in Andre Norton and Phyllis Miller, *House of Shadows* (New York, 1984), 57–60, 88–90, 122–27; my thanks to Janet Anderson for this discovery. For the later New York State renters strike, see Henry Christman, *Tin Horns and Calico: An Episode in the Emergence of American Democracy* (New York, 1945).

33. My book *Singing the Master: The Emergence of African American Culture in the Plantation South* (New York, 1992), involves accounts of plantation life at festive times, such as the harvest. The planters themselves encouraged their slaves to display themselves in their most African styles. Among themselves the planters and their families imitated their slaves at play, an imitational format that developed into the first great American popular culture form, the blackface minstrel show. This is paralleled in American show business by another kind of spectacle, the Wild West Show, which featured the symbolic presentation of American Indians carrying out attacks on white settlers, a more than casual reference to the Indian raids that lay behind the various forms of White Indian displays.

34. Robert Beverley, *History and Present State of Virginia,* ed. David Freeman Hawke (New York, 1966), 3. In this identification, as many commentators have noticed, Beverley was flying in the face of John Smith's very early account: "They are inconstant in everie thing, but what feare constraineth them to keep" and subject to worst kinds of excesses in bodily cleanliness, eating habits, dependability (*Travels and Works of Captain John Smith,* ed. Edward Arber and A. G. Bradley (Edinburgh, 1910) 2:464. Cf Bernard Sheehan, *Savagism and Civility: Indians and Englishmen in Colonial Virginia* (Cambridge, 1980), 50.

35. Beverley, 3–4.

36. See here the images in Hugh Honour, *The New Golden Land: European Images of America from the Discoveries to the Present Time* (New York, 1975), 126–34. Sheehan surveys the literature, 49–51.

37. Edwin Patrick Kilroe, *Saint Tammany and the Origin of the Society of Tammany or Columbian Order in the City of New York* (New York, 1917), notes that Horatio Hale "says the words are not of the Delaware language, but of Iroquois origin, and mean 'I am master wherever I am' " (26). The motto was engraved on a thirty-two-pound cannon presented by the Schuylkill Fishing Company to the Association Battery for use in the defense of Philadelphia in 1747. That this motto was being used that early in the history of the company suggests that the self-identification with Tammany and the stereotype of the Indian regarding making war and peace with honor and dignity antedates the adoption of the costume and the other emblems of membership.

38. The evidence is sorted out nicely by Kilroe, 108–10.

39. The best resource for this history remains Kilroe's doctoral dissertation. He draws heavily on the work of Francis Von A. Cabeen, "The Society of the Sons of Saint Tammany in Philadelphia," *Pennsylvania Magazine of History and Biography,* 26

(1902) and 28 (1903). More recent studies drawing on this material include: Rayna Green, "The Tribe Called Wannabee: Playing Indian in America and Europe," *Folklore* 99 (1908): 35–36; Donald A Grinde, Jr., and Bruce A. Johansen, "An American Synthesis: The Sons of St. Tammany or Columbian Order," in *Exemplar of Liberty: Native America and the Evolution of Democracy* (Los Angeles, 1991) 169–89; Nicholas Varga, "America's Patron Saint: Tammany," *Journal of American Culture* 10 (1987): 45–51; Alan Leande MacGregor, "Tammany: the Indian as Rhetorical Surrogate," *American Quarterly* 35 (1983): 391–407.

40. Ebenezer Hazard to Jeremy Belknap, in *Belknap Papers* (Boston, 1891), I:335. Hazard was born in Philadelphia, January 15, 1744, and was graduated from Princeton in 1762, and became a well-known classical scholar, antiquarian, and patriot. See Kilroe, 75.

41. Cited in Cabeen, 218, from *Freeman's Journal,* May 7, 1783.

42. Eddis, p. 115.

43. The article by John Witthoft, "The Lenape as Peacemakers of the Forests," *Keystone Folklore* 4 (Summer, 1992): 49–58, gives an overview of the literature on how the Lenape were viewed by their neighboring groups of Indians as peacemakers, thus certainly contributing to the attribution of this character to Tammany.

44. Kilroe, 79.

45. The study of the growth of voluntary associations in their European origins has been initiated by Margaret C. Jacob, *Living the Enlightenment: Freemasonry and Politics in Eighteenth-Century Europe* (New York, 1991). She suggests that with formation of the Freemasons we may locate the "earliest moments in the formation of modern civil society." "The lodge, the philosophic society and the scientific academy became the underpinning . . . for the republican and democratic forms of government that evolved slowly and fitfully in Western Europe from the late eighteenth century on." Addressing similar developments in America, Mary Ann Clawson, *Constructing Brotherhood: Class, Gender and Fraternalism* (Princeton, 1991), 13, provides an interesting feminist reading of the role of Freemasons and other such organizations in American life: "Fraternalism was one of the most widely available and persistently used forms of collective organization in European and American history from the Middle Ages onward. Any explanation of this must take into account its ritual character. Initiations and other ceremonies were dramatic enactments. . . . In the case of Masonic fraternalism . . . the image of one particular social actor, the artisan, dominated the reality-defining drama/discourse of fraternal ritual." The Indian with his robe, feathers, and buckskin was substituted for the Masons apron and other paraphernalia by the Sons of St. Tammany, but they otherwise shared a great deal, both in constitution of the group and the chartering myths and rituals they developed.

46. J. Hector St. John de Crèvecoeur, *Letters from an American Farmer* (1782) (New York, 1957), 57 ff.

47. John Eliot, "The Learned Conjectures" (1650), quoted in George H. Wil-

liams, *Wilderness and Paradise* New York, 1962), 102. See also Roderick Nash, *Wilderness and the American Mind,* rev. ed. (New Haven, 1973), 29.

48. Nash, 28–30; Roy Harvey Pearce, *Savagism and Civilization: A Study of the Indian and the American Mind,* rev. ed. (Baltimore, 1965).

49. For a detailed description of this achievement see the masterworks of Norbert Elias, *The Civilizing Process* (New York, 1978); and Fernand Braudel, *Civilization and Capitalism, 15th–18th Century,* tr. Sian Reynolds, 3 vols. (New York, 1981).

50. Crèvecoeur, 216.

51. Ibid. See also James Axtell, *The Europeans and the Indians* (New York, 1981), 168–206; Annette Kolodny, *The Land before Her: Fantasy and Experience of the American Frontiers, 1630–1860,* 68 ff.

52. Quoted in William Cronon, *Changes in the Land: Indians, Colonists and the Ecology of New England* (New York, 1983), 5.

53. Crèvecoeur, 215.

54. Ibid.

55. Sheehan surveys the arguments, 37–64.

56. The article from the *Independent* is reprinted in Cabeen, 443–45.

57. Howard Mumford Jones, *O Strange New World: American Culture, the Formative Years* (New York, 1964), 70.

58. My thanks to: Marion Nelson Winship for first directing me to the Tammany materials; Bob St. George at all stages in helping to work out this argument; to Peter Thompson, for help in understanding voluntary organizations in Philadelphia during this period; to Rhys Isaac and Michael Zuckerman for pointing to further materials, leading to a larger scale understanding of this phenomenon during this period; to Caroll Smith-Rosenberg and Michael Roth for informed and enthusiastic readings along the way and to Janet for doing the hard editing.

TWO KINDS OF
"NEW HISTORICISM"
FOR PHILOSOPHERS

Ian Hacking

COULD PHILOSOPHICAL ANALYSIS have anything to do with the activity that Michel Foucault called the history of the present? Yes, I say. No, says almost everyone else. So I have some explaining to do.

Philosophical analysis is an activity, a way of doing philosophy, defined in part by its practitioners. It used to think of itself as analyzing concepts, and then turned to words. I think of J. L. Austin, C. D. Broad, Paul Grice, G. E. Moore, Bertrand Russell, Gilbert Ryle, Ludwig Wittgenstein, but of course there are many very much younger, very much American, and very much alive analysts today. The men whom I have mentioned knew, in some cases, a great deal about the past and in particular about ancient philosophy. Some felt intellectual kinship with Aristotle. But a sense of the past played little role in their most creative work. Analytic philosophy is widely regarded as the very antithesis of historical sensibility. It needn't be, or so I contend.

I have no desire to make peace between different traditions. Attempts to reconcile continental and analytic philosophy are at best bland, lacking the savor or pungency of either. I should add that in connecting philosphical analysis with certain techniques used by Foucault I am not making a point about recent French thought in general. I am discussing one kind of use of the past, represented by some of Foucault's books. Finally, although I in no way dissociate myself from analytic philosophy as at present practiced in America, my list of heroes in the second paragraph shows my connection with those roots primarily concerned with the analysis of concepts. There are other roots, those of the Vienna Circle, that are less germane.

My title speaks of two uses of history. One I've just mentioned: philosophical analysis and the history of the present. But I was invited to discuss something more general: philosophy under the rubric "History and . . ." The invitation alluded to the ways in which Richard Rorty has combined history and philosophy. That, then, is the other use of history for philosophy to which my title refers.

I begin in section I, "The Mandate," by describing what I was asked to say about history and philosophy. In II, "Antihistory," I record the plain fact that most American philosophers working in anything like an analytic tradition have little use for history in their philosophical work. In III, "Undoing," I note how Rorty uses history for philosophical ends, namely, to undo much philosophy, and not only the analytic type. In IV, "Taking a Look," I describe another use of history, applied to more specific ideas and situations than those considered by Rorty. In V, I draw some brief connections between philosophical analysis and Foucault's history of the present. I take this to be a continuation of the sorts of "taking a look" that are the topic of IV.

I. THE MANDATE

"Our various papers," so went my invitation to discuss History and Philosophy, "will not consist of case studies or histories of the disciplines."[1] We were asked to "concentrate on the ways in which the kind of knowing in which each field is engaged is affected by consciousness of and connections with the past." In section II I state, for the record, the obvious fact that most philosophy written in English is *not* much affected by consciousness of or by connections with the past.

"How is the new historicism, or philosophy as conversation, connected with philosophy as problem-solving?" "Problem solving" must refer to analytic philosophy in the twentieth century, for the self-description of philosophy as problem solving is at best minor in other traditions. "Philosophy as conversation" adverts to a theme of Richard Rorty's book, *Philosophy and the Mirror of Nature.*[2] And "new historicism" must denote a historicism that has recently appeared or reappeared in philosophy written or spoken in English. Hence my mandate was to focus on recent events connected with philosophy and history in an English-language milieu.

"New historicism, or philosophy as conversation": philosophy as conversation is not, for me, identical to the new historicism. I shall insist that it denotes only one kind of new historicism. But what's historicism?

Something like this: the theory that social and cultural phenomena are historically determined and that each period in history has its own values that are not directly applicable to other epochs. In philosophy that implies that philosophical issues find their place, importance, and definition in a specific cultural milieu.

That is certainly Rorty's opinion, and, aside from some qualifications stated in section III, it is mine too. He reaches a subversive conclusion about the nature of philosophy by analyzing the philosophical tradition in which he himself grew up. He holds that traditional topics of mind and matter, of the foundations of knowledge, and refutation of skepticism, freedom of the will and the problem of universals—the kit and caboodle of metaphysics and epistemology—had a place in earlier pieces of European history but are now defunct. Philosophy shall absent itself from a postphilosophic age. I am perhaps out of step when I see this less as a new historicism than as an example of a historicism that is recurrent among philosophers. I shall say something about that in III. It is an old-fashioned historicism that pays little attention to the complex interweavings of past and present. But perhaps that is what is intended: a fly-by-night encounter with the past, more story than history.

It does matter that philosophy as conversation is not the only sort of "new" historicism around. In IV I describe another kind. The individual concepts traditionally of interest to philosophers are not, for it, timeless objects. Instead "normalcy," "chance," "cause," "person," "evidence," "guilt," or "abuse" are structures whose roles and power have been determined by specific histories. This is a local historicism, attending to particular and disparate fields of reflection and action. It discourages grand unified accounts, but it does demand taking a look at lots of little facts. Rorty's use of history is in contrast global, drawing conclusions about the whole of philosophy and indeed everything else, for chemistry and literary criticism are alike ruled part of conversation.

II. ANTIHISTORY

The invitation mentions that "in the wake of structuralism's and functionalism's celebration of the synchronic, the significance of historical knowing is far from clear." This remark is germane to some disciplines, but there has been no significant interaction between structuralism and American philosophy. The exception proves the rule. Noam Chomsky's ideas about generative grammar, Cartesian linguistics, and innate mental structures did attract young philosophers of language. He has also been recognized as a structuralist. I say he proves the rule that structuralism had no impact on American philosophy, because the selfsame philosophers who took up his work thought of it as readily fitting into ordinary analytic philosophy. They were astonished to hear it given the alien name of structuralism.

Structuralism has emphasized the synchronic. Analytic philosophy could so readily engage Chomsky's grammar not because it is synchronic but because it is achronic. Thus it is like many other philosophical reflections that have no temporal dimension. The few "professional" historians among philosophers have commonly declined to be historicist when doing philosophy. Hume's *History of England* made him the first man to earn a good living from the sales of his books. For years Leibniz was paid to do historical hackwork. But Leibniz's philosophy is nonhistorical. Hume's is positively antihistoricist—as befits the original Whig historian. The old historicism in philosophy was the work of amateurs like Hegel, and it is amateurs (like Rorty or myself) who practice new historicisms today.

I shall be talking about how some kinds of history matter to some ways of doing philosophy. But I would be disloyal to many of my friends if I did not report what they believe: "There's history, and then there's philosophy. There's the history of philosophy (and the philosophy of history) but philosophers today need be no more conscious of their history than any other kind of thinker!"

This attitude is not some freakish disposition of analytic anglophones. Popular tradition says philosophy is about the eternal verities. A dictionary says that philosophy is the rational investigation of being, knowledge, and conduct. Philosophers have wanted to know what kinds of things there are, how we find out or what we can know, and what we ought to do. To say it a third time in Greek, philosophers do metaphysics, epistemology, and ethics. These are thought of as timeless inquiries. That sort of thinking spills out into several distinguishable attitudes, each well represented by able young American philosophers. I shall sketch them in order of decreasingly virulent antihistoricism.

Present-Timeless. We want to understand things such as duty, reason, causation, personal identity, existence, truth, and the difference between the universal and the particular. We try to understand excuses for not doing what one promised to do; we need to understand promises and how

or why they bind. We need to know the differences between explanations
in history, in the deterministic sciences, in the statistical sciences, and in
matters of personal behavior. We may salvage some good ideas from dead
thinkers (says Present-Timeless), but consciousness of the past is irrelevant except as a warning against pitfalls and bad mistakes. Hence we have
no historicist sensibilities. As teachers of philosophy we would be happier
if the interesting bits of the history of our subject were taught partly in
the Western Civilization and Culture Series, and the rest taught elsewhere
as a specialist subject, no more part of philosophy than the history of science is part of science, or the history of art part of art.

Pen-Pals. A milder position notes the persistence of certain philosophical interests. Older philosophers set the stage and made permanent contributions. It is a slightly surprising matter of fact that many of their
concerns remain vital. We profit by reading and analyzing their ideas,
clarifying their conclusions, refuting their errors. Old philosophers are to
be studied as pen friends: one-way discussants across the seas of time. We
don't care about them because of their role in *their* day. The problems peculiar to fourth-century Athens or seventeenth-century Amsterdam don't
matter to us. We care about only the old books that speak to us. (A Pen-
Pal can also be a [moderate] Present-Timeless. For a good example, take a
sequence of five excellent, alternating books by Jonathan Bennett: *Rationality* [1964], *Locke, Berkeley, Hume: Central Themes* [1971], *Linguistic Behaviour*
[1976], *A Study of Spinoza's Ethics* [1984], *Events and Their Names* [1988].)[3]

Doing-and-Sharing. A yet gentler suggestion: philosophy is not a kind of
knowing but an activity. Despite our practice of writing books, Socrates
should be our archetype. One kind of apprenticeship that distinguishes
philosophy is the reading of canonical philosophers and discussing their
work—with a teacher. Do not blush at philosophy's perennial themes.
Unlike the natural sciences it is not in the progress business. And do not
be misled by the fact that philosophical minds have long been turning in-
choate conceptual messes into natural sciences; that is a hobby that comes
with the trade, and when it works a new kind of professional is created,
not a revamped philosopher. No matter how many topics it creates and
then evicts into the province of science, philosophy will continue to deal
with fundamental aspects of the human condition and the human mind.
Dead philosophers speak to us not because, as Pen-Pal thinks, they got a
foot in the door of some difficult problem that helps us pry it open further. They speak to us directly about matters of joint concern.

Getting-Inside. Our Pen-Pals hear whatever they want to hear. It is no criticism that they take the words of the dead philosopher totally out of context (if that's what they want to do). Let one be Whig in his reading and the other Tory. What the dead philosopher himself meant is of no moment to either reader, for a *Pen-Pal* values only what helps him to do his own philosophizing. But *Doing-and-Sharing* has a difficulty. If we are engaging in a discourse with the dead, we had better understand them. Even if they do speak to something mysterious called the human condition (read "Western tradition"?) they speak in the words of their day, in their settings. We must become engaged in the interpretation of texts. We must work our way into a circle of meanings. We must become hermeneutical.

This classification is evenhanded. It caricatures all parties. Caricature yes, but those parties are out there in abundance. I thought it improper to proceed to history-and-philosophy without putting that on record.

My sketch glides over one question that does trouble me. It was posed in my invitation. I shall neglect it, although it was part of my mandate. "In what way does a precontemporary philosopher's ability to speak directly to some of us alter our notions about the importance, or irrelevance, of historical understanding to philosophical understanding?" I don't know the answer. More candidly, the fact that dead philosophers can speak directly doesn't *alter* my notions at all. But I would like to understand the phenomenon better. I find it *astonishing.* I put my perplexity as vividly as I could in the first two parables of my "Five Parables."[4] I think it is paradoxical that Descartes can speak directly to sophomores whose conception of the world seems to be distressingly achronic—yet the better you know the text the more you realize that only the most arduous hermeneutical scholarship can make much sense out of it at all.

A mild version of this paradox lies in the fact that all four ways of not doing history are OK. All are honorable ways in which to be a philosopher. Do not think, however, that the path from Present-Timeless to Getting-Inside takes us to a more and more historicist practice of philosophy. It does involve the use of more and more old sentences. Pen-Pal takes the ones he likes. Doing-and-Sharing should attend to all the sentences in some major texts of certain great authors. Getting-Inside must enter the entire discourse which a text exemplifies. Yet by the end of the process I would have a certain sympathy with the crass interjection of a particularly antihistorical Present-Timeless. He says that there is nothing peculiarly philosophical about the task of interpreting texts. We (continues P.-T.) are members of the republic of letters. So we do care about a rereading of the *Laches?* We care equally about the re-presentation by Octavio Paz and others of the sumptuous poetry of Sister Juana Ines de la Cruz. The fact that an ancient Greek philosopher wrote the former does not make it intrinsically more relevant to today's philosopher than the latter.

III. UNDOING

Philosophers have never lacked zest for criticizing their predecessors. Aristotle was not always kind to Plato. Scholastics wrangled with unexcelled vigor. The new philosophy of the seventeenth century was frankly rude about the selfsame schoolmen. But all that is criticism of someone else. Kant began something new. He turned criticism into self-reflection. He didn't just create the critical philosophy. He made philosophy critical of philosophy itself.

There are two ways in which to criticize a proposal, doctrine, or dogma. One is to argue that it is false. Another is to argue that it is not even a candidate for truth or falsehood. Call the former *denial,* the latter *undoing.* Most older philosophical criticism is in the denial mode. When Leibniz took issue with Locke in the *Nouveaux Essais* he was denying some of the things that Locke had said.[5] He took for granted that they were true-or-false. In fact, false. Kant's transcendental dialectic, in contrast, argues that a whole series of antinomies arise because we think that there are true-or-false answers to a gamut of questions. There are none. The theses, antitheses, and questions are undone.

Kant was not the first philosophical undoer. The gist of Bacon undoes the methodology of scholastic thought. But Kant is assuredly the first celebrated, self-conscious, systematic undoer. Pure reason, the faculty of the philosophers, outsteps its bounds and produces doctrines that are neither true nor false.

Kant occasionally adverts to this or that famous thinker ("the good Berkeley"), but little in his three Critiques is historical. He is close kin to Present-Timeless and Pen-Pal. But Kant, the last great philosopher of the Enlightenment, lived when the romantic era in Germany had begun. The conception of language not as mental but as a public object with a history—an idea that we associate with Hamann, Herder, and Humboldt—was being established as Kant aged. The philosophy of language became historical like much else. Life, culture, and one's identity as a person and moral agent were seen as essentially embedded and indeed as constructed in a historical tradition.

Undoing thus became historicist, but not just with the likes of Hegel; one thinks, for example, of Comte's post-Kantian historicist positivism. Comte's kind of progress is the suppression of defective earlier stages of human consciousness—the abandoning of beliefs that in reality lack truth value. They are replaced by a cast of propositions that really are up for grabs as true or false. It is as if Comte thought that revolutionary history could replace the transcendental analytic.

But it is not Kant, let alone Comte, that we think of when we mention *historicism, progress, undoing.* We think of Hegel. No one thinks of Hegel and Comte in the same sentence anymore, so it is well to have a little classification into which these people and others fit naturally enough.

The history of philosophical doctrines: a sequence of propositions was advanced over the centuries, one or more of which might in essentials have been true, but most of which were false. *And* we are progressing, for we are winnowing away false notions while adding true ones. Comte is the post-Kantian version of this, with early doctrines rejected as neither true nor false, and a new method to pick out what is true within the true or false.

Undoing by antinomies: two theses opposed to each other both possess seemingly compelling arguments. Each is based on presuppositions shown to be untenable by the critical philosophy. Neither is true or false. *And* with this discovery we are progressing, indeed making a decisive conceptual step akin to that of Copernicus. But our progress is partly one of limitation, through the Kantian realization that many of our aspirations to knowledge were misconceived.

Historicist undoing: ideas are presented as thesis countered by antithesis in a historical setting. They are superseded by a replacement of both by synthesis. In consequence neither thesis nor antithesis can strictly be regarded as true or false. Such a sequence is not the passive discovery of truth and elimination of error. Nor is it Comte's revolutionary discarding of what was neither true nor false. Nor is it Kant's undoing by limiting the possibilities of pure reason. The process of thought in the course of human history is itself proposed as the making of Truth and Possibility. It is more than the manifestation of Mind. It is Mind Making Itself. Hegel married rampant historicism to Kant's practice of undoing. *And:* the ring that bound the two together was progress. This progress was not merely something that was happening (how lucky we are to be alive in these times, and so forth). The process of history was essentially Progress, Mind superseding its past to make of itself the future.

There are three handy dimensions to this banal trio of *undoing, historicism,* and *progress.* Some twentieth-century philosophies can be graphed upon this framework. To take only some trite labeling for figures not yet mentioned:

. . . Undoing: progress based on a bold new method, but no historicism (logical positivism).

. . . Undoing: some historicism, and lots of progress (Dewey).

. . . Undoing: lots of historicism, the whole idea of progress untenable thanks to historicist reflection, but if we could restart everything, after reflective total undoing, that would be something (Heidegger).

. . . Undoing: no historicism, pessimism, and probably no progress (Wittgenstein).

Everything interesting is omitted in such a scheme, but it enables me to leap back to my mandate. How, I was asked, do I "see philosophy being affected by its recent attempts to come to terms with its past. How is the new historicism, or philosophy as conversation, connected with philosophy as problem-solving?" When we hear of philosophy's "recent attempts to come to terms with its past" and "philosophy as conversation," we know that the reference is to Richard Rorty's *Philosophy and the Mirror of Nature.* Where is Rorty on my set of coordinates? I put the question this way to remind us that his work is not anomalous: it has a place in a well-orchestrated if simpleminded schematism.

Rorty is a historicist undoer, and in a sense he believes that progress has been made (thank goodness philosophy's over). That's not novel. It's *what* he undoes historically that makes him profoundly original. No matter how loosely we construe membership in an analytic and primarily anglophone tradition, Rorty was the first member to apply the technique of historicist undoing to that tradition. He clearly feels an affinity for Dewey, but Dewey's prose was never so trenchant as Rorty's, nor did he have the same analytic tradition both to deploy and to undo. That's one reason to call Rorty, not Dewey, the source.

Rorty sees philosophy as constantly foundational, as setting itself up as judge over the other fields of human thought and activity. Analytic philosophy—within which Rorty not only includes but emphasizes logical positivism—was a final stage in an attempt to provide foundations and to provide criteria of good and bad thought. Its apparatus, notably the ana-lytic/synthetic distinction, falls into disarray. Correspondence theories of truth collapse. The very concept of being true to a real world of facts be-comes idle, and various sorts of realisms and antirealisms become Mickey Mouse. The paraphernalia of analytic philosophy came to be seen as such, as rigamarole. A thrust in that direction can be extracted from the best thinkers, from Sellars, Davidson, Goodman. If there is a name for what's left, it is pragmatism. "James and Dewey," writes Rorty in the introduc-tion to *Consequences of Pragmatism,* were "waiting at the end of the dialec-tical road which analytic philosophy traveled," and now wait for Foucault and Deleuze (p. xviii).

I would emphasize that Rorty's undoing is undoing by tracing the path of programs and projects in philosophy. He is not much concerned with the concepts and how they are constructed. It is seldom an undoing by asking into the origin and formation of concepts. There is his impor-tant discussion of the "invention of the mind." He has some things to say about "knowledge." But the book is interestingly non-Kantian, non-Hegelian, and, I venture with trepidation, non-Heideggerian; certainly non-Wittgensteinian. He does not say of the dead philosophers whom he condemns to the past that their doctrines can now be seen as neither true nor false. He is saying that they are wrong, or have come to be wrong be-cause of other historical developments.

Rather surprisingly, Rorty's way of undoing is more in the spirit of the Vienna Circle than of Kant or Hegel or Heidegger.[6] It is plain, bluff, middle-American. It differs from the Vienna Circle in that there is no progressive theme of a new method in philosophy. The theme is re-trenchment. Let us tolerantly put the past aside, have no new philosophy as such, encourage stability, and engage in conversation without threat, without revolution, above all without programs. "Every generation finds its philosopher," I hear some cynic muttering, "and middle America in the eighties found its own."

One reason for the enthusiastic reception of his book was that all the British and American students who had felt angry, oppressed, and im-potent in the face of a hegemonic analytic philosophy were told, almost from the inside, that it had committed suicide. That is also one reason why the book was greeted, in other quarters, with resentment. Rorty him-self makes humane pleas for pluralistic tolerance in these matters. Sharing Rorty's pluralism, I find the ephemera of acceptance and resentment unimportant—certainly to my present mandate. But I was asked how "philosophy as conversation connected with philosophy as problem-solving?" Officially, not at all. This is made especially plain in "Philosophy in America Today," the last essay in *Consequences of Pragmatism* (211–30). Rorty states as a matter of brute fact that there is no shared recognition of problems, and that a problem for a Cornell Ph.D. may not be seen as a problem or even as philosophy at UCLA. And that's within mainstream establishment analytic philosophy. He also talks of "programs which seem to have a shorter and shorter half-life" (216).

I do think that specific programs of research and inquiry in philosophy have short half-lives. I think that's been true through much of Western philosophy, unless you take "rationalism" or "nominalism" or another such jargon "ism" as a program. Problems—"the problems of philosophy"—seem to me something else. Perhaps we suffer from equivocation. I am sure that there are people now or recently at both Cornell and UCLA thinking and talking and writing about the problem of free will. *The* problem is the same in both places, although in one place, a person will be wrestling with a complicated logic of tense and modalities intended to represent freedom—that will be the UCLA problem and program, say. At Cornell, perhaps, it may be an examination of common law and its attributions of responsibility. Of course the members of this pair of programs and problems share little—except both address the problem of free will.

I must tread cautiously here. I don't think that philosophy is only or even mainly for solving problems. "Problem solving" may have been an ephemeral feature of philosophy. I once cheerfully dated its fruition as 1910–12. James, *Some Problems of Philosophy* (text, 1909–10);[7] Moore, *Some Main Problems of Philosophy* (text, 1910–11);[8] Russell, *The Problems of Philosophy* (1912):[9] these three books examine different problems, but there is an enormous overlap. Overlap on what? Since we are discussing Rorty, let James the pragmatist speak. He wanted to. *Some Problems of Philosophy* was written at the end of William James's life. He needed to return to problems to round out pragmatism, "which now is much like an arch built only on one side."

What are these problems? "No exact definition of the term 'metaphysics' is possible, and to name some of the problems it treats of is the best way of getting at the meaning of the word" (29). James proceeds to list twenty-one problems. For example, "What are 'thoughts,' and what are 'things'? and how are they connected?" (29). "In knowledge, how does the object get into the mind? Or the mind get at the object?" "We know by means of universal notions. Are these also real? Or are only particular things real?" (30). He also includes among his problems the issue of objective validity (or not) of moral and aesthetic judgments.

I would not express James's twenty-one problems with quite the words that he thought to use for the students of 1910. But they're almost all with us, including the three I've quoted. I won't quarrel with a romantic who says they're all in Plato. That's 2,300 years ago. The half-life of problems is short? I'm guessing we're nowhere near the half-life of these issues yet.

Nor is Rorty himself uninterested in certain traditional "problems of philosophy." On several recent occasions he has taken Bernard Williams to task for, in effect, saying that there is something fundamentally different about ethical discussion and scientific research.[10] Aren't there certain hallowed names for what's at issue—for example, "fact/value distinction"? People have been a long time asking, in all sorts of idioms, whether there is such a distinction. If there is, what is it? Does it lie in objectivity? In method? In reference? Are there intrinsically different ways of settling disputes? Or is it all a matter of degree? Is one relevant difference that between verifiability and meaninglessness, as the Vienna Circle urged? Is it the case that the moral concepts that we have of people are in significant ways distinct from the nonethical concepts that we apply to things?

We return, in short, to variations on one of William James's problems. What's notable is that when Rorty takes up a problem of philosophy no hint of a historical consideration is adduced. Problems appear to be addressed in the old antihistorical analytical way. Rorty may be more true to James than he noticed. *Philosophy and the Mirror of Nature* may also be "much like an arch built up on only one side." A return to problems may be building up the other side—but not in a historicist way.

IV. THE LOCKEAN IMPERATIVE:
TAKING A LOOK

Now I turn to a combination of history and philosophy that is in some ways the exact opposite of Rorty's. It does not apply history to the whole sweep of philosophy, but it does conceive of many philosophical problems as being essentially constituted in history. I sometimes think of the project as Locke plus history.

Locke's *Essay concerning Human Understanding* is as nonhistorical a work

as we could imagine, yet its project is amenable to historicization.[11] It is
about the origins of ideas and the origins of knowledge. Many readers find
that it emphasizes foundations for human knowledge. The book aims,
on that reading, at overcoming any skepticism residual after Descartes.
It also does its professed work as "underlabourer" to the Fellows of the
Royal Society of London. It is a perfect example of what Rorty takes to be
the core project of modern philosophy (that is, Western philosophy from
Descartes to almost now): epistemological foundations.

Where others rightly spot foundations, I also see a quest for analysis
and genesis. Locke thought that we understand concepts and knowledge
better when we understand what puts them in place, what brings them
into being. I call this the Lockean imperative: to understand our thoughts
and our beliefs through an account of origins. The fancy name is to be set
beside another one, "genetic fallacy," according to which it is foolish to
expect that the content of an idea, or the credibility of a proposition, can
in any way be illuminated by our routes to it. I think that "genetic fallacy"
is insubstantial name-calling.

Locke is the model empiricist: our ideas and our knowledge originate
in experience. But his methodology is rationalist. His book is one great
thought experiment. Aside from anecdotes, he almost never takes a look.
This is true of the entire tradition of the *idéologues*—Berkeley, Hume, Con-
dillac, Maine de Biran, or whomever. A transition occurs only at the end
of the line, namely, Condorcet, and in the work of his great historicist ad-
mirer, Auguste Comte.

Positivism began as a historicist doctrine. It was a theory about the successive transformation of knowledge. The *Cours de philosophie positive* does
more than take a look at the evolution of knowledge.[12] It bores us by
being all too comprehensive. In contrast, what philosophers now commonly call positivism, that is, logical positivism, urged that we attend
not to "the context of discovery" but to the "context of justification."[13]
To think that the context of discovery meant anything to what was discovered was to commit the genetic fallacy. Logical positivism was better
named logical empiricism, that is, positivism made nonhistorical.

Logical positivists admired the natural sciences. Their antihistorical
notion of knowledge became standard among anglophone philosophers
of science. It was battered by Kuhn's famous opening sentence: "History,
if viewed as a repository for more than anecdote or chronology, could

produce a decisive transformation in the image of science by which we are now possessed."[14] Kuhn proposed to take a look.

Kuhn's theses, his style, and the needs of readers at the moment turned *The Structure of Scientific Revolutions* into a compulsive best-seller. It also got a lot of other people to examine how the most seemingly adamant, well-tested but abstruse items of human knowledge get there. Comte, who had bitterly campaigned for the creation of a chair of the history of science some 125 years earlier, might have felt justified. But not happy: for many of Kuhn's readers began to reach skeptical conclusions about the very nature of science. That seemed to scare empiricist philosophers. Yet Kuhn was following the empiricist adage — "take a look."

Kuhn is too well known to need discussion, but the present generation of post-Kuhnian students of science isn't, yet. It takes *social construction* as its motto. In the matter of taking a look it has been courageous. We have Bruno Latour, trained as an ethnographer, who became a participant observer in a biochemistry laboratory, breaking a lot of glass in the process, and coauthoring *Laboratory Life: The Social Construction of Scientific Facts*.[15] We have Andy Pickering venturing into the holiest of holies, high energy physics, incidentally providing a first-class "objective" account of what has happened in the subject over two decades, but concluding with a philosophical thesis encoded in his title, *Constructing Quarks*.[16]

It is unimportant how one labels work like this. History? (Historians of science don't like that.) Anthropology? (New tribes to study: denizens of the laboratory.) Sociology? (These workers practice nothing remotely like American sociology.) Microsociology, chronologically recounted? ("Microsociology" was one of Latour's buzzwords.) Nothing fits well. No matter. In the present institutionalization of America, these people by and large get co-opted into philosophy or paraphilosophy departments. Kuhn, once adamant that he was a member of the American Historical Association and not of the American Philosophical Association, now works at M.I.T. in "Linguistics and Philosophy" and is president of the Philosophy of Science Association.

It is true that the people I have mentioned have tended to include something other than philosophy in their training. They have not been generated by the vast machinery of the philosophy departments that they later join and indeed adorn. Perhaps it is precisely because they know something about something that they are so given to what I nonchalantly call "taking a look." Nevertheless, their motivation is none other than the Lockean imperative. And the general conclusions at which these workers drive are original but mainstream philosophy. Here are two examples, one about knowledge, one about kinds.

The *knowledge* about a particular tripeptide produced by the hypothalmus of mammals, or the *established hypothesis* of quarks, is best described not in terms of *discovery* but in terms of *social construction*. These authors don't therefore think that the product of the construction is not "really" a fact (now)—only that the unthought world doesn't come in facts. The factization of the world is a human activity.

The *kinds* in terms of which the world is described (and the corresponding ideas, concepts, categories, classifications, or what have you) are not kinds with which the world is ready-equipped and which we elicit by probing. They too are constructed. It needs no insight to locate the philosophical thrust. These authors are addressing the problem of universals. They are propounding a somewhat novel historicist nominalism. Its roots are in the Lockean imperative to investigate the origin of ideas. The conclusions would, I hope, have cheered Locke, if not the Fellows of the Royal Society. But the procedure is un-Lockean, in that it takes a look at how the concepts did come into being in real life.

Note that *one* of the things that writers such as Pickering and Latour are doing is conducting historical inquiries, even if they are taking a look at rather recent events. In the same spirit, Simon Schaffer and Steven Shapin study the seventeenth-century battle over the experimental method of reasoning. In *Leviathan and the Air Pump: Hobbes, Boyle and the Experimental Life* they tell how a new style of scientific reasoning was put in place.[17] These histories, whether they be of the 1970s or the 1650s, are not done out of curiosity about the past. They are intended to show something about our present reality, our present reasoning, our present modes of research. They may not unfittingly be called histories of the present.

Such workers put historical substance on the bare scaffolding of Nelson Goodman's *Ways of Worldmaking*.[18] Where Goodman wrote pithily about versions of the world and right and wrong categories, these men say what the versions and categories are and how they come into being. Note that the conclusions about knowledge and about kinds directly address two of William James's twenty-one problems.

The conclusions of a Latour, a Pickering, or a Shapin and Schaffer will not seem striking to some established philosophical schools that are skeptical about the natural sciences. "Just what we expected all along," say the know-nothings, briefly forsaking logorrhoea: "The scientists make it all up." Such a priori antiscientism appeals only to the ignorant. The books I've mentioned are something else. They are based on a very serious working knowledge of the very sciences about which they are, in a certain sense, skeptical. The nominalism of authors like this is combined with a high level of *facticity* (or is it just plain curiosity?).

It was not my intention to advertise recent historicist work in the philosophy of science. For me it leads on to another observation. It is remarkable that this ferment should chiefly be happening in connection with natural science. We can see how that came to pass. There are three reasons. First, after Kuhn, a snowball. Second, if you're going to be iconoclastic and constructionalist, the idols to bash are those of natural science. Third, the Lockean imperative, unstated but present. Genetic accounts of ideas and knowledge have always tended to focus on the concerns of Locke's old friend the Royal Society.

But what about arenas where we would be more likely to find concepts molded by history? Arenas where what pass for facts bear on human nature and behavior? What about conduct, ethics, morality? We are curiously lacking, particularly in English, any serious philosophical-historical consideration of moral kinds and moral knowledge.

Perhaps philosophy of natural science was lucky. Tired old cultural relativism in morality has been with us (it feels) forever. No jejune relativism had comparable currency among those well acquainted with a natural science. Then Kuhn came bounding in with what many of his readers took to be all the trappings of "relativism" in science, "mob psychology" and the like. Two decades later we had work of the sort I've just touched upon.

Compare the abstract topic headings of metaphysics and ethics. We have reality, truth, fact, . . . on the one hand, and right, good, justice, . . . on the other. In the natural sciences we have been taking a look at the material circumstances under which truth, reality, and fact are constructed from case to case (with no obligation to tell the same story in every case). This meant investigating not truth, reality, and fact but truths, real things, and facts. In ethics, especially in English, there has been too much fixation on the abstract, on the good, the right, and the just.

J. L. Austin tried to get us to focus on what is small and alive rather than grand ("A plea for excuses").[19] Unfortunately his legacy has been the study of speech acts rather than the analysis of language. Even fewer paid heed when novelist-philosophers told moralists to deal with thick concepts. Bernard Williams's *Ethics and the Limits of Philosophy* recently repeated the plea.[20] But he has not urged us to think about thick moral concepts as historical entities whose form and force have been determined by their past. He has written a Pen-Pal book about Descartes, but he has not attempted any historicist reflection on any thick moral concept.

"Moral" inquiries not far removed from what I have in mind have been undertaken in all sorts of piecemeal and goal-directed ways. No one commonly recognizes them as either philosophy or history. There is for example the "Social Problems" school, stemming from Garfinkel, and responsible for Labeling Theory. It is interested in, among other things, how the invention of a classification for people, and its application, does several things. It affects how we think of, treat, and try to control people so classified. It affects how they see themselves. It has strongly to do with evaluation, with the creating of values, and, in some cases considered (homosexuality, juvenile delinquency) with manufacturing a social problem about the kind of person, who must then be subjected to reform, isolation, or discipline. An almost entirely independent type of work is done by the Agenda-Setting school, pioneered by Gusfield's study of how "drunken driving" became firmly fixed on the political agenda. Note the title: *The Culture of Public Problems: Drinking-Driving and the Social Order.*[21] Often, I believe, public or social problems are closely linked with what are called problems of philosophy.

Gusfield and Garfinkel provided quasi-historical studies of kinds of behavior—not natural kinds but social kinds and I would say moral kinds. For a mature adult to drive under the influence of drink is immoral. If impaired judgment is an excuse, then to begin to drink, knowing that one will drink more and then drive, is immoral. Everyone here knows that, but not, perhaps, how it *became* immoral. That leads to a question both historicist and philosophical: How do the conditions of formation of this conception determine its logical relations and moral connotations? We here arrive at philosophical analysis, conducted in terms of the origins of the concept. That leads me to my final section. I have been discussing uses of history to philosophical students of science. Now I wish to be more general, considering for example not science but ethics, and at the same time more specific, considering not just philosophy but what I call philosophical analysis, and considering not just history but what Foucault called history of the present.

V. PHILOSOPHICAL ANALYSIS
AND HISTORY OF THE PRESENT

Philosophical analysis is the analysis of concepts. Concepts are words in their sites. Sites include sentences, uttered or transcribed, always in a larger site of neighborhood, institution, authority, language. If one took seriously the project of philosophical analysis, one would require a history of the words in their sites, in order to comprehend what the concept was. But isn't "analysis" a breaking down, a decomposition into smaller parts, atoms? Not entirely; for example, "analysis" in mathematics denotes the differential and integral calculus, among other things. Atomism is one kind of analysis, to be sure, and in philosophy is exemplified by Bertrand Russell's Theory of Definite Descriptions. (Even that did not analyze the definite article, "the," but it did analyze sentences in which the article occurs.) J. L. Austin did not analyze sentences in the sense of exhibiting their elements but in the sense of providing an analysis of what we do with them and of what their uses are. Similarly to invoke the history of a concept is not to uncover its elements but to investigate the principles that cause it to be useful—or problematic.

If one embraced more specific conjectures about the ways in which the condition for emergence and changes of use of a word also determined the space in which it could be used, one would be well on the way to a complex methodology. In the third of my "Five Parables" I have half-seriously described one of my own attempts at that.[22] But whatever the methodology, one thing is clear. Such an attitude invites one to take a look. It is prompted by the Lockean imperative. Because of the post-Kuhnian events mentioned in IV, it was natural to take such looks at scientific concepts and their sites. Hence I have tried to display the network of possibilities and constraints that have been built into our present conceptions of chance, determinism, information, and control.[23]

But what about ethical concepts, following the transition suggested in IV? The example of this sort on which I have myself done most work is child abuse.[24] Child abuse is not just immoral. It is at present an absolute wrong. Last year I told a young man I was going to interview a lawyer who defends child abusers. He replied, "How could someone do *that*? Murderers have to be defended in court, but child abusers?" I believe I can show that our category "child abuse" is less than thirty years old and has been molded throughout that period into its present shape. And if it be said, "Very interesting, but what has that got to do with philosophy and in particular ethics?" *One* reply: here is a living example of how an "absolute value," a prima facie absolute wrong, gets constructed before our very eyes. What if this is of the very nature of what we experience as absolute value? Discussions about ethical relativity come to life when substance such as this is breathed into them. Child abuse is used as an example for metaethics. A second reply: here is a thick moral concept demanding analysis and understanding both in its own right and because its structure is probably similar to a lot of other moral concepts being constructed this very day. (There are lots of other replies.)

Child abuse both describes a kind of human behavior and evaluates it, messily mixing fact and value. It is easier to argue that it has been constructed in a macrosociological set of exchanges than that Pickering's quarks and Latour's thyrotropin-releasing factor have been constructed in the microsociology of the laboratory. But just because it is evaluative it has an effect upon the investigator quite different from that of quarks. One becomes involved in the subject itself. I began looking at it merely as an example of the ways in which we make up kinds of people. No longer. Child abuse involves pressing moral (not to mention social, political, and when one gets down to cases, personal) issues in itself. It is an *intrinsically moral* topic.

It is also *extrinsically metamoral.* By this I mean that it can be used to reflect on evaluation itself. The reflection can be done only by taking a look into the origin of our idea. That is fulfilling the Lockean imperative. But the look must be into the social rather than the personal formation of the concept. It involves history. The application is to our present pressing problems. The history is history of the present, how our present conceptions were made, how the conditions for their formation constrain our present ways of thinking. The whole is the analysis of concepts. For me that means philosophical analysis.

I know of only one sustained philosophical model for this sort of inquiry, namely, some of the work of Michel Foucault. *Discipline and Punish* is numerous things: an account of a transformation in the nature of the prison and in the treatment of criminals; a study of our very concepts of criminality, recidivism, punishment, "correction" (as in California Department of Corrections), and prison reform.[25] In my terminology it is an extrinsically metamoral book about the intrinsically moral. As proof that the author found the topic intrinsically moral one sees his inevitable engagement as a leading figure of a collective dedicated to the reform of the French penal system. Some people blame his book *Madness and Civilization* for the discharge onto the streets of thousands of helpless people who would otherwise be in the care of lunatic asylums.[26] But his topics are also extrinsically metamoral. As Foucault said in a 1977 interview, "When I think back now, I ask myself what else it was that I was talking about, in *Madness and Civilization* or *The Birth of the Clinic,* but power?"[27] People who accuse Foucault of something they call nihilism fail to see that one can be extrinsically metamoral and intrinsically moral at the same time, or at least, in the same person.

Foucault has become a cult figure, but there are plenty of analytic philosophers who have great trouble with what he is doing. I have never had this trouble, and so seem to be anomalous. My work has been seriously influenced by Foucault (or by successive Foucaults) for exactly twenty years. Books I have written and books I am writing reek of his effect on me. Yet I was trained as a purebred analytical philosopher with primary emphasis on philosophical logic. I still regard myself as such, as one whose mind was formed by Frege, Moore, and Russell. It is perhaps significant that despite my respect for many logical positivists, they had little effect on the way I think. This is perhaps the fundamental way in which I differ from Rorty. He is still fighting people to whom I never paid much attention. At any rate I feel no inconsistency between my analytic instincts and my ability to use some aspects of Foucault. I regard my investigations of chance or of child abuse as pursuing the Lockean imperative. It is also, manifestly, the history of the present in the sense intended by Foucault. One conducts the analysis of the words in their sites in order to understand how we think and why we seem obliged to think in certain ways.

Philosophers are more than metaphysicians. Those whose roots lie in the tradition of philosophical analysis are concerned with concepts less grand than James's metaphysical twenty-one. Plenty of philosophical problems surround concepts such as "normal" (said of human behavior, characteristics, or customs) or "chance." Or, to pursue the Foucauldian chain: "mad," "criminal," "diseased," "perverse." I believe that specific details of the origin and transformation of these concepts is important to understanding them and for understanding what makes them "problematic."

Thus I conclude by returning to one of the mandated queries: "How is the new historicism, or philosophy as conversation, connected with philosohpy as problem-solving?" What I have been describing is not *the* new historicism, but in philosophy it is rather new. I mention Kuhn and Foucault as mentors with decisive impacts on the subject. It is historicist. It is not philosophy as conversation. It is philosophy as hard work. Or to use understatement, it is less talking than taking a look. How is this activity connected with problem solving?

There is a wonderful idea, rightly called Hegelian, that if you understand the source of a problem, you thereby make it go away. We find this conception in Freud and Wittgenstein alike. There is more than a whiff of it in *Madness and Civilization* and other early work of Foucault's. I think that is just a mistake. I do not see, for example, my investigations of chance or abuse as solving the problem of free will or of the respective rights of state, parents, and children. I certainly do not have the ludicrous self-indulgent conception that the problems go away when I am through. But I can show why these matters are problematic, whereas before we knew only that they were problematic. Sometimes one can hope to make a concept more problematic than before, for example, "information and control." And of course to use history for the understanding of philosphical problems is not to resign one's birthright to be a philosopher in the Present-Timeless mode.

When the concept—the words in their sites—at which one takes a look is a moral one or one that bears on action, the investigation will be what I have, with heavy hand, been calling extrinsically metamoral. One may also have aspirations toward influencing the ethical decisions in which that concept is clothed. That is a step not toward problem solving but toward intrinsically moral action. That is a matter of deeds, not analysis. This distinction between deeds and analysis I owe to Moritz Schlick.

NOTES

1. All quotations are from Professor Roth's letter dated 11 Mar. 1986.

2. See Richard Rorty, *Philosophy and the Mirror of Nature* (Princeton, 1979).

3. See Jonathan Bennett, *Rationality: An Essay towards an Analysis* (New York, 1964); *Locke, Berkeley, Hume: Central Themes* (Oxford, 1971); *Linguistic Behaviour* (London, 1976); *A Study of Spinoza's Ethics* (Indianapolis, 1984); and *Events and Their Names* (Indianapolis, 1988).

4. Ian Hacking, "Five Parables," in *Philosophy in History,* ed. Richard Rorty, J. B. Schneewind, and Quentin Skinner (Cambridge, 1984), 103–24.

5. See Gottfried Wilhelm Leibniz, *New Essays on Human Understanding,* ed. and tr. Peter Remnant and Jonathan Bennett (Cambridge, 1981).

6. "Kant or Hegel or Heidegger" is of course a Rortyism. Take the following occurrences of the name "Foucault" in *Consequences of Pragmatism (Essays: 1972–1980)* (Minneapolis, 1982): "Foucault and DeLeuze" (xviii); "Kuhn and Foucault" (xli); "Dewey, Foucault, James and Nietzsche" (xlii); "Habermas and Foucault" (76); "Heidegger, Sartre and Foucault" (86); "Nietzsche, Nabokov, Bloom and Foucault" (158); "Borges and Nabokov, Mallarmé and Valéry and Wallace Stevens, Derrida and Foucult" (136); "Hegel-Marx-Nietzsche-Heidegger-Foucault" (226). I take it that Rorty is aware of his practice (see xl, 65, 92). But it also illustrates the observations I make in this paragraph.

7. William James, *Some Problems of Philosophy* (London, 1912). Possibly the title was chosen by his son Henry, as William James did not complete this "beginning to an introduction of philosophy." The terminology of "problems" occurs throughout.

8. G. E. Moore, *Some Main Problems of Philosophy* (London, 1953). The text is a compilation of lectures given in London under that title starting in 1910.

9. Bertrand Russell, *The Problems of Philosophy* (London, 1912).

10. I have been privileged to hear Rorty speak to this issue in both Charlottesville, Va., and Jerusalem; it is in print as a lecture at Notre Dame, so we cannot dismiss this as a passing interest. See Richard Rorty, "Is Science a Natural Kind?" in *Construction and Constraint: The Shaping of Scientific Rationality,* ed. Ernan McMullin (Notre Dame, 1988), 49–74. The text by Williams that is discussed is *Ethics and the Limits of Philosophy* (Cambridge, Mass., 1985), 139.

11. See John Locke, *An Essay concerning Human Understanding* (1690; Oxford, 1975).

12. See Auguste Comte, *Cours de philosophie positive* (Paris, 1830–42).

13. Hans Reichenbach, *Elements of Symbolic Logic* (New York, 1947), 2.

14. Thomas S. Kuhn, *The Structure of Scientific Revolutions* (Chicago, 1962), 1.

15. Bruno Latour and Steve Woolgar, *Laboratory Life: The Social Construction of Scientific Facts* (Beverly Hills, 1979); 2d ed., main text unaltered but with "Social" deleted from subtitle (Princeton, 1986).

16. Andy Pickering, *Constructing Quarks* (Edinburgh, 1984).

17. Simon Schaffer and Steven Shapin, *Leviathan and the Air Pump: Hobbes, Boyle and the Experimental Life* (Princeton, 1986).

18. Nelson Goodman, *Ways of Worldmaking* (Indianapolis, 1978). Goodman speaks of his "constructionalist" orientation; Latour calls himself "constructionist."

19. See J. L. Austin, "A Plea for Excuses," in *Philosophical Papers,* ed. J. O. Urmson and G. J. Warnock (Oxford, 1970), 175–204.

20. See Bernard Williams, *Ethics and the Limits of Philosophy* (Cambridge, Mass., 1985).

21. Joseph R. Gusfield, *The Culture of Public Problems: Drinking-Driving and the Social Order* (Chicago, 1980).

22. In the third of the five parables, see n. 4.

23. Ian Hacking, *The Emergence of Probability* (Cambridge, 1975); *The Taming of Chance* (Cambridge, forthcoming).

24. Ian Hacking, "The Sociology of Knowledge about Child Abuse," *Nous* 22 (1988): 53–63; "The Making and Molding of Child Abuse," in *Coherent Worlds,* ed. Mary Douglas and David Hull (Princeton, forthcoming).

25. Michel Foucault, *Discipline and Punish: The Birth of the Prison,* tr. Alan Sheridan (New York, 1977).

26. See Michel Foucault, *Madness and Civilization,* tr. Richard Howard (New York, 1965).

27. Michel Foucault, "Truth and Power," in *Power/Knowledge: Selected Interviews and Other Writings, 1972–1977,* ed. and tr. Colin Gordon (New York, 1980), 115.

RESPONSE TO IAN HACKING

———◄═►◄○◄═►———

David A. Hollinger

BY INVOKING WILLIAM James's figure of the unfinished arch and by connecting that figure to our own discourse about history and philosophy, Ian Hacking suggests that we might yet construct an arch in which at least some kinds of history might be joined with at least some kinds of problem-solving philosophy. It is to classical problems of philosophy of the sort listed by James in 1910 that we must attend, it would seem, in order to complete the arch, while the section already in place is apparently—if I read Hacking correctly—the more fully historicist side, the side made by "taking a look."

I am attracted to Hacking's vision of history and philosophy joining to create such an arch, but I'm not sure the structure Hacking would have us build is truly an arch, its two parts joined by a sturdy conjunction, or simply two separate slabs leaning precariously against each other at the top, ready to be hauled off to separate locations should a construction gang of conventional philosophers or conventional historians decide to appropriate one or the other for their own use.

Clifford Geertz, in speaking about history and anthropology, has urged us to take care of the conjunctions and to trust that the nouns in our cross-disciplinary discourse would take care of themselves. I want to try to follow that advice in my remarks on Hacking's paper. I will react sympathetically to the main element in Hacking's historicist program, which he calls "taking a look." After that, I'll express my puzzlement about the ambivalence Hacking betrays toward Michael Roth's conjunction question, which I would paraphrase as "What does historicism have to do with how we answer questions traditionally asked by philosophers?" But first I want to speak up loudly for philosophy as problem solving, and urge that the soundest parts of Richard Rorty's work—upon which much of Hacking's paper is a commentary—be taken as consistent with the traditional problem-solving mission of philosophy.

In this initial set of reflections on Rorty, I, as a historian, am trying to warn my philosopher friends that they might better serve themselves and our society by reforming analytical philosophy along historicist lines than by abandoning analytical philosophy altogether in order to practice history. I offer this friendly warning not out of any turf jealousy, nor out of any resistance to the development of a more philosophically sophisticated historiography than we now have; on the contrary, my friendly warning derives simply from my honest sense that history has less to offer philosophers than it is now fashionable to admit in public. Perhaps it is easier for a historian than for a philosopher to stand up and say this? As it was left to the Republican Richard Nixon to open relations with China because liberal Democrats were afraid of being soft on Communism, so it may be left to historians to say a friendly word about analytical philosophy because philosophers are afraid of being soft on logical positivism.

Of course we need no conjunction at all if we take literally Rorty's hyperbolic announcement that philosophy is "over," a human project of some historical significance which, like the Ottoman Empire and accordian bands, eventually passes into history and is replaced in the conversation of humankind by something else, like the PLO and heavy metal. I share Hacking's appreciation for Rorty's historicist undoing of the foundationalist presuppositions of the epistemological project of modern philosophy, but I believe that Rorty, reacting against the pretensions of his philosopher colleagues, has become so self-effacing on behalf of the philosophic guild that he now threatens to undervalue the skills that trained philosophers can bring to the answering of questions about the true, the good, the right, and the just. Rorty concedes that these issues will continue to be debated even in the chastened atmosphere Rorty now calls "ethnocentric," in which we recognize our own historicity and therefore refrain from making essentialist and transcendent arguments on behalf of the entire species.[1] But what kind of critical discourse are we to have in this atmosphere? In his eagerness to end the monopoly of philosophy departments on the relevant discourse and to get literary critics and historians and novelists involved, I believe Rorty slights the virtues of specialization. John Rawls's *A Theory of Justice* can enrich conversation of exactly the chastened, historically self-aware sort that Rorty wants to encourage, but the book is a monument to the discipline, patience, and specialized skill that formal philosophical training can provide.[2] Rorty's own work trades extensively on that analytical heritage, without which his own writings would surely have much less to teach us.[3]

I am also troubled by the apparent extent and intensity of Rorty's denial that we need philosophers in their capacity as "specialists in universality." Rorty is surely correct to fault philosophers for having so often confused the parochial practices and notions of their own culture with "human nature" or "the universe," and he is right to identify historians and anthropologists as the "specialists in particularity" who, by displaying the diversity of human life, can give the lie to spiritually imperialistic claims.[4] Yet the pluralism Rorty associates with the work of historians and anthropologists sometimes becomes too uncritical, at least for me. In his cautious defense—insufficiently cautious, I believe—of "ethnocentrism," Rorty proposes that we all divide the world's population into two groups, those "to whom one must justify one's beliefs" and "the others." The first group, "our" group, are those "who share enough of one's beliefs to make fruitful conversation possible."[5] Rorty knows he is being provocative. I suppose I'm the kind of person he has in mind when he remarks that some folks "will be repelled by this suggestion that the exclusivity of the private club might be a *crucial* feature of an ideal world order. It will seem a betrayal of the Enlightenment to imagine us as winding up with a world of moral narcissists, congratulating themselves on neither knowing or caring what the people" in some other club are like.[6] Rorty should be more troubled by this prospect than he has so far shown himself to be. He does grant, in one of the most intriguing sentences he has published recently, that "ideal of procedural justice and human equality" may be "parochial, recent, [and] eccentric," but on that account are no "less worth fighting for," and may be "the best hope of *the species*."[7] To justify that proposition, we might well use the services of specialists in universality.[8]

I would not have said so much about Rorty were his work not so clearly in the background of Michael Roth's call to this conference and were not Hacking's paper so antiphonal—and appropriately so—to Rorty's work. I want now to turn directly to Hacking's paper.

"Taking a look" is Hacking's name for a specific type of historicism he says can be congenial even to a philosopher preoccupied with philosophical concerns that are "present" and ostensibly "timeless." The aim is to enrich our understanding of the concepts we use, the beliefs we hold, and the questions we address by coming to grips with their historical origins. This program of "taking a look" is pretty much that previously endorsed by Hacking and a number of other contributors to the important collection of 1984, *Philosophy in History,* co-edited by Rorty, Quentin Skinner, and J. B. Schneewind. As Peter Hylton put it in that volume, the "emphasis" is "not so much on solving philosophical problems as on gaining a deeper understanding of what a given problem is, why it arises, what gives it its force, why it grips us or fails to grip us." Such historical studies, Hylton remarks, have already "been undertaken for a variety of subjects, including the more prestigious sciences." [9]

Indeed they have, and Hacking is justified here in identifying post-Kuhnian historiography of science as a heuristic for studying the comings and goings of moral imperatives, such as our currently acute sensitivity to the abuse of children. Yet the historical study of ideas about the good, the right, and the just does not strike me as quite so novel as Hacking makes it sound. No doubt the studies he wishes to undertake and to encourage are more rigorous than many we now have on our bookshelves, but in fact the rise and fall of value systems has long been of interest to historians and sociologists. I suppose we cannot be reminded often enough that the Kuhnian transformation of our ideas about science consisted very largely in the applying to scientific truth of historicist perspectives long since applied to the rest of culture, including our aesthetic ideals, our moral imperatives, our political ideologies, our standards of justice, and our systems of religious belief. If Kuhn's work on scientific truth can inspire a more adequate and rigorous historical study of the good, the right, the beautiful, and the just, I'm delighted, but it does mean hauling coal to Newcastle.

I doubt if historians of science have nearly as much to say to Hacking in this regard as do the political and intellectual historians now arguing about the origins of antislavery sentiment in the English-speaking world in the late eighteenth and early nineteenth centuries. This issue would seem to fall in the same class as the sudden decision in our own time that child abuse is an intolerable evil. I refer especially to David Brion Davis's *The Problem of Slavery in the Age of Revolution,* and to the critiques of that book recently offered by John Ashworth and Thomas Haskell. [10]

In any event, Hacking's "taking a look" is an enterprise historians will easily recognize and appreciate. That such an enterprise might appeal to philosophers of the "present-timeless" cast of mind is all to the good. But here we come to Michael Roth's conjunction question ("What does historicism have to do with how we answer questions traditionally asked by philosophers?"), and I am puzzled by Hacking's gingerly, circumspect approach to it.

Hacking suggests that the very notion that philosophers engage in "problem solving" is a brief historical moment, something that turned up in England and America about 1910, a bubble on the ocean of philosophical time. It is true, as Hacking notes, that James, Moore, and Russell signal the infatuation of that generation of philosophers with a *Wissenschaftliche* vocabulary, according to which philosophy, like physics or philology, addresses a series of discrete "problems," but Hacking may be putting too fine a point on language. On the very pages Hacking quotes from James's *Some Problems of Philosophy,* James uses the then-trendy word "problem" interchangeably with the older word "question."[11] James and his contemporary philosophers were committed to formulating and defending answers to what they took to be the vital questions of philosophy—metaphysics, epistemology, ethics—and the distinction between up-to-date "problem solving" and old-fashioned "question answering" was, for them, not so momentous. Hacking is closer to the right track, it seems to me, when he points out that James's list of "problems" or "questions" contains continuities running back to Plato and when Hacking acknowledges that even today lots of these questions are still worth thinking about. Philosophy as "problem solving" may not be such an exotic and idiosyncratic moment in the intellectual history of the West.

The cautious character of Hacking's approach to Roth's conjunction question is also apparent in Hacking's lengthy excursus on "undoing," which is, after all, a decidedly negative way of constructing the role historical consciousness might play in answering philosophical questions. That role would seem to be one of undercutting the very enterprise of problem solving cum question answering by demonstrating the futility of *foundationalist* solutions and answers. But if historicist undoing serves to cast doubt on foundationalist styles of question answering, what does it do for nonfoundationalist styles, such as that developed in Don Herzog's book, *Without Foundations?*[12] Hacking's account of historicist undoing leads me to welcome historicist undoing, and to encourage it, as far as it goes, but in its wake the conjunction Roth has urged us to look for remains elusive.

It remains all the more elusive, for me, at least, when Hacking calls at the end of his talk for the completion of the arch by way of "working . . . in one's own way" on the "problems" of philosophy which turn out, on Hacking's representation of them, to be prior to the various specific programs through which they have been carried from Plato down to ourselves. If the problems are indeed timeless, as Hacking seems to say at the end, then I see no arch, no conjunction, but just the two big slabs leaning awkwardly against each other, ready to be carried off to decorate business-as-usual departments of philosophy and history. "Taking a look" and "historicist undoing," Hacking explains earlier in the paper, may "bear directly on philosophical problems," but not on their "solution." This would suggest that when Hacking is "taking a look" or engaged in some "historicist undoing" he's carving gargoyles on one slab, and when he's trying to answer the preprogrammatic, persistent, Plato-derived "problems" of philosophy he's simply embellishing the other slab. But Hacking's message may be more radically historicist: he may be saying if we are serious about "taking a look" and "historicist undoing" we will stop short of even trying to formulate and defend answers to the persistent problems of philosophy, we will simply have to settle for an "understanding" of these questions. If that's our program, the arch we shall build will be an arch of history, without offering even nonfoundationalist, provisional answers to the questions James thought it important to try—with appropriate historical self-awareness, to be sure—to answer. Such an arch might be wonderful to have, but it's not the one James wanted to build, nor the one implied as an ideal by Roth's conjunction question.

But Hacking can join with anyone he wants to build any arch he wishes, and if he, as an individual, wishes to join us historians, he would not only be welcome, he'd have a lot to teach us. Indeed, we have been speaking about history and philosophy in terms of what insights or challenges historicist perspectives might offer to philosophy, but the serious interest in history we find in Hacking provides a good opportunity for reminding ourselves that the best conjunctions facilitate two-way travel.[13] The controversy over the Davis thesis on antislavery is, again, an example of how a little philosophy can go a long way in sharpening issues and deciding how to assess evidence. I have encouraged analytical philosophers in general to attend to the virtues in their own disciplinary tradition, simply because I continue to believe specialists are needed in the formulation and defense of provisional answers to philosophical questions. But if individuals like Hacking choose to give up on problem solving and devote themselves to problem understanding, I am happy—on behalf of historians—to welcome Ian Hacking to "our"club.

NOTES

1. For Rorty's effort to develop a sympathetic interpretation of "ethnocentrism," see his "On Ethnocentrism: A Reply to Clifford Geertz," *Michigan Quarterly Review* 25 (1986): 525–34. See also Rorty's "Solidarity or Objectivity?" in *Post-Analytic Philosophy*, ed. John Rajchman and Cornel West (New York, 1985), 3–19, esp. 13.

2. See John Rawls, *A Theory of Justice* (Cambridge, Mass., 1971).

3. In an earlier appreciation of Rorty's splendid *Philosophy and the Mirror of Nature* (Princeton, 1979) I have emphasized Rorty's willingness to build critically upon this heritage rather than to ignore it; see David A. Hollinger, *In the American Province: Studies in the History and Historiography of Ideas* (Bloomington, 1985), 167–75.

4. Rorty, "Ethnocentrism," p. 530.

5. Ibid., 13.

6. Ibid., 533; emphasis in original.

7. Ibid., 532; emphasis added.

8. Some of the same suspicions of, and uncertainties about Rorty's new "ethnocentrism" I voice here are developed more extensively in an essay that came to my attention only after the Scripps Symposium: see Edward Davenport, "The New Politics of Knowledge: Rorty's Pragmatism and the Rhetoric of the Human Sciences," *Philosophy of Social Science* 17 (1987): 377–94, esp. 388–94. Since the Scripps Symposium Rorty himself has dealt more forthrightly with some of the difficulties that have troubled Davenport and me and others. I want particularly to call attention to the last page of Rorty's new book, *Contingency, Irony, and Solidarity* (Cambridge, 1989), 198. There, Rorty endorses the "ethnocentrism" of a "we" dedicated not to self-enclosure but "to enlarging itself, to creating an ever larger and more variegated *ethnos*." It is the ethnocentrism, Rorty adds, of "the people who have been brought up to distrust ethnocentrism." For a similar, but less ample qualification, see Rorty, "Science as Solidarity," in *The Rhetoric of the Human Sciences: Language and Argument in Scholarship and Public Affairs*, ed. John S. Nelson, Allan Megill, and Donald N. McCloskey (Madison, 1987), 43.

9. Peter Hylton, "The Nature of a Proposition and the Revolt against Idealism," in *Philosophy in History: Essays on the Historiography of Philosophy*, ed. Richard Rorty, J. B. Schneewind, and Quentin Skinner (Cambridge, 1984), 393.

10. Especially pertinent is Thomas L. Haskell, "Convention and Hegemonic Interest in the Debate over Antislavery: A Reply to Davis and Ashworth," *American Historical Review* 92 (1987): 829–78. Haskell's notes contain references to the other contributions to this debate.

11. William James, *Some Problems of Philosophy* (Cambridge, Mass., 1979), 22.

12. Don Herzog, *Without Foundations: Justification in Political Theory* (Ithaca, 1985).

13. For a discerning appraisal of recent work by some of the most philosophically self-conscious of today's historians, see John Toews, "Intellectual History after the Linguistic Turn: The Autonomy of Meaning and the Irreducibility of Experience," *American Historical Review* 92 (1987): 879–907.

RESPONSE TO
DAVID A. HOLLINGER

———❧·◦·☙———

Ian Hacking

THE ARCH

I AM GRATEFUL TO David Hollinger for his lucid positive observations and for providing an opportunity for clarification. The metaphor of an arch was James's, not mine. I take one slab to be pragmatism, the other, problems. I do not take one slab to be philosophy and the other to be history and regret having given the impression to the contrary. I repeated James's metaphor to remind us that the president of the pragmatists himself thought that his philosophy needed a side devoted to problems.

THE CONJUNCTION

Hollinger's point about slabs of history *and* philosophy—about Roth's conjunction—is nevertheless well taken. Hollinger thinks that I "may be saying if we are serious about 'taking a look' and 'historicist undoing' we will stop short of even trying to formulate and defend answers to the persistent problems of philosophy, we will simply have to settle for an 'understanding' of these questions."

First, undoing is not my way. It is others who are serious about it. I respect Hollinger's very clear statements about Rorty's work. Taking a look is my way, and I claim that all that it can do is to provide understanding or perhaps increasingly problematize (as in my example of "information and control"). But historicist taking a look is not the only thing that I commend! To use a certain kind of historicizing to comprehend problems is not to cease to be an analytic philosopher who addresses problems. Philosophy, for me, is not a matter of earnestly grinding along a single track: it is a gigantic shunting yard of motley activities.

PROBLEMS

Hollinger wants philosophers to go on trying to solve problems. In using James I was unclear. He was talking about The Big Problems of Philosophy. When I was talking about taking a look and about problems, I was talking more about the small problems of conceptual analysis. There's a relation between the two in that the small problems often bear on The Big Problems. I'll give a new example, which incidentally will affirm that, contrary to Hollinger's fears, I have not ceased to speak in the Present-Timeless voice.

There has been some popular and some scientific discussion of an "anthropic cosmological principle." I recently argued that one use of this principle commits a fallacy in probability reasoning—a fallacy of an elementary sort, of general application, but one which has not, I think, been diagnosed before.[1] I claim that my discussion bears on one use of the anthropic principle, urged by distinguished astrophysicists, and which they do not distinguish logically from other uses. My discussion also bears on the most common popular objection to the argument from design for the existence of God. (If the universe is old enough we would have got here by chance; God is not needed. I claim that's a fallacy.) It is to be observed that:

1. This is pure conceptual analysis.

2. It is entirely Present-Timeless.

3. It is closely connected with the argument from design, and my discussion speaks, in a Pen-Pal way, of Hume.

4. It bears on an antinomy (Was there a beginning to the universe or not?) that Kant thought he had undone, that most people since thought had been undone, but that now excites some cosmologists.

5. The Big Problem on which my little fallacy bears is one that most people in at least the Western tradition would hold to be philosophical: How did we get here?

I do not directly address, let alone solve, The Big Problem. A number of writers who use the anthropic principle do not only address but claim to solve that Problem. I claim that some of them commit a fallacy. I claim that there is a little problem of logic, and I do claim to solve that. That bears on Big Problems like how we got here and the argument from design. It bears on the latter in a doubly negative way, arguing that the most common objection to the argument is itself a fallacy. That is how it is with much philosophical analysis, and I well understand why many people, including many historians, have no taste for such talk. I relish it.

None of that has anything to do with historicist taking a look. I give the example to recall the many things that philosophers do, and will go on doing. Could one practice historicist taking a look in this area? I distinguish the argument from design (3) from how we got here (5). The argument from design came into being or was resurrected at certain very specific junctures, the most important being late seventeenth-century England, another being a decade ago in cosmology. I believe one would understand a lot more by engaging in some archaeological spadework, which might even lead to a little undoing of the argument in a way that could be more conclusive than Kant's. But that would be entirely compatible with the sort of Present-Timeless fallacy-mongering of my own that I have mentioned. Philosophers do many things.

The Big Problem, how we got here (5), does not I think yield to my kind of taking a look because the topic is always there. There is no historical moment or epoch or civilization to which it is peculiar and at which one might look. But perhaps there is still something to be done by way of taking a look. It has been little noticed that Foucault's final works could serve as a model for the historicized investigation of the eternal. But I don't know how to follow that lead, yet.

THE CLUB

Hollinger generously says that if people like me choose to give up on problem solving and devote themselves to problem understanding, he is happy to welcome us to the club of historians. That I don't give up on problem solving is now, I hope, clear. More relevant is my response to Hollinger: "First I better distinguish two kinds of problems." That is the ancient voice of another club speaking, a club of which Socrates is one of the earlier members on record. Locke, whom I did mention, is after Hobbes the charter member of the club writing in English. Those men represent another way of thinking, not one from which historians are constitutionally barred, but one which is not, by and large, to the historical taste. Conceptual analysis is a name for it. It is completely untouched by

Rorty's undoing of foundationalism in philosophy. In replying to Michael Roth's initial questions I was trying to show how those who think my way would now bring to their labors a historicized understanding of those innumerable little but critical concepts, words in their sites, that so engaged Socrates.

NOTE

1. See Ian Hacking, "The Inverse Gambler's Fallacy: The Argument from Design: The Anthropic Principle Applied to Wheeler Universes," *Mind* 96 (1987): 331–40. For three distinct criticisms, see M. A. B. Whitaker, "On Hacking's Criticism of the Wheeler Anthropic Principle"; P. J. McGrath, "The Inverse Gambler's Fallacy and Cosmology"; and John Leslie, "No Inverse Gambler's Fallacy," *Mind* 97 (1988): 259–64, 265–68, 269–71, respectively.

SOMETIMES, ALWAYS, NEVER: THEIR WOMEN'S HISTORY AND OURS

Lillian S. Robinson

THE PROBLEMATICAL CONJUNCTION in the title of the conference for which this essay was originally prepared, the "and" that—at once innocently and provocatively—linked history to the participants' several modes of inquiry and discourse, set me thinking about some other small but significant words. These are not conjunctions but adverbs, modifiers of the verbs that constitute the motors of history; they're the adverbs of choice (multiple choice, to be sure) of the standardized test: sometimes, always, and never.

As I attempt to take hold of the distinction between "women's history," on the one hand, and "history *and* women's studies," on the other, these adverbs become the operative terms in categorical statements about the lives of women. Feminists—including feminist scholars who are not historians —look to history to furnish ammunition for such categorical statements:

Women have *always* . . .

Women have *never* . . .

But *sometimes* women *did* . . .

Precisely because the history of women was for so long denied and unwritten, those who are most concerned with our present and future condition want to see the past neatly and definitively packaged. It even seems as if that is the only way it can be readily available as a whole, in a context where, though anatomy may not be destiny, memory just may be.

But there is something essentially ahistorical about such statements, something that resides in the very adverbs that express historical time. Historians understand the kind of statements that *can* be made about women's historical experience and be considered true to be of quite a different order. At times, I fear that the two conceptions of history are on a collision course, about to confront each other head-on at high speed. At other times, I fear that they will merely go right past each other in directions so opposite as to represent an equally grave if less dramatic threat to feminism and to women.

As a commentator, I am rather uncomfortably situated with a foot in each camp. Feminism, to me, entails the collective vision of a just social order and the means to its attainment. It is in the interest of this vision that, as a nonhistorian, I ask history quite literally to refresh my memory —that is, not only to remind but thereby to revitalize. For feminist activists, scholars, and theorists, the process that Virginia Woolf called "thinking back through our mothers" is intricately bound up with the essential project of thinking forward with our sisters and through our daughters and nieces in a common search for a usable past. But my commitment as a cultural historian demands that we be reconciled to far less certainty than the commitment to feminism seems to call for. It means learning to make peace with contradiction, ambiguity, anxiety. The images evoked by the conditions of certainty are history as a sword or a road, whereas the conditions of uncertainty call up nothing more dignified by way of a metaphor than, say, a hotfoot on the route to Armageddon. What the two sets of images have in common is the notion of change and the vital importance for its furtherance of coming to see how it has occurred in the past. What separates them is their contradictory conceptions of the kinds of assurances we need from the past in order to intervene in effecting change.

No one has yet written a history of women's history. But I think I can indicate some of the major points such a summary would encompass.[1] It would begin with feminist historians' critiques of the discipline's habitual (one might say historical) neglect of women's experience, deriving from the "bias against women implicit in the events usually considered worthy of historical attention, those from which all other changes are understood to follow: wars and diplomacy, politics and law [so that] the almost total omission of women from traditional historical writing flow[s] quite naturally from the discipline's characteristic focus on . . . public activities."[2] Feminists have also pointed out the ways in which the imposition onto history of male-biased assumptions not only distorted representation of those exceptional women who did make it into the purview of the "great men make public events" model but also limited the usefulness of the new social history, despite that approach's greater interest in mass experience, personal relationships, family, sexuality, and consciousness.[3]

The summary would go on to outline the scope and content of the remarkable reappropriation of our past that women's history has accomplished so far. The history of women in classical antiquity, under feudalism, in the transition to capitalism, in the Industrial Revolution and the political upheavals contemporary with it, in the Russian Revolution and the two world wars, under agrarian, mercantile, and industrial societies; as factory workers, teachers, students, doctors, midwives, house servants, mothers, field slaves, and secretaries; as creators and participants in the movements for women's suffrage, abolition, trade unions, birth control, and civil rights; as builders of religious denominations, temperance societies, women's colleges, settlement houses, correctional institutions, and discussion clubs; as mystics, executives, artists, and theorists; as the lovers of men and of other women; as victims of oppressive conditions who made their lives — including their patterns of resistance — *within* those conditions.[4]

But no matter how full the detail and how much the narrator glories in it, any overview of women's history very soon leads to some theoretical challenges to longer-established paradigms of thinking about history and its boundaries. Almost every item on my list either calls attention to women's participation in one of the acknowledged great events of history (thus also calling into question what we thought we knew about those events) or forces us to confront the larger problem of which events are to be considered the proper concern of history. From there, the next logical step, taken by feminist historians more than a dozen years ago, is to redefine the history of women so as to privilege women's gender-specific history over reinterpretations of "participation in" or "contribution to" a male-defined reality.

The inferences that the late Joan Kelly drew from the refocusing of historical attention onto women's activities result in even more dramatic revaluation of existing historical paradigms. In her 1976 essay "The Social Relations of the Sexes: Methodological Implications of Women's History," Kelly maintains that "in seeking to add women to the fund of historical knowledge, women's history has revitalized *theory*, for it has shaken the conceptual foundations of historical study. It has done this by making problematical three of the basic concerns of historical thought: . . . periodization . . . the categories of social analysis, and . . . theories of social change."[5]

An approach that puts women — and particularly their status relative to men—at the center of its inquiry, Kelly argues, will "unsettle . . . accepted evaluations of historical periods," for those eras that have been understood as reflecting "progress" for humankind—meaning *mankind*—cannot be judged in the same way once the male experience is no longer taken as the sole human norm (SRS, 3). What is called for is not necessarily a simple reversal of the received judgment but rather an acknowledgement that, if we look at the experience of both sexes, we get a more complex and disturbing picture. "Suddenly," says Kelly, "we see these ages with a new double vision—and each eye sees a different picture" (SRS, 3).

One of the most radical aspects of Kelly's position is her assumption that an evaluative judgment is, in fact, built into the very division of history into particular periods. In marking off "the Renaissance," say, as a historical epoch, historians are already making a statement about its existence as a positive era. So if we ask, as Kelly herself does in the title of another well-known essay, "Did Women Have a Renaissance?" we are questioning not only whether the centuries usually encompassed by the acrobatically flexible term *Renaissance* were salutary for women but also, if they were not, what sense it makes to talk about them as constituting a meaningful period.[6]

Once the old periodizing concepts are called into question, Kelly observes, new ones may be proposed based either, as certain feminist historians have suggested, on the turning points in women's gender-specific experience—in reproduction, for example—or, as Kelly herself prefers, on "relational" categories that would understand structural changes as crucial to the extent that they affect and are affected by the relative power and status of the two sexes. This is a schema that makes it possible to retain existing categories without that retention's meaning that we retain them uncritically (SRS, 4).

Traditional periodization certainly influences the way nonhistorians view history. (Convention has made it impossible for any of us to conceptualize the American nineteenth century *not* divided into two unequal parts by the Civil War.) Nonetheless, the essential challenge of rethinking periodization is primarily a challenge to the historical discipline. But Kelly's thesis goes further. She holds that failure to take the status of women into account—in, for instance, the evaluation of the "good" periods in Western culture—is the result of historians' acceptance of a prevalent ideology that considers the subordination of women to belong to the natural rather than the social order. Insistence on the socially constructed (hence the alterable and, in fact, changing) status of women and relations between the sexes has implications that reach far beyond disciplinary borders, linking theoretical concerns about how we perceive and interpret history to theoretical concerns about how we are to change the world.

The connecting concept, for Kelly, is the term *social relations*. Historians, she argues, have not only accepted the notion that the subordination of women is natural—hence not subject to critical interpretation—but have perpetuated it through historical description. By contrast, understanding gender as a social category means an expansion of "our conception of historical change itself, as change in the social order" (SRS, 8). To the extent that it constitutes a declaration about the conceptualization and representation of historical change, this is still a statement about the discipline. But, by explicitly joining women's history to her third category, theories of social change, Kelly situates it in relation to the future, as well as to the past, which is to say to history as lived and not only as written.

On this basis, Kelly makes the case for considering the private and domestic aspect of human life as a fundamental part of history and an appropriate object of historical scrutiny. The most novel and exciting task of the study of the social relations of the sexes is still before us, she concludes. It is the task of appreciating "how we are all, women and men, initially humanized, turned into social creatures by the work of that domestic order to which women have been primarily attached. Its character and the structure of its relations order our consciousness, and it is through this consciousness that we first view and construe our world" (SRS, 15). This is the sense in which Kelly states that "a dominant reason for studying the social relations of the sexes is political," for she sees understanding the social forces and interests served by the existing order to be "in itself liberating" (SRS, 15).

Get that: Understanding something is in itself liberating. Knowledge of our history as women is liberating. Understanding the place of domestic experience, one of the new areas examined by women's history, in the formation of consciousness is liberating to both women and men. These are unequivocally political claims. But, although I once saw a neoconservative historian literally tremble with fury as he cited them, they are nonetheless rooted in a sense of the historical discipline's possibilities *and* limitations. They are a historian's claims.

In an article whose intentions are to suggest the outlines of a broad theoretical position, Kelly does not stop to make the case that I believe

to have been one of her underlying assumptions, namely, that all historical inquiry is similarly political in that it is ideologically motivated and
serves ideological ends. But her unadorned statement about *feminist* political motivations leaves us all vulnerable to the claim that it is only we
who act with political motivation and that, therefore, at one end of some
great intellectual spectrum, we have women's history, which is politically
tainted, and, at the other, distinct from it, "real" history, which is ideologically neutral, value free. Kelly says that to know is in itself liberating,
while her opponents call into question the validity of what we think we
know and our methods of finding it out, once it is announced that the
goal is liberation.[7]

But the larger problem is not—or not primarily—an epistemological
debate among historians. When I said Kelly's claims for women's history
were a historian's claims, I was careful to precede that declaration with a
reminder that, as a member of the historical profession, Kelly recognized
the discipline's limits as well as its possibilities. One of the most obvious
limits is that issues having to do with liberation, unlike questions of epistemology, cannot be restricted to the confines of any academic discipline.
It is, of course, one *kind* of liberation for the mind that has been restrained
by old intellectual paradigms to break through those bonds to a wholly
new perspective. When the paradigms, old and new, entail lived experience of the actual person whose mind is thus freed, the process is that
much more liberating. But insight, as psychiatrists never tire of telling us,
is only the first and often the easiest stage of therapy, and understanding
how something oppressive came into being is only the first step toward
changing it. From a position outside the preoccupations of the historical
discipline, true liberation comes only with the change, not the understanding. So the problem that I have characterized as "larger" comes into
being when assumptions like Kelly's, a historian's assumptions, encounter
assumptions about liberation that situate the struggle in quite a different
arena and view women's history as a potential weapon in that other locus.

I have chosen two examples to illustrate some of the issues that arise
in such an encounter, one involving a nonhistorian's applying what she
would call historical evidence and reasoning to more general questions
of social theory, the other involving the application of arguments from
women's history to a legal dispute over the rights of working women. The
former is embodied in Riane Eisler's book *The Chalice and the Blade,* while
the latter is reflected in the participation of historians Rosalind Rosenberg

and Alice Kessler-Harris in a lawsuit with the catchy title *Equal Employment Opportunity Commission versus Sears, Roebuck and Company.* (We may call this overview Zipping through History: From the Great Mother to the Mall.)

The Chalice and the Blade, subtitled *Our History, Our Future,* is one of those eccentric books that come along from time to time drawing very large conclusions about what Mary Beard called the "long history" of women.[8] It is hard to avoid granting rather greater importance to this one than to other specimens of the genre since it comes to us featuring Ashley Montague's claim (against a bright red background and next to a statue of the Great Mother of Sernobi) that it is "the most important book since Darwin's *Origin of Species.*" Moreover, Eisler herself, an attorney whose previous publications have focused on issues concerning women and the law, is described on the same dust jacket as a "futurist." This may have caused me to wonder, for a cynical moment, whether, in that case, all historians may be qualified as *passéistes,* but I am drawn to the specific vision of the future that Eisler advocates, and terrified—as I think all of us must be—of the alternative.

Essentially, Eisler looks forward to a future in which the "dominance model" of human relationships is replaced by a "partnership model" and in which, therefore, a more cooperative and altruistic human community lives at peace with itself and with nature, thus avoiding the twin evils of nuclear war and ecological disaster. Partnership can be attained by eliminating the form of dominance that Eisler claims is the basis of all the others, gender dominance, through a return to a respect for that which is life-generating and nurturing, in preference to that which is death-oriented and destructive. The word *return* is used advisedly, because the historical position on which Eisler bases her argument is that a cataclysmic turning point once "occurred during the prehistory of Western civilization, when the direction of our cultural evolution was quite literally turned around" from worship of the life force to worship of lethal power (*CB,* xvii).

The mission Eisler has taken on is even more candidly ideological than the one that Kelly lays out for women's history. Not only must Eisler demonstrate the existence of societies where what she calls "gylanic" values prevailed, she has to show that the prevalence of such values actually led to social structures based on gender partnership. She does the first of these sloppily, the second not at all. Rather, she takes it for granted that "spiritual values" do determine social patterns.

If your overview of Western cultural evolution begins with prehistory and ends the day before yesterday, it is bound to rely on sweeping generalizations. A scholar would wish to be particularly careful, in these circumstances, to make sure that the generalizations at least depended on cogent presentations of credible evidence. Eisler, however, allows her reasoning to become as sweeping as her conclusions, indulging in what one reviewer called "excesses of free association and sleight of hand."[9] That reviewer, Rachel Sternberg, identifies the lacunae in that portion of Eisler's argument centering on prehistoric cultures: the amazing logical leaps the author takes to get over a thousand-year discrepancy here, an apparent blade there where the argument requires a chalice, the use of a surviving myth in yet another place where there's not even enough material evidence to misinterpret. Sternberg goes on to say that Eisler is "on firmer ground when she moves to history. At least there are contemporary documents to work with . . . that reflect social relations far more clearly. . . . From ancient Greece to Christian Rome to Europe during the Enlightenment, she reclaims a place for women and tries to show that the more say women have, the healthier the world" (19).

Sternberg does point out that this produces a rather simplistic view of such complex events as the rise of the Nazis, but she does not realize that Eisler's historical ground is no firmer than her prehistorical speculations. Eisler's brief treatment of Elizabethan England, for example, contains errors of fact and method that are typical of her procedure throughout.

Eisler begins her animadversions on the Elizabethan age with a paragraph uncritically citing G. Rattray Taylor's 1954 volume *Sex in History.* "Uncritically" means that she not only quotes Taylor without comment but characterizes his wildest speculations as "data." Thus she allows Taylor to adduce as evidence for the "mother-identified" or "feminine" values that Elizabeth's reign brought to the fore "an awakening conscience of responsibility for others, expressed, for instance, in the institution of the poor law."[10] This reminds me of a *New Yorker* cartoon from the Vietnam War period showing a meeting of Pentagon brass; all the others are pointing, jeering and incredulous, at one of their number, saying, "You mean you thought pacification meant *peace?*" Can Taylor really have thought and led Eisler to think that the poor laws, draconian coercion of a population impoverished by economic changes that both of them completely ignore, actually meant *caring* for the poor?

After continuing the citation of Taylor's rhapsodies attributing "the

new love of free learning" and the flowering of the arts to the motherli-
ness of Elizabeth (who, popular tradition tells us, claimed for herself only
"the heart and stomach of a *king*"), Eisler goes on in her own voice: "It
is also significant . . . that during periods of gylanic resurgence such as
the Elizabethan age, the time of the troubadours, and the Renaissance,
upper-class women obtain relatively more freedom and greater access to
education. For example, Portia and other Shakespearean heroines were
notably learned women, reflecting the somewhat higher status of women
in the period. But, as the treatment of Shakespeare's heretically rebellious
Kate in *The Taming of the Shrew* and other literary works indicates, even before the Elizabethan age drew to a close, the violent reassertion of male
control was already under way" (*CB*, 142).

Even Eisler recognizes in her footnotes that some of these categorical assumptions about which places and periods were infused with gylanic
energy are highly controversial. Of all the wrong or wrong-headed assertions in that passage, however, I am most struck by the remark that "Portia
and other Shakespearean heroines *were* highly learned women." For what
Portia and other Shakespearean heroines were in the first instance was invented literary characters. On the one hand, the statement about *The Taming of the Shrew,* though couched in a peculiarly passive discourse, seems to
be acknowledging the role of the author in designing a literary situation
to carry a certain ideology, that of male control in this case; on the other
hand, the educated noblewomen apparently really "were," those invented
literary characters merely "reflecting" social reality. Here, I think, is the
real crux of the problem, Eisler's inability or refusal to distinguish between ideas and things. In fact, much of the interest of the strong women
characters in Elizabethan literature resides precisely in the *contradiction* between the use of "woman" as a concept, a symbolic and intellectual instrument, and the evidence of a quite different reality for actual contemporary
women. This contradiction does not lead to neat certainties but to anxiety,
but it is from creative anxiety that honest feminist scholarship comes.

There, if you will, is a value-laden term: honest feminist scholarship.
For I would suggest that the problem is not distinguishing between ideological and nonideological interpretations of history, but between honest
and dishonest ones. In the case in point, the notion of contradictions in
general and, in particular, the subtle interweaving of contradictions and
congruences between a society and its official ideology would be very
useful to Eisler—at least, if demolishing her entire thesis can be con-

sidered a useful act of preliminary housecleaning. Eisler has to postulate some of the dottier things she does about the gylanic values of long-dead cultures because "it . . . seems logical that women would not be seen as subservient in societies that conceptualized the powers governing the universe in female form—and that 'effeminate' qualities such as caring, compassion, and non-violence would be highly valued in these societies." By the same token, she says, "the root of the problem lies in a social system in which the power of the Blade is idealized" (*CB,* xvi, xviii).

Unfortunately, though, it is not "logical" to assume anything about actual social relations in a society on the basis of the fact that it conceptualized the creative spirit as female; "they *must* have" is not a claim based on logic, in any case, but on wishful thinking. Similarly and even more fundamentally, the problem may not be a long and ignoble tradition of idealizing the Blade but the contradictory operation of social forces that led to the idealization.

But questions and contradictions do not suit Eisler's goals which, by demonstrating the preexistence of a partnership model of relationships and a "chaos" theory of sudden social change, aim to put us back on the track to planetary salvation. The question is whether, in order to have world peace, we have to accept as true a science-fiction scenario in which macho invaders "from the peripheral areas of our globe" and the "dark order" they established caused a traumatic reversal in the peaceful direction "we" would otherwise have pursued. (In fact, I don't know about you, but when I hear language about "peripheral areas" and "dark orders," I worry more about racism than outer space.)

And yet, precisely because the social forces impelling us toward war and environmental destruction are more complex than Eisler admits, precisely because history itself is a more contradictory process than she allows, it is an area in which a good book could help, but where there is a limit to the damage a bad one can do. In my other example of women's history in the public arena, the stakes are by no means as global—after all, what could be?—but they really are the stakes.

The case at issue is the EEOC's sex discrimination suit against Sears, Roebuck for failure to implement an affirmative action program that would place women in traditionally male areas of employment within the organization, specifically commission sales on big-ticket items. Not only was the case, including the participation of historians, argued at a venue well outside the halls of academe with their conventional towers of ivory, but the historians' role itself was widely discussed in the popular press before it could be debated at the more stately pace characteristic of professional journals and scholarly books. And although the official title of the case suggests, reasonably enough, that it was the defendant, Sears, Roebuck, that was on trial, the headlines in both kinds of publications tell us that it was in fact women's history.

But what would women's history have been on trial *for?* The question is absurd, yet it embodies the sense — so strongly supported by reports of the trial — of an embattled discipline, where disagreement between expert witnesses was as sharp as that between the actual parties to the suit, but where resolving those intellectual differences, had that been possible, would not necessarily have had a predictable impact on the case itself. In fact, neither the two feminist historians involved nor subsequent commentators have even been able to agree about the real nature of the issue in the Sears case. It has been variously presented as a matter of control over the application of feminist research;[11] as a struggle between "politicizing" our work and retaining scholarly integrity;[12] and as a conflict between essentially incongruous discourses.[13] I tend to see it as a version — albeit a rather odd one — of the problem with which I began, the different conceptions of the uses of women's history held by feminist historians and by other feminists. It is a conflict that is readily posed in terms of disparate languages but where discourse is, in fact, the name of the question, not the answer.

History and historians entered the case because Sears offered a novel defense against the government's charge of sex discrimination. Instead of countering the indisputable statistics showing that Sears had not succeeded in putting enough women to work in commission sales, the company attempted to demonstrate that discrimination was not the reason for the skewed statistics. The problem, as they framed it, was that women did not want these jobs that certainly paid better but that involved an element of insecurity as to earnings, forced workers to compete for sales, required longer and later hours, and often entailed going out of doors or coming into contact with the kind of bulky, greasy, hard items typically sold on commission. Sears's position was that women are different from men and the differences dictate different labor market choices. But how to turn such cultural commonplaces into admissible evidence? A chorus of male managers coming in and "explaining" to the court that women work for pin money, really prefer noncompetitive part-time jobs at earlier hours and a fixed wage, value cooperation and nurturance over competition, and don't want to soil their pretty little hands or risk their hairdos, would not only be unconvincing but might even constitute further evidence of discriminatory attitudes. What Sears needed was an authoritative explanation for the preference they attributed to working women operating in an inferentially free market of choices. They sought that explanation in recent research on the history of women.

More to the point, what they sought was a feminist *historian* who could give testimony supporting an alternative explanation in which discrimination against women did not figure. Sears's attorneys brought in historian Rosalind Rosenberg, whose interpretation of the past two decades of research in women's history, with its emphasis on women's culture and the differences that inform it, supported the position that women's choice rather than the company's policy or practices was responsible for the discrepancy between hiring goals and realities. To offer an alternative interpretation of the historical evidence, the EEOC asked Alice Kessler-Harris, who had turned down the role that Rosenberg played for the defense, to testify for the prosecution. Her testimony, which acknowledged differences in male and female experience and values but also understood those differences—well—differently, supported the assumption that discrimination was a key factor in the statistical pattern presented by the prosecution. The rest, so to speak, is history.

The historical interpretations on both sides—entitled, respectively, the "Offer of Proof concerning the Testimony of Dr. Rosalind Rosenberg" and "Written Testimony of Alice Kessler-Harris"—have been published in the Archives section of *Signs: Journal of Women in Culture and Society*.[14] They make interesting reading, not because they introduce new scholarship about the history of women, but because of the interpretive strategies that the summaries serve. The richness of the research itself and the new areas of speculation that it opens up are apparent even through the numbered points and tight precis called for by the juridical context. If women's history was indeed on trial, it was not to determine whether it was a legitimate and authentic area of intellectual inquiry. Lawsuits do not, in any case, tend to be about the intellectual reputability of academic specialties. What this one did to *put* the field on trial was to call into question the larger ideological applications of scholarship whose practitioners would presumably have been the first to acknowledge that it was indeed ideologically motivated.

It is worth noting that neither historian commented—nor was expected

to—on the *specific* "history" under litigation, the differential hiring patterns at Sears, Roebuck. Their role in the trial did not come into being
with the policies and practices that the government was defining as discriminatory. Rather, it was created by Sears which, in so doing, deflected
the burden of attention from its own labor relations to the almost infinitely larger topic of women, in general and in employment. Once this
shift occurred, it is not surprising that both historians designed their testimony as a series of "gross generalizations about the entire history of
working women" (SC, 169).

After the findings of women's history were introduced, there were two
sets of "facts" in the case: Sears, Roebuck's practices and the history of
working women. Ironically, in a courtroom arena where there is constant
reference to the facts and, beyond them, to the truth, neither set was in
dispute. The case resided in interpreting the relationship that subsisted
between them. As with Riane Eisler's conclusions about the kind of social
conditions that "must" have existed in cultures that worshiped the maternal spirit, Rosenberg's case, carefully examined, amounts to a claim that
the two sexes' different cultural and social experience "must" uniformly
have led women to make job choices reflecting these differences, without attention to economic motivations. Kessler-Harris argued for greater
variety in women's response to their experience and, even more importantly, for the possibility that economic considerations might outweigh
socialized expectations—both one's own and other people's. In short, in
valorizing the lure of higher wages to low-paid women workers, Kessler-
Harris was asserting the power of material relations themselves over the
culture that reflects them.

Because the real argument was based on inferring meanings and thus
attributing causality, much critical attention has been devoted to the differences between the way truth is claimed in a court of law and in an
academic journal. The disjunction was particularly striking in the cross-
examination of Kessler-Harris by Sears's lawyers, who insisted on unadorned "yes-or-no" answers that ignored all the nuances of her original
testimony. The opposing counsel's restriction of the way the testimony
was presented was one way of censoring the content of the testimony. In
the courtroom, Kessler-Harris's "multiple interpretations were found to
be contradictory and confusing, while the judge praised Rosenberg for
her coherence and lucidity" (SC, 170). The more complex and qualified
analysis Kessler-Harris presented makes far better scholarly sense, whereas

Rosenberg's "Offer of Proof," couched as it is in a discourse of certainties, of facts marshaled to back unqualified assertions, makes far better *legal* sense.

It is not hard to see how the differences between the academic and legal frames of reference, reflected precisely in differences between their characteristic modes of expression, might suggest that the essential problem is a discursive one. The two discourses are different and the conflict was being played out on grounds entirely determined and dominated by one of them. It is very important to distinguish, here, between acknowledging that different discourses are appropriate for different frames of reference and reducing the contradiction to one between opposing modes of expression.

Joan W. Scott, for instance, points out that Sears (or, more accurately, the Sears "team") "constructed an opponent" against whom they asserted that man and women differ (SC, 168). (In short, they strongly implied that the government and its historian-witness were denying the existence of sexual difference.) Needless to say, this act of construction was a purely rhetorical one. The strategy was not so much discursive as forensic; it was a strategy of fighting, not one of talking. The danger in seeing it differently is that it obscures some essential political realities.

Thus, Scott calls attention to Rosenberg's rebuttal, noting the way it labels as subversive the view that all employers might have some interest in sex-typing the labor force (SC, 171). But Scott herself goes on to agree that this view and the Marxist perspective that informs it exist outside of the present boundaries of American political discourse and hence cannot be heard in the courtroom. If this is so—and the Sears trial certainly suggests that it is—the problem is not with the discourse itself but with which interests it exists to foster and which it exists to suppress. The inadmissibility of speech about the employers' vested interest in the sex-biased status quo tells us nothing about speech and a great deal about employers and courts of law, which is to say, about power.

The significance of this distinction is apparent in Kessler-Harris's own account of the case. Kessler-Harris points out that the sexual-difference aspect of the argument was never controversial, insofar as "Rosenberg's testimony offered an interpretation to which many of us had come. Namely that women's social and cultural differences from men could and should be the object of historical analysis." But she adds that "no student of the history of working women that I know of inferred from that interpretation what was suggested by Rosenberg."[15] In short, Rosenberg's opinions are as bizarre among academic specialists in the field as Kessler-Harris's are in a law court. But the particular struggle is within the judicial context, the law court's home ground. So it doesn't much matter—in the short run—that the other point of view is dominant in the professional world in which historical research is carried out and interpreted.

It is for this reason that a response based on assumptions about how we understand different sectors of discourse is inadequate. Scott claims that what is required in addition to the assertion of difference in the face of gender categories "is an analysis of fixed gender categories as *normative statements* that organize cultural understandings of sexual differences" (SC, 175, italics mine). But it is insufficient to identify a story as a story, even as a prescriptive one, when different narrators have differential access to telling the story and only some can literally lay down the law as well.

Moreover, although Kessler-Harris's version is the more "narratively" narrative—admitting more complexity, variety, contradictions, and shades of meaning—it was only her story that was smeared as "political." Her own position attributes ideological motivation to both sides, averring that "there is no point in obscuring the essentially political perceptions or the political decisions that followed from them. Neither of us would have been selected as expert witness had we come to the opposite conclusions" (PA, 52–53). Rosenberg's position, however, is that "scholars must not subordinate their scholarship to their politics, even if the scholarship appears to be heading in a politically dangerous direction. If the scholars allow their politics to drive their scholarship, they will be left with bad scholarship and misguided public policy" (HP, B1). The clear implication here is that it is she who does not flinch from the truth, politically unpleasant though it may be, and that, therefore, her position is not politically motivated. Moreover, those who consider her testimony wrong in some sense (the term having been used with both factual and moral connotations) *must* be asking her to stifle the truth in the interest of policy goals. In fact, however, Kessler-Harris also thinks the matter comes down to "the nature of truth and the possibility of claiming it in a case of this kind and under the conditions that a court of law offers" (PA, 52). She is saying that the question of what kinds of truth it might or might not be appropriate to suppress in the interests of what sort of higher good *does not arise* in this case. And that no one was asking Rosenberg to tell anything less than the whole historical truth, but that she could not accept Rosenberg's interpretation as *reflecting* the truth.

We have come a long way from Joan Kelly's assertion that certain understanding is "in itself liberating." If, as Riane Eisler claims, future liberation depends on allegations about the past that turn out not to be true, *which* knowledge is liberating? If the truth will make us free and Rosalind Rosenberg believes that testimony other than what she delivered would have been untrue, how does that liberate the victims of invidious employment practices at the nation's second-largest employer of women? And did Kessler-Harris's equal conviction, accompanied by her more nuanced sense of what historical truth is, work in the cause of liberation? Ah, but Kelly said understanding, *knowledge* is what is liberating. She just didn't go on to say what knowledge is or how we know when we've got it. Or how it changes in different lights.

Fortunately, I am not called upon to provide neat answers, only to identify some of the questions and predict that there will be many more of them in the years to come. My only advice comes from a source neither feminist nor historical, from *Hill Street Blues,* in fact, which offered all of us the weekly admonition "Be careful out there."

NOTES

In revising this paper for publication, I became aware of just how much I owe to Professor Deena Gonzalez of Pomona College, who served as my commentator on the original "History and . . ." panel, and to my sister-members of the Spring 1988 Scholars Seminar at the Stanford Institute for Research on Women and Gender. My thanks, also, to the Institute's Marilyn Yalom Research Fund, which supported the work of revision.

1. For some discrete pieces of that history, see Ellen Carol DuBois, Gail Paradise Kelly, Elizabeth Lapovsky Kennedy, Carolyn W. Korsmeyer, and Lillian S. Robinson, *Feminist Scholarship: Kindling in the Groves of Academe* (Urbana, 1985), 18–21 and 48–58; Christine Fauré, "Absent from History," tr. Lillian S. Robinson, *Signs: Journal of Women in Culture and Society,* 7 (1981), 71–80; and Joan Wallach Scott, "Women's History," and "American Women Historians, 1884–1984," in her collection *Gender and the Politics of History,* Gender and Culture series (New York, 1988), 15–27, 178–98.

2. DuBois et al., *Feminist Scholarship,* 19.

3. Ruth Rosen, "Sexism in History, or Writing Women's History is a Tricky Business," *Journal of Marriage and the Family* 33 (1971): 541–44; and Ellen Ross, "Women and Family," *Feminist Studies* 5 (1979): 181–89.

4. In addition to the works cited elsewhere in these notes, see, for the very tip of the iceberg: Marylin S. Arthur, Renate Bridenthal, Joan Kelly-Gadol, and

Gerda Lerner, *Conceptual Frameworks for the Study of Women's History* (Bronxville, N.Y., 1976); *Sexual Asymmetry: Women in Antiquity*, ed. Josine Blok and Peter Mason (Amsterdam, 1987); *Connecting Spheres: Women in the Western World, 1500 to the Present*, ed. Marilyn S. Boxer and Jean H. Quetaert (New York, 1987); Patricia Branca, *Women in Europe since 1750* (London, 1978); *Becoming Visible: Women in European History*, ed. Renate Bridenthal and Claudia Koonz (Boston, 1977; augmented ed., 1988); *Liberating Women's History: Theoretical and Critical Essays*, ed. Berenice Carroll (Urbana, 1976); Nancy F. Cott, *The Bonds of Womanhood: "Woman's Sphere" in New England, 1780–1835* (New Haven, 1977) and *The Grounding of Modern Feminism* (New Haven, 1987); *A Heritage of Her Own: Toward a New Social History of American Women*, ed. Nancy F. Cott and Elizabeth Pleck (New York, 1979); Natalie Zemon Davis, "Women's History in Transition: The European Case," *Feminist Studies* 3 (1976): 83–103; Carl Degler, *At Odds: Women and the Family from the Revolution to the Present* (New York, 1980); Ellen Carol DuBois, *Feminism and Suffrage* (Ithaca, N.Y., 1978); *Women and Power in the Middle Ages*, ed. Mary Erler and Maryanne Kowalski (Athens, Ga., 1988); Elizabeth Evans, *Weathering the Storm: Women of the American Revolution* (New York, 1975); Estelle B. Freedman and John d'Emilio, *Intimate Matters: A History of Sexuality in America* (New York, 1988); Linda Gordon, *Woman's Body, Woman's Right: A Social History of Birth Control in America* (New York, 1976); *"To Toil the Livelong Day": America's Women at Work, 1780–1980*, ed. Carol Groneman and Mary Beth Norton (Ithaca, N.Y., 1987); *Clio's Consciousness Raised*, ed. Mary S. Hartman and Lois Banner (New York, 1979); Martha C. Howell, *Women, Production and Patriarchy in Late Medieval Cities* (Chicago, 1986); *Women's America: Refocusing the Past*, ed. Linda K. Kerber and Jane D. Mathews (New York, 1982); Alice Kessler-Harris, *Out to Work: A History of Wage-Earning Women in the United States* (New York, 1982); Mary Kinnear, *Daughters of Time: Women in the Western Tradition* (Ann Arbor, 1982); Claudia Koonz, *Mothers in the Fatherland: Women, the Family and Nazi Politics* (New York, 1987); Asuncion Lavrin, "Latin American Women's History," *Latin American Research Review* 13 (1978): 314–18; Gerda Lerner, *The Creation of Patriarchy* (New York, 1986) and *The Majority Finds Its Past: Placing Women in History* (New York, 1979) and, as editor, *Black Women in White America: A Documentary History* (New York, 1972); *Ambiguous Realities: Women in the Middle Ages and the Renaissance*, ed. Carole Levina and Jeanne Walsa (Detroit, 1987); Maria Mies, *Patriarchy and Accumulation on a World Scale: Women in the International Division of Labour* (London, 1986); Ruth Milkman, *Gender at Work* (Urbana, 1987); Linda Richter, "The Ephemeral Woman in Urban Histories," *International Journal of Women's Studies* 5 (1982): 312–28; Rosalind Rosenberg, *Beyond Separate Spheres: Intellectual Roots of Modern Feminism* (New Haven, 1982); Sheila Rowbotham, *Hidden from History: Rediscovering Women in History from the Seventeenth Century to the Present* (New York, 1974); *Women's Search for Utopia: Mavericks and Mythmakers*, ed. Ruby Rohrlich and Elaine Hoffman (New York, 1984); Mary Ryan, *Womanhood in America from Colonial Times to the Present* (New York, 1975); Janet Sharistanian, *Gender, Ideology and Action: Historical Perspectives on*

Women's Public Lives (Westport, Conn., 1986); Rosalie Silverstone, "Office Work for Women: An Historical Review," *Business History* 18 (1976): 98–110; *Women in Medieval History and Historiography,* ed. Susan Mosher Stuard (Philadelphia, 1987); Louise A. Tilly and Joan W. Scott, *Women, Work and Family* (New York, 1978; reissued 1987).

5. Joan Kelly, "The Social Relations of the Sexes: Methodological Implications of Women's History," *Signs: Journal of Women in Culture and Society* 1 (1976): 809–23; rpt. in *Women in History and Theory: The Essays of Joan Kelly,* Women in Culture and Society series (Chicago, 1984), p. 1, my italics; hereafter cited in text as SRS.

6. Joan Kelly, "Did Women Have a Renaissance?" in *Becoming Visible: Women in European History,* ed. Renate Bridenthal and Claudia Koonz (Boston, 1977); rpt. in *Women in History and Theory,* 19–50.

7. I say "opponents" advisedly. The gentleman who nearly succumbed to apoplexy as he attacked this essay figures only in memory and (hence) in anecdote, but G. R. Elton's vicious attack on Kelly's book ("History According to Saint Joan," *The American Scholar* 54 [1985]: 549–55) is the stuff of respectable footnotes.

8. See Mary R. Beard, *Woman as Force in History* (1946; rpt. New York, 1971), esp. ch. 12, "Woman as Force in Long History," 279–340. The book under discussion here is Riane Eisler, *The Chalice and the Blade: Our History, Our Future* (San Francisco, 1987); hereafter cited in text as *CB.*

9. Rachel Sternberg, "Archaeology and Prehistory: Everybody Gets Their Digs In," *In These Times,* 27 Jan. 1988, 19; hereafter cited in text.

10. G. Rattray Taylor, *Sex in History* (New York, 1954), 151, as cited in Eisler, 142. In contrast to her uncritical use of odd works like this one, Eisler bolsters her argument by invoking long lists of feminist scholars *without* specific citations.

11. See Ruth Milkman, "Women's History and the Sears Case," *Feminist Studies* 12 (1986): 375–400.

12. Samuel G. Freedman, "Of History and Politics: Bitter Feminist Debate," *New York Times,* 6 June 1986, B1; hereafter cited in text as HP.

13. See Joan Wallach Scott, "The Sears Case," in *Gender and the Politics of History,* 167–77; hereafter cited in text as SC.

14. "Women's History Goes to Trial: *EEOC v. Sears, Roebuck and Company,*" *Signs: Journal of Women in Culture and Society* 11 (1986): 751–79.

15. Alice Kessler-Harris, "*Equal Employment Opportunity Commission v. Sears, Roebuck and Company:* A Personal Account," *Feminist Review* 25 (1987): 58; hereafter cited in text as PA.

HISTORY AND CULTURAL STUDIES

Elazar Barkan

THE PROLIFERATION OF cultural studies under various names has reached the discipline of history over the last few years as the new cultural history. This attraction to cultural studies as a multicounterdisciplinary occupation is being filtered into history through renaming old interests, "updating" social history, and incorporating identity studies. Methodologically, cultural historians are shifting their alliances from social scientists to literary critics and postmodernist rhetoric. Yet history's disciplinary culture of maintaining a commitment to extratextual reality may be said to distinguish the historian from the literary critic. But perhaps this is more of a residue than a dichotomy. The preoccupation of new cultural historians is to apply the approach of history from the bottom-up to larger and more diverse subaltern groups. Recounting the past thus carries new political and intellectual ramifications, as historians pay an increased attention to issues of representation and interpretations. Especially poignant is the work of Edward Said.

Edward Said's publication of *Culture and Imperialism* (1993), 15 years after his path-breaking *Orientalism* and 120 years after Matthew Arnold's *Culture and Anarchy,* may suggest a new postcolonial cultural closure. Said places himself at the end of a long genealogy of cultural critics and postcolonial writers who have called into question the imperialist hegemonic West and have articulated categories for resisting domination. It is an optimistic closure. Back in 1978, Said argued in *Orientalism* that Orientalists (all Westerners who studied the East) constructed the Orient as the inverse of their own image: irrational, exotic, sexual, and mysterious. Despite its shortcomings—primarily, seeing all Western writing on the East as a unified message of exploitation— *Orientalism* charted a new discourse. Specifically, it initiated a novel way of thinking and writing about the relations of the West to its Others and challenged traditional disciplines to question venerable presuppositions. Said had a clear and explicit agenda: to expose the biased attitudes of scholars in the West toward the Middle East. Many have argued that Said's partisan agenda obscured the significance of his approach.[1]

In the meantime, Said's treatment of orientalism as a discourse has been explicated further by numerous writers, which has led to a more nuanced interpretation. Following his own lead, Said of the 1990s is a more pragmatic, thoughtful, and sensitive critic who at times maintains his old spirit of resistance and political sharpness. His new synthesis is informed by highbrow theoretical criticism but privileges the need to view culture from several perspectives rather than hold a commitment to any absolute truth. Affirming the canon even as he reinterprets it, Said sounds more like a leading professor in a major university and a preeminent scholar in his field (which he is) than a representative of marginal resistance voices (as he presents himself). This "positionality"—a marginal voice speaking from the center—is manifested in Said's view of the world, which highlights that "all cultures are involved in one another; none is single and pure, all are hybrid, heterogeneous, extraordinarily differentiated, and unmonolithic" (xxv). The "new alignments" in the global multinational-diasporic culture "now provoke and challenge the fundamentally static notions of identity" (xxv), but he is cognizant that "old authority cannot simply be replaced by new authority" (xxiv). Thus, Said's approach offers a synthesis. Not infrequently, however, this rhetoric, which emphasizes harmony, is contradicted by the "real" political conflicts, not merely the paradoxes, in the text.

Consider Said's thesis. Said argues for the centrality of "Empire" to every facet of Western culture, even when the action takes place off stage. In order to understand the West, one has to investigate its relations to its margins. For example, in discussing Jane Austen's *Mansfield Park,* Said points to the fact that it was money earned in the colonies that provided the resources for the affluence of English life. Characters in this and other novels suddenly appear from the colonies to shape the narrative. In this sense, the empire is central even in its absence, as Occidental and non-European cultures are written "against" the center, constructing realities that must be historically informed. This historical reading of the empire transforms the culture of the Occident—which in the past had been viewed as appropriating everything—into a universal culture. Quoting C. L. R. James, Said declares that Beethoven belongs as much to West Indians as he does to the Germans, "since his music is now part of human heritage" (xxv). Said does not explore what exactly are the consequences of such hybridity, of renaming the West as the world, or the world as the West. However, as he insists that culture is about telling different stories, such a shift is not without consequences. I shall return to the question of universalizing later.

Said defines his subject in *Culture and Imperialism* in familiar terms as "the general pattern of relationships between the modern metropolitan West and its overseas territories," that is, the reciprocal impact of Europeans and non-Europeans. But Said maintains the traditional supremacy of the center in the postcolonial world. Not only does he work in New York, where the book was written, he also privileges New York as "the exilic city par excellence." How so? because it "contains within itself the Manichean structure of the colonial city described by Fanon" (xxv). One presumably does not have to be an anticolonialist or a theorist to subscribe to the view that New York embodies "all" global contradictions. Said, however, describes the historical changes that transform New York from the center of power to the embodiment of the contemporary pluralistic city as a move from colonialism to anticolonialism and resistance and finally to postcolonialism. Said as omnipotent postcolonial critic establishes a harmony even in the midst of a "Manichean structure." It is therefore not self-evident how, despite his historical construction, which is informed by global movements and writers, Said's perspective from the political and the academic center is distinct from previous Western appropriations that translate the other into familiar terms.

As a "New York story," Said's book is a tour de force in affirming culture in Matthew Arnold's nineteenth-century sense of "the best that is thought and known." Said begins with the traditional literary pantheon (including Conrad, Austen, Kipling, Yeats, Gide, and Camus) and broadens it to include representatives of both the West and the rest. But even in the description of the nonoccidental cultures, Said's main focus remains a small, elite group of writers who have enjoyed international recognition (Achebe, Fanon, Naipaul, Rushdie, Ngugi), or in other instances are among the most prominent in their own academic subfield (such as Ranajit Guha in "Subaltern" studies). One may well wonder whether any of these writers, or Said himself, belong less to the Occident than Beethoven does to human history? At a certain level, Said's highbrow disposition excludes popular culture altogether and addresses only the most established historical and contemporary writers. The music is Verdi's and the texts are all classical. There is no hip-hop or rasta. Said explains his selection principle: "First of all I find [the choices] estimable and admirable works of art and learning, in which I and many other readers take pleasure and from which we derive profit" (xiv). Despite Ruskin's racism and Said's egalitarianism, and their polarized rhetoric, the anticolonial critic's aestheticism is not fundamentally different from the Victorian's connoisseurship. The post-Marxian, postdeconstruction theoretical frame ends in a pragmatic, historically informed postmodern rationalism. For Said, the choice of a text is aesthetic, its understanding is historical.

Said's "homemade resolution" (194) is a historical move to replace the Hegelian linear dialectal history with a "contrapuntal analysis." Despite the musical metaphor, his binary oppositions often maintain certain old boundaries that "we may consider" as "absolute" (108). Said's story retraces the old evolutionary models by recreating, not deconstructing, the Occidental representations. He begins with nineteenth-century images of differences among peoples as "species" (Carlyle), rapidly moving through the racist litany to the rhetoric of "benevolent" Darwinian imperialism, to the impact of imperialism on the daily life of the subjugated peoples, and finally to the reciprocal hegemonic influence of the empires and the metropolis. It is in this historical context that the distinct "imperial personality" constructed in numerous modernist texts has shaped Occidental culture. For Said, the key is a historical analysis not a moral approach, which he rejects as leading only to condemnation or ignorance of the traditional canon (xiv).

Drawing on the overall immense reservoir of admiration his previous work generated, the "later" Said is writing from the position of a statesman. No longer does he approach Occidental writings with the moral indignation that characterized *Orientalism*. For a "reformed" Said, every writer has to be understood on their own terms. The model for a new and better representation is described by Said in his commentary on contemporary representations of the Middle East. While the description is of texts written by Arab women, the criterion is offered as a universal paradigm: "Such works are feminist, but not exclusivist; they demonstrate the diversity and complexity of experience that works beneath the totalizing discourses of Orientalism and . . . nationalism; they are both intellectually and politically sophisticated, attuned to the best theoretical and historical scholarship, engaged but not demagogic, sensitive to but not maudlin about women's experience; finally, while written by scholars of different backgrounds and education, they are works that are in dialogue with, and contribute to the political situation of women in the Middle East" (xxiv). One may replace orientalism and nationalism with patriarchy or any hegemony to achieve the "ideal" contemporary cultural text. Said presents a new model for postcolonial representation that at once includes postmodern insights but abandons their uncertainty. This new intermediate position, a kind of a postanticolonial critique, takes into account anticolonialist-poststructuralist sensibilities while examining them in the light of more traditional pragmatic, commonsense approaches.

Said's move from an us-versus-them perspective to a more nuanced vision is the most significant modification of his earlier stance in *Orientalism* and is emblematic of the shift in cultural studies. For Said, postcolonialism is a call for inclusion, not destruction; it is a richer study of the cultural treasures of the West and its Others; and most of all, it depends upon developing the historical context of the empire and its aftermaths. The uniqueness of Said's text is that unlike other postcolonial writers, he aims at a master narrative, not a theoretical essay, not an explication of a particular text or region, but at a global history of culture and imperialism. Such homogenization treats the various ethnic and gender identities as modular components that can be filled into an expansive "otherness."

Said's antiessentialist canonization is inclusive, representing without challenging current academic culture. In the decade and a half since *Orientalism*, a growing number of people of various marginal alliances have been incorporated into the center and have become part of the very power structure which we/they had criticized and often continue to challenge in our work. The centers as institutions, in contrast, have changed very little. American universities retain their world superiority better than any other sector of the American economy and face no real competition from elsewhere in the world. Within academia, traditionally prominent campuses have preserved their preeminence by opening up to new groups (even if the pace is far slower than any member of these groups would find satisfactory). One could therefore say that the traditional method of mediating among conflicting notions of truth through power has been upheld. Power clearly belongs to certain Ivy League and major campuses' professorships and not to others. While the centers remained essentially the same, some of their occupants have changed. Representatives of marginal groups have moved into positions of power and have been crucial in the reconfiguration of the intellectual agenda. The current situation is still far from satisfactory, but a sufficient number of "resistance voices" have enough of a stake in the system to come to terms with the consequences of being the new owners of "the master's house." It is from these positions of power that cultural studies are now charting their future.

I would like to suggest that Said's *Culture and Imperialism* exemplifies cultural studies of the 1990s and represents the incorporation of marginality into the center. Said himself exemplifies especially the generation of the elder culturalists and their new hybrid "positionality," stemming from the transformation of their role in the last generation; from leading the movement for curricular reforms and being a symbol for the cultural politics of the academy, to being considered the most prominent intellectuals in the country. Their current popularity may at times seem as though it is turning into the preoccupation of the humanities. In the guise of interdisciplinary and comparative work, these and other scholars in the various "identity studies" have been reshaping their shared concerns as cultural studies. For example, Stephen Greenblatt and Giles Gunn edited *Redrawing the Boundaries: The Transformation of English and American Literary Studies* (1992) and devote about two thirds of the essays to different aspects of cultural, gender, postcolonial, and postmodernist studies. Comparing this volume to La Capra's *Soundings in Critical Theory* (1989) and his interest in Marxism, psychoanalysis, and deconstruction, the theoretical cross-disciplinary affinity becomes apparent.

Among historians the trend has been dubbed *The New Cultural History,* the title of Lynn Hunt's popular edited volume (1989), which perhaps represents more of a common epistemological approach to the subject of culture than disciplinary coherence and which has attracted many adherents among previously social and intellectual historians. These three volumes share a moderately eclectic theoretical approach (primarily Marxism, psychoanalysis and French postmodernisms) to a variety of texts that deal with gender and ethos in various configurations. One reading of the popularity of the study of culture sees it as a move toward integrating history with the latest wave of nontraditional disciplines.

CULTURAL STUDIES

"A conjunction of historical changes—the collapse of the colonial empires, the effects in Britain of the modern diaspora of peoples of color,
the fragmentation of gender identities and the complexities of identities
politics in the postmodern world—have led cultural studies writers to
combine Gramscian politics with poststructuralist notions of subjectivity
in a search at once for ways of explaining and intervening in the contemporary world."[2]

The "new" coherent eclecticism is beautifully illustrated in the user's-
guide-like *Cultural Studies,* from which the above quotation is taken. In the
"guide," the volume's thirty-nine articles are rearranged into sixteen sec-
tions in order to "represent their multiple [theoretical and material] investments and interventions." The table of contents, in contrast, is arranged
alphabetically. The editors' solution suggests a theoretical and political coherence that cannot be subdivided without concurrently undermining the
enterprise. Such coherence, beyond disciplinary boundaries is, however,
relatively new, and institutionally the practitioners of cultural studies often
still belong to the various "identity studies" of the last generation, those
that more often than not are still "programs" rather than full-fledged academic departments. Though often characterized by fragile administrative
status and a lack of tenured budgetary lines, these have often been at the
forefront of intellectual and theoretical shifts. Growing out of political
radicalism, "studies" and "criticism" have thus reconfigured the academy
and at present portray a pragmatic coalition.

In certain instances, as in the case of American Studies, academic politics have been sufficiently inoffensive (not to say nationalistic) as to permit
a reasonably easy digestion of the transcending of disciplinary boundaries.[3] In other cases, primarily where ethnic and gender programs are
involved, the turf battle has been more contentious. One way to examine
the development of identity studies as a component in the genealogy of
the new cultural studies is to focus on the intellectual innovation that led
to the reconfiguration of social and political understanding of their subject matter. The incorporation of gender-based analysis (feminist, homo-
and heterosexual, masculine) as well as ethnic approaches, the privileging
(and limitations) of theoretical approaches, the greater attention paid to
technological changes in the production of culture, the mutual appropriation among disciplines of texts and methodologies, the egalitarian claims

about high and popular culture, non-Western and Occidental cultures—
all of which have created the set of concerns which inform cultural studies.

Yet the harsh rhetoric of the accompanying cultural wars during the
1970s and 1980s alluded on both sides of the barricades to destruction and
oppression rather than renovation. However, the popularity of the new
studies resulted not from political intimidation or "political correctness"
but rather from the intellectual success of the new approaches. While
opponents decried its standards, the new scholarship often expanded and
enriched previous research. Suddenly (by academic time scales, which
are somewhere between historical and biological) disciplines were overturned, canons were questioned, and prestige was being challenged. The
trends that received earlier exaltation in several academic journals such
as *Critical Inquiry* or *Representations* have proliferated and have now been
picked up even by university presses. At present, new positions in these
disciplines as well as others are advertised in a way that includes a "cultural" component or is open to cultural studies. If in earlier days ethnic
minorities and women were implicitly denied credentials because of their
identities, identity studies in contrast contested the legitimacy of the traditional hierarchy of white males to speak in the name of everyone else.

As the dynamic umbrella term, cultural studies has been framed in
its latest institutional postulation as an amalgam of methodologies, approaches, subject matter, and rhetoric that goes beyond any specific discipline or identity. Traditional departments in English, history, anthropology, art history, comparative literature, and religion, to mention the
major ones, have been in the last few years changing the content of the
canonical curriculum to take account of these new tendencies. Such eclecticism at times frightens critics, especially because it is informed by "real
life" situations of the weaker members of society. The reaction denigrated
these studies as victimology, and in response, and as an effort to achieve
a higher legitimacy, practitioners of cultural studies at this stage invest a
major effort in an attempt to provide the subject matter with a theoretical
coherence and an academic rhetoric that go beyond political justifications.
A different focus may reveal the new intellectual coherence to be the professional consequence of the inclusion of "new" intellectual workers on
cultural studies. While specific ethnic or gender-based political backing
was often crucial for the success of identity studies, their adopted French
aura lent them an intellectual panache typically lacking among groups that

suffer discrimination and was especially significant in facilitating the new academic vogue.

Professionally, the genealogy of the gentrification of cultural studies includes the success of earlier interdisciplinary studies that had reacted against overspecialization in research and teaching in traditional disciplines. The allure of deeper knowledge and understanding has often, notwithstanding various canons, had a darker side in the increased ignorance of scholars in areas they do not consider their expertise. The specter of the academy where scholars even within one discipline were unwilling and unable to talk to each other has sustained pessimism for a long time. So while generally such alienation occurred, and disciplines became administrative units organized as coalitions sharing resources rather than professional communities striving for intellectual coherence, a weak but visible countertrend brought interdisciplinary work to public attention. Interdisciplinarity provided an attraction both for scholars who found their interests ignored in the traditional setting and also as a model for the new identity studies. This is not to say that bread-and-butter issues were less crucial under these circumstances. On the contrary, because the relevant decisions were often made in distant administrative units (the traditional departments, with their mired interest groups), interdisciplinary and identity groups had to bridge methodological and curricular gaps (mutual ignorance) in order to accumulate the sufficient minimal resources to initiate a program, to assemble a critical mass.

THE FORTUNES OF RADICALISM

"We thus came from a tradition entirely marginal to the centers of English academic life, and our engagement in the questions of cultural change—how to understand them, how to describe them, and how to theorize them, what their impact and consequences were to be, socially—were first reckoned within the dirty outside world. The Center for Cultural Studies was the locus to which we *retreated* when that conversation in the open world could no longer be continued: it was politics by other means. Some of us—me, especially—had always planned never to return to the university, indeed, never to darken its doors again. But, then, one always has to make pragmatic adjustments to where real work, important work, can be done."[4]

By the late 1980s, just as academic politicking got juicier and out of hand, identity studies had come of age and became "respected"; transformed into cultural studies. Having been around for long enough, scholars in the cultural studies stream have inadvertently established a canon, and perhaps even more important, a tradition. The signs that cultural studies have "made it" are manifest: recognizable academic jargon, a proliferation of successful and prestigious journals, a generational differentiation with a familiar roster of founding mothers and fathers, the appearance of new fields of research. And plenty of prestigious academic appointments. Cultural studies is becoming an establishment. This raises the question of what happens to an oppositional group whose identity initially stems from its challenge to authority once it acquires authority?

Or one may ask how the growth of identity studies into cultural studies affected the status of academic radicalism? How were intellectual endeavors that began characteristically from an initial oppositional radical posture combined with a professional and a social highbrow disposition, such as the one manifested by Said? As a question in the sociology of knowledge, to use an old-fashioned designation, one may examine the possible relationship between a new academic discipline and specific ideological and political commitments. A recent history of cultural studies underscores the radical stance as "a return of the repressed, accompanied by a radical politics and concern with other oppressions (gender, race) besides those enforced through class."[5] Naming ethnic and gender studies as "cultural studies"—as a new professional activity—is a retelling of the stories we have been narrating in the recent past in a conscious effort to form new entities and in the process reconfigure new professional identities. The "new" identities that now constitute cultural studies and have populated over the past generation various other academic departments are currently producing an imprecisely demarcated but spectacularly popular terrain.

Stuart Hall's construction of the origin of cultural studies in Birmingham, certainly high on anybody's list of the founding myths for culturalists, portrays the predicament of identity studies in their efforts to institutionalize radicalism yet avoid academic seclusion. One may find another example in a manifestolike document from the mid-1980s that stated that cultural studies should be formulated as "counter disciplinary," to be practiced by "resisting intellectuals" whose role is defined as "a counterhegemonies practice that can both avoid and challenge it." Such duality was to be achieved in "an oppositional public sphere," not to "be conceived as a 'department' or as part of the boundary separating professional activities from those of amateurs." The vision of the writers was that "resisting intellectuals must develop and work with movements outside the limiting contours of the disciplines, symposia, and reward systems that have become the sole referent for intellectual activity."[6] These sentiments, which drove identity studies, especially women's, ethnic, lesbian and gay groups in their earlier years, are at present in stark contrast to the high visibility and intellectual prominence of the practitioners.

The growing pains of "institutionalization" may involve more nostalgia for a marginal position than real hardship. What happens when the criticism of appropriation and colonialism is done from the colonial center, from the most powerful and prestigious positions? Connecting activists and scholars, the radical move of the Birmingham group, has become the catchphrase of the nineties for intellectuals and foundations alike. The impact of such co-opting is hard to predict. One may like to think that a significant reformulation of the system is possible, yet it is just as possible that efforts to connect today's activism to the academy may end with present-day activists preferring to be gentrified rather than remaining "authentic." If one goes by the communal academic experience of the past generation, lucrative and prestigious positions remain exactly that. Hall describes his own, Richard Hoggart's and Raymond Williams's turn to the academy as a retreat from a real world that was too hard, a defeat in the face of a dialogue that cannot be maintained. So while the title of Williams's *The Long Revolution* might have been revolutionary for Cambridge at the time, whatever radicalism the work possessed was mediated by Williams's prestigious academic position.[7] While radical politics may be viewed as noble, the structural inability of academics to divorce themselves from their institutional ties or to reject the lucrative temptations of the system in order to pose a "real" opposition (presumably one that is not self-serving), often transforms the intended "politics" into a "narration," very often one that can easily be confused with the fictional. Short of rare academic radicalism such as seen on the 1960s campuses, the academy serves more to domesticate radicalism than to nurture it. The focus on radicalizing language, for example, has often achieved the very opposite of radical politics, isolating activists and often amounting to no more than renaming academic activities. Hence "*public*-actions" seems to stand for actual "repolitization." (In this particular case the "actions" were purported to include legitimizing writing reviews and books for the general public and naming these as taking place in "an oppositional public sphere."[8] Not quite the making of a social revolution.)

Such sterilized politics is aggravated by the selection process of graduate school, the relatively long training for immersion in the critical vocabulary, and the competition for visibility in the "central" departments, conferences, journals. Thus, because the older elitism associated with Arnoldian culture was the target of much of the rebellion, current cultural studies, with its new elitism, presents a dilemma. But in contrast to identity studies as the politics of validation, cultural studies may have to mediate the relationship of the various identities not at the expense of any but by recognizing that no coherent political agenda is a likely outcome. Yet political efficacy could be developed by embarking on coalition building, which delineates an achievable intellectual and political agenda. Which is very much the current practice, if not the theoretical disposition, among culturalists.

As the reverberations in the academy of the various identities have proliferated, it seems no longer possible or desirable to concentrate (or limit) the study of "an identity" to a particular department in the university. From not being "worthy" of departmental status, the study of gender/race/identity has moved exceedingly rapidly to a situation in which it may no longer be possible or advisable to be confined to a department. Women's studies for example, perhaps the most fully evolved "studies," have become such a crucial part of any curriculum—from the sciences to the professional schools, to the social sciences and to the humanities—that nobody envisions any longer collapsing it into a single department. The days of feminism as a radical movement in the academy have passed. No longer do generic feminists lead the onslaught on established patriarchy. Feminism is criticized for being too universalizing (read colonialist), overlooking the multiplicity of "voices," entangled by polarized opinions. Traditional feminists often find themselves compelled to defend their position against criticism from women of color or lesbians, who decry earlier feminists critiques for obscuring differences among women. Yesterday's radicals are today's conservatives. The radical critique of feminism that began around 1980 has turned within a few years into dogma. One could almost say that "vanilla feminists" are now swallowing the bitter pill of radicalism they prescribed for mainstream academia a generation ago. Feminist theory is at a stage when it has to articulate strategies to investigate the incongruity between universalizing womanhood and the innovative research that illuminates the diverse experiences of women along ethnic and class lines. How is feminism to go beyond the homogenization of women? The multiple-jeopardy (women of color are doubly victimized) answer is appropriate only in certain instances, but often the multiple identities are in competition. Do these multiple identities create an internal conflict in which neither ethnic nor gender identity can be referred to independently? Given the political and intellectual significance of feminist pluralism, what does the contradiction of identities do to the politics of oppression? Or put differently, how is one to deal with the apparent reluctance to move beyond cumulative victimization?[9]

Other identity scholars find themselves in a similar predicament. African-American, Chicano, and gay scholars face a plurality that confronts the very essence of shared authenticity. Although pushing diverse agendas, the various ethnic and gender-based studies' unifying claim was frequently that a position can best (and at times, only) be represented by it's subjects. "Subject position," "positionality," "essentialism," and "reductionism" were among the more genial buzzwords in the debate. (The other side included terms such as *racism, fascism, misogyny, homophobia,* etc.) The politics of exclusion and reclaiming one's identity were indeed very powerful in the earlier days, when a small group of writers was validating new areas of scholarship. A unified front was essential for the legitimizing process to succeed. Within a short time, however, the participants in these debates have multiplied dramatically, and a synergy of diverse disciplines and publications proliferated. The success, however, by its sheer number of prominent practitioners has undermined the argument about exclusive authenticity. (Although the number of African-Americans on the campus is declining, the overall number of "minorities" is greatly increasing.) The growing disagreements among practitioners undermined the very notion of authenticity as the production of a single voice. In a society that privileges multiple identities, identity studies created a predicament: how is one to mediate among various claims of authentic knowledge?

Within identity studies, class provides a somewhat different dilemma. If one ascribes the academic transformation to the inclusion of racial minorities, women, and open homosexuals in the power structure, then the reshifting of attention to class creates a new parity if not homogeneity beyond the validation of difference. Yet the likelihood for such a return to class is minimal. Historically, self-interest has proved the single most influential factor in mobilizing scholars in support of antidiscriminatory,

pro-activist scholarship. Hence a scholar's identity or a liberal-left ideology is most likely to explain one's participation in supporting a particular cause. Class affinity is fundamentally different. Although a small
number of the poor and the underclass do enter the academy, their impact as a group is minuscule because they go through an instantaneous
transformation by becoming middle class. The very aspiration (and acting
upon it successfully) creates a dissonance with the authenticity of poverty.
While women, ethnic and racial minorities, or homosexuals do not change
their identity because of academic gentrification, the poor cannot help it.
An academic discussion about poverty is by necessity paternalistic. And
paternalism, at present at least, is held in low esteem. It is thus unlikely
that class—the only one of the contemporary triad that rarely has an authentic academic representation—would become central to cultural interpretation or would gain such "authentic" voices in the near future. The
legacy of the Center for Contemporary Cultural Study in Birmingham and
the place of Raymond Williams, E. P. Thompson, and Eric Hobsbawm
among other British Marxists in the genealogy of cultural studies, as well
as the liberal ideological sympathies of other practitioners, suggest that
questioning the ability to represent the poor and the lower classes in the
academy authentically does not express the self-perspective of those practitioners. Yet the centrality of class as a category and subject matter should
obviously not be conflated with authenticity.

A different possible coalescence for cultural studies is around the victim's point of view. Viewed from a conservative perspective, identity
studies resulted in what came to be denigrated as "victimology." In contrast, the practitioners view the use of conventional or newly fashionable
methodologies to challenge traditional power structures as the renovation
of the master's house with the master's tools. The perspective of the victim as a concept is coming into prominence as the great homogenizer
across cultures, identities, and disciplines. Given the rejection of violence
as the last liberal universal bastion, victims of violence maintain the general middle-class empathy. Yet the victim's perspective may be problematical precisely because it includes the vast majority of the world population,
and one may doubt whether anybody is ever excluded. Generally concepts
that overexplain have not been more successful in the past than those that
only give partial answers. Yet as opposed to the poor, who are co-opted by
academic institutions, survivors of violence remain survivors, sharing and
at times competing for the validation that comes from their experiences.

And while the term *victimology* originated as a denigration, as so often happened in the past, a derogatory castigation may turn into an identity. Victimology could turn out to be the next cultural paradigm. There is a great deal to study about suffering, comparing different manifestations, investigating the relationship of reality as actuality and memory, probing the unspeakable.

A generation older, and notwithstanding diverse disciplinary influences, cultural studies seems to have developed a coherent (many would argue too coherent) answer to the social and cultural changes that face society and are reflected in the academy, producing in the process a cross-disciplinary canon. Said's version may be most representative. One may well focus the inquiry of this canon on the centrifugal international forces produced by the postcolonial struggle that transformed the academy in the West. While the new players have led to the proliferation of approaches and subject matter of the academy, the trend simultaneously produced centripetal attraction, which presented a risk of homogenizing cultural differences. This was especially pertinent in the debate over political correctness and the accepted conventions of the new cultural frontiers that proliferated on the main campuses in the United States. For example, "minority discourse"—by 1990 a fad in various configurations—provided an ideal administrative intellectual niche for constructing a global minority identity, where the Others are playing musical chairs. The actors change, but the structure has become universalized. The issue is complexified when identity is advanced as a critique against conservative readings—such as by Achebe of Naipaul's replicating Conrad—while at the same time providing the validating epistemology of the radical critique.[10] The next step is the recognition that the multiplicity of indigenous—touristic—authentic culture can no longer be reified into a single primordial authenticity, and cannot be distinguished either within academic or "real" inscriptions.[11] Although the recognition of history as merely a text is strongly resisted among historians, the multiplicity of histories as text by literary critics and anthropologists among others is likely to move the debate beyond its current focus on theory and highbrow intellectual inclination.[12]

Where does all this leave History? One perspective can be gleaned from a report by the American Comparative Literature Association on the state of the discipline at the end of the century.[13] I point to the report because it frames the debate in practically identical terms to the debate surrounding contemporary cultural history in a discipline that has been consciously elitist and is pondering the possibility of mending its ways. In this case, disciplinary boundaries become mirrors more than obstacles. While taking account of all of the contemporary gallery of concepts and identities, the report maintains a traditional emphasis on quality, standards, while attempting to face the challenge of decentralization and draw attention to new areas outside Europe. The issue of methodologies, primarily the study of literature in the original languages—the sine qua non of the discipline—is largely maintained, with the allowance, however, for marginal literatures to be taught in translation. This is a postcolonial, pragmatic sense of how to uphold standards while offering diversity, to include marginal voices without violating the traditional privileging of authenticity. The result is a neopragmatism that, it could easily be argued, perpetuates paternalism and "exotic" authenticity by giving in to real-life limitations of who knows what languages. The issue is which cultures are seen as necessarily studied in the original, and which "others" are not. Rejecting translation is justified by the inability to convey the full sophistication of a culture, but such a crucial consideration is suspended where the study of the original is simply not feasible, especially in non-Western and Third World languages. The alternative to translation is even less attractive, that is, not to study "remote" cultures. The committee's intention is commendable, but the unavoidable result is that the center does, and will, indeed hold. Very much in line with Said's contrapuntal historicity.

Cultural studies presents history with a methodological challenge. As, for example the ACLA report suggests, history should inform all new critical theories, and these ought to be based on training that provides a "historical basis for [analysis]."[14] As a result of this methodological turn toward history that has been evident in other disciplines, historical methodology is flourishing outside history departments. Having been liberated from a semi-exiled existence (which lasted roughly from the Great Depression to the end of the Vietnam war, a period in which history was mostly subsumed under the social sciences), historians are perplexed and delighted by the now not-so-new popularity of the discipline.[15] The deluge both enriched and further fragmented the profession. In short, history has become, if not always reflexively, postmodern. Dangling between the world as text and representations as reality, historians have been pondering the new possibilities and limitations embedded in these methodologies. Concurrently, the approaching end of the century (as well as of the millennium) has provided further motivation for reflexive and historical accounts and a general awareness of the way we tell stories. Faced with this seemingly imminent closure, "noble dreams" of cumulative objective knowledge are confronted with a growing cognizance among historians of their need to adjudicate between fiction and reality. In those not so distant times before cultural studies, historians were already becoming engaged with the question of what types of stories we tell. Because the epistemological angst of historians may have risen during the last generation, it is perhaps somewhat surprising that the stories of the postcolonial have remained so similar to each other. A structuralist narration of cultural history in seven words or less may sound like: elite/canon, radicalism, politics, interdisciplinary studies, institutionalization, elite/canon; describing how young radicals are institutionalized into the canon. Yet the discipline seems to have practitioners who occupy each of these categories. Whether for professional eminence or other identity marks, each (new) cultural historian finds a place within this cycle as "radical" or "established." Subject to the limitations of the discourse, historians configure their own loci within this cycle and contribute to the communal story.

History as a discipline had an ambivalent role in the emergence of cultural studies: it is more a disciplinary manifestation of larger intellectual developments than a professional innovation. Institutionally it played a secondary role, while intellectually it supplied a major gateway for many of the competing approaches. Granting the limitations of a general overview, the genealogy of the new cultural history resembles the action of an omnivore. Cultural history did not follow a coherent linear intellectual evolution, one that brought into prominence a particular component at distinct points; rather it included every possible cultural and methodological innovation. The new cultural history can be said not to reject any approach, topic, or methodology. Nor does it rank these along any hierarchy. Historically, in addition to the role of identities, the genealogy of the new cultural history incorporated the methodologies of the Annales, literary criticism, and anthropology. The description of the discipline may focus on Princeton as a locus, where social history was transformed into cultural history, or trace it to Britain with its various Marxist and neo-Marxist schools, and end up either in the Open University or in New Historicism. In any of these constructions one is most likely to consume French and German main dishes with Italian and Russian dressings, with non-Western players and postcolonial theorists providing the dessert.

In attempting to delineate the subject matter of the new cultural history, the prominence and popularity of certain topics may present a predicament. Although the outsider may be confused, there is no need epistemologically, nor is it possible, to adjudicate and construct a coherence among the various constituencies of cultural studies. Notwithstanding this eclecticism, there is no sense of anarchy among the practitioners. Like members of an exclusive club, insiders just know. When did historians move from Foucault and Derrida to Gramsci, oops, is it now Wittgenstein and Benjamin? When was the move from Martin Guerre to the Marquis de Sade completed? What was the meaning of such a shift? There is nothing surprising in asking such questions in a profession that prides itself on "reflexivity." However, the meaning of reflexivity often depends on a construction that names the act of asking as naive, as an indicator of liminality, a tolerated outsider, but perhaps not more. One may look to the "distant" discipline of history of science and the fortunes of the concept of paradigm. Historians of science would generally not use Kuhn's paradigm because it is seen as too simplistic, not sufficiently precise, conveying too many contradictory meanings, while in other disciplinary cultures the concept maintains its attraction. Yet one need not despair. Training and the initiation ceremony on campus called graduate school—the New Age "final clubs" where currently textual postmodernist sexuality stands for much else since famously "there is nothing outside the text"—may still deliver one to the promised land.

In the proliferation of interdisciplinary approaches, traditional history may still provide a methodological segue between fiction and the claims of cultural studies to external reality. At present, history is done in several disciplines and the results differ at most by degree and perhaps by the temperament of the practitioners. However, historians most often learn by example from previous works with marginal innovations. The effort to engage in a revolutionary new writing is at present more of a hope than a practice, largely shaped by the high value historians place on the nonfictional character of their work, which constrains creativity. Yet the introduction of theoretical considerations into historical writing as well as the growing awareness of theoretical considerations by practicing historians is on the rise. As the demarcation from literary criticism is blurred and a greater number of practitioners from several disciplines participate in different professional meetings as partial and new insiders, the likelihood of maintaining older boundaries wanes.

A theoretical predicament for new culturalists as historians, and perhaps even more so as activists, is the need to bring the story to a close. How is one to negotiate the postmodern milieu and the theoretical emphasis on the limited or nonexistent "agency" and multiple readings yet maintain a comfortable coziness with nonfictionality? At present it seems that while critics privilege the view that emphasizes activism as scholarship, this view does not include the prescriptions of how to overcome the theoretical predicament of agency and discourse. This predicament empowers pragmatic centrist interpretations. These comments do not mean to diminish the significance of radical politics but rather to point to the difficulty of translating the postmodernist insights into concrete action on one hand and historical narratives on the other. It has been the (mostly frustrated) goal of culturalists to bridge activism and scholarship, evident in history as in other disciplines. The frustration often results despite (or because of) the substantial success in informing the academy about the real world. The movement has become a powerful force in reforming the academic curriculum while inspiring activism and informing the political system. Yet academic filters are structured to bring disillusionment. Despite changes in the academy, once community concerns are reinscribed, abstracted, and metamorphosed into theory, the temperament and goals of activism are hardly recognizable, as is becoming the case in cultural history. Activism cannot apparently sustain academic discourse in a direct manner over the long haul and has to be mediated in order to be institutionalized. If the pace of activists energizes academic discourse, the longer "metaview" of scholars provides activism with "serious," "deep" analysis and what often amounts to policy options. The permanent revolution cannot it seems survive even in the academy. A crucial reason seems to be the different "corporate culture" between activism and scholarship, which differ perhaps more in their time scale, not targets. Their coexistence, through disagreements, may in the next academic generation be influential.

The precise process of how the impact of the activist will be mediated is the major challenge of the discipline during the next decade. Earlier efforts of privileging activism and excluding "nonauthentic" voices have encountered major obstacles and will most probably be further marginalized in the future. Over the long run, the hate of DWEMs is not better than misogyny, nor is black racism superior to other xenophobia. The question of identity activism can also be addressed as one that inquires into the types of identity that may continue to present challenges in the future. One may begin with the observation that as a result of activism and scholarship during the last 50 years (and others may say 150), issues of race and gender have been transformed dramatically. When assessing the impact of activism, it is worthwhile to remember that a couple of generations ago, even the application of the concept of equality was controversial, as was the legitimacy of studying minorities or women. As these categories have become the consensus, they create new meanings. In a society when new concepts such as "multiple identities" are fast becoming a cliché, the question may well be asked what would be the next set of categories that would captivate cultural studies. That a historical answer is privileged in this volume may not be wholly surprising.

NOTES

1. For a favorable criticism, James Clifford, *The Predicament of Culture* (Cambridge, Mass., 1988), 255–76.

2. Lawrence Grossberg, Cary Nelson, and Paula A. Treichler, eds., *Cultural Studies* (New York, 1992), 18.

3. Patrick Brantlinger, *Crusoe's Footprints: Cultural Studies in Britain and America* (New York, 1990), 26–33.

4. Stuart Hall, "The Emergence of Cultural Studies and the Crisis of the Humanities," *October* (1990): 11–23.

5. Antony Easthope, *Literary into Cultural Studies* (London, 1991), 7.

6. Henry Giroux, David Shumway, Paul Smith, James Sosnoski, "The Need for Cultural Studies: Resisting Intellectuals and Oppositional Public Spheres," *Dalhousie Review* 64 (1984): 472–86.

7. Hall.

8. Giroux, et al.

9. Chandra T. Mohanty, Ann Russo, Lourdes Torres, *Third World Women and the Politics of Feminism* (Bloomington, 1991); Nupur Chaudhuri and Margaret Strobel, eds. *Western Women and Imperialism: Complicity and Resistance* (Bloomington, 1992).

10. Chinua Achebe, *Hopes and Impediments* (New York, 1989), 1–21.

11. Marshall Sahlins, "Goodbye to *Tristes Tropes*: Ethnography in the Context of Modern World History," *Journal of Modern History* 65 (1993): 1–25.

12. This is, for example, evident in Saul Friedlander, ed., *Probing the Limits of Representations* (Cambridge, Mass., 1992), which brought even Hayden White and Dominick LaCapra to admit to the "reality" of history beyond the text.

13. "A Report to the ACLA: Comparative Literature at the Turn of the Century," chaired by Charles Bernheim, May 1993.

14. Ibid.

15. Student enrollment in history declined by over 60 percent from 1970 to 1985. The increasing enrollment since (especially graduate enrollment) is disproportionally high both as compared to all fields and to all the humanities and the arts (Barbara Alpern, "Rising Enrollment Challenge for the Future," *Perspectives* 31, no. 8 [1993]: 13–14).

HISTORY... BUT

⟨━━━━➤◆◀━━━━⟩

Robert Dawidoff

The small survivor has a difficult task
Answering the questions great historians ask.
—Edwin Denby, "On the Home Front—1942"

Time was when the voices in historical narrative were standard ones. Now history is open, to workers, to popular culture, to the middlebrow, to the built and natural environment. And this is a good thing. But without questioning the sincerity of the eager embrace of history to include all manner of phenomena, I do wonder at its capacity to do them justice. And as other disciplines rush to assimilate historical methods, this historian's wonder increases. The historian would speak both for history the discipline and for History the enveloping occurrence. The historian's embrace is inevitably an explanatory one; the place being offered by the historian is a place in History. That is what history has to give, the matter-of-fact security of historicity.

History's current attraction for other disciplines in part reflects their recognition that history is a way of looking at things that makes it possible to regard a discipline in a way that replaces some of its self-examination with the genetic account of its existence. It is a way around theory at a time when many scholars are tired out with theory. At the same time, one hears from many quarters a certain unease with the resurgence of the historical. Along with the admission of reluctant need, there is a recognition of all that history claims and an anxiety like that expressed by the King of Siam in *The King and I:* "If allies are strong with power to protect me, might they not protect me out of all I own?" A fear of annexation. Most of the disciplines are old rivals of history—parents, siblings, children of history; they have learned to beware their own need for what history does, even as, nowadays, they diagnose in themselves a deficiency requiring a dose of history.

The professional scholarly study of history is not good for all the things that History is good for. It is what you might call prescription history and may need to be used only on doctor's advice and under controlled circumstances. Over-the-counter history is a less controlled and less specific remedy, the generalized fix. And the history cure draws on many sources and sometimes forgoes altogether the compounds of scholarship for the herbal and spiritual, the voodoo and homeopathic remedies of histories that, as with many remedies, work on certain populations because of traditions outside the stream of modern science and because of what those populations need.

If what ails someone is ignorance of the history scholarship knows about, there are usually over-the-counter popular remedies, information and interpretation, that historical science has developed for common usage; these include textbooks and general histories and the kind of history you can include in biographies and critical studies, history as a decided-upon addition to something. Consulting the historian to find out things need not entail altering one's method in the light of his advice. The recent uses of history by other disciplines have sometimes meant to go beyond this to more serious interventions, intending not so much relief as metabolic or systemic change. These (medicinal) interventions by prescription seem to involve the doing of a kind of history itself, which is not unprecedented, of course, but which often challenges and changes aspects of the patient-discipline's routine and self-understanding.

The history that scholarship can prescribe answers comparatively sophisticated questions and makes many assumptions about who wants to know what and how much about what. Much of the knowledge and the interest of present-day historical scholarship is rarefied. Communities held together by truth are not necessarily communities held together by truth believed according to the standards of scholarly professions. Art, human expressive fabrication, which moves people to share identity or views or to a common cause does not have the same criteria of selectivity as historical scholarship. What scholarly history cures is only sometimes what ails the history-deficient. This applies not only to the doctor but to the remedy. Some curative agents, like popular culture, may not be altogether effective in the historian's preparation. What the historian may have to do to turn these into medicine may take the healing power out of them. It is a case of the historian's capacity not only to prescribe for others but to master the proper effects of the possible remedies.

There are many kinds of history deficiencies, and it is not always clear which plague our fellow disciplines, chronic internal deficiencies or tension headaches brought on by theoretical stress. History soothes theoretical stress. Its inclination is to view it as all in the mind of the patient anyway, and the bias of the historical profession is not to take all that seriously what is only in the mind. The historian resembles that up-to-date television general practitioner Marcus Welby, who can assimilate all the new drugs—he even kind of knows about Freud—to a soothing Dutch uncle's persona, so that the latest remedies are dispensed with unblushing countertransference and aggressive bonhomie. This aspect of the historian's practice yet clings to the profession's self-understanding. And it is soothing to the discipline, troubled by the conflicting claims and apparent dilemmas that often accompany the attempts to reconcile scholarly practice with contemporary theory, to be told essentially that it is all in your mind, that it isn't the real world, that history is realer than theory.

In part this reflects the ease with which history as a subject of interest moves through the various levels of schooling and interest. A Civil War buff has more to say to the most sophisticated scholar of the Civil War than, I think, a philosophy autodidact to a philosophy professor, or a voracious reader to a literature professor. History still does most of its work within the framework of its simplest and most widely shared functions, telling people about their stories and the stories of other peoples and things they are interested in, the once-upon-a-time stories that make up History, whatever else historians or history might happen to mean. (And this despite some historians' desire to remake the discipline in the model of other disciplines, such as science, social science, and the other humanities, to become more like them in the pursuit of history.)

The voice of the modern scholar is by definition distinct and detached from the phenomena studied. The scholar, however, characteristically spends more time and becomes more identified with a subject's work or deeds than the subject did in the first place. It takes longer to study the life than to live it, longer to interpret the work than to create it, longer to understand the event than it took to happen. Very often the historian's stake in the subject exceeds in intensity and force the original participants'. J. H. Hexter's shrewd saw about how he spent his "historian's day" in the Renaissance was a subtle indoctrination, in the no-nonsense historian's tone, into the historian's mysterious craft. It proposed that to devote one's day to the mastery of the detail of long-gone societies was a likely way to understand them objectively. That is one way to do it, of course, and Hexter exemplifies a remarkable historical method. But it is not clear that all historical things are best understood by those who devote their days to them after the fact, or at a scholar's distance, or with a scholar's intensity or joy. This is especially true with what is called popular culture. How do you write about something that is a challenge to a way of looking at the world in the language of the world it challenges?

I have never seen a rock lyric quoted in scholarship without feeling uneasy. It seems immediately ungainly, because the cadence of the sentence is by definition different from the rhythm of the song. Prose influenced by the music, hip prose, does not mate easily or well with the prose of selective scholarly knowledge. The kinds of connections and attributions and scholarship necessary to the study sound funny often as not. I do not think there is much wrong with the study. I do it too. But I worry, because the scholarly tone sounds pompous, and it often destroys the pleasure of the thing by transforming the pleasure into a concentration, does more than quote with its quotation marks.

The scholar's awkward agenda is not as off-putting as the *faux* scholarship of so many rock writers, but it seems to engender a generation gap. The historian sounds old, the journalist less old, and the rock music sometimes just sounds better unhistoricized. The liner-note history of the music represents a history of the music itself. But the inclusion of the music into historical narrative tends to be awkward, arch, pointed, condescending, whether it is written by a fan or a nonfan: the fan sounds like a groupie, the nonfan like a groupie's parent. The writing of cultural history from the rock music and what it represents seems, in turn, homemade, ill-informed, parochial, and devotional.

The study of popular culture is a cure for what ails the study of expression and society, but its availability to self-conscious examination is problematic, and its assimilation to cultural history is especially so. The adjustment to popular materials by scholarly disciplines inevitably challenges those disciplines. That is part of the point of inclusion. Cultural history is only one way of approaching popular material. Cultural history's openness to this material, its agenda of inclusion, has a moral. And if the moral has changed so that it is inclusive as well as judgmental, then the sentence-by-sentence writing of history is still judgmental.

At the heart of Hayden White's project of historical criticism is his identification with the perception by novelists that there was something in history that ruined the fun, took the joy and life out of the things it chronicled and the people who chronicled it. The materials I work with show me some of the problem. I recently wrote about Sophie Tucker's relation with Jean Paul Sartre (in the person of that disgusted provincial historian Roquentin in *Nausea*) during the fateful encounter of modernism with African-American culture in the twentieth century, an elegant if far-fetched association.[1] And for the life of me, I felt a kind of empathy for Soph, in there with all the brains and swells. By the time I was done with the whole business, using the insights of social history, African American history, feminist history, the history of popular culture, immigrant history, the history of liberalism, even modern European intellectual history, historicizing the last of the red-hot mommas, she was imprisoned, looking back out at me, reproachfully, as if to say, "This is the thanks I get for all that good singing?"

I suppose she might also have been flattered at the company she was keeping. She would surely have laughed at me, both my earnest historicizing and my worry, advised me to relax and enjoy myself and not to worry about her; she'd met royalty, after all, and had played many a tougher joint than the quarterly into which I was booking her. She would have been proud that one of her fans was a professor. She would have reminded me that it doesn't matter what they say about you, so long as they're talking about you.

But there is a loss when you make culture out of expression, history out of culture, especially with the stuff of nonhigh culture—when, say, you put a popular song you love to sing or hear behind the bars of analysis. Context is imprisoning because, by making the subject a part of history, you somehow risk knowing the stuffings out of it, when what you wanted to do was to keep what in it so beguiled you alive forever, as you experienced it. In the name of craft, history licenses the passion you feel for a subject without examining the passion, trapping you and what delights you into becoming unconscious actors in the film noir of the cultural justice system.

Cultural history has its own agenda. It may be an agenda of inclusion, but it wishes cultural expression to be included in the narrative of attributed meaning and somehow to fit in with what historians know about societies. It requires a certain kind of mind and education, and the history it writes reflects them. There is probably nothing wrong with this. The historian's literary art, transformed by the ever-fresh wonder of history itself, writing about the past so that you remember what you never knew, can work wonders with most material.

But the bias of history is there, toward event, toward common sense, and toward a kind of old-fashioned good sense about things. History is not exactly burdened by philosophy, but it has one; and it is itself notoriously the examples from which philosophy and literature teach. Being principally about the things people do makes history in some ways more conservative than if it were equally about the things people think or imagine—intellectual and cultural history were not Clio's firstborn.

Cultural history brings to the thinking and imagining, to expressivity, the balancing grounding of history, but its bias is toward narrative as a kind of control or discipline and toward change and continuity as the essence of life. That is not just Professor Lovejoy's "great chain of being." Historians tend to be skeptical of psyche and emotion and tend not to do them justice. History is not very good at feeling or ruminative thinking. Narrative and change/continuity are history's schemes of life, but not necessarily life itself, or what it means to people, just one way of looking at it, as if from a distance. The historian has long explored the necessary difference between describing and being Napoleon. If historians mean to continue to expand their narrative beyond traditional high-culture subjects to a broader range of representative phenomena and voices, they will need to adjust their thinking to the cases.

History makes cultures; professional scholarship legitimizes cultural production; contemporary historical scholarship is open to a wider range of productions and in some ways is motivated by a more generous and egalitarian attitude. Everybody gets into historical heaven nowadays. But the tone of the legitimacy, what the phenomenon must undergo to get the wings, has not necessarily changed. And something inside the listener, the wonderer at, the person motivated by insatiable curiosity to study things in the first place, is affronted. What does history do to art, to feelings, to secrets, in making culture out of them?

History has a confident air, to some extent a confidence built on its apparent closeness to human experience. It is a scholarly activity that parents and detectives and novelists and singers and religious people and musicians and criminals and lawyers and just about everybody ends up doing. Historians gain a confidence from the seeming naturalness of their activity. And the popularity of history right now reflects that interesting confidence, its lowness to the ground of experience. The theory wars have exhausted many scholars and the widely perceived isolation of the academic has made the commonness of the historical ground attractive. But history's seductive way of working by inclusion is to some extent based on its enfolding momentum. And it is never more dangerous than when it is most blandly inviting, when it is readiest to take the burden of self-consciousness off the shoulders of those who seek its counsel.

I remember the eagerness with which, as a student, I, a nonreligious Jew, took to Puritanism. I now realize how vibrant and exciting an introduction to the moral world that was to me. Reading Jonathan Edwards for the first time was a revelation, you might say. I had the sort of reaction to Puritanism, and to other subjects I studied in history, of excitement and mastery of details and even possession, that friends had studying philosophy, literature, theater, physics, and so on. The study of intellectual history was the medium for my own investigation of a structure of conscience and piety that was not readily available to me in late-sixties America on terms that suited my own insides. Not surprisingly I took to and remain took with Perry Miller.

I remain entranced by Miller's distillation of the Puritans as a moral reproach to liberalism and his delineation of the Augustinian strain of piety, that deeply self-critical, impassioned attempt at self-forgetting, with its moral seriousness tied to a shower of delirious hope of escaping the rational from the top of the intellectual pyramid, rather than from its base. I welcomed his construct of a Puritan mind and bathed in the details, the logic of Petrus Ramus, the economy of salvation, the fragile, complex Edwardsian solutions.

I was a student of divinity, I took all the advantages of the Puritan solution, except of course the advantages of belief or the disadvantages of its discipline. I was a Puritan, if that meant mastery of the details. And I resented, as if a Puritan, the moralistic compromises of the benevolent American successors. I feared Edmund Morgan's remarkable *The Puritan Dilemma,* because I could see that he rendered what I believed an unnegotiable agony into a formidably practical solution.[2] My historical judgments were founded on the rock of my own pseudosalvation. My historian's day was spent with what I craved, away from what unnerved me, on terms that protected me from both and rewarded me with the odd reversal of investment.

I remember the seminars, the outside discussions, the papers we all wrote, the articles and books we read, the deep delving into the details of a long-outworn faith. The Puritans are dead, long live Puritanism. I remember, too, the intense immersion in the details that all of the history graduate students had to acquire. History was our obsessive subject and historiography our informal medium of communication. We learned to express our feelings, our gossip, our aspirations, our everything, in the terms of professional scholarly history. That intense maneuvering of the details of someone else's culture, that need, and that intensity feed scholarship, initiating the graduate student into the days one must live, as Hexter says.

Years later, I taught graduate students who were also believing Christians and who explained to me, with admirable patience, that my understanding of the delicate balance of Puritanism could not be correct. It was not Christian. They knew their faith, and I knew its history, and we disagreed across an unbridgeable chasm. I think I was right. That is not the point. The point is that my delight, following Miller, in the culture of the Puritans was based on my not wanting Grace, my not believing in it, my doing it in the most intense detail possible but without the faith that motivated it. It freed my intellectual synthesis of the most important element of its creation—not as a fact, this I had mastered, but as a compelling, motivating apprehension, something my accounting for inevitably fell short of. That made an important element in the study of cultural history, one that was never discussed even in our too few philosophy of history classes. Our training prized and trusted our immersion in the detail and indeed regarded it as the baptism one must undergo in the historian's creed. My delight in the detail was also balanced by my need for the discipline. I was uneasy with what interested me most. I welcomed the discipline of history to control my passion for its details. And although I realize that my associates, then and now, would not recognize themselves in this, I must say I recognize them, at their best and at their blandest.

The question is not whether immersion in details is a necessary or bad thing, but which immersions reflect professional or subjective choices, why some are OK and others not, and what is to be believed and what not. History, as a profession, arrives in any epoch at a certain tone to take toward the materials of history; it allows certain kinds of questions to be answered with certain kinds of answers. What historians always agree upon is claiming a certain distance from what is studied. This creates particular difficulties in the study of expressive subjects, worth at least a hesitation, a reflex suspicion of the consequences of inclusion, its dangerous capacity to function as a kind of control.

Writing gay history, for instance, one wonders what to believe and what to write. The narrative of cultural history has survived for years on certain assumptions—that being gay did not matter, was not very significant to cultural production. Writing about gay men in American culture, one is reinterpreting the contribution to and part played in that culture by figures like Walt Whitman, Herman Melville, Henry James, George Santayana, Langston Hughes, Lorenz Hart, F. O. Mathiessen, and Thornton Wilder, who have been central to its cultural history and definition, and whose sexual identity it has been a part of that history to suppress. It is a contentious subject, one that makes one question the history itself.

More than the history of the group, the secret history and the relation of the group to the majority culture are troubled. What does one believe? Conventional sources will not yield the answers one is looking for, because part of the point of conventional sources is not to disclose gay identity or influence. One falls back on the ancient sources of history: recollections, secrets, gossip, intuition, clues, reinterpretation, imagination. But in deciphering subversive and secret places in culture, the loss may be great.

Part of the job in writing a history of gay men in American culture is to bring out of the closet a treacherously double-edged situation. Gay men were secret about themselves, creating a secret world, and also gave in tribute to the culture a defining and participatory energy that, stripped of its own interest, could make the culture see itself as it wished to be seen. To do this subject, you need to study the secret gay subculture and the selfless and often self-denying work gay men did in the larger culture. To represent the subculture, you listen for the signals, you give the knock, the wink, and you find out about secrets and pain, but is the knowing research or joining, the telling history or betrayal? And what does the private culture sound like when the coded language you need to gain entry to understand and live within it is translated, when it is made to sound like just one more subset of the historicized normal, when the private cynicism and mockery become a category, reified into neutral jargon, yet another "contribution"—to what, I wonder, to what?

And the perspective of this secret world on the world at large, its special edge and its particular dualities, can be lost when made too easily the subject of historical discourse. You experience a stubbornness when you care about something, be it culture or habits or privacy or perspective, lest it should come too trippingly off the tongue, be too easily placed. And in writing it, do I become like my religious graduate students unable to accept scholarship's Puritans? How will the history I write affect my membership in the cultures I belong to? Will I sacrifice the special views of the conventional, the tones of a gay sensibility, by insisting on their place in the narrative of American history? Will I lose my professional identity in my subjective engagement in the scholarship?

Can the loss involved in doing history be balanced by the gain? You tell about the past because it isn't there. So you gain the story in lieu of the thing. But by extending its range, cultural history increases its control and the potential loss felt by its interested readers. There is some vitality and something passionate and idiosyncratic and just unsayable lost in the transformation of expression into cultural production, enshrined in the historicized accounts of it. What does making history of something do to one's experience of it? This is the question posed by any attempt at representation. But, even in the absence of any satisfactory answer, it needs asking. The concern it expresses is part of the process of the recovery of the past for delight's or interest's sake.

Troubling as this is with great books, to some extent the exchange is fair, because history, like criticism, is a way to make them seen and heard, and the confidence of the classic is that it can survive any contextualization and triumph over any understanding; as Soph says, don't worry so long as they're talking about you. . . . The frailer work, however, may have more trouble. The occasional, the evanescent, the momentary, the sensual have a harder time with the kind of life preserver history offers, perhaps overburdened by the price in significance that must be paid to be joined to the great chain of explanatory historical being. Sometimes the pleasure is weighed down by the ways in which people see them, by how seriously they must be taken, talked about, and regarded, and by how weary they must feel. And sometimes passing pleasure is the essence of historical truth.

The notion that the best history comes from a certain distance is a problem. Who but a gay would know to rewrite homophobic history to rescue the whispered voices of the closet? Actually, some might and have done, but not many. The thought that the assumptions and methods of contemporary history can go unchanged by an inclusion of a new subject matter, which really does question the assumptions of much of the history that came before, is problematic. The aplomb with which history includes any new subject by, well, including it, is infuriating. History keeps meeting one's objections by confidently, obtusely, agreeing to include them in its narratives, inevitably on its narratives' smothering terms. And then there is the loss you feel as you turn something you love, secrets you share, ambitions you harbor, passions you have known and identities you feel, history you have lived, something as real as a song and as secret as gay history, into the narrative. Can the narrative redeem your loss? Should it?

Dealing with the effect of AIDS on gay male culture, for instance, one encounters a literature that is meant for certain fundamental purposes: to find things out, to save lives, to mourn, to entertain, to warn; and the means—protest, the quilt, spiritual writings, anger—do not blend with the standards and the methods of history writing. One's interest in this history, whose writing it is in turn meant to serve, is sometimes at odds with professional scholarly history. As you turn it into the cadences of the profession, you feel a loss, you feel an anxiety, and those feelings are worth more than a moment's hesitation. They make you think about who reads what we do and why it is written and what it is for. In the same way that cultural production should challenge the narrative and the easy, historicizing explanations and give voice back to the historian, it should stay for a moment our narrating hands. Does the history have important work to do in the world, for people actually living in it? Do contemporary events require that we rewrite history and not write them into history, after their moment has passed or even as it passes?

Those moments of hesitation and doubt may amount to nothing other than anxiety, as history, like Time, marches on. But this anxiety, this worry about loss, is properly the business of anyone who takes up history as the solution to disciplinary issues and problems. It is ordering, and it makes an interesting way around certain problems, and it does retain the freshness of all good old things. But the resurgence of history requires also a proper caution. History's method is to annex itself to a narrative discourse. The discourse itself supersedes with explanation and context even that which we might, for a moment, wish to observe as if, like our lives themselves, it was worth regarding in a singular way, for all it might make us feel and think, with the illusion of independence of time and circumstance, with the illusion of originality, with all the illusions that history properly records as illusion, but which human expression must believe in and cultures must protect in order to do what we love them doing.

Engaged in writing gay history, wanting to write more about songs, one feels the anxiety of potential loss. I want to write history so the stories will not get lost and the plight will stay clear, to honor and understand and remember, to enthuse, and to change. You say to yourself (or your training says to you) that history writing is superior to quilts and pictures, memories, recollections, folktales and dish, because it is the medium that preserves them—and that it is superior to secrets and private discourse too. And yet there is something to what historians do that is like good embalming. What a way to keep something alive, to preserve its lineaments in memory!

It is great to tell and hear a story, but, although it makes us more at home in the world to know the narrative of what we are doing, that once-upon-a-timeness of history is a problem for those of us whose motive for writing history is not altogether professionalized or historicizing but also direct: to remember the things in life that most move and express us and to act on them. Formal culture seems to lose less in the translation into cultural history, or maybe it is that most of the formal culture I know is already historicized. The materials I am working on, popular culture, democratic culture, gay culture, the issues of the lives, their impact, their moral and expressive dimensions, seem to resist the very history one wants to write.

On the one hand, I am driven to historicize the Grace out of the Puritans and the "hotcha" out of Sophie Tucker; on the other, I am moved to protect the secrets and the activist consciousness of gay men from historicization—and probably from criticism. And the more history I attempt, the more intense the struggle between my training and my passions. At this point, of course, I should say that this intense conflict leads to vital, productive history writing. I hope it does, but I mistrust that resolution. I am of two minds. And that suggests rhetorical and, perhaps, moral caution.

There is an anxiety historians of culture I know feel when we begin to turn what we love into culture, into history, into sentences that legitimate at the same time that they vitiate the mysterious and inexplicable way the best expressive things feel. I worry that what gets lost in the telling is what made me want to tell in the first place. At the very least, it seems to me, one must keep this awareness alive as a hitch in the process of historicizing, more than a moment's hesitation and doubt. So to "History and . . ." I suppose I am presenting "History but . . . ," which expresses a historian's anxiety about the loss in the telling.

NOTES

1. See Robert Dawidoff, "Some of Those Days," *Western Humanities Review* 41 (1987): 263–86.

2. See Edmund Sears Morgan, *The Puritan Dilemma: The Story of John Winthrop* (Glenview, Ill., 1958).

HISTORY AND
THE STUDY OF CULTURE

—————⟫•◦•⟪—————

Carl E. Schorske

HISTORY IS ONE of the few disciplines to boast a muse, Clio, thanks to the academic intelligentsia of Alexandria who assigned her to our craft. The muses are, of course, female. If any among them has partaken more than others of the nature and destiny of woman in a man's world, it is Clio.

Look at the very purpose and structure of this conference. It is organized as a series of pairings or couplings. Although at the center of the inquiry, history does not pose the questions. We are foregathered to scrutinize Clio's value as a partner, present or future: Is she a satisfactory helpmeet? Can she, does she, could she enrich the performance of her partners from other disciplines in the academic quadrille?

How shall Clio deport herself in this dating game?

For good and for ill, the only thing she is really good at is dates. In both senses of the word: *date* as a measure and locus in time, and *date* as an exploratory erotic encounter that can lead to a gratifying relationship of indeterminate duration. Clio's fixation on dates in the first sense is deep and serious. The calendar is for her a kind of sacred book, but it has ill equipped her to establish an autonomous existence or a full-bodied faith. Every other discipline defines itself either by its subject matter, the terrain or objects of its study (like anthropology, literary criticism, biology), or by pursuing principles through rigorous internal mental procedures to create a world of meaning (philosophy, mathematics). Not so history. It has neither turf nor principles of its own. Historians may choose their subject matter from any domain of human experience. At times, we have had universal historians, who have aspired to make the whole world their oyster. In more modest moments, historians have made the oyster their world—

as when they study a small episode: a diplomatic incident or, nowadays, a peasant festival or a single text. But always historians have been concerned with describing their objects of study under the aspect of change, under the ordinance of time. They may delineate a subject with the purest linear simplicity or with the densest textual complexity, but always they stick to the elemental conviction that the beginning of wisdom is to know whether something happened before or after something else. Thus a historian will not let a poem or a text stand alone as a literary analyst does, letting it illuminate its self-enclosed particularity, but seeks meaning by relativizing the poem to other objects in a time series. He or she will not listen to the angry cry of E. E. Cummings, "Let the poem be"—a cry later echoed by the New Critics in literature and their intratextualist successors in every field of the arts, after years of bondage to the flattening effect of historicization on the arts. There is something partial and unreliable about the historian's fidelity to the object compared to that of the specialist in a discipline defined by subject matter. The historian pursues the analysis of the object's particularity (whether it be a poem, an institution, or a unit of culture) only to the extent that he or she can appropriate it as an element in weaving a plausible pattern of change.

If we turn from subject matter, the domains and objects of the historian, to the principles or concepts historians use in organizing them, we find again a certain limit to their commitment. A political scientist or philosopher strives to formulate concepts and to develop a series of mental operations to prove their validity. The historian is singularly unfertile in devising concepts. It is not too much to say that historians are conceptual parasites. Here is where the dating game begins.

Historians do not demonstrate the truth of the concepts they borrow, but only use them as a means, in order to give plausibility or cogency to the unfolding gestalten in which they reconstitute a past. Thus, historians might use the Freudian concept of narcissism to explain the behavior of a historical actor, but they feel no obligation to prove that concept, let alone to subscribe fully to the psychoanalytic system that generated it. They adopt principles and concepts not to prove or even illustrate their truth but to lend authority, explanatory force, and meaning to the convergence they are plaiting into a temporal process or configuration.

Confined to no single domain of human experience, historians move into any terrain in search of the materials they will organize into a temporal pattern with the help of the concepts borrowed from those fields of learning that generate principles. They reconstitute the past by relativizing the particulars to the concepts and the concepts to the particulars, doing full justice to neither, yet binding and bonding them into an integrated life as an account under the ordinance of time.[1] In the tapestry the historian weaves, diachronic dynamics are the warp, synchronic relations are the woof. Clio, in short, is on the distaff side. She spins her yarn partly from materials she has chosen and carded but not grown, partly from concepts she has adopted but has not created. Her special skill is to weave them together into a meaningful account on the loom of time—a loom that is truly her own. Her skill in plaiting makes Clio prized by others, sometimes to be wooed, sometimes to be enslaved. She herself necessarily wills her involvement in relationships with other branches of culture, for without them she would lose her power to realize her own identity. The problem, now more than ever, is to choose those relationships freely and to make them meaningful, fruitful.

II

Given the core of history as a mode of knowing and being as I have described it, what has been the orientation of history toward the study of culture? I cannot avoid treating the problem historically; that is the only way for me, a self-reflexive modern like the rest of you, to get a fix on it. Thus I shall try, *en bon historien,* to address the kinds of intellectual relations that characterize history in the field of cultural study today by the special form of distancing that the past provides.

Let me not frighten you if I begin with Herodotus. He is not far from the problem of history and cultural studies today. Arnaldo Momigliano correctly observed the "strange truth that Herodotus has really become the father of history only in modern times."[2] The reason for this is that Herodotus allowed culture (in the wide, anthropological sense) to play a critical role in his *Histories.* While the narrative core of his work was the Persian Wars, he treated the conflict between Greeks and barbarians as a clash of cultural systems. Herodotus' integrated historiography was unseated by the sharper but narrower political historiography of Thucydides. Thucydides too had what we would think of as interdisciplinary external relations—ties to sophistic philosophy, Hippocratic medicine, and Sophoclean dramaturgy. But with all his breadth, he shrank Herodotean cultural analysis down to the dynamics of power within the framework of the Hellenic polis system. With Thucydides, politics became the central concern of the historian, and its field was ethnocentrically defined.

Herodotus' very breadth was held against him thereafter. The Alexandrians, to be sure, prized him as fabulist and artist—no mean status in a culture that valued history as a branch of literature. They honored him by attaching the name of a muse to each of the nine books of his *Histories*. But Greco-Roman and Christian "universalism" produced a kind of high-culture ethnocentricity that doomed Herodotus' multifaceted cultural approach to history to incomprehension for two thousand years.

The reception of Herodotus' *Histories* gives access to the changes in Clio's intellectual alliances and epistemological fashions perhaps better than any text in our craft. I shall not pursue it here. But let me give you, by means of an image of the historian's work (fig. 1), two benchmarks in the story—one from 1716, the other from 1980. The engraving shows how Herodotus—and with him, cultural history—was seen in the beginning of the eighteenth century, when he began to be restored to favor. An allegorical frontispiece to a Dutch edition of the *Histories,* it pictures Herodotus being crowned by the muses. As befits their Dutch patrons, these muses use a map, indicated on a great parchment unfurled to memorialize Herodotus' work. On it are pictured the great movements of the barbarian hosts and the Greek defenders, the political and military struggles that, in the eighteenth-century view, constituted Herodotus' central focus and claim to Clio's crown of laurel. Across the shadowy portion of the picture on the left are scattered the symbols of the non-Greek cultures described by Herodotus the ethnographer: the Egyptian pyramids and the image of a scribe; the tripod—is it the golden one that Croesus, king of Lydia, gave to Delphi?; a horse's head bridled in the Scythian manner; a Persian sun symbol and winged lion; in the far rear the city of Babylon with its tower. These cultural remains are presented in disorganized array, reminders of the ethnographer and mythographer Herodotus, whose accounts could amuse, but not instruct, as the political ones did. By 1716, their connection with the narrative of great events had long been lost to the reader. They were lost even to Clio herself, as represented in the engraving. She directs our gaze away from the symbols of culture as she points insistently to the great parchment that validates the coronation of Herodotus as a historian of great actions.

If some of our cultural historians were to prepare a similar tribute to Herodotus today, the subject matter on either side of the panel would be switched. Clio would point her approving finger at the parchment, but the map would be erased, and the white sheet would be labeled *écriture*. On it would be displayed the symbols of the non-Hellenic cultures taken

Fig. 1. From [Herodutus, History] Herodotou Halikarnesseos, *Historion logoi [9] epigraphomenoi mousai.* ed. Jacob Gregorovius (Leyden, 1715). (Photograph courtesy of Brown University Library)

from the lower half. (There might be some dispute among the muses as to whether the symbols should be organized systematically, in the manner of anthropologists, or disposed as random bricolage to be caught for a moment in a kaleidoscopic frame, in the manner of Theodore Zeldin or Eugen Weber.) Herodotus would win his laurels as historian for his services in constructing a synchronic representation of past culture, complete with burial rites, kinship systems, child-rearing customs. Meanwhile, consigned to the shadows in the left and lower half of the picture in our 1980s version would be the images of the great Persian and Greek hosts, reminders of Herodotus' interest in politics, warfare, and cataclysm that have largely lost their commanding position as subjects for historians.

The fact is that I found the engraving of 1716 in a recent work of anthropological and textual history, published in 1980.[3] Its author, François Hartog, has reproduced it as an emblem of the historiographical tradition he intends to overcome. Hartog has chosen a title for his excellent book that marks it clearly as on the cutting edge of cultural study today: *Le Miroir d'Hérodote: Essai sur la représentation de l'autre* (The mirror of Herodotus: An essay in the representation of the other). The book focuses on one of the barbarian cultures that Herodotus found especially engrossing, the Scythian. Hartog, brushing aside the question of what Scythian culture could have been, shows how Herodotus constructed a picture of the Scyths that would serve as a kind of magic mirror for defining Hellenic identity, one that would reinforce the Greek cultural values that Herodotus shared. The "other" itself, Scythian culture, is swallowed in the Greek view of it; and the Greek view in turn is swallowed in Herodotus' mental and literary construct, the text. Hartog's study shows the characteristic fruits of Clio's new partnerships with literary criticism, linguistics, and anthropology: subtle and convincing textual analysis and the exploration of the mental organization of social perception. But some of the burning questions that Herodotus posed get lost: How did the Greeks and the barbarians come to fight? (In Herodotus' words, "What were the grounds of their feud?") What is the effect of war on the cultures of the belligerents? These problems of interlinked temporal transformation of power structure and cultural values recede in favor of more static dimensions of culture: the image of the other, its role in identity definition, and the construction of the text.

III

What lies between the two uses of the frontispieces to Herodotus? I do not wish to argue that Clio's transfer of affections from politics to culture is complete. Yet there has surely been a great displacement—almost an inversion—of concerns. Once again I must turn to history itself to get a fix on the present ways in which history approaches culture. The central focus here is on the rise and fall of Clio as queen of the disciplines.

The eighteenth century is decisive for the reinvention of cultural history in Europe. Since the Middle Ages, Clio had been the servant of Church and State. Appropriately to the modest function of her discipline in the power structure of academic culture, historians were placed in the faculties of either theology or law.[4] They provided moral example and practical lessons in the support of more august disciplines. In German universities there were no separate chairs in history until the end of the eighteenth century. Clio remained a handmaiden, and her intellectual purposes and even her tools for meaning-making reflected her actual subordination.

In the eighteenth century, theology ceased to be the queen discipline in the European world of learning, and philosophy began to replace it in a secularizing culture. When philosophy began to define in a very general way the goals of society as part of the realization of Reason, history found a new mate—and a new calling. That politics was involved in the bonding of history and philosophy few would deny. The seductive idea of terrestrial progress, replacing the supratemporal teleology of religion, was the brainchild of philosophy and history. Voltaire, and even the skeptical Gibbon, saw themselves as philosophic historians, judging and ordering history not only according to the criteria of Reason but in the light of the progress of Reason. The history of Mind and the history of Society were seen as inextricably linked, and the destiny of humankind as at stake in that union. The Encyclopedists sketched the outlines of an intellectual history centering on the history of science. History as the study of culture— strongly oriented toward a philosophic politics of freedom under law— was born. Kant, lowering his guard for a moment in his euphoric faith in Reason, predicted correctly that historians in the next century—the nineteenth—would devote themselves to constitutional history and international history, the spheres in which humanity would develop its freedom by placing the realm of action under the expanding power of rational law.

I do not wish to maintain that there was general acceptance of the extravagant claims of French *philosophes* and German idealists that history would actualize the potential of Reason for ordering the world of man and nature. But I would argue that, in and out of the academy, even those who resisted such claims found themselves accepting history as the ground on which the problems of man's destiny would have to be debated. History as a mode of thought soon penetrated virtually every branch of European high culture even as the extravagant hopes and fears attached to it in the French Revolution receded, while the mythic analogues from which it had never been far removed spread through politics into the populace. As for the academy, chairs of history were established all over Europe and fields of humanistic learning new and old organized their teaching on historical premises. Clio, whose whole career had been lived in dependence on other branches of learning, seemed to win not just her autonomy but sovereignty over all. She became queen of the human sciences. As philosophy had once overmastered theology as the ultimate guide of life and learning, so history now replaced philosophy.

During Clio's short reign as queen of disciplines in the nineteenth century, political history maintained a clear priority within the field of history itself, as Kant had prophesied. With it was associated a continuing commitment to a teleological orientation. Though political history broadened its substance from the rulers to the ruled, from states to nations and peoples, the nonpolitical forms of historiography had difficulty in asserting themselves, as did other kinds of social analysis, such as sociology, that arose to challenge history's narrative mode of understanding. It was in this context that cultural history, the other half of Herodotus' concern, began to emerge from the shadows. The principal pioneers in this field—Burckhardt and Fustel de Coulanges, and in some ways Tocqueville—were conservatives who rejected the nineteenth-century liberal sociopolitical system, its belief in progress, and the political historiography that expressed its aims. Against the prevailing teleological orientation of history, with its diachronic emphasis, they developed a counterproject: history organized in synchronic tableaux, in which the most diverse, often clashing components of cultural life—institutions, intellectual and artistic production, mores, social relations—could be displayed in cross section, a horizontal panorama. Burckhardt especially displayed for the first time the colligative power of history, its potential for confronting in coherence the most nonhomogeneous materials of culture. Time certainly did not stop in the construction of these masters, but it was, one might say, slowed down.

Not transformation, but cultural coherence became the focus of attention. It is worth observing, for the understanding of the contemporary situation in American historiography, that these authors aroused intellectual excitement and achieved canonical status among the educated in our country only after World War II, when the identification of history with progress began to dissolve.

In America, the favored form for history's engagement with culture was intellectual history. The subject matter here was not culture in the broad, anthropological sense but in the narrower sense of history of ideas as generated within the educated class. The term itself, *intellectual history,* carries the mark "Made in the U.S.A." It appeared first in close connection with social history. Some of you will remember college history courses entitled "Social and Intellectual History of . . ." Today this bracketing would be almost unthinkable. These courses carried into education the ideas of the New History of the turn of our century, when a generation of reforming intellectuals that included John Dewey, Charles Beard, and James Harvey Robinson sought to reanimate the Enlightenment tradition and update it for a modern industrial world. Though they did not reject political history, the New Historians fought against its narrow institutional focus by expanding history to include popular social movements and social conditions on the one hand and the ideas that furthered or resisted the reformer-intellectual's democratic project of political empowerment and social justice on the other.

In the manner of the Enlightenment, whose traditions these Americans reanimated, the progress of ideas and the progress of society seem to advance together and transform each other. The "culture" that such a historical outlook found worthy of note tended to be either religious or political. Its history of ideas was construed in a narrow but dynamic diachronic mode—the opposite of the cultural history of European conservatism à la Burckhardt, with its somewhat static, synchronic comprehensiveness and its abjuration of narrative.

The New History, social *and* intellectual, certainly felt itself, not unlike its European cousin, Marxist history, to be if not queen of the disciplines, then certainly autonomous. It cultivated the social sciences within itself. It patronized and utilized humanistic culture, especially political thought and philosophy, but only to the degree that this culture could be related to its sociopolitical project. The arts were seen not as constituents of history but as illustrations of social and political processes.

IV

History-as-actuality undermined the American New History's vaulting conception of Clio's nature and function. More: it altered Clio's standing in the belief system of modern society. Two world wars dealt a series of blows to the confidence that Western liberal culture, especially American culture, had placed in history as the scene of progress, of collective, rational self-realization. With the loss of faith in progress, history was also weakened as a mode of understanding the various domains of human culture, from the arts to the economy. The ties to the past were loosened. Although the complex process of breaking from tradition in the arts and other branches of elite culture reaches back into the nineteenth century, it was accelerated by the crisis of progress.

Somewhere about the 1950s, the break with history acquired the force of a generalized paradigm shift in academic culture. One discipline after the other in the human sciences cut its ties to history, strengthened its autonomy with theory and self-oriented critical analysis, and produced its meanings without that pervasive historical perspective that in the nineteenth century had permeated the self-understanding of almost every branch of learning. While the social sciences turned to behaviorism and natural-scientific models, humanistic disciplines developed self-referential formalistic criticism. Rosalind Krauss, drawing on Clement Greenberg, has well expressed the internalistic orientation of the modernist paradigm shift: "[A] modernist culture's ambition [is] that each of its disciplines be rationalized by being grounded in its unique and separate domain of experience, this to be achieved by using the characteristic methods of that discipline both to narrow and 'to entrench it more firmly in its area of competence.'"[5]

The consequence of this ambition was that the human sciences as a whole became not just specialized but, as a group, polarized. While the social sciences gravitated toward scientific abstraction (mathematical economics, quantification and behaviorism in sociology and politics, and so on), the humanities decontextualized their inquiry and treated their objects wholly internalistically. The social sciences tried to be hard, less humanistic; the humanities abstract and less social.

Where did the paradigm shift, the dehistoricization of academic culture, leave Clio? And what have been its consequences for history in the study of culture?

I can approach an answer to both questions most easily by reminding you once more of that early twentieth-century course entitled "Social and Intellectual History of . . ." What the old New History had thus joined together around 1900, a variety of New Histories put asunder in the 1960s and 1970s. For within history as a discipline the polarization of the human sciences repeated itself. "Social and intellectual history" came to mean not complementarity but antithesis. Clio, overthrown as queen, was not only no longer courted, but found herself in a bed of Procrustes in her own house, pulled apart between historians who looked for inspiration to the dehistoricized social sciences and historians who looked to the dehistoricized humanities.

Clio now plunged into a real identity crisis that lasted about twenty years. I think she is now emerging from it with a more modest and clearer idea of her powers, and perhaps with a firmer sense of her need for freedom of choice in her relationships.

One can follow well the identity crisis of history in the pages of *History and Theory,* founded in 1961 with the aim of consciousness-raising, of bringing history into the age of self-reflection and methodological sophistication. But much of the periodical's effort—and this seems to me the particular characteristic of history's essential nature that surfaced only in the general context of dehistoricization—was devoted to discussion of other disciplines for the light and help and criticism they might offer our very untheoretical field. In the first four years, roughly one-third of the articles was devoted to developing a scientific method for historians. In 1966, quantification emerged as a strong subtheme, with thirteen articles appearing between 1964 and 1983–and a special Beiheft in 1969. The approach to history from anthropology, of all social sciences the one most directly concerned with the mental world of culture but traditionally the least concerned with temporal transformation, was the subject of eleven articles in roughly the same time period. At the end of the disciplinary spectrum was the domain of high culture from which intellectual history had drawn its subject matter. There the new methods of literary criticism—textual, structural, and linguistic—began to be explored for their applicability to history. Hayden White performed perhaps the boldest act of historical self-criticism when he lifted historiography entirely out of time and specific historical context by analyzing it as a literary genre. White's *Metahistory* generated no less than fourteen articles in *History and Theory* since it appeared in 1975, and a separate Beiheft as well.[6] More importantly, it opened the door to other attempts to redefine intellectual history as a metahistorical field with the armamentarium of intratextual analysis. Until now, that school has devoted its attention mostly to critical reflection, and has seldom tried to write history.

Between these two poles, one can also find in *History and Theory* the attempts of Anglo-Saxon analytic school philosophy to clarify historical explanation as well as discussions of hermeneutics. Since 1983, the new topic of representations has inspired eight articles. Meanwhile, psycho-analytical and Marxian approaches to history continue to be explored, and narrative is recuperated as a bottom-line form of historical thought.

The striking feature of the articles in *History and Theory* is the continuously even distribution of the various positions represented in it. It is not what I expected from my personal experience; namely, a strong weighting in the direction of social history and its affiliated social sciences during the sixties, followed by a strong predominance of *discours sur le discours* inspired by literary criticism in the eighties. Not so. The various positions appear quite evenly distributed over the two decades.

In terms of short-term interests, one could—and still can—perceive historians proclaiming the beginnings of a New History based on some new interdisciplinary partnership and gathering followers who productively work the new vein. But each group's militant expectation of prevailing in victory over other modes quickly evaporates.

History and Theory's record speaks the higher truth: that history cannot find a clear identity based on privileging a given discipline outside history as partner. I submit that history has taken into its own body the autonomization of academic disciplines. History is accordingly proliferating a variety of subcultures. Its universalist tradition dead, it can create no macrocosmic frame or grand periodization. Instead it addresses a vastly expanded subject matter in microcosmic ways. Correspondingly, the need for different extra-historical disciplines, new alliances, is exponentially expanded. Cultural history, both popular and elite, is being transformed by the new modes of analysis which the other disciplines have generated in their posthistorical period. Politics both inside and outside the academy also gives rise to new subdisciplines within history. Groups struggling for social power outside the academy—lower classes, minorities, and women —produce both old-fashioned epic history and a new kind of cultural social history within it.

The history of science can serve us here as model for a principal way in which contemporary intellectual history is addressing its task. The history of science lent itself most readily to a purely internalistic treatment on a progressive premise shared by both the natural scientists and the public. Historians who sought to embed scientific insight in a social matrix were resisted, in part justly, for their inadequate scientific understanding, but also because they tampered with the mythology of the autonomy of science and discovery prevailing in the scientific guild. The main prerequisite to advance in the history of science was mastery of science itself. It required that the historian be formally educated in the subject by professionals in it. To that training the historian of science would add, from history, philosophy, and sociology, such knowledge of context and social-analytic techniques as to construct a convincing relationship between scientific thought and other aspects of the relevant cultural and social space in the past. The history of science still suffers from the division between internalists and contextualists. But the presence of both as participants in the same enterprise raises the standards of performance.

Only recently have historians working in literature and the arts and even psychology imposed similar demands upon themselves. Previously, secure in the centrality of their social or political account, historians simply skimmed the ideological cream from the artistic thought they appropriated. The advent of formal analysis in the arts poses demands for rigor that undermine such an impressionistic approach. Graduate education reflects the change. I learned about the methods of other disciplines from my colleagues, late and not too rigorously. Students of history today enter seminars in art or literature—or even psychoanalytic training—to acquire the analytic techniques of the subject they wish to explore historically. And in our history seminars appear students from the other disciplines, likewise seeking a more professional way of casting history's light upon their subject. A generation thus educated, as we all know, is just beginning to produce works combining rigorous analysis and well-plaited historical texture.

V

Looking at history today, one may well speak of glasnost. The hierarchical order of disciplines has been shaken to its foundations. For the first time in her long life, Clio is playing the dating game on her own terms. She has lost the illusion of being queen, monarch of all she surveys in the scholarly scene. She is no longer bonded in service to theology or law, nor is she wedded to philosophy in order to realize with her partner liberal bourgeois projects in the world of politics. Now she chooses her own partners freely.

At one level, the new glasnost is exhilarating. We are erupting with new creations at the frontiers of system and convention, just as music is. But let us not be overcome with the euphoria of our pluralistic freedom. There are potential losses too. In relating to other systems of thought, history can forget one of her few fundamental commitments: to chart not only continuity, but change. Anthropology, the discipline that has enriched cultural history more than any other in recent years, has been synchronically oriented, though it too is now developing a more diachronic orientation. It would be a loss (*pace* Herodotus) if the cross-sectional recuperation of past culture were pursued at the price of the charting of change and the struggles that produce it. Foucault's example, and the linguistic turn that has accompanied it, similarly leads toward a cross-sectional rather than a processual ordering of historical life. Here the model of Herodotus, with his interactivist dynamic, can still serve us well.

Will glasnost usher in a perestroika? Surely not in the sense of some overarching systemic notion such as inspired the universal historians in the past or the progressives in the nineteenth century. More probable is an institutional dissolution of history as a discipline, with its practitioners joining other departments from which they draw their subjects and their concepts. But I doubt that fate will befall us. I count on the strength of Clio's consciousness of her nature as guardian of the temporal experience, her fidelity to the calendar, and her pride in the distaff where her yarns are spun.

However *dépaysée* she may become, Clio has been strengthened in her weaving ability by the experience of our fragmented, dehistoricized culture. She is making a new start under the sign: "Have loom, will travel."

NOTES

1. For a fuller statement of this position, see Leonard Krieger, "The Horizons on History," *American Historical Review* 63 (1957): 62–74.

2. Arnaldo Momigliano, "The Place of Herodotus in the History of Historiography," *Studies in Historiography* (London, 1966), 141.

3. François Hartog, *Le Miroir d'Hérodote: Essai sur la représentation de l'autre* (Paris, 1980).

4. See the excellent analysis of historiography in terms of the teaching function of historians in Josef Engel, "Die deutschen Universitäten und die Geschichtswissenschaft," *Hundert Jahre Historische Zeitschrift, 1859–1959* (Munich, 1959), 223–78.

5. See in this volume Rosalind E. Krauss, "The Story of the Eye."

6. See Hayden V. White, *Metahistory: The Historical Imagination in Nineteenth-Century Europe* (Baltimore, 1973).

AFTERTHOUGHTS: HISTORICAL INTERVENTION AND THE WRITING OF HISTORY

➤◆◄

Ralph Cohen

I

ALTHOUGH THIS COLLECTION is called "History and . . . ," it might, perhaps more appropriately, have been called ". . . and History." Most of the contributors are not historians and they write from disciplines other than history. What they consider is the intervention of history in the writing of philosophy or anthropology or literature or folklore. Most of the contributors are not particularly concerned with defining or analyzing or describing the different conceptions of history; rather, they discuss their views of history only as these intervene in disciplinary discourses.

Intervention is a charged term in our time; it refers to the military and political intercessions that have taken place and continue to take place in the name of humanity, peace, conquest, war, and other such noble purposes. Previously, it was of course a form of colonial acquisition and domination. It is also applied to medical practices that invade the body; the use of a military metaphor to describe what was once thought a pure act of medical wisdom.

When applied to a discipline, historical intervention is seen as broadening the scope of the discipline by drawing attention to its past history or to disciplinary problems or dimensions that were previously overlooked. But historical intervention is treated as a necessary practice by Marxists who insist on historical interpretation of texts. Intervention is thus seen as a kind of writing or acting that can be dangerous or desirable depending upon the agent, victim, or host of the provocation. As writing, intervention interrupts the narrative by introducing a virus or a remedy.

"Intervention," however, need not be historical. The introduction of a

396

discourse from another discipline or an interpolated story or a poem in a novel creates an interruption that challenges the narrative it enters, creating ethical, gendered, political, and philosophical irregularity.

In writing of intervention, I accept the fact that philosophy or music study or literary criticism develops discourses that treat the problems pertinent to their disciplines: philosophical analysis or deconstructive readings or analyses of musical scores. Historical interventions thus introduce a historical interpretation into a narrative that was without it.

Interventions are always partial; if interventions are historical, other parts of the discourse remain unhistoricized. This is clearly presented in Clifford Geertz's suggestion that historical interventions should compose alternate chapters in an anthropological study. The other chapters would be disruptive and analytical details of particular events—deep studies of situations and events. A text that has historical intervention contains at the very least a historical and a nonhistorical discourse. Discussions of interventions would seem to require an analysis of the interaction between the historical and the nonhistorical. In addition, one would look to two types of distinction. The first would refer to the partial version of history that does the intervening. "All histories," writes Paul Veyne, "are partial,"[1] and he means by that that no history can represent all possible versions of history. Any historical intervention in this framework is both partial and interdependent. The second distinction discriminates the type of history that intervenes.

There are, however, attempts to rehistoricize histories of a discipline or to offer new or alternative histories. This is evidenced in claims for new historical histories of literature or in feminist or minority histories offered as alternatives to conventional histories. Such claims assume that history writing is a unified, coherent narrative and that oppositional history is disunified, fragmentary, characterized by multiple discourses. But there is no reason to assume that traditional history is without gaps or mixed discourses or that alternative histories are without some coherent as well as contradictory discourses. It may in fact be reasonable to assume that versions of history when incorporated in traditional genres are ideologically inconsistent.

In some of the essays included in this volume, historical interventions are identified with political power and social domination when inserted in the discourses of literature, sexuality, cultural studies, even history itself. But the very fact that they are inserted in texts that are nonhistorical or historical in different ways demonstrates that they are combinations of mixed discourses. Why have scholars brought historical discourses into nonhistorical narratives at this time? One obvious answer is that external social changes resulting from the changed status of women and minorities have introduced masses of texts that have caused the rethinking of our premises about the past in relation to the present. Members of these excluded groups are now writing narratives that deliberately set out to replace the conventional views of the past with specific reference to their past exclusions. The abandonment of scientists' claims to objectivity mimicked by nonscientists has been replaced by another scientific model: that of collaborative scholarship. Humanists find that their disciplines have historical interrelations that had been overlooked. The development of new disciplines like film study and performance study require a historical justification of their origin and development. And history has invaded traditional disciplines like philosophy and history because scholars seek to justify them in the marketplace of competing intellectual products. In the changes that are taking place from modernism to postmodernism, from reality to virtual reality, history in its numerous versions is invoked to explain the cultural transformations.

Putting the question of history as intervention prejudges the reply because it assumes that history as an imperial discipline is invading the others. But we can reverse the question about historical intervention and ask whether any disciplines are intervening in history. We can then note that discourses of literary theory, anthropology, psychoanalysis, gender, sexuality, statistics, and other disciplines are intervening in the history writing of Hayden White, Linda Orr, Lynn Hunt, and others. It is not merely that we are witnessing historical interventions in other disciplines but that disciplinary discourses are multigeneric.

If we realize that multiple interventions rather than merely historical interventions are characteristic of contemporary writing, then we may discover connections between multiple ("United Nations") military and political interventions and those in narrative. Indeed, the revisionary discourses of gender, the family, and the nation-state include terms and metaphors that are revising our understanding of history as well as the disciplines of literary study, psychoanalysis, sociology, and political theory. Just as our views of human nature are being altered by the technologies of reproduction, so our discourses are being altered by the invasion of disciplines into each other. Interventions do not undo disciplines; they reconstitute them.

The essays in this volume are limited to historical interventions. But historical discourses are not all of the same kind; they relate the past to the present by attending to the varieties of change and continuity based on considerations of data, distance in time, gender, class, and other factors relevant to contexts. Ian Hacking, for example, points out that philosophical analysis does not require historical writing, but analysis of certain behavior does call it forth. Child abuse is one such act. It is not only intrinsically immoral; it is "extrinsically metamoral": "By this I mean that it can be used to reflect on evaluation itself. The reflection can be done only by taking a look into the origin of our idea. . . . But the look must be into the social rather than the personal formation of the concept. It involves history. The application is to our present pressing problems. This history is history of the present, how our present conceptions were made, how the conditions for their formation constrain our present ways of thinking." This view of history involves reflecting upon the origin of a moral idea, how it came to be constructed, and how it shapes our present way of thinking.

This is Hacking's way of relating a specific philosophical analysis to history. He traces social changes that lead to legal changes. These then call forth a philosophical reconsideration of child abuse as a moral issue. Victimization of the helplessly innocent is immoral. This, I take it, is what Hacking means when he refers to the conditions of formation of the moral issue that constrains how we think.

Hacking is not in this essay interested in philosophical history but in the historical genealogy of an ethical concept. Of course, any attempt to deal with the history of philosophy can refer to works in their context. And Quentin Skinner and other contemporary philosophers have tried to understand past philosophies by reference to the very terms and contexts that made their writing possible. But such views of historical intervention have come under attack. Historical intervention, some philosophers argue, uses present concepts and facts to reveal the political and philosophical inadequacies of past thinking. Historical intervention in this practice requires a desirable use of anachronism or noncontextual history. Historical intervention should not hesitate to imply progress. Jonathan Rée writes: "If you want to describe and explain the past as well as pos-

sible, you must make constant use of concepts and facts which were unknown or even inconceivable at the time. After all, you ought to aim to
understand better than, say, Hegel did, why his argument lost its way at
a certain point; you should try to know, better than Dickens, how techniques for the representation of speech work in his novels; and you should
certainly seek to explain, better than contemporaries could, the problems
of disease, politics, production, nutrition, and economics which troubled
earlier societies."[2]

Rée argues that explanations of the past in order to be the best possible
explanations require of us the introduction of present concepts and facts.
Historical intervention should serve to support and confirm the concepts
that we find usable in the present. But a somewhat different version of history seeks to explain the formation of present concepts, not their present
utility. It also is far less sanguine about the validity of contemporary concepts of rhetoric, representation, and politics. If we treat history as an
evolutionary process, we need to study more than the achievements of the
present; we need to know how such achievements both advance and constrain present knowledge. The historical intervention controversy I am
describing is not about change, for Hacking and Rée agree that change
has taken place in time. It is not even about the use of present knowledge,
though Hacking is less certain than Rée about the unconstrained value
of this knowledge. The controversy about intervention refers to how past
knowledge is transformed. Hacking argues for knowing how the origins
of a moral problem have come to be transformed into its present state so
that its present usefulness can also be seen as limited even though it cor-
rects past versions. If child abuse is immoral, how should child abusers
be dealt with? Rée finds that present knowledge serves to replace past
ignorance or inadequacies but he does not trace the limitations that this
transformation introduces. What we have then are two versions of historical intervention: originary and anachronistic.

Historical intervention figures prominently in various feminist discourses, but "intervention" here refers to the discipline of writing and rewriting history. Feminist histories are alternative histories; they intervene
in the discipline by offering new data and new interpretations of received
data. They redefine such terms as *class, gender, sexuality, gaze,* and *feminine* by
applying them to information previously ignored or unknown. The essay
in this collection by Lillian Robinson indicates how two feminists can disagree about the legal and ethical implications of historical intervention.

And other feminists have rewritten history with a sharp awareness of distinctions that need to be made especially in the language of historical discourse.

Carol Smith-Rosenberg, for example, has written of the dilemma of cultural change "in which language both serves and wars against the unifying forces of social cohesion" and she sees the need to rethink terms like *class* and *gender* in developing a feminist history: "The tension between the two meanings of *gender* and *class* (as sociological description and as cultural prescription) played a critical role in the construction of a middle-class identity. While the one reflected the uncertainties of a world in flux, the other constituted an attempt by new middle-class women and men to impose a sense of order on the economic and demographic disruptions of their time. The 'ordered' vision women and men sought to impose differed as widely as their experiences of social change."[3]

She uses Bakhtin's linguistic model for cultural history and argues that it both encourages and attacks the unifying forces of class cohesion; for her, language becomes a synecdochic representation of class itself. "It permits us," she writes,

> to use the development of language competency as a metaphor for the formation of class identity. The following questions then suggest themselves: Which specific social and gender groups originated the "unitary language" of class identity? Who taught it to whom (that is, to which other social, gender, and generational groups)? What techniques and technologies did they use to disseminate their words? Did those groups who learned the language (rather than originate it) transpose it in the process of learning, so that it more accurately reflected their sociostructural location, their anxieties, and their angers? Did they speak a second language altogether, one that either directly confronted or less overtly subverted the unitary language of class cohesion? If so, were they able to maintain their social dialects against the forces of uniformity? How did the next generation of speakers alter the varied languages they inherited?[4]

Smith-Rosenberg seeks to relate the alteration of language to the alteration of class. Her version of historical intervention is class intervention. Although she tends to see class as a unitary group — a position called into question by other feminists — she is aware that some process of mixed discourse takes place in any class change. Moreover, she is uneasy with the concept of a "unitary language," and although she distinguishes between the originator of the class language and "those groups who learned the language," she might just as readily have argued that the originators are like the learners because they replace their language with the new one. What is impressive in Smith-Rosenberg's study of the American Female Moral Reform Society in the 1830s and 1840s is her awareness of the linguistic and ideological contradictions in studying shifts from one class to another.

She is among the select group who recognize the dilemma of historians who even in their alternative histories nevertheless leave traces of the dominant class they seek to reject. Although she is referring to the group she is studying, her questions about the relation of language to class identity pose a persistent dilemma for writers of alternative histories.

In her writing there is the excitement and discovery of a change that matters in one's life as well as in one's scholarship. What is notable in Smith-Rosenberg's history is her attention to the personal and social basis of her writings. She conceives her social and political role in society as requiring resistance to a world she did not make. The personal nature of this version of historical intervention is its connection with autobiography, with the educational life of the historian. Historical discourse as conventional history is intervened; the ideal of the neutral or objective historian has been replaced by the writer's personal history or by intertextual alliances with Foucauldian, Marxist, Freudian, and Lacanian premises.

One such alliance is used by Carolyn Porter to provide a theoretical alternative to traditional literary history with its patriarchal and hierarchical construction. In "History and Literature: 'After the New Historicism,'" (1990) she opposes any history that employs formalist or transcendental discourses in an account of literature. Literary history should depict "the potential for subversion and resistance in the discursive field." A proper history of literature would be a "continuously heterogeneous discursive field in which dominant and subjugated voices occupy the same plane." The reader would, by contemplating this level field, discover the depths of conflict. Through this array of heterogeneous discourses, the voices of those othered by the dominant discourses would acquire new authority and even the dominant voices would struggle with each other. This history would, I assume, make formalism itself a voice or voices in the heterogeneous discourses.

Porter grants multiple discourses and multiple interventions, but her version of history creates an ideological problem because she assumes that dominant and subjugated voices occupy the same plane. But interventions, although given the same prominence, do not possess the same authority. Contradictory writings do not possess equal authority even though they appear in the same publication; it is a matter of the reader's involvement in a text, in its values and insights. While Porter's solution gives voice to those now subjugated or silenced, it does not empower readers to respond equally to each voice. Patriarchal and other dominant voices may still prove more persuasive than those who deserve support.

This historical intervention with its potential for subversion and resistance differs not merely from Smith-Rosenberg's class language but from Hacking's genealogical history or Jonathan Rée's evolutionary anachronism. Although in the essays in this volume feminists share a desire not to be trapped by patriarchal discourse, they have considerable disagreements about what histories ought to replace it.

Rena Fraden offers a sympathetic but telling criticism of Porter's argument about leveling or equalizing all discourses. Even if it could be achieved, it would be undesirable. Fraden writes: "I wonder whether it is inevitable that the embrace of multiplicity means that I must concede hierarchy or metaphors of depth to the traditional humanists. Depth may not be something I am willing to give up altogether—at least with respect to morality and politics, if not aestheticism. Are we saying that giving agency to those who have been denied it is the extent of our intellectual morality? Are exclusion and inclusion the sole grounds on which we base morality, aesthetics, politics? Sometimes I think that what is being articulated in the vision of multiplicity is utopian democracy."

II

Historical intervention in music study seems to represent a rather special case. Leo Treitler suggests that the received view of scores and notation was called into question by a study of medieval music and by the technological developments that made the performance movement of comparative receptions readily accessible. He writes: "Questions about works, scores, notation, and performance have become newly activated through our awareness that the medieval music culture, in which we locate the roots of our Western tradition, lacked all the conditions that have been for us the premises for the possibility of a history of music: a transmission founded on the written score, a work concept, the idea of musical structure, the idea that the musical work is autonomous. Recognizing that these are not universals, we are, in effect, challenged to understand why we have thought them to be."

Musicology represents a special case—like that of art and architecture—in the inquiry into historical intervention. It is the verbal study of a nonverbal art. Musical scores may reveal continuities and discontinuities, but writing about such scores, even when the score is included in the verbal text, the scholar is always engaged in a translation exercise. Treitler's reference to the historical performance movement is an example of the shift in the interpretation of performance. Originally used to argue for an "authentic" performance, an antiquarian return to the past, it underwent a "radical shift of focus" to the conviction that a "dedicated performance practice has its own authenticity."

This shift raises the question of the purposes to be served by such historical intervention. Treitler refers to the hermeneutical view of Paul Ricoeur to explain the present focus of performance: "The interpreter moves between two poles, aiming at one for the restoration of meaning from a primary attitude of respect for the text, and at the other for a critique of the text from the standpoint of the interpreter's own hermeneutic position, that is, for a demystification of the text. It is not a matter of choosing between these two stances but of recognizing the necessity of interpreting the text from both stances, which are inextricably linked."

Treitler suggests, following Ricoeur, that the interpreter should both restore and demystify a text. This suggests that historical intervention should restore the text in its time and interpretation should indicate its current ideological implications. But this hermeneutic approach to music of the past leaves unanswered the question of what "music" is. Treitler's essay leaves the reader open to assess the critical functions performed by contemporary composers rather than interpreters.

The compositions of John Cage and George Rochberg and others who compose electronic music confront us with questions about the nature of "music" and "noise." They lead us to inquire into the grounds for change from received public performances to those of contemporary composers.

In developing countries traditional performance may be a way of constructing a national tradition. In Western societies this procedure may form the basis for calling national music traditions into question. There is also another performance issue that should be considered as historical intervention in music: public performance of rock and rap and the availability of videos. These ought to be considered as historical interventions into the structure of music audiences since they create generational appeal. They not only offer alternatives to received music, they often select deliberate targets for subversion.

Interventions in musicology as Treitler points out are interrelated with those in literary theory, art criticism, and anthropology. Such interconnections led Clifford Geertz in 1980 to express his uneasiness at which he considered a disordering of genres. In an essay entitled "Blurred Genres," he noted the new connections (the varied interventions) that texts were displaying:

> The properties connecting texts with one another, that put them, ontologically anyway, on the same level, are coming to seem as important in characterizing them as those dividing them; and rather than face an array of natural kinds, fixed types divided by sharp qualitative differences, we more and more see ourselves surrounded by a vast, almost continuous field of variously intended and diversely constructed works we can order only practically, relationally, and as our purposes prompt us. It is not that we no longer have conventions of interpretation; we have more than ever, built—often enough jerry-built—to accommodate a situation at once fluid, plural, uncentered, and ineradicably untidy.[5]

The fixity and tidiness of genre writing were being supplanted by texts that described actual behavior rather than wise behavior or expert behavior. Geertz then saw the changes that connected action to its sense as redirecting inquiry from what knowledge is to "what it is we want to know." And he hesitated then to predict how this new relation between thought and action would affect how we would live. "The relation between thought and action in social life can no more be conceived of in terms of wisdom than it can of terms of expertise. How it is to be conceived, how the games, dramas or texts . . . have the consequences they do remains very far from clear. It will take the wariest of wary reasonings, on all sides of all divides, to get it clearer."

Geertz, however, was mistaken in assuming that blurred or mixed genres were the symptoms of a search for explaining behavior by rationales rather than by determinants. The blurring or mixing to which he pointed emphasized the generic multiplicity that had previously been rarely noticed. But the blurring was no blurring; it was a characteristic of texts occasionally noted by critics, one that became readily noticeable when Bakhtinian works began to be translated and accepted. Geertz interpreted a symptom as the disease.

When invited to consider the relation between history and anthropology, he continued to seek an ordered balance, not a "blurring" between anthropology and history. By 1988, Geertz had two sets of examples that indicated how the new history and anthropology might be joined. One was that of the Melbourne school which provided a text in which a chapter that offered a historical, diachronic narrative was followed by a chapter offering an anthropological, synchronic one. The second example included texts responding to a series of questions conceived by semiotical anthropologists and institutional historians. These questions continue to be asked and, Geertz ironically remarks, some may even be answered. The dilemma that he pointed to in his early essay is still present and what the relation between history and anthropology will lead to still remains unclear for him (though perhaps somewhat less so than in his earlier essay):

> The recent surge of anthropologists' interest in not just the past (we have always been interested in that) but in historians' ways of making present sense of it, and of historians' interest not just in cultural strangeness (Herdotus had that) but in anthropologists' ways of bringing it near, is no mere fashion; it will survive the enthusiasm it generates, the fears it induces, and the confusions it causes. What it will lead to, in surviving, is distinctly less clear.
>
> Almost certainly, however, it won't lead much further than it already has either to the amalgamation of the two fields into some new third thing or to one of them swallowing up the other.

But it is precisely this "new third thing" that Renato Rosaldo declares now exists. There are scholars who "occupy the borderlands between the two disciplines [history and anthropology] and between their academic colleagues and their minority lay communities. Their research encompasses classic notions of historical periods and whole cultures as well as a sense of inconsistencies and interactions within and between cultures. Their worlds are more polyglot than monolingual." If Geertz is most concerned with the conjunction between history "and" anthropology, Rosaldo is concerned and angered by the American histories that order narratives to deny authority and presence to nonwhite heritages: "Who is included in that magical 'we' which excludes a number of historical heritages from its dominant narrative? Why should I not see my heritage reflected in the mirror of American history? For us Chicanos such blind-spots comprise more than intellectual errors. They wound, they offend. They grow out of largely unconscious patterns of white supremacy."

What Rosaldo urges in response to Geertz's solution is that minority heritages should be inscribed within a history that includes the dominant narrative. He urges not an isolated intervention but one included as a necessary narrative of heritages. The anger and resentment in his questions indicate that intervention derives from personal hurts and resentment of insults that are not always deliberate. Implicit in the response to Geertz is the assumption that equal but separate cannot be a satisfactory historical solution. Rosaldo suggests that "the disciplines are undergoing change in part because once-sovereign scholars must now engage in dialogue with natives who are both objects of analysis and analyzing subjects." This results in a different kind of historical writing. Natives who were the object of anthropological inquiries have themselves become subjective inquirers. Anthropologists now include those who were previously the object of inquiry.

The exchange between Geertz and Rosaldo brings to the fore an important dilemma in historical intervention. Geertz insists on the continuity of anthropological procedures. He grants the introduction of a new kind of history, but he considers it as a discipline with its own premises and articulation. Rosaldo, too, does not wish to undo anthropology or dominant history. He does, however, wish to see it in relation to heritages it previously ignored. Intervention would thus include the new vision within the dominant history.

Robert Dawidoff, a cultural historian, devotes his paper to exploring the frustrations that cultural history writing entails. The intervention loses the expressive aspects of people and events. Cultural history creates order and in doing so loses the passion and pleasure of one's experience. He writes:

> But there is a loss when you make culture out of expression, history out of culture, especially with the stuff of nonhigh culture—when, say, you put a popular song you love to sing or hear behind the bars of analysis. Context is imprisoning because, by making the subject a part of history, you somehow risk knowing the stuffings out of it, when what you wanted to do was

to keep what in it so beguiled you alive forever, as you experienced it. In the name of craft, history licenses the passion you feel for a subject without examining the passion, trapping you and what delights you into becoming unconscious actors in the film noir of the cultural justice system.

Dawidoff is aware of the value of rewriting history by making it inclusive, genealogical, open to various explanatory methods. But he laments his incapacity to write history that would display the moral and experience dimensions of his subjects. "And the more history I attempt, the more intense the struggle between my training and my passions. At this point, of course, I should say that this intense conflict leads to vital, productive history writing. I hope it does, but I mistrust that resolution. I am of two minds. And that suggests rhetorical and, perhaps, moral caution."

Dawidoff finds himself trapped in his view of how cultural history has to be written. His uneasiness derives from a sense that history legitimates narrative and that one cannot write history unless one is detached from the phenomena studied. But this view is called into question when the writer is himself the object of inquiry as in the situation of minority historians. The act of intervention is an irregularity, a disordering of narrative. It confronts the writer with a challenge to alter how personal history can rewrite public history. The desire to capture the passion of actors in history and one's feeling about historical events is a problem for narrative construction. History as a genre can include autobiographical comments, memoirs, letters, songs, and stories. If writing can capture the passions that we feel, then historians can seek the narrative that will reveal them. It seems that Dawidoff has succeeded in conveying a historical dilemma in the very passion and ordered disorder he believes he cannot achieve.

Historical interventions are provocations for altering the narratives they invade. When they invade parts of a narrative, they demonstrate interdisciplinary alliances. And when they rewrite history they create combinatory narratives such as the story of the American Female Moral Reform Society. The very procedure of historical intervention suggests narrative disruption. And it calls attention analogously to fragments and segments. Roger D. Abrahams in writing of history and folklore notes that maskings, riddles, and proverbs are no longer seen as unaccountable fragments of past traditional practices. They are considered part of a network of belief systems and have ideological implications as do interventions.

My "Afterthoughts" draw attention to the present historical situation in which history writing is a multiple enterprise. The original conference papers can be understood as a generic response to Michael Roth's historical inquiry. If we think of these as a family of papers, then subsequent additions can be considered an extended family. The construction of this collection exemplifies one type of transformation that illustrates the combinatory process in writing. Historical intervention offers different versions of history in a common procedure of interceding. Intervention both consumes and subverts disciplinary discourses.

The combinatory relationship is not, however, what is innovative. I have implied that generic writing has always been latently combinatory. What is contemporary is the overt insistence on the interdisciplinarity of disciplinary discourses. Such writing is a deliberate effort to posit restructuring of texts and institutions. In this respect combinatory writing confronts the reader with ideological and moral ambiguities. If we begin to recognize the combinatoriness of historical interventions, then we may wisely be preparing ourselves for discourse and disciplinary combinations considerably less comforting than those in this collection.

NOTES

1. Paul Veyne, *Writing History,* tr. Nina Moore-Rinvalucri (Middletown, 1984), 42.
2. Jonathan Rée, "The Vanity of Historicism," *New Literary History* 22 (1991): 979.
3. Carroll Smith-Rosenberg, "Writing History: Language, Class and Gender," *Feminist Studies Critical Studies,* ed. Teresa de Lauretis (Bloomington, 1986), 33–34.
4. Ibid., 36–37.
5. *American Scholar,* 49 (Spring 1980): 166.

CONTRIBUTORS

ROGER D. ABRAHAMS is Professor of Folklore and Folklife at the University of Pennsylvania. His most recent book is *Singing the Master: The Emergence of Afro-American Culture in the Plantation South* (1992).

ROBERT ALTER is Class of 1937 Professor of Hebrew and Comparative Literature at the University of California at Berkeley. His two most recent books are *The World of Biblical Literature* (1992) and *Hebrew and Modernity* (1994).

ELAZAR BARKAN teaches history and is the Director of the Graduate Humanities Center at the Claremont Graduate School. He is the author of *The Retreat of Scientific Racism* (1993).

JOHN BRENKMAN teaches English at the City University of New York. He is the author of *Culture and Domination* (1989).

RALPH COHEN is the Director of the Commonwealth Center for Literary and Cultural Change at the University of Virginia. In 1992, he edited *Studies in Cultural Change*.

ROBERT DAWIDOFF is Professor of History at the Claremont Graduate School, where he codirects American Studies. His most recent books are *The Genteel Tradition and the Sacred Rage* (1991) and, with Michael Nava, *Created Equal: Why Gay Rights Matter to America* (1994).

CAROLYN J. DEAN teaches history and cultural studies at Brown University. She is the author of *The Self and Its Pleasures: Bataille, Lacan and the History of the Decentered Subject* (1992).

RENA FRADEN teaches English at Pomona College. She is the author of *Blueprints for a Black Federal Theatre: 1935–1939* (1994).

CLIFFORD GEERTZ, an anthropologist who has worked in Indonesia and Morocco, is Harold F. Linder Professor of Social Science at the Institute for Advanced Study, Princeton. His most recent book is *Works and Lives, the Anthropologist as Author* (1988).

SANDER L. GILMAN is Professor of German, Professor of the History of Science, and Professor of Psychiatry at the University of Chicago. His most recent books are *Freud, Race and Gender* (1993) and *The Case of Sigmund Freud: Medicine and Identity at the Fin-de-Siècle* (1993).

IAN HACKING teaches philosophy at the Institute for the History and Philosophy of Science and Technology at the University of Toronto. His most recent book is *The Taming of Chance* (1990).

DAVID A. HOLLINGER teaches history at the University of California at Berkeley. He is the author of *Morris R. Cohen and the Scientific Ideal* (1975), *In the American Province: Studies in the History and Historiography of Ideas* (1985), and is coeditor (with Charles Capper) of *The American Intellectual Tradition* (1989).

E. ANN KAPLAN is Professor of English and Comparative Studies at the State University of New York at Stony Brook, where she also directs the Humanities Institute. Among her recent books are *Rocking around the Clock: Music, Television, Post Modernism and Consumer Culture* (1987) and *Motherhood and Representation: The Mother in Popular Culture and Melodrama* (1992).

W. D. KING teaches theater at the University of California at Santa Barbara. He is the author of *Henry Irving's Waterloo: Theatrical Engagements with Arthur Conan Doyle, George Bernard Shaw, Ellen Terry, Edward Gordon Craig, Late Victorian Culture, Assorted Ghosts, Old Men, War and History* (1993).

Rosalind E. Krauss is Distinguished Professor of Art History at Hunter College and the Graduate Center, City University of New York, and the cofounder and coeditor of *October*. Her books include *The Originality of the Avant-Garde and Other Modernist Myths* (1985) and *The Optical Unconscious* (1993).

Carolyn Porter is Professor of English at the University of California, Berkeley, and the author of *Seeing and Being* (1981).

Lillian S. Robinson's books include *Sex, Class, and Culture* (1978), *Monstrous Regiment: The Lady Knight in Sixteenth-Century Epic* (1985), and, as coauthor, *Feminist Scholarship: Kindling in the Groves of Academe* (1985).

Renato Rosaldo teaches anthropology at Stanford University. He is the author of *Ilongot Headhunting, 1883–1974* (1980) and *Culture and Truth* (1989).

Michael S. Roth is the Hartley Burr Alexander Professor of Humanities at Scripps College and Director of the European Studies Program at the Claremont Graduate School. He is the author of *Psycho-Analysis as History: Negation and Freedom in Freud* (1987), *Knowing and History: Appropriations of Hegel in Twentieth Century France* (1988) and editor of *Rediscovering History: Culture, Politics and the Psyche* (1994).

Carl E. Schorske is Dayton Stockton Professor of History Emeritus at Princeton University. He is the author of the Pulitzer prize–winning book *Fin-de-siècle Vienna: Politics and Culture* (1979), and coeditor, with Thomas Bender, of *Budapest and New York: Studies in Metropolitan Transformation* (1994).

Leo Treitler is Distinguished Professor of Music at the Graduate Center of the City University of New York. He is the author of *Music and the Historical Imagination* (1989).